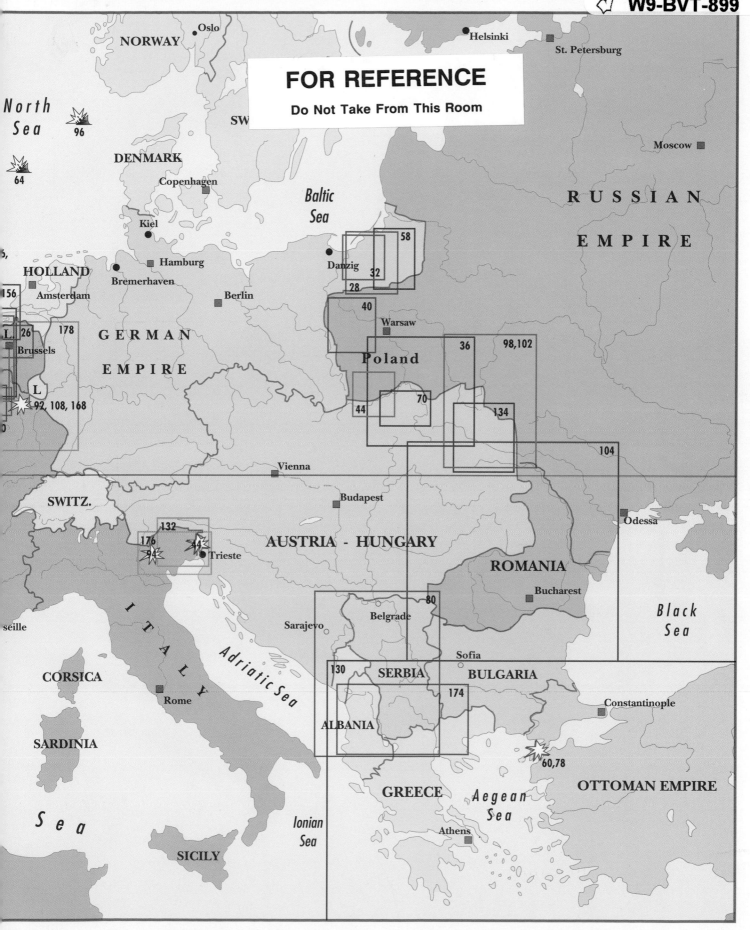

W9-BVT-899

FOR REFERENCE

Do Not Take From This Room

THE HISTORICAL ATLAS OF WORLD WAR I

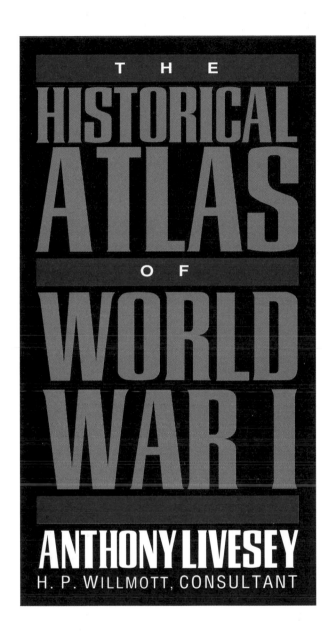

THE
HISTORICAL
ATLAS
OF
WORLD
WAR I

ANTHONY LIVESEY
H. P. WILLMOTT, CONSULTANT

A HENRY HOLT REFERENCE BOOK
Henry Holt and Company
New York

R
940.410223
L78h

A Henry Holt Reference Book
Henry Holt and Company, Inc.
Publishers since 1866
115 West 18th Street
New York, New York 10011

Henry Holt ® is a registered
trademark of Henry Holt and Company, Inc.

Copyright © 1994 by Swanston Publishing Limited
All rights reserved.

Published in Canada by Fitzhenry & Whiteside Ltd.,
195 Allstate Parkway, Markham, Ontario L3R 4T8

Library of Congress Cataloging-in-Publication Data
    Livesey, Anthony.
        The historical atlas of World War I / Anthony
Livesey; consultant H. P. Willmott. — 1st ed.
            p.   cm.   — (A Henry Holt reference book)
    1. World War, 1914–1918—Campaigns.   2. World War, 1914–
    1918—Maps.   I. Title.   II. Series.
    D521.L56   1994   93–47649
    940.4'1'0223—dc20   CIP
ISBN 0-8050-2651-7

Henry Holt books are available for special promotions and
premiums. For details contact: Director, Special Markets.

First Edition—1994

Printed in the United States of America
All first editions are printed on acid-free paper.∞

10 9 8 7 6 5 4 3 2 1

272855

What passing bells for these who die as cattle?
Only the monstrous anger of the guns.
Only the stuttering rifles' rapid rattle
Can patter out their hasty orisons.

from *Anthem for Doomed Youth*
Wilfred Owen (1893–1918)

Contents

The difficulties of Italian mountain warfare as illustrated by J. Matania, 1914–15

Introduction

"It must come to a fight." The dying words in 1913 of Field Marshal Alfred, Graf von Schlieffen, Chief of the German Great General Staff between 1891 and 1905, reflected the absolute certainty of one of the most influential military minds of his time. For at least a decade before 1914, the major European powers had been arming and preparing themselves for war.

No leader or government actually wanted war, none consciously plotted it; but almost all citizens of every major nation in Europe had come to share Schlieffen's conviction by the beginning of the second decade of the twentieth century. This near-unanimity seems inexplicable from the perspective of the 1990s. The nineteenth century, unlike its predecessor, had seen few wars in Europe, and no major European war at all after 1871. The European population had risen by 10 percent every decade from 1870 to 1900, and the same period had seen the rapid spread of industrialization and the transformation of the entire European economy to a basis in manufacturing. Growing prosperity, a perceived advance in living standards, increasingly enlightened social legislation and effective parliamentary representation had helped to ease internal social tensions in most states by 1914. In a real sense the industrialization of Europe before the First World War had brought with it, besides increasing literacy and slowly improving social conditions, a rise of hope, of optimism for the future.

But the years of prosperity also saw the unprecedented militarization of society, and the elevation of nationalistic fervor – in its semi-respectable guise as patriotism – to the status of prevailing ideology in every European state, even those such as Austria-Hungary which were ostensibly multinational in make-up.

The militarization of society was felt at all levels, including the personal. Among the new obligations which accompanied increasing prosperity in most European states was conscription for military service. Conscription was made possible by the increasing reach of state bureaucracy; it was deemed desirable almost everywhere following the war of 1870–71, when the French Army, for over a century the army of Europe, was crushed in a matter of weeks by German armies that owed their victories in part to sheer weight of numbers. By 1914 Germany could maintain a peacetime army of 1,500,000 men and a reserve of 3,500,000. France, despite her demographic inferiority, matched Germany by achieving a call-up rate of some 87 percent of the eligible male population (compared to 57 percent in Germany). Whereas in 1870 France had mobilized 300,000 men at the outbreak of war, in 1914 Serbia, not even the most important of the second-grade powers, maintained a standing army of 204,000 men. This sheer number of citizens with some experience of military life by 1914 helps to explain the evident blurring of the distinction between military and civil society in much of Europe.

The cost of this militarization was enormous, since rapid technical advances necessitated the re-equipment of both armies and navies with increasing regularity after 1870. Such expenditure could be justified in democratic societies only in terms of comparison with neighbors; hence neighbors were increasingly portrayed as potential enemies in both official and unofficial propaganda. The wider availability of newspapers and journals, and the spread of literacy, gave new power to such nationalistic messages. In France, in Germany, in Britain, Russia, Austria-Hungary and Italy in the early years of the twentieth century, politicians, newspaper magnates and magazine editors vied with each other in the identification and dissemination of the true essence of the nation. Increasingly, too, they plundered histories both ancient and modern to uncover the nation's "natural" enemies. Germans were reminded of their civilizing mission among the Slavs and of the constant danger of a Russian revival; they were urged also to maintain unslackened vigilance along the Rhine against the French expansionism which had seen Napoleon reduce the German nation to a French satellite. The French, aggrieved at their defeat by Germany in 1870–71, traced a succession of reverses at the hands of their eastern neighbor back to the Battle of Bouvines (1214). Russians brooded on the thankless role of their nation as bulwark against the Turkish infidel to the south and victim of German and Polish rapacity in the west. Italians saw in Austria, the enemy of their nation's unification, a continued obstacle to recovery of Roman greatness in the Balkans. For citizens of the Austro-Hungarian Empire, ancient ethnic and religious differences with the Balkan Slavs were identified as the cause of internal strife within the Empire, and overlaid upon equally long hatred of the Italians and the Turks. Only Great Britain seemed to lack enmity toward the nation's traditional enemy, France; the British instead were encouraged to see in the burgeoning economic power of Germany a direct threat to the world empire which proclaimed British greatness.

The media, through which such messages were broadcast, were limited by today's standards. In Great Britain, for example, the *Daily Mail*, the first newspaper to achieve a mass circulation, sold only some one million copies a day; few owned a wireless (the contemporary term for the newly-invented radio). Nevertheless, the growth of popular news media was unprecedented throughout Europe in the late nineteenth and early twentieth centuries, following the rising curve of literacy. Moreover, national history – and a nationalistic slant to history – featured at the core of education in schools, and mass education, at least to a limited age, became the norm in most of Europe after about 1880. If few even in western Europe (let alone in the plains of Hungary and the interior of Russia) knew much about the detail of international affairs, there were even fewer who can have escaped entirely exposure to persuasive nationalistic and sentimental images of their own country and its neighbors.

Other factors contributed to this nationalistic mentality. The first Olympic Games of modern times in 1896, for example, much heralded as a new, peaceful rivalry between potential antagonists (as in Ancient Greece where wars were halted for the games), in fact inflamed national rivalry and was widely lauded for inducing in the young and fit – the potential soldiers – the military virtues of obedience, loyalty, fortitude and fitness.

A spirit of jingoism was by 1914 deeply ingrained, and as the political crises of that year developed, such sentiments proved strong enough to silence the voices advocating restraint. This jingoism was to prove extraordinarily resilient, despite the war's long duration and appalling losses; only in Russia in 1917 and in Germany and Austria-Hungary at the very end of 1918 did sufficient numbers of soldiers and civilians begin to question such views to make continuation of the war itself impossible. In one respect, the history of

World War I can be seen as the story of the slow and bloody decline of militaristic nationalism in the face of the harsh and unsentimental realities of modern warfare.

The war envisioned
All speculations on the nature of the coming war were anachronistic, for reasons which had as much to do with the advance of technology and the long years of relative peace as with the sentimentality of much late nineteenth-century chauvinism. Despite the contrasting examples of the nature of warfare in the American Civil War (much reported in European newspapers), the Boer War and the Russo–Japanese War – to say nothing of the almost constant conflict in the Balkans – the models of warfare which most impressed themselves on public consciousness, both military and civilian, were the Austro–Prussian War of 1866 and the Franco–Prussian War of 1870–1; the most influential theorist of war was undoubtedly Napoleon I, whose theories passed to the early twentieth century through the works of Jomini and Clausewitz.

The years before 1914 witnessed, in France and Britain particularly, an extraordinary proliferation of fictional accounts of "the next war" (the only survivor in print in English today is Erskine Childers' *The Riddle of the Sands*, which is somewhat peripheral to the genre). Almost all the authors envisaged warfare in Napoleonic terms with infantry charging in massed ranks, cavalry winning the decision. Events, it was thought, would also be quickly decided as in Napoleon's time, often in a day. Technological advances since Napoleon – most notably the network of railways across much of Europe – would, most authors predicted, merely enable greater concentration of the twentieth-century's larger armies, thus making conflict even more decisive. Two major battles at most would decide the issue – and indeed this had been the case at Sadowa in 1866 and Sedan in 1870. Too little attention was paid to the lessons of recent wars in America, South Africa and Manchuria precisely because they failed to accord with the prevailing image of this style of warfare.

This image prevailed among professional soldiers as strongly as among civilians. Many senior Russian commanders had actual experience of the true implications of technology on modern warfare through the 1904–05 conflict with Japan, but even they believed the coming war would conform with Napoleonic principles. Perhaps the only professional soldiers who had truly begun to adapt to the realities of modern warfare were a small number of British officers and NCOs who had had experience in the Boer War; as commanders in the smallest army among the major European powers, their influence on the expectations with which Europe went to war in 1914 was slight.

Another problem was that commanders in all armies expected to be able to exercise the sort of personal direction that had characterized the generalship of Marlborough, Frederick the Great and Napoleon. Among many, the belief had grown up that the issue of an order was tantamount to its fulfilment on the spot, for the advance of technology since the late nineteenth century (field telephones and despatch riders in particular) had induced the belief that such parade-ground expectations were realistic on the battlefield too. Thus on all sides both military and civilians viewed the coming war with confidence: the mass armies of Clausewitz's "nation in arms" would concentrate in overwhelming force at the battlefront, and the resulting action, efficiently conducted in imitation of the genius of Napoleon, could not fail to be decisive.

Plans and forces

The armies raised to meet these confident expectations varied greatly in size, in quality, in equipment and in objectives. The plans with which they went to war in 1914 ranged from the tightly timetabled to the vague.

Germany

German strategy was based on Schlieffen's plan, adopted in 1905. This was designed to address the fundamental weakness in Germany's position: the fact that since 1891 the Germans had faced the prospect of simultaneous war against both France and Russia, both west and east. Schlieffen proposed a massive blow at maximum speed in northern France, achieving decisive victory within six weeks; then, using Germany's efficient interior rail system, the victorious formations were rapidly to be ferried east to destroy Russia's armies before their cumbersome mobilization was completed.

Schlieffen had ordered the German left wing in Alsace Lorraine to be lightly manned (he was prepared to accept temporary French penetration into Germany), while the right flank in the north was to comprise massed formations. These were to execute a rapid enveloping movement through Flanders and Picardy and then take Paris from the west. The subtle-ty of the maneuver lay in the fact that, if it succeeded, the Germans would take the French center and right in the rear, forcing them to fight with their backs to their own fortifications along the German border. One drawback was that the flanking advance envisaged would necessitate violation of Belgian (and, ideally, Dutch) territory, and Belgium's independence had been guaranteed by Great Britain since 1839. The risk of British involvement was, however, one which Schlieffen was prepared to run, provided the heavy initial blow against France proved decisive. Success depended on mass and momentum.

The German system for raising the necessary mass armies in 1914 dated from the reorganization of the Prussian Army after its defeat by Napoleon at the Battle of Jena in 1806 and was based on the Clausewitzian concept of the "nation in arms". Every able-bodied man was liable for service from the age of 17, for two years' full-time enrollment in the infantry or three in the cavalry or horse artillery. Thereafter, though nominally a civilian, he was obliged to serve in the Regular Reserve for four or five years, depending his arm of service. He was then enrolled in the "first levy" of the Landwehr for five years, then the "second levy" up to the age of 39, and the Landsturm until he was 45. In this way, massed reserves were at all times available.

The military profession in Germany carried a greater prestige than any other, and this had one significant drawback: higher command was considered an occupation for aristocrats, rather than professional soldiers selected by merit. In the war against Austria, 65 percent of Prussian officers were aristocrats. By 1914 this percentage had fallen to some 30 percent, but they retained the important posts and commanded the most important regiments. Individual initiative by the commander on the spot had been encouraged under the Elder Moltke, with great emphasis on experience and observation rather than theory; the extraordinary thoroughness with which the German General Staff planned and timetabled every detail of Schlieffen's grand scheme greatly reduced this emphasis, partly as a deliberate effort to compensate for the indifferent quality of some senior commanders. The greatest strength of the German armies, and the true source of their professionalism and fighting spirit, lay rather with the lower ranks, bourgeois junior officers and, most especially, non-commissioned officers, for it was they who trained and led the massed ranks of conscripts. If the German Army was the driving force behind World War I, the professionalism of German NCOs drove the German Army. Whereas the professional core of the small British Army was very largely dead by 1915, the NCO core of the much larger German Army survived merciless attrition until the beginning of 1918, and the resilience of the German Army as a whole began to erode only once these men had disappeared.

France

Following defeat by Prussia in the war of 1870–71, the French senior commanders had devised numerous plans against renewed war with Germany. All hinged on the newly strengthened eastern frontier forts, of which Verdun was one. French strategy was essentially based on an initial defensive campaign followed, when opportune and prudent, by a decisive counter-stroke. But in the years immediately preceding 1914, a new, more aggressive thinking came to dominate the French staff. The leading proponent of this non-defensive strategy was Colonel Louis Loizeau de Grandmaison, Director of Military Operations and author of the notorious "Plan XVII". In a remarkable demonstration of the triumph of sentimental nationalism over reason, he advocated all-out attack – offensive à l'outrance – as more suited to the French military spirit. Arguing that deployment of the new 75 mm field gun in any event gave French armies tactical superiority on the battlefield, he proposed an offensive immediately upon commencement of hostilities. First and Second Armies would invade Lorraine, while Third and Fifth Armies on their left would attack north of Metz – or, if German forces crossed into Belgium, strike them in the left flank. The offensive spirit which Grandmaison claimed was intrinsic to his countrymen was bolstered by such devices as the omission of any reference to defensive tactics in the 1913 training manual for infantry officers.

Plan XVII is comprehensible in the light of the French nationalistic imperative toward the recovery of Alsace and Lorraine from Germany, and its basis in the harnessing of a much-mythologized French offensive spirit is in accord at least with the Clausewitzian principle of uniting the whole nation, both physically and spiritually, in the war effort. In military terms, however, the plan was grotesquely misconceived, for it ignored all historical evidence of the possible, particularly in its miscalculation of German strength. In the first week of conflict, the Plan XVII counted only 45 German front divisions in the west; in the event, 83

were to be deployed. Military history showed clearly that an attack had a chance of success only if it had numerical superiority in a ratio of at least 3:1; in August 1914 the Germans outnumbered the French on the Western Front by 3:2.

The most populous nation in Europe outside Russia at the beginning of the nineteenth century, France had been in demographic decline since about 1850, and this decline had been emphasized by the rise of Germany. The mass army with which France sought to retain parity with Germany was raised only at the cost of strenuous effort in conscription. A program of military reforms due for completion by 1916 had encompassed before 1914 a lengthening of the period of service for conscripts – a development of which the significance was not lost upon German observers, and which certainly contributed to the military brinkmanship of the immediate pre-war years. In contrast to the view in Germany, however, French conscripts were regarded mainly as reserves, suitable for such tasks as garrison duty. The professional army of some one million men was expected to win the opening campaign, and with it the war.

Austria-Hungary

Austria-Hungary's plans, under the direction of the forceful Chief of Staff, General Franz Conrad von Hötzendorf, provided for two eventualities: war against Serbia alone and war against both Serbia and Russia. In the former case, Conrad's Plan B called for a combined offensive into Serbia by Fifth and Sixth Armies from Bosnia and Second Army from the province of Voivodina, north of Belgrade. In the latter case, under Plan A, Fifth and Sixth Armies were to guard the Serbian border, while First and Fourth Armies struck north-eastwards from Galicia into Poland to link with the expected German advance, and Third Army and the redeployed Second Army were to drive eastward from eastern Galicia into Russia itself. The weakness in these plans was the required redeployment of Second Army should political developments necessitate a change in mobilization; subsequently, one of Conrad's six armies became unavailable for immediate deployment on either front when he ordered advances into both Serbia and Galicia. In any event, Austria-Hungary lacked sufficient resources to maintain momentum for two simultaneous offensives.

Both economically and militarily, Austria-Hungary was altogether the junior partner in the alliance of

A French 75 mm field gun "soixante quinze", December 1914

the Central Powers. Covering a vast area of central Europe, the Austro-Hungarian Empire suffered from the centrifugal effects of nationalism in a multinational state, from a steady decline in military and political prestige since the mid-nineteenth century, from very uneven industrial and economic development, and from a large and inefficient bureaucracy. Conscription, though modelled on the efficient German system, in fact produced more problems than solutions; units tended to be racially homogeneous (though senior command positions were monopolized by Germans or Hungarians) and thus frequently unwilling to serve on fronts where they might face opponents of the same race or culture. Prewar dispositions had therefore to be made for ethnic, not purely military, reasons. The Austro-Hungarian Army as a whole was hampered by language difficulties, by an aristocratic domination of senior command positions nearly as marked as that of the German Army, and by chronic difficulties of supply and equipment, manifesting themselves most notably in a serious weakness in artillery other than the heaviest siege pieces. The peacetime strength of the army, some 415,000 rising on mobilization to nearly 3.5 million, thus looked more formidable on paper than it was in fact on land.

Russia

Just as Germany's problem was to avoid fighting on two fronts simultaneously, Russia, though having only one front, had to face two potential enemies – Germany and Austria-Hungary. The former was correctly identified as the more dangerous, and implementation of alternative plans drawn up by the Russian General Staff was dependent on whether Germany's opening blow was directed at France or at Russia itself. The military dispositions were identical whichever was implemented. First and Second Armies were positioned in the northwest facing East Prussia, the Third, Fifth and Eighth Armies the southwest, facing Austria-Hungary. Another army, the Fourth, was stationed in rear, to be deployed to either the northern or the southern front as events might dictate. If Germany first attacked eastward, all Russian forces were to retire – in the manner so successfully employed by Field Marshal Kutuzov in the face of Napoleon's invasion in 1812 – then to counter-attack when opportunity arose. If, on the other hand, the Germans remained at first inactive in the east while attacking in the west, both army groups were immediately to advance into East Prussia and Galicia. If successful, the whole might of Russia could then be redeployed for an attack on central Germany, bringing the war swiftly to a conclusion.

The Imperial Russian Army, a conscript force with a peacetime strength of 1,200,000, was the largest standing army in Europe. In the Russian Empire as a whole, the fit male population of military age was estimated in 1911–12 as some 26 million, and the sheer size of this potential force made Russia a major consideration in the war plans of all European powers. This almost limitless resource was, however, severely reduced in effectiveness by a rail system so chronically inefficient that large numbers of available men could be transported across country only by laborious stages. Reforms introduced after the disasters of the Russo–Japanese War of 1904–05 had resulted in a largely effective system of promotion to field rank on the basis of merit, but the senior command and the supply structure of the Russian Army as a whole was severely weakened by corruption and inefficiency. Like those of Austria-Hungary, the Russian forces suffered from dependence on a relatively weak industrial base, and consequent shortages of equipment, when compared to Germany.

The Russian Army, however, had one considerable advantage: the conscript infantrymen was generally not only well led but well accustomed to a life of considerable privation – and therefore able to improvise and to continue to fight in circumstances which would have proven intolerable to many of his enemies.

Great Britain

While all the other European powers measured their military strength in armies, Great Britain was a case apart. Traditionally Britain was a great – indeed the leading – sea power, with no need for conscription or a large standing army. The expeditionary force earmarked for France in 1914, all volunteers, numbered a mere 160,000, formed into six infantry divisions. These professionals represented, in Liddell Hart's felicitous phrase, "a rapier among scythes" by comparison with the Continental conscript armies, but their impact on the events of August 1914 was necessarily slight (Chancellor Bismarck had earlier commented that a policeman would prove sufficient to deal with the British Army). Moreover, the role of the BEF in France in 1914 was in any event unclear, since no plans had been developed beyond the vague notion of deployment on the left wing of the French line.

The aristocratic domination of the German Army's higher ranks was not so evident in the British Army (or indeed in the French): the purchase of commissions been had abolished in 1871, and in any case the military profession carried less prestige in Britain. Nonetheless, the proportion of higher officers who approached the coming war with unwarranted confidence in their own abilities and in the power of modern technology was still considerable.

Artillery

Calculations from the Franco–Prussian War of casualties caused by infantry fire and by artillery had yielded a ratio of approximately 85 to 6; despite evident advances since 1871 in the design and manufacture of guns, it is unlikely that many observers in 1914 would have predicted any great change in the coming war. The perfection of the machine gun notwithstanding, it is in fact arguable that failure to appreciate the vastly increased importance of artillery over the intervening period was the single greatest failure of military foresight in World War I. German statistics even for 1914 show a ratio of 49 casualties caused by artillery to 22 by infantry.

The standard British field gun was the 18-pounder, with a range of 7000 yds/6400 m and a rate of fire up to eight shells per minute. The range of equivalent

guns in the other armies was similar. Outstanding among field artillery weapons was the French "75", which had a buffer recoil action, allowing it to be fired repeatedly without re-laying. It had a range of 9000 yds/8230 m and could fire in excess of 15 rounds a minute. All field artillery in 1914 was supplied with a high proportion of shrapnel shell, for maximum effect against infantry formations in open ground.

Heavy guns had been developed by all armies to demolish enemy fortifications. Of these, the most versatile was the Austrian 30.5 cm Skoda – indeed, so effective were they that Austria was to lend batteries to Germany to help reduce Belgian fortress-cities during the invasion in 1914, since the corresponding German guns, the 30.5 cm and the 42 cm Krupp weapons, were less mobile. Each 30.5 cm Skoda could fire a 1786 lb/810 kg shell every six minutes.

The types and relative numbers of field guns with which the armies of the major powers were equipped in 1914 were indicative not only of the strength of the respective armaments industries, but also of the various tactical doctrines in favor at the time. The contrast between French and German provision was particularly significant. The quick-firing "75" was regarded as an all-purpose weapon by the French Army, and supplied to all infantry divisions, where its rate of fire and maneuverability were expected to be ideal in support of infantry attacks. Standard provision at divisional level was 36 guns, all "75s". The standard German 77 mm field gun was a much less effective weapon, but all German infantry divisions were also equipped with three batteries of 150 mm field howiters, giving a total of 72 guns at division level. The German 150 mm field howitzer was an efficient weapon, capable of firing five rounds per minute at an effective range of 9300 yds/8585 m; its availability at divisional level was to give German infantry divisions a decisive advantage over their French opponents in 1914, in both defense and attack.

Rifles

The infantryman's rifle differed little from army to army, all being bolt-action weapons – the British Short Magazine Lee-Enfield Mk III, the French Lebel M 1916, the German Mauser M 1898 and the Russian Moisin-Nagant M 1891. Some had individual advantages such as greater reliability but none was markedly superior.

There was one distinction, however. The Continental powers produced heavier rifles, holding fewer rounds. These were used for unaimed shots, fired from the hip during mass advances. The British, on the other hand, were trained to shoot rapidly from a prone position, aiming at a target.

Machine guns

The main purpose of the machine gun was to provide rapid fire from crews of one, two or at most six (a conservative estimate calculated that the fire of one gun was equal to that of 80 riflemen; a rate of 600 rounds per minute was typical). Machine guns had considerably greater range than rifles, and were therefore capable of providing indirect supporting fire for an attack as well as defending a position. It was again only in the small and professional British Army that the devastating effect of machine-gun fire on a massed attack had been recognized, partly as a result of experience in South Africa, and British infantry attacks were theoretically made in open order to minimize casualties during the advance.

By 1914, however, only the German Army had appreciated the advantages to be obtained by deploying machine guns in batteries (rather than dispersed among infantry formations). This tactical development led to the belief in the war's early stages that German divisions were equipped with greater numbers of machine guns; in fact, Allied and German infantry divisions all included 24 guns in 1914.

Transport

For strategic mobility, the crucial transport arm was the railway. The military importance of the railway was well understood – railways had influenced strategy in both the American Civil War and the Franco–Prussian War – and rail movement was fundamental even to the mobilization plans of most European nations. However, for short and medium distance mobility, despite the fact that by 1914 a British division included nearly 900 motor vehicles, all armies relied on the horse to an extent that is now difficult to appreciate. And on the battlefield itself, all armies moved on foot. This disparity between strategic mobility and relative tactical immobility was a technological paradox whose implications had not impressed themselves on any observer in 1914. The unshakeable conviction that the first clash of arms would prove decisive effectively stifled any detailed consideration of the possibility that the strategic mobility of reserves might swiftly turn a prolonged campaign into stalemate.

In contrast to the other major combatants, Great Britain did not operate a system of conscription and instead relied entirely upon volunteers. Efficient propaganda and recruiting initiatives enabled the British Army to avoid conscription until 1916

Aircraft

Today, the failure of any of the major powers to recognize the full potential of aircraft seems to be perhaps one of the greatest tactical oversights of the wartime planners. By 1914 all the largest armies had formed an air corps or division but airplanes were thought to be very limited in their usefulness with minor reconnaissance missions considered to be the utmost extent of their capacity, and certainly no aircraft armament had been developed. The first recorded operation in which aircraft adopted an offensive role was during the war between Italy and Turkey in 1911, when an Italian pilot dropped hand-grenades on Turkish positions. The example of this innovative pilot seems to have been largely lost on his contemporaries and as late as 1914 the French General Foch remarked that "aviation is good sport, but for the army it is useless".

By 1914 the German navy did possess a large fleet of Zeppelins but the vulnerability of these hydrogen-filled airships was soon made apparent and their contribution to the German war effort was minimal, despite optimistic pre-war predictions.

Navies

Since the Battle of Trafalgar in 1805 the British Navy had ruled supreme. Supremacy, however, led to complacency and by the end of the 19th century the British Navy was extremely outdated. In Germany, in 1898 and 1900, two navy laws were passed which outlined clear-cut plans for a massive extension of the German fleets. Furthermore, it was evident that Germany's new navy was designed to operate in the North Sea – Britain's traditional perserve. The British Admiralty was galvanized into action and, with the appointment of Admiral Sir John Fisher to the post of First Sea Lord, Britain embarked upon an ambitious restructuring of its naval power base.

The single most important development during what subsequently became known as the "Naval Race" was the construction of HMS *Dreadnought* which, with its armament and speed, rendered every other battleship in the world obsolete. By the outbreak of war, Germany had done much to reduce Britain's lead, and had introduced its own dreadnought-class construction program, but Britain still enjoyed a numerical superiority and now her ships were the most advanced examples of naval design afloat.

Treaties and Alliances

The four years preceding the commencement of hostilities witnessed an unprecedented flurry of diplomatic activity in Europe. The single most potent factor influencing Europe's leading politicians was the unification of Germany. Central Europe, for so long a heterogeneous collection of small city-states and minor principalities, had bonded to become a nation capable of withstanding the aggression of its territorially acquisative neighbors and, indeed, of adopting an aggressive stance itself. The prime mover in the struggle for unification was the "Iron Chancellor", Otto von Bismarck, and it was Bismarck's machinations which were to eventually result in the formation of a chain of alliances which committed the signatories to mutual support in the event of aggression being directed toward them.

Bismarck's primary concern was to ensure an atmosphere of stability in which the infant German nation could consolidate its gains, politically, economically and territorially. His first overtures were directed at Austria-Hungary and Russia, but it soon became evident that conflicting aims in the Balkans made the latter nations uneasy partners, and even prospective enemies. In the face of this dilemma, Bismarck inclined toward Austria-Hungary, influenced by the fact that the Austrian army was more efficient and better equipped than that of Russia, and the Austro-German

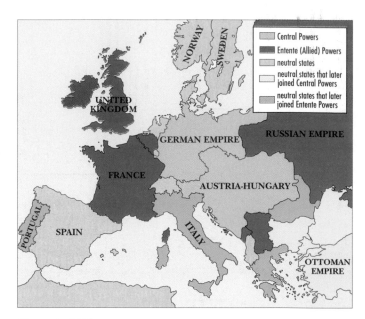

Europe in 1914

alliance (1879) proved one of the more enduring of the Chancellor's maneuvers. Perhaps the most important provision of this treaty was that, while neither partner was committed to military action if the other was attacked by France (or any power other than Russia), Russian aggression, or aggression by any third party supported by Russia, committed both partners. Russia, however, was not dismissed from Bismarck's thoughts and Russia again became temporarily allied to Germany and Austria-Hungary with the signing of a treaty which made provision for possible disagreements in the Balkans.

Italy, already inclined toward alliance with Germany and her partners, was pushed toward ratification of the Triple Alliance (1882) by French aggression in colonial north Africa. This treaty committed Germany, Austria-Hungary and Italy to mutual support in the event of French aggression, and to benevolent neutrality in the event of hostile activity directed toward France. This agreement was periodically renewed up to the outbreak of the war.

The network of alliances built-up between 1871 and 1890 was the brainchild of Bismarck, and with his dismissal from office by the new Kaiser, Wilhelm II, the system soon began to collapse. Believing alliances with both Austria-Hungary and Russia to be incompatible, the Kaiser's government allowed the treaty with Russia to lapse, thereby offering Russia encouragement to seek security in other quarters. In 1893, a treaty was ratified which assured both Russia and France of the other's military intervention in the event of invasion by Germany, or by Germany in support of any of her partners. Again, Germany faced the possibility of a war on two fronts. Furthermore, despite Bismarck's hopes for stronger links with Britain, the Kaiser had supported the Boers in the Boer War of 1899–1902, thereby alienating British public opinion.

Britain itself was slowly moving away from its traditional policy of "splendid isolation" and in 1902 the Anglo-Japanese alliance was signed. This treaty assured

Wilhelm I of Prussia is proclaimed Emperor of Germany in the Hall of Mirrors, Versailles, 18 January 1871

each party of the other's aid in the event of a conflict in the Far East. Britain also sought to strengthen links with the U.S.A., though no formal treaty was signed. Though traditional enemies, France and Britain were moving rapidly toward increased amity. Colonial disputes over Egypt and Morocco were largely resolved with the formation of the Entente Cordiale (1904) and Britain's links with France implied a unity with Russia.

Fearing the implications of the Entente Cordiale, Germany attempted to divide Britain and France by interfering with France's Moroccan possessions. These attempts failed to provoke any division and, in fact, further cemented Anglo-French relations. In 1907, Britain's links with Russia were confirmed by an entente between the two nations. Within a few short years, Bismarck's carefully planned diplomatic maneuvers had been nullified and Germany, though having been able to stabilize through forty years of peace, had become more isolated than it had been in 1871. Only Austria-Hungary could be counted on as a reliable ally.

It should, however, be emphasized that the alliances which had been formulated between 1871–1914 were, without exception, defensive in orientation and none of the powers involved committed itself to assist an ally in aggressive action. This fact constitutes a powerful refutation of any claim that the web of international treaties caused World War I. Though Germany still had territorial aims in 1871, Bismarck's primary goal was to ensure a stable peace through negotiation and through the establishment of diplomatic deterrents. He was so successful that Europe enjoyed uninterrupted peace for nearly half a century.

German soldiers depart for the front

PART I
1914

By the summer of 1914, the diplomatic situation in Europe was tinder-dry. In June, Archduke Franz Ferdinand, heir to the Austro-Hungarian throne and Inspector General of the imperial forces, was to inspect the army in the Bosnian capital Sarajevo.

Bosnia-Herzegovina was a recent Habsburg acquisition, administered by Austria-Hungary since 1878 but annexed only in 1908. The inhabitants were Turks (that is, Moslems), Serbs and Croats. Most of them – especially the young – resented Habsburg rule, and many were agitating for some sort of political union with neighboring Serbia. When the Archduke's visit was announced, six students, all idealistic patriots and members of a political group called the "Young Bosnians", resolved to assassinate him. They received both encouragement and basic weapons from a Serb secret terrorist organization known as the "Black Hand".

On Sunday 28 June, the Archduke and his wife, the former Countess Sophie Chotek, drove through the streets of Sarajevo in an open car. It was both their wedding anniversary and the feast of St Vitus – the most important festival in the Serb national calendar. Despite lax security, the assassination attempt nearly failed: one of the conspirators failed to draw his revolver; another took pity on the Archduke's wife; and a third threw his bomb but missed the Archduke's car, injuring some 20 onlookers. As a result of this last incident, the Archduke's security advisors recommended return by a different route. Possibly confused by the change, the Archduke's chauffeur took a wrong turning and came to a halt. Gavrilo Princip, one of the six Young Bosnians, saw before him – doubtless to his amazement – his intended victim in a stationary car. He stepped onto the running-board and shot the Archduke and his wife. They both died almost immediately.

At 18 years old, Princip was too young to face the death penalty, so he was incarcerated near Prague, in the fortress town of Theresienstadt (later to achieve notoriety as the Nazis' "showpiece" concentration camp). There Princip died, of tuberculosis, just months before the war he had triggered ground to its bitter conclusion.

His act was more than an assassination: it was a challenge to Austria-Hungary's role as overlord of Bosnia. Austria-Hungary sought redress, and proof – of which none was found – that the Serbian Government had instigated the plot. An ultimatum was dispatched on 23 July by the Imperial Government to Serbia, so worded as to be unacceptable. Serbia, however, abjectly stomached the terms, save for two which violated its status as an independent nation. Austria-Hungary then broke off diplomatic relations and mobilized. The march to war had begun.

First events
Russia, self-appointed protector of the Balkan Slavs, could not permit Serbia to be overrun, and mobilized in response, though only against Austria-Hungary and without any declaration of war. In other circumstances than the Europe of 1914, and among diplomats more skilled than those employed by Germany since the abandonment of Bismarck's carefully-constructed European order, the Russian response might have been interpreted correctly as the warning which was intended – and some diplomatic compromise have been found to satisfy both Austria-Hungary and Serbia. Instead, there were many in positions of authority in both Germany and the Habsburg Empire whose diplomatic judgment was faulty, and more than a few in Germany at least who had calculated from observing Russian railroad construction and French military reforms that war sooner was preferable to war later. Germany at once sent an ultimatum to Russia, demanding Russian demobilization within 12 hours; Russia refused to comply, not least because of the physical impossibility of countermanding complex and extensive mobilization orders on such short notice. On 1 August Germany declared war on Russia and, on the 3rd, without pretext or warning but in full accordance with Schlieffen's mobilization time-

table, on France. The following day German troops invaded Belgium. The British Government, unwilling to risk German hegemony in Europe, found in an 1839 treaty guaranteeing Belgian independence a neat pretext for declaration of war on Germany (and the first of many propaganda coups to boot). Austria-Hungary declared war on Russia the following day. Thus by 5 August all the major European powers were officially at war.

In the West, the grim drama of Schlieffen's Plan and the bloody farce of French offensive strategy were now in full swing. In the East, four Russian armies invaded the Austrian province of Galicia (now southern Poland) on 10 August; two days later, two further armies crossed into East Prussia. In the former campaign, the Russians scored an impressive success, driving the ill-organized Austrian forces back to the Carpathian Mountains. In the north, however, initial successes were soon followed by a crushing defeat at the hands of the Germans at Tannenberg.

On the Western Front, a French corps-strength

Russian civilians indicate their support for the war and their rejection of German demands for demobilization

advance into Upper Alsace on 7 August was quickly halted, and seven German armies, comprising 1,500,000 men, were in position by the 12th to deliver a massive blow toward Paris. French reinforcements resumed the attack in Alsace on l9 August, but pressure to the north obliged these formations to be transferred there. The main French thrust into Lorraine, by 19 divisions in all, was launched on the 14th, but was broken in the Battle of Morhange Sarrebourg by the 20th.

A global war

The war rapidly assumed global dimensions: Portugal confirmed its intention to honor treaty obligations to Britain on 7 August, Japan joined the Allies on 23 August, and the teetering Ottoman Empire, committed by secret treaty, on 29 October. The German colonies in Africa all adjoined those of Great Britain, France, Belgium or Portugal and, except for the Cameroons (where fighting lasted into 1915) and German East Africa – now Tanzania – (where an extraordinary guerilla campaign led by Paul von Lettow-Vorbeck was waged with remarkable success until November 1918), they quickly fell (page 48). Meanwhile Australian and New Zealand forces seized German colonies in New Guinea, the Solomon, Caroline and Marshall Islands, and Samoa. In November, British and Indian troops occupied Basra in what was then the Ottoman province of Iraq, while their Japanese allies bombarded and then captured the German naval base at Tsingtao in China. At sea the Royal Navy, having boxed in the German High Seas Fleet, was able to devote overseas units to hunting down and sinking German commerce raiders from the South Atlantic to the Indian Oceans.

While the war spread across the globe, the combatants enlisted troops from the furthest reaches of their empires to serve in Europe. Within weeks of the outbreak of war, an Indian Expeditionary Force was fighting in Flanders, and 30,000 Canadians, 20,000 Australians and some 8000 New Zealanders were on their way to Europe (South Africa was to send troops in 1915). A division of Moroccans was fighting with the French army as early as the Battle of the Marne; they were soon joined by troops from French West Africa, including the famous Senegalese tirailleurs. German forces in East Africa

The British Army was quick to ensure that it took full advantage of its colonial troops. Britain was reluctant to issue arms to its African subjects but in India there was a long tradition of native regiments

consisted largely of locally-recruited Askaris, although Germany lacked the means of transporting colonial forces to the European fronts. The Russians recruited Muslims from Central Asia to fight on the Eastern Front, a practice that eventually provoked an uprising, while Arab units formed a significant part of Turkish strength.

Stalemate

Once the great German advance through France had been halted at the Battle of the Marne (page 34), both sides tried to maintain the war of maneuver by turning the northern flank of the other in a series of leapfrogging movements popularly (though misleadingly) termed "The Race to the Sea", after which the German High Command launched a very heavy attack on initially-fluid Allied positions around Ypres with the same intention. After the failure of these actions, troops on both sides everywhere on the Western Front began to dig themselves in, creating trenches of increasing complexity and permanence simply to protect themselves from enemy shellfire and bullets. Nowhere on either side was the intention to create permanent fortified positions; in all cases both commanders

and troops on the ground saw entrenchments as a temporary measure, to be held until the war of movement could be resumed after the next offensive. The great stalemate in the West was thus evident on the ground long before it intruded on the perceptions even of those most directly involved in the fighting.

Home fronts

The scale of the miscalculation on all sides of the nature and cost of the war in 1914 was largely kept from the civilian populations of the Allies and Central Powers alike by censorship. Newspaper correspondents were not allowed near the fronts. The unconcealable truth that the confidently predicted victory had not yet been achieved was acknowledged by default only on all sides, and official statements implying that victory was nevertheless still imminent formed the basis of a concerted official campaign in all the major powers to whip up even greater patriotic fervor; for no civilian population could believe, or be allowed to believe, that victory had been missed by default or miscalculation on the part of their leaders. A spirit of renewed effort by every means evolved, and with it growing intolerance. In most belligerent countries enemy aliens were interned, enemy shops looted in major cities. In Great Britain, the Suffragette campaign went into abeyance along with all other forms of political activism; many young women now embraced the fatuous habit of presenting white feathers – a symbol of cowardice – to any man of serviceable age not in uniform. Anti-German manifestations in Britain ranged from the decision of the Royal family to abandon their historic German surname in favor of the more British Windsor to a mindless series of attacks on dachshunds because of their German origin.

Industrial action (a feature of the pre-war world in all European countries) declined rapidly along with all other forms of class-based political activity. Industry itself began to undergo the transformation necessary to supply a modern war, though even by the end of 1914 the true scale of the requirement for weaponry, munitions and uniforms was not accurately judged, even in Germany – and was misjudged badly in Britain, where no tradition of supporting a mass army existed. Huge profits could be made in the expanding wartime production of materials and much of the energy and imagination of pre-war Revolutionary propaganda was diverted into the depiction of war profiteers as fat men in top hats and immaculate clothes, drinking champagne while young men perished at the front.

Propaganda

Official, or semi-official, propaganda likewise burgeoned as the war was dimly seen to be neither won nor lost. Photographs, cartoons, posters and medals all proliferated. The British produced postcards in great number depicting the German "rape" of "Brave Little Belgium" and others of the proud British lion standing in defiant guard on the white cliffs of Dover. Still others showed Britannia and Marianne (France) dancing in accord or otherwise extolling the Entente Cordiale. A famous French pair of illustrations contrasted the ill-treatment and despair of the population of an Alsatian village under German occupation after 1871 with their joy after liberation by France in 1914. Cards depicting commanders, or favorable caricatures of them, abounded. Marching songs, and adaptations for children, became popular in all countries. The effort to foster national enthusiasm for the war effort was, of course, particularly strenuous in Britain, where the army in 1914 (and indeed until 1916) was entirely made up of volunteers, so that posters calling for enlistment were essential. More sinister was the ever-growing license permitted to caricaturists – and indeed journalists and other ostensibly objective commentators – to demonize the enemy. In the Allied camp, the stereotype German became increasingly ape-like, while German commentators responded to propaganda stories of German atrocities in Belgium with increasingly lurid accounts of the murder of German soldiers by Belgian civilians, including priests and medical personnel.

Much propaganda was, of course, directly related to appeals for public financial support for the war effort. Austrian artists produced patriotic Vivat bands, printed on silk, for sale in support of Austrian war charities. In Germany, a Hindenburg cult emerged after the general's great victory at Tannenberg and, in a deliberate attempt by the German Great General Staff to deflect attention from the failure of the Schlieffen Plan in the west, he was represented as invincible. Most bizarre, perhaps, was the creation of enormous wooden statues of Hindenburg into which, for a donation toward the war effort, Germans could drive a nail to turn him into a man of iron.

Thus civilians on both sides were kept largely in the dark and, since they were so ill-informed, they relied on rumors, which became more grotesque at each telling. In a famous example, a German newspaper report that, on the fall of Antwerp, bells were rung in churches throughout Germany, became by stages perverted in Allied minds to the belief that recalcitrant clergy were tied to the bells and used as clappers. Many such stories were extraordinarily graphic by the standards of normal peacetime sensibilities of the period: Germans were accused, for example, of severing the hands of Belgian babies and the breasts of Belgian nuns, among other atrocities. Although some acts of brutality were undoubtedly committed against civilians, most of these reports were later found to be without substance; moreover, the extent to which such stories were artificially fostered, particularly on the Allied side, can be gauged by the fact that widespread genuine atrocities (such as those perpetrated by Austrian soldiers against the civilian population of Serbia in the course of the invasions of 1914) were given far less prominence in the Allied press. The fact that belief in German atrocities was so prevalent and persistent reflects both the mood of the public and the effectiveness of Allied propaganda.

A huge and enthusiastic crowd gathers in Königsplatz, Berlin to listen to pro-war propaganda speeches in August, 1914

Just a few of the many casualties suffered by the German Army. In the optimistic bulletins regularly released to the press exact figures were carefully avoided

The reality

Censorship and propaganda could not, however, long conceal the fact that by the end of 1914 France and Austria had suffered huge casualties which had all but crippled their military capabilities, at least in the short term, Germany had suffered enormous losses without gaining the decisive victory which might have justified their sacrifice, the northern arm of Russia's offensive had been unceremoniously amputated by the German victory at Tannenberg, and more than half of the BEF who had crossed the English Channel to France in August were casualties, and one in ten of them were dead. Nor could any official effort conceal the hard truth that, in the East as in the West, the opening campaigns had ended in stalemate.

Yet in all the major powers enthusiasm for the war continued unabated, in part because the most terrible losses were yet to come, in part because of an excess of zeal in the name of security, which in turn meant secrecy. Thus the British War Office censored all cables and foreign correspondence as well as soldiers' letters from the front. The Defense of the Realm Act (disparagingly known as "Dora") was likewise applied to newspapers – the principal channel for information – with the threat of prosecution for publishing unauthorized news. Moreover, a form of self-censorship quickly evolved. Bad news was simply not reported. Newspapers not only encouraged their readers to believe in the justice of the cause, but also quite deliberately made light of the dangers facing men at the front. British newspapers of 1914, for example, habitually reported claims by officers that their men "now laugh at German shells".

Nor were civilians enlightened by their clergy – another source of information – for many clergymen were of the class which had led their countries into the war, and almost all were equally ill-informed and fearful of growth in atheism following pointless sacrifice; and many believed their proper role in wartime was to console the bereaved rather than preach the fundamental Christian truths of peace and forgiveness. In fact, the clergy, with some notable exceptions, were often among the most patriotic, and therefore bellicose, of all groups. The result was that war produced a surge of patriotism throughout all classes and all combatants, which stilled other passions and preoccupations. This would remain true, at least in Britain, France and Germany, until the losses in the great battles of 1916, when scarcely a village or hamlet on either side was left untouched by human loss. Enthusiasm for the war actually grew during 1914 – but left unanswered the daunting question of how to win and end it. To this, though few as yet recognized it, nobody had the answer.

Timeline 1914

The Steps to War
June – November 1914

28 June	Assassination of Archduke Franz Ferdinand at Sarajevo
2 July	Austria assured of German support by German ambassador
13 July	Austrian emissary to Sarajevo reports his inability to locate any evidence implicating the Serbian Government in the assassination
14 July	Austrian Council of War Ministers resolves on action against Serbia
22 July	Austria warned by Russia against drastic action in Serbia
23 July	Austrian ultimatum to Serbia; agreement to its terms demanded within 48 hours
25 July	Russia declares that it cannot divorce itself from events in the Balkans
25 July	Serbia orders mobilization
25 July	Serbia accepts Austria's terms, except for the clause allowing Austrian investigation into Serbian affairs. Austrian minister leaves for Vienna
25 July	Serbian government requests Greek support, as laid down by earlier treaty, against any Bulgarian threat; Greece agrees

26 July	Mobilization of Austria
26 July	Mobilization of Montenegro
26 July	Churchill orders British fleet to move to war bases after the naval review
28 July	Austria declares war on Serbia
1 Aug	Germany declares war on Russia, following Russia's refusal to demobilize
3 Aug	Germany declares war on France
4 Aug	Germany declares war on Belgium
4 Aug	Great Britain declares war on Germany
5 Aug	Montenegro declares war on Austria
12 Aug	Great Britain declares war on Austria
23 Aug	Japan declares war on Germany
2 Nov	Russia declares war on Turkey
6 Nov	Great Britain and France declare war on Turkey

Key to Maps

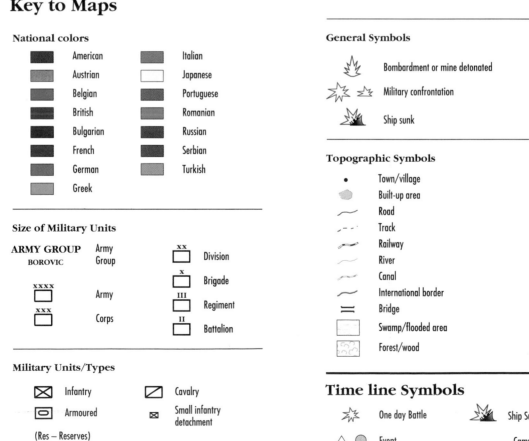

National colors

■	American	■	Italian
■	Austrian	□	Japanese
■	Belgian	■	Portuguese
■	British	■	Romanian
■	Bulgarian	■	Russian
■	French	■	Serbian
■	German	■	Turkish
■	Greek		

Size of Military Units

ARMY GROUP BOROVIC	Army Group	xx □	Division
xxxx □	Army	x □	Brigade
xxx □	Corps	III □	Regiment
		II □	Battalion

Military Units/Types

⊠	Infantry	⊘	Cavalry
⊡	Armoured	⊠	Small infantry detachment

(Res – Reserves)

General Symbols

💥	Bombardment or mine detonated
💥 💥	Military confrontation
💥	Ship sunk

Topographic Symbols

•	Town/village
⬡	Built-up area
⌢	Road
- - -	Track
~	Railway
~	River
~	Canal
~	International border
=	Bridge
▢	Swamp/flooded area
▢	Forest/wood

Time line Symbols

💥	One day Battle	💥	Ship Sunk
△ ●	Event		Campaign or extended Battle

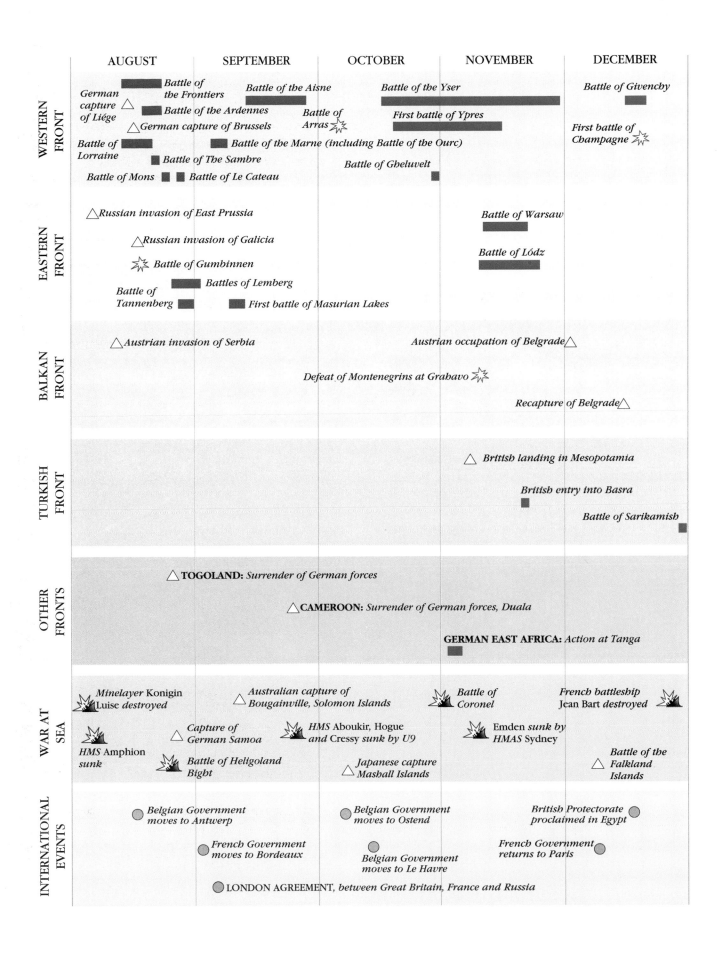

Battle of the Frontiers August 1914

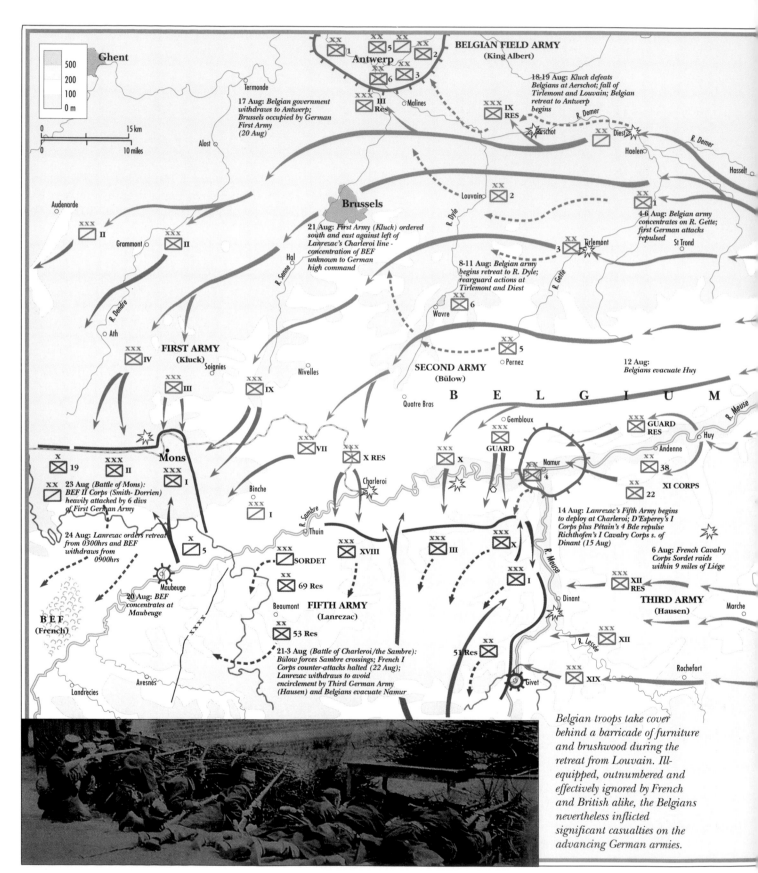

Ghent

500
200
100
0 m

0   15km
0   10 miles

Termonde

Alost

Audenarde

Grammont

R. Dendre

Ath

FIRST ARMY
(Kluck)

Soignies

XXX II

XXX II

XXX IV

XXX III

Mons

X 19

XXX II

XXX I

XX 23 Aug (Battle of Mons): BEF II Corps (Smith-Dorrien) heavily attacked by 6 divs of First German Army

24 Aug: Lanrezac orders retreat from 0300hrs and BEF withdraws from 0900hrs

X 5

Maubeuge

20 Aug: BEF concentrates at Maubeuge

BEF
(French)

Landrecies

Avesnes

BELGIAN FIELD ARMY
(King Albert)

XX 1

XX 5

XX

XX 2

Antwerp

XX 6

XX 3

XXX III Res

Malines

18-19 Aug: Kluck defeats Belgians at Aerschot; fall of Tirlemont and Louvain; Belgian retreat to Antwerp begins

XXX IX RES

R. Demer

Aerschot

XX Diest

Haelen

Hasselt

R. Demer

17 Aug: Belgian government withdraws to Antwerp; Brussels occupied by German First Army (20 Aug)

Brussels

21 Aug: First Army (Kluck) ordered south and east against left of Lanrezac's Charleroi line - concentration of BEF unknown to German high command

Hal

R. Senne

Louvain

XX 2

R. Dyle

XX 3 Tirlemont

St Trond

4-6 Aug: Belgian army concentrates on R. Gette; first German attacks repulsed

8-11 Aug: Belgian army begins retreat to R. Dyle; rearguard actions at Tirlemont and Diest

R. Gette

XX 6

Wavre

XX 5

Pernez

XX 1

12 Aug: Belgians evacuate Huy

SECOND ARMY
(Bülow)

Nivelles

Quatre Bras

B E L G I U M

Gembloux

XXX GUARD

XXX X

Namur

XXX 4

R. Meuse

Huy

Andenne

XX 38

XXX GUARD RES

XX 22

XI CORPS

XXX VII

XXX X RES

Charleroi

Binche

XXX I

R. Sambre

Thuin

XXX SORDET

XX 69 Res

Beaumont

FIFTH ARMY
(Lanrezac)

XX 53 Res

21-3 Aug (Battle of Charleroi/the Sambre): Bülow forces Sambre crossings; French I Corps counter-attacks halted (22 Aug); Lanrezac withdraws to avoid encirclement by Third German Army (Hausen) and Belgians evacuate Namur

XXX XVIII

XXX III

XXX X

XXX I

XX 51 Res

Givet

14 Aug: Lanrezac's Fifth Army begins to deploy at Charleroi; D'Esperey's I Corps plus Pétain's 4 Bde repulse Richthofen's I Cavalry Corps s. of Dinant (15 Aug)

6 Aug: French Cavalry Corps Sordet raids within 9 miles of Liége

R. Meuse

Dinant

XXX XII RES

THIRD ARMY
(Hausen)

Marche

XXX XII

R. Lesse

XXX XIX

Rochefort

Belgian troops take cover behind a barricade of furniture and brushwood during the retreat from Louvain. Ill-equipped, outnumbered and effectively ignored by French and British alike, the Belgians nevertheless inflicted significant casualties on the advancing German armies.

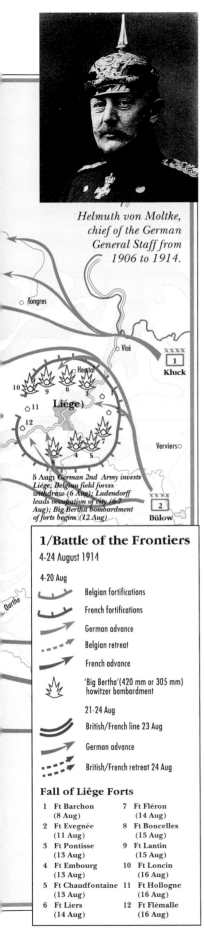

Helmuth von Moltke, chief of the German General Staff from 1906 to 1914.

5 Aug: German 2nd Army invests Liége; Belgian field forces withdraw (6 Aug); Ludendorff leads occupation of city (6-7 Aug); Big Bertha bombardment of forts begins (12 Aug)

1/Battle of the Frontiers

4-24 August 1914

4-20 Aug

⌣⌣⌣	Belgian fortifications
⌣⌣⌣	French fortifications
→	German advance
⇢	Belgian retreat
→	French advance
💥	'Big Bertha'(420 mm or 305 mm) howitzer bombardment

21-24 Aug

⌒⌒	British/French line 23 Aug
⟶	German advance
⇢⇢	British/French retreat 24 Aug

Fall of Liége Forts

1	Ft Barchon (8 Aug)	7	Ft Fléron (14 Aug)
2	Ft Evegnée (11 Aug)	8	Ft Boncelles (15 Aug)
3	Ft Pontisse (13 Aug)	9	Ft Lantin (15 Aug)
4	Ft Embourg (13 Aug)	10	Ft Loncin (16 Aug)
5	Ft Chaudfontaine (13 Aug)	11	Ft Hollogne (16 Aug)
6	Ft Liers (14 Aug)	12	Ft Flémalle (16 Aug)

War came in the west within 24 hours of German mobilization: the 16th Division entered Luxemburg at 1700hrs on Saturday 1 August. The inexorable timetable of the Schlieffen Plan meant that from the 6th, 550 trainloads of men and munitions were crossing the Rhine daily. By 12 August seven German armies were in place to deliver a massive blow.

But the clarity of purpose with which Schlieffen had designed that blow had been lost. Both fear of a French invasion across the Rhine and the recollection of his uncle's successful double-envelopment of Napoleon III's armies at Sedan in 1870 had led Moltke to strengthen the forces in Alsace and Lorraine at the expense of his all-important right wing. His failure of nerve was to prove fatal to an already questionable Schlieffen Plan.

First moves

Belgian resistance to the German advance was vigorous, despite the shock destruction of the Liége forts by Krupp 420mm and Skoda 305mm siege howitzers. As the German Second Army advanced on Namur and Charleroi, the surviving elements of the Belgian Army withdrew behind the defences of Antwerp, mounting a series of largely ineffective sorties against the German right and rear during the ensuing campaign.

Reports of the German advance into central Belgium did not sway the French high command from their faith in Plan XVII - and in any event no alternative plan had been prepared (see Strategic View). The casualties inflicted on the massed columns of Kluck and Bülow's armies by the Belgians were swiftly dwarfed in the bloody and unexpected repulse of the French main forces, driven back on their fortifications with losses of over 300,000.

The open flank

Meanwhile, I and II Corps of the BEF (French), some 80,000 men, had landed at Le Havre and Boulogne on 9 August, and by the 20th had concentrated at Maubeuge, on the left of Lanrezac's Fifth Army. With little intelligence of the size or location of the forces opposing them and no coordination at all with the Belgians, these forces found themselves assailed from the north by the German First and Second Armies and from the east by the Third (Hausen). Lanrezac, warned on 23 August of the imminent fall of Namur, issued orders to withdraw – an action which led Joffre to dismiss him on 3 September for lacking fighting spirit.

The BEF, having resisted repeated German attacks at Mons on the 23rd, was left exposed; French ordered a similar withdrawal from 0900hrs on 24 August.

Strategic View: Joffre

German movement into Belgium suggested to the French commander in chief that Moltke planned only a limited outflanking maneuver. Having despatched Lanrezac's Fifth Army to guard the lower Meuse, Joffre turned to the chief objective of Plan XVII, an invasion of Alsace and Lorraine intended to derail any possible German offensive plans. Dubail's First Army entered Alsace on 7 August. A German counter-attack on the 10th reversed his initial successes, so Joffre threw Pau's new Army of Alsace (A) into the increasingly bloody struggle. His last reserves, some 37 Territorial and Reserve divisions, were assembled on the 12th into

Maunoury's Army of Lorraine (L), and Dubail and Castelnau (Second Army) then attacked on that part of the front: here too the French were heavily defeated. These costly setbacks to a Plan which had made no provision for failure kept Joffre's attention firmly fixed on the south, and delayed his realization that the main German forces were elsewhere. Lanrezac appealed on the 14th for protection for the left (that is, western) flank of his position at Charleroi, but it was only with the fall of Liége and Belgian warnings that over 200,000 German troops had crossed the Meuse that Joffre was persuaded to turn his attention northward.

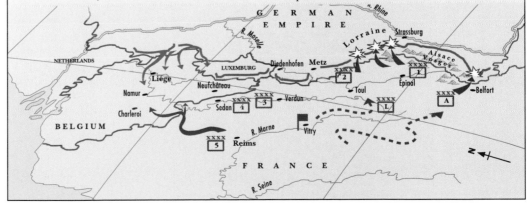

Tannenberg The Russian Advance 13–23 August 1914

Despite a cumbersome mobilization program, the Russian high command responded swiftly to French appeals for help by bringing forward their planned invasion of East Prussia. General Jilinsky, commander of the Russian northwest group of armies planned a westward advance by the First Army to draw forward German forces; two days later, the Second Army was to advance northwestward from Poland into the German rear, cutting off their retreat over the Vistula.

This plan was not without its problems: poor railways and roads in the border area would make movement difficult and the two armies would be separated by the Masurian Lakes.

The campaign

Rennenkampf's clash with Prittwitz at Gumbinnen (Map 1) had dramatic consequences. Warned of Samsonov's advance, Prittwitz panicked and informed Moltke that he intended to retreat behind the Vistula. Moltke immediately replaced him with General Paul von Hindenburg and General Ludendorff. He also dispatched to the Eastern Front two corps from the German right wing in France, with serious consequences in the west (page 30).

As Prittwitz lost hope, so Jilinsky became more over-confident. He urged Samsonov to advance further west before turning north, hoping to encircle even greater numbers of Germans. This increased still further the distance between the two Russian armies.

A German response was set in motion by Colonel Max Hoffmann, deputy Chief of Staff of the Eighth Army. Hoffmann's plan, for which Ludendorff was largely to be given credit, was for the Eighth Army to disengage from Rennen-

kampf's First Army, leaving merely a cavalry screen, and move troops by rail and on foot to strike at Samsonov's Second Army in the south.

I Corps and 3rd Reserve Division were to be taken by train to the right flank of XX Corps (Map 2) which would retreat slowly before Samsonov's advance. Meanwhile, XVII Corps and I Reserve Corps were to march southward and take up station on XX Corp's left wing. Samsonov would thus advance into a trap. Jilinsky made matters worse by urging Rennenkampf to press forward; Samsonov thus faced almost the entire Eighth Army, with no hope of reinforcement from First Army.

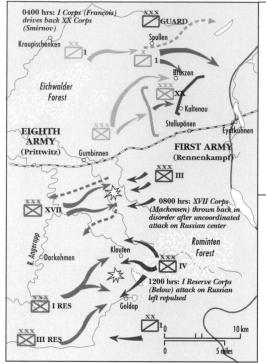

1/Battle of Gumbinnen
20 August 1914

⤴ Russian XX Corps positions, dawn

⤳ German attacks, dawn

⇢ Russian retreat, morning

➜ German attacks, 0800 hrs and midday

➜ Russian counter-attacks

⇢ German XVII Corps retreat

⤴ Russian positions, evening

"The XVII Corps is heavily engaged and cannot advance, nor is there any good news from XX Corps. I may be obliged to retreat behind the Vistula."

General Prittwitz report to Moltke on 20 August

Russian troops launch an attack in East Prussia, 1914. Four men have already become casualties, out of fourteen visible in the picture, and this wave of attackers is clearly still some distance from its objective. The Germans forces enjoyed considerable technical superiority over their Russian counterparts, it was essential that German commanders take full advantage of this together with better communications in order to make Hoffmann's plan work.

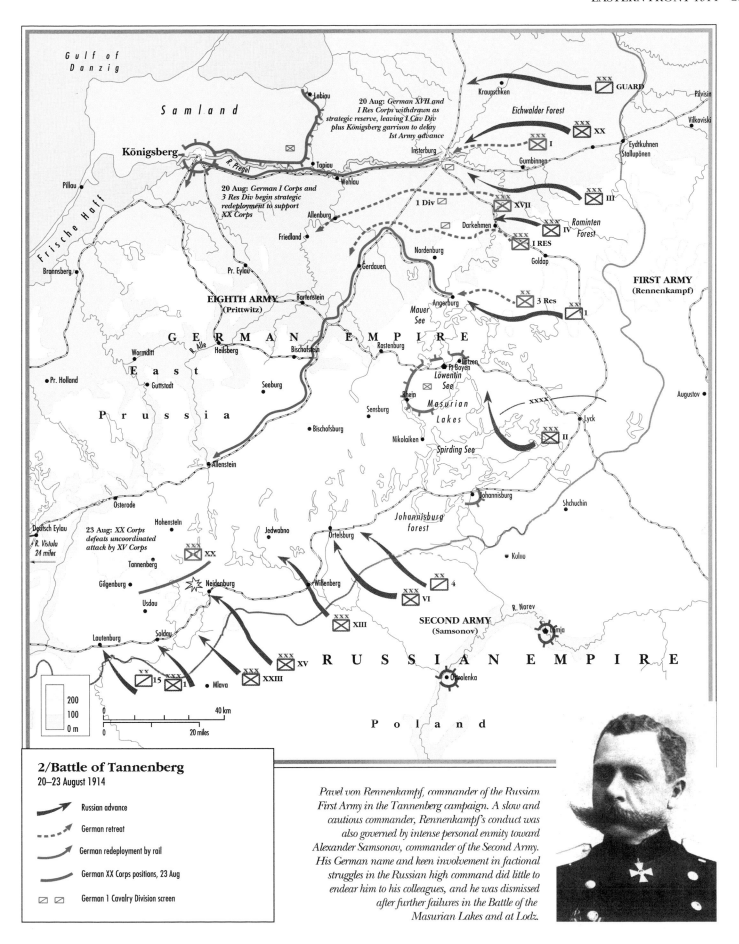

Gulf of Danzig

S a m l a n d

Labiau

20 Aug: *German XVII and I Res Corps withdrawn as strategic reserve, leaving I Cav Div plus Königsberg garrison to delay 1st Army advance*

Kraupschken

Eichwalder Forest

Pilvisin

Vilkoviski

Königsberg

Tapiau

R. Pregel

Wehlau

Insterburg

Gumbinnen

Eydtkuhnen
Stallupönen

Pillau

20 Aug: *German I Corps and 3 Res Div begin strategic redeployment to support XX Corps*

1 Div

Allenburg

Darkehmen

Rominten Forest

Goldap

Brannsberg

Friedland

Nordenburg

I RES

Frische Haff

Pr. Eylau

Gerdauen

FIRST ARMY
(Rennenkampf)

EIGHTH ARMY
(Prittwitz)

Bartenstein

Angerburg

3 Res

Heilsberg

Bischofstein

Rastenburg

Mauer See

Wormditt

R. Alle

G E R M A N   E M P I R E

Lötzen

Ft Boyen

E a s t

Pr. Holland

Guttstadt

Löwentin See

Augustov

Seeburg

Rhein

Masurian Lakes

P r u s s i a

Sensburg

Spirding See

Lyck

Bischofsburg

Nikolaiken

II

Osterode

Johannisburg

Shchuchin

Deutsch Eylau

R. Vistula
24 miles

Hohenstein

Jedwabno

Ortelsburg

Johannisburg forest

Kolno

23 Aug: *XX Corps defeats uncoordinated attack by XV Corps*

Tannenberg

XX

Willenberg

4

Gilgenburg

Neidenburg

VI

Usdau

SECOND ARMY
(Samsonov)

R. Narev

Lautenburg

Solday

XIII

Lomja

15

1

Mlava

XXIII

XV

R U S S I A N   E M P I R E

Ostrolenka

200
100
0 m

40 km

20 miles

P o l a n d

2/Battle of Tannenberg
20–23 August 1914

→ Russian advance

⇢ German retreat

→ German redeployment by rail

— German XX Corps positions, 23 Aug

⊡ ⊡ German 1 Cavalry Division screen

Pavel von Rennenkampf, commander of the Russian First Army in the Tannenberg campaign. A slow and cautious commander, Rennenkampf's conduct was also governed by intense personal enmity toward Alexander Samsonov, commander of the Second Army. His German name and keen involvement in factional struggles in the Russian high command did little to endear him to his colleagues, and he was dismissed after further failures in the Battle of the Masurian Lakes and at Lodz.

GUARD

XX

I

III

XVII

IV

1

The Great Retreat   August – September 1914

On 29 August, Joffre ordered the Fifth Army, though hard pressed by the German Second Army, to attack the left flank of the First Army to relieve pressure on the BEF as it retreated after Le Cateau. Lanrezac's I, III, X and XVIII Corps counter-attacked at Guise on that day. The Fifth Army retreated the following day to avoid encirclement but the counter-stroke had achieved its purpose.

There was, however, no alternative for the Allies but continued retreat. But an additional significant factor emerged: Kluck was convinced that the BEF had been destroyed at Le Cateau and that the French Fifth Army was now the Allied left flank. The Schlieffen Plan was abandoned and the advance shifted to the southeast to roll up the Fifth Army. This was originally at the request of Bülow who, when Lanrezac counter-attacked, had asked Kluck for assistance; when this proved unnecessary Bülow pressed Kluck to wheel in nonetheless to cut off Lanrezac's retreat. Kluck referred the request to Moltke, who gave his consent to change of direction.

Kluck thus passed east of Paris where, unknown to him, French forces, taken from the fortresses on the German frontier, were concentrating. These were to be formed into the Sixth Army (Maunoury).

Kluck thus unwittingly exposed his right flank to the Sixth Army. Galliéni, military governor of Paris, sought permission from Joffre to exploit this, despite the specific designation of his army to the defense of Paris.

By 2 September, Kluck's left flank was on the Marne at Château-Thierry, his right on the Oise at Chantilly. Joffre ordered the Sixth Army to complete its concentration in the Paris area and the general retreat to continue until the Fifth Army was safe from envelopment. Meanwhile,

the newly-forming Ninth Army (Foch) was to continue its concentration between the Fourth and Fifth armies.

Moltke's conflicting orders

On 3 September, Moltke, while agreeing with Kluck's change of direction, ordered him to guard the right flank of the Second Army. But the First Army had been moving faster than the Second and was farther south than Moltke realised. Nor did Moltke fully explain his order. Kluck knew that to obey the explicit part of the order (to provide flank protection for the Second Army) would halt his army for two days, allowing the French either to escape or to rally, while trying to comply with Moltke's apparent intentions (to ensure that the French were driven southeast of Paris) would leave the right wing of Second Army exposed. He took the latter to be his main duty, his army being ideally positioned for the task.

Kluck continued his southward march across the Marne on 5 September, his right flank protected by a weak detachment of three brigades and limited cavalry only. The existence of the French Sixth Army was still unknown to him.

French infantry on the attack in 1914. The retreat to the Marne revealed unexpected French resilience in defense.

Joseph Joffre, French commander-in-chief in the first part of the war. After the disastrous failure of Plan XVII (which he had helped to formulate), his imperturbable handling of the Allied retreat ultimately ensured the failure of the Schlieffen Plan.

Strategic View: Joffre
After the failure of the defensive actions at Mons and Charleroi, Joffre set about transferring all available forces from the French right to the extreme left of his line (dashed arrow), while holding together the left and center as they withdrew. He was prepared even to abandon Paris if necessary. Kluck's change of direction to the southeast at last seemed to offer the chance of a counter-blow.

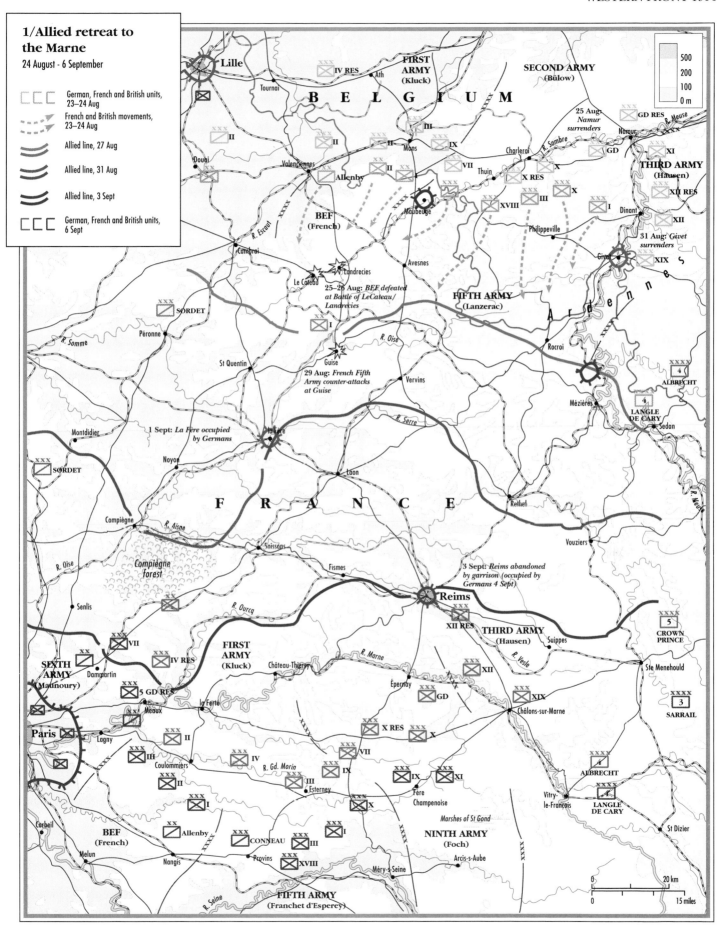

1/Allied retreat to the Marne

24 August - 6 September

⊏⊏⊏	German, French and British units, 23–24 Aug
⇢⇢⇢	French and British movements, 23–24 Aug
⌒⌒	Allied line, 27 Aug
⌒⌒	Allied line, 31 Aug
⌒⌒	Allied line, 3 Sept
⊏⊏⊏	German, French and British units, 6 Sept

BELGIUM

FIRST ARMY (Kluck)

SECOND ARMY (Bülow)

500
200
100
0 m

Lille

IV RES

Ath

Tournai

III

II

II

H

Mons

IX

25 Aug: Namur surrenders

GD RES

R. Meuse

Namur

Charleroi

R. Sambre

VII

Thuin

GD

XI

THIRD ARMY (Hausen)

Dougi

Valenciennes

XX II

Allenby

II

Maubeuge

X RES

X

XII RES

XVIII

III

X

I

Dinant

XII

BEF (French)

Cambrai

R. Escaut

XXXX

Avesnes

Philippeville

31 Aug: Givet surrenders

Givet

XIX

Ardennes

Landrecies

Le Cateau

25–26 Aug: BEF defeated at Battle of LeCateau/ Landrecies

FIFTH ARMY (Lanzerac)

SORDET

Péronne

R. Somme

St Quentin

I

R. Oise

Guise

29 Aug: French Fifth Army counter-attacks at Guise

Vervins

R. Serre

Rocroi

Mézières

XXXX
4
ALBRECHT

4
LANGLE DE CARY

Montdidier

1 Sept: La Fère occupied by Germans

la Fère

Laon

Rethel

Sedan

R. Meuse

SORDET

Noyon

F R A N C E

Vouziers

Compiègne

R. Aisne

Compiègne forest

Soissons

Fismes

R. Oise

Senlis

XX

R. Ourcq

3 Sept: Reims abandoned by garrison (occupied by Germans 4 Sept)

Reims

XII RES

THIRD ARMY (Hausen)

Suippes

R. Vesle

XXXX
5
CROWN PRINCE

VII

SIXTH ARMY (Maunoury)

XX
Dammartin

IV RES

FIRST ARMY (Kluck)

Château-Thierry

R. Marne

XII

Épernay

GD

XIX

Châlons-sur-Marne

Ste Menehould

XXXX
3
SARRAIL

5 GD RES

la Ferté

Meaux

Lagny

II

X RES

X

VII

ALBRECHT

Paris

III

IV

IX

IX

XI

Fère Champenoise

R. Gd. Morin

III

Coulommiers

Esterney

X

Vitry-le-François

4
LANGLE DE CARY

Corbeil

I

Marshes of St Gond

St Dizier

BEF (French)

Melun

XX
Allenby

CONNEAU

III

Provins

XVIII

Nangis

I

Méry-s-Seine

Arcis-s-Aube

NINTH ARMY (Foch)

0   20 km
0   15 miles

FIFTH ARMY (Franchet d'Esperey)

R. Seine

Tannenberg The German Triumph August 1914

Alexander Samsonov, commander of the Russian Second Army, committed suicide on the 29th August, when the full extent of the Russian defeat was realised.

On 23 August, Samsonov's center made contact with the German XX Corps, but the Second Army was extended over 60 miles (97km) and its two wings were separated from the center. The Germans thus had the prospect of double encirclement, for as the Russians advanced the German XX Corps gave way.

The Russians drove the Germans back in this sector, then, on 26 August, Ludendorff ordered François's I Corps to smash the Russian left wing. François determined to get behind the

1/Battle of Tannenberg,
23-31 August 1914

23-26 Aug

⌒⌒⌒ German fortifications

⟶ Russian advance

⟶ Rail movement of German I Corps

⟶ German attack

- - -> Russian retreat

27-31 Aug

⟶ Russian advance

☑ German 1 Cav Div screen

⟶ German attack

- - -> Russian retreat

⟶ Final position of Russian XII, XV and XVIII Corps

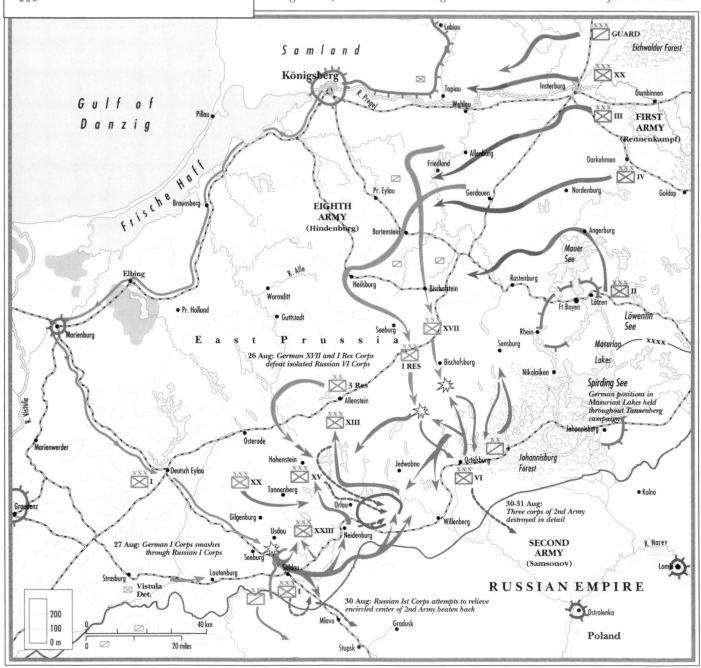

26 Aug: German XVII and I Res Corps defeat isolated Russian VI Corps

27 Aug: German I Corps smashes through Russian I Corps

30 Aug: Russian Ist Corps attempts to relieve encircled center of 2nd Army beaten back

30-31 Aug: Three corps of 2nd Army destroyed in detail

Spirding See: German positions in Masurian Lakes held throughout Tannenberg campaign

RUSSIAN EMPIRE

Poland

> *" A man rushed up shouting that the German Cavalry was on us. There are signs of nerves."*
>
> Colonel Knox, British Military Attaché, immediately prior to François's attack on the Russian left.

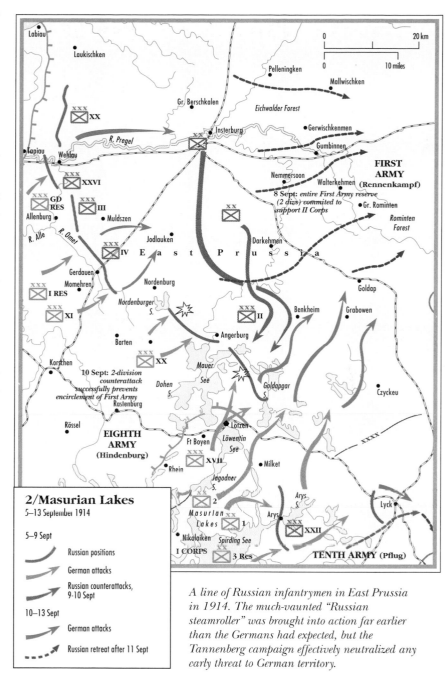

Russians and cut them off from retreat eastward. He therefore made a token attack on the Russian left, seemingly obeying his orders, while positioning his troops for his purpose.

Also on the 26 August, the Russian right wing, already seperated from the center, was repulsed and forced to retire to Lake Bossao. The Russian right flank fell into retreat southward for some 20 miles (32km).

The next day François attacked the Russian left which retreated in disorder. He then moved to get behind the Russian rear. Samsonov now inexplicably ordered his center to strike northward, rather than reassembling his flanks to attack.

On 28 August the Germans attacked at first light. Russian collapse was imminent, for the Second Army's rear was now closed, its flanks shattered. The destruction of the Russian centre continued throughout 29 August. During 29 and 30 August the desperate, unco-ordinated Russians made repeated attempts to break through the encirclement but were everywhere and always driven back. By 31 August their resistance was at an end.

2/Masurian Lakes
5–13 September 1914

5–9 Sept

⟶ Russian positions
⟶ German attacks
⟶ Russian counterattacks, 9-10 Sept

10–13 Sept

⟶ German attacks
⟶ Russian retreat after 11 Sept

Aftermath

After this great victory, the Germans were free to turn on Rennenkampf's First Army (Map 2). On 5 September the Germans made a sustained attack on Rennenkamf to hold his attention, while on the 9th François cut-off his rear. Rennenkempf had no option but to retreat eastwards into Russia. He first ordered two divisions to counter-attack in the center on 10 September, halting the German XX Corps for 48 hours. Rennenkempf's First Army thus escaped, pouring back along the route they had earlier taken in expectation of victory.

Schlieffen's plan (p 27) had been reversed: the Germans were held to a stalemate in the west while delivering a knock-out blow in the east, precisely the opposite of what the great German architect had planned.

A line of Russian infantrymen in East Prussia in 1914. The much-vaunted "Russian steamroller" was brought into action far earlier than the Germans had expected, but the Tannenberg campaign effectively neutralized any early threat to German territory.

First Marne September 1914

Early on the evening of 3 September, Galliéni, commander of the defense of Paris, sought Joffre's permission to attack Kluck's First Army with units of the French Sixth Army now arriving in the city. He argued that French salvation lay in counter-attacks along the entire line north of the River Marne, from Paris to Verdun; Sir John French, however, had learnt of plans to evacuate the French Government to Bordeaux, and was considering withdrawing the BEF to the Channel ports.

France saved

By passionate argument both in person and by telephone, Galliéni finally won over both Joffre and French. Meanwhile, Kluck, believing that the forces opposed to him were still in retreat, continued his advance south.

The Battle of the Marne proper began at about 1430hrs on the afternoon of 5 September, when advance units of Maunoury's Sixth Army collided with a corps of Kluck's flank north of Meaux. On the following day all the Allied left-wing armies had turned about for a full scale attack. Kluck shifted the bulk of his army westward on 6–7 September (see Strategic View) to mount a ferocious counter-attack. This halted the French advance and forced Maunoury's Sixth Army onto the defensive between 7 and 9 September (see Map 1). The German advance was only stemmed when Galliéni rushed forward reinforcements, some in commandeered Paris taxicabs.

By now the action was general along the whole front west of Verdun. Kluck's maneuver had, however, lengthened a gap, now of some 30mls/48km, between his army and Bülow's Second, still moving south, which the Germans had no reserves to fill. Into this gap now marched the BEF and the left-wing formations of the French Fifth Army (d'Espérey).

Moltke, far behind the front and inadequately informed of events, had reached the point of mental collapse. He instructed a young staff officer, Lieutenant-Colonel Hentsch, to visit the command centers of all the German armies to assess and report on the situation. If it were in fact the case that the BEF was across the Marne and moving into the gap between the First and Second armies, then Bülow should retreat to the Aisne.

Hentsch arrived at Second Army's headquarters simultaneously with reports that its right flank was being turned by the French. Bülow advocated retreat; Hentsch agreed, and later the same day (9 September), in Moltke's name, ordered Kluck's First Army, the left flank and rear of which were threatened by the BEF's advance, also to withdraw to the Aisne. By the afternoon the Battle of the Marne was over.

The Allies, slow in pursuit, failed to consolidate their gains; the German armies retired in an orderly, unmolested fashion to the line Noyon–Verdun, where they quickly organised new positions. Thus, though the Allies had won a strategic victory, arguably making the war's outcome inevitable, however the immediate effect of the battle was indecisive.

Consequences

The campaign nevertheless caused enormous loss of life. German casualty figures were never

Joseph Simon Galliéni was appointed Joffre's deputy just before the outbreak of the war, despite his ill-health. He played a crucial role in the Battle of the Marne, seizing the opportunity to counter-attack the right flank of the German advance even though Joffre favored retreat beyond the River Seine.

" *The pursuit had been thrilling. Through the intermittent thunderstorms and heat and glare of the early September days we had pressed on... Every hour a fresh situation developed, sharp actions, bursts of shrapnel, sudden pursuits.* "

**Captain Arthur Osborn
Royal Irish Dragoon Guards**

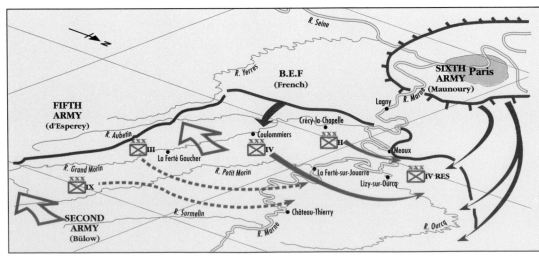

Strategic View: Kluck
Kluck reacted slowly to the French Sixth Army advance on his right because he believed that the BEF and the French Fifth Army were still in retreat southward, and also because he recognized the danger of losing touch with the Second Army. On 6 September he was forced to withdraw II and IV corps to meet the threat on his flank, then on 7 September the two left-flank corps; this did indeed open a yawning gap between his army and Bülow's.

published (though 15,127 German prisoners were taken), but French losses for 5-10 September alone were about 80,000.

The Battle of the Marne concluded the first phase of the war on the Western Front. Moltke was relieved of his command on 14 September and replaced by Erich von Falkenhayn. The price Germany paid was dreadful. Military successes elsewhere might lead to a negotiated peace, but all chance of the swift, total victory envisaged by Schlieffen was gone.

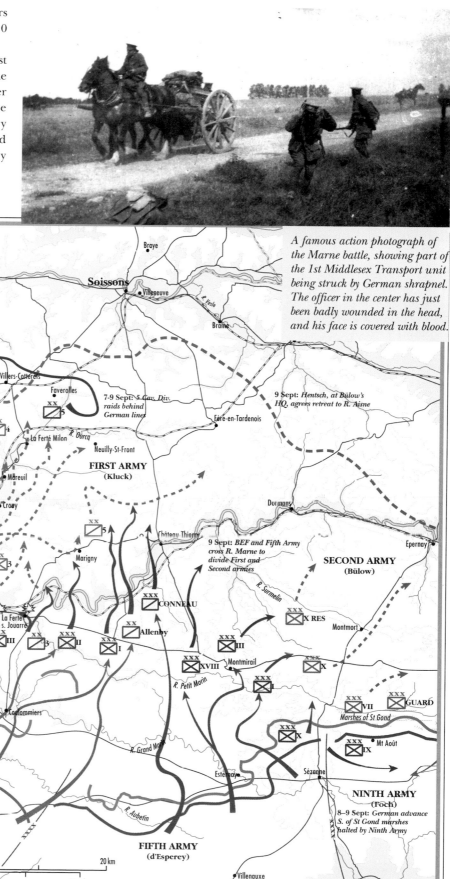

A famous action photograph of the Marne battle, showing part of the 1st Middlesex Transport unit being struck by German shrapnel. The officer in the center has just been badly wounded in the head, and his face is covered with blood.

1/Battle of the Marne

5 – 10 September

5 – 8 Sept

⟋⟋⟋ Allied lines

━━━ German lines

➤ Allied advance (BEF and Fifth Army only)

5 – 8 Sept

⊏⊏⊏ Dispositions, 9 Sept (AM)

⟿ Allied movements

⇢ German movements

⇠ German line, 10 Sept

✳ Bridge destroyed

Map labels:

Estrées-St-Denis • Compiègne • Braye • Soissons • Villeneuve • R. Vesle • Braine

X 43

7–9 Sept: Kluck begins to force Sixth Army back on Paris

Villers-Cotterêts • Faverolles

7-9 Sept: 5 Cav. Div. raids behind German lines

Fère-en-Tardenois

9 Sept: Hentsch, at Bülow's HQ, agrees retreat to R. Aisne

Crépy-en-Valois

XXX IX • XX 4 • XX 5

X 1 & part 3 • XXX IV • Napuil • R. Ourcq • La Ferté Milon • Neuilly-St-Front

FIRST ARMY (Kluck)

XXX VII • XX 7 • Mareuil • Crouy

XX 4 • XX 8/7R

Dormans • Epernay

XX 62 • Dammartin • XX 56 • XX 22R • XX 9 • XX 3 • Marigny • XX 5 • Château Thierry

9 Sept: BEF and Fifth Army cross R. Marne to divide First and Second armies

SECOND ARMY (Bülow)

R. Sormelin

XX 45

SIXTH ARMY (Maunoury)

Meaux

Paris 12 miles 19 kms • Claye-Souilly

X • La Ferté s. Jouarre • XXX III • XXX 3 • XXX II • XXX I • XX Allenby

XXX CONNEAU

XX X RES • Montmort

XXX III • XXX XVIII • Montmirail • XXX X

R. Petit Morin • XXX I

Crécy-la-Chapelle

Coulommiers

XXX VII • XXX GUARD • *Marshes of St Gond*

XXX X • XXX IX • Mt Août

B.E.F. (French)

R. Grand Morin

Estérnay • Sézanne

NINTH ARMY (Foch)

8-9 Sept: German advance S. of St Gond marshes halted by Ninth Army

200 / 100 / 0 m

20 km / 10 miles

XXX

FIFTH ARMY (d'Espérey)

R. Aubetin • Villenauxe

Galicia and Serbia   August – September 1914

The outbreak of war found Conrad von Hötzendorff, chief of the Austrian General Staff, resolved on immediate offensive action on both Russian and Serbian fronts (see Strategic View). Intelligence reports indicated that on the 20th day of mobilization, Russia would be able to deploy some 31 divisions to Austria's 30; 10 days later, Russia would have 52 divisions on the frontier, Austria only 39: the case for a quick offensive was plain.

Nikolai Ivanov, commander of the Russian southwestern front, in fact began the ensuing campaign with about 1,200,000 men to some one million Austrians, since Russian mobilization had proceeded much more quickly than foreseen. Ivanov expected an Austrian advance eastwards, and had deployed his stronger armies - to meet it; Conrad, promised a German advance into Poland from East Prussia, mounted an offensive northward from Galicia to crush the expected main Russian concentration in western Poland against the Germans. The Battle of Gumbinnen (page 28) ensured that no such German co-operation was possible, and the Austrian First and Fourth armies blundered head-on against Russian forces expecting to take their advance in the flank or rear.

The campaign

In the battles of Krasnik (23–24 August) and Komarow (25 August – 1 September), Austria achieved some initial success (Map 1). But in the battle of Gnila Lipa (26–30 August) the Russian Third and Eighth armies drove back Brudermann's Third Army towards Lemberg. Auffenberg turned southward to meet this threat at Rawa Russka, but was forced to retreat by the resumed advance of Plehve's Fifth Army, which he had mistakenly assumed defeated. Facing strategic encirclement from the north and steady Russian advance from the east, Conrad was forced to abandon Lemberg and withdraw to the River Dunajec and the Carpathian passes. Austrian losses were over 500,000, approximately twice the Russian casualties.

War in Serbia

Austria, brought almost to ruin in Galicia, had meanwhile again become locked in an indecisive struggle in Serbia (Map 2). Austrian forces had bombarded Belgrade on 29 July and crossed the rivers Save and Drina into Serbian

territory on 12 August. The Serbs, commanded by the redoubtable Radomir Putnik, counterattacked on 16 August, driving the Austrians back. The Austrian commander, Oskar Potiorek, - again advanced across the Drina on 7–8 September, and the Serbs were obliged to withdraw to stronger defensive positions southwest of Belgrade, which the Austrians occupied on 2 December.

Resupplied by the French through Salonika, Putnik mounted a vigorous attack, driving the Austrian forces back (Map 2). Belgrade was retaken on 15 December, ending a disastrous season of campaigning for Austria.

Austrian infantry take advantage of the natural defensive position formed by a dry stream bed, Galicia, 1914.

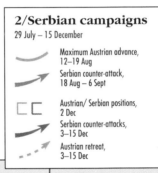

2/Serbian campaigns
29 July – 15 December

Maximum Austrian advance, 12–19 Aug

Serbian counter-attack, 18 Aug – 6 Sept

Austrian/ Serbian positions, 2 Dec

Serbian counter-attacks, 3–15 Dec

Austrian retreat, 3–15 Dec

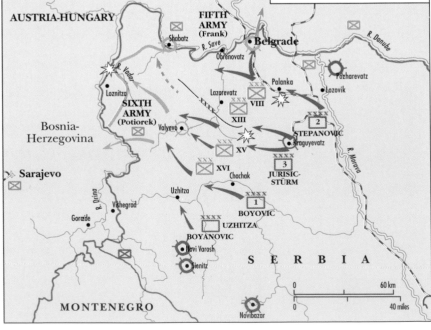

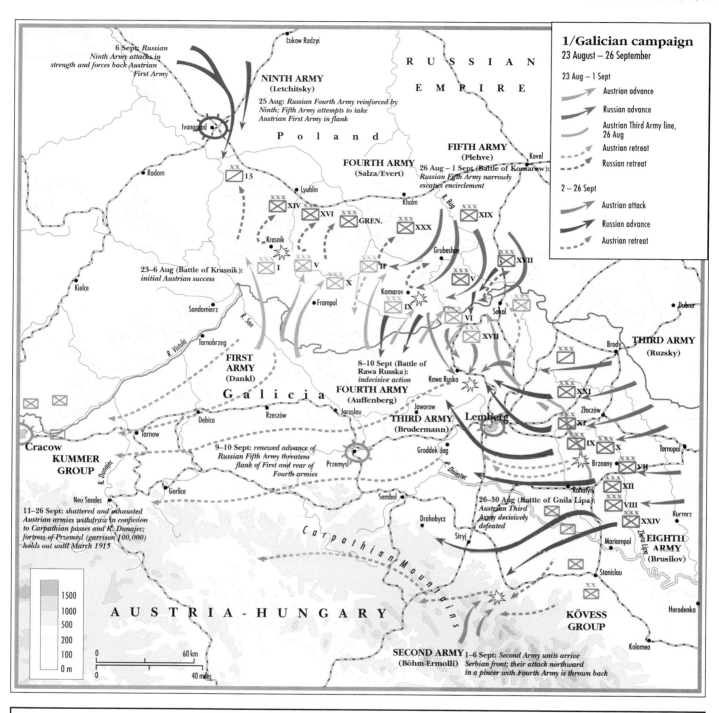

6 Sept: *Russian Ninth Army attacks in strength and forces back Austrian First Army*

NINTH ARMY
(Letchitsky)

25 Aug: *Russian Fourth Army reinforced by Ninth; Fifth Army attempts to take Austrian First Army in flank*

P o l a n d

R U S S I A N

E M P I R E

FIFTH ARMY
(Plehve)

FOURTH ARMY
(Salza/Evert)

26 Aug – 1 Sept *(Battle of Komarow): Russian Fifth Army narrowly escapes encirclement*

Kovel

Łukow Radzyi

Ivangorod

Radom

XX 13

Lyublin

Kholm

XXX XIV

XXX XVI

XXX GREN.

XXX XIX

XXX XXX

Kielce

Krasnik

XXX I

XXX V

XXX II

Grubeshev

XXX XVII

23–6 Aug *(Battle of Krasnik): initial Austrian success*

Sandomierz

XXX X

Frampol

Komarov

XXX IX

XXX V

Sokal

Dubno

R. Bug

Brody

VI

XVII

XXX XVII

8–10 Sept *(Battle of Rawa Russka): indecisive action*

Rawa Ruska

THIRD ARMY
(Ruzsky)

R. San

Tarnobrzeg

FIRST ARMY
(Dankl)

FOURTH ARMY
(Auffenberg)

XXX

XXX XXI

Złoczów

G a l i c i a

R. Vistula

Debica

Rzeszów

Jaroslau

Jaworow

THIRD ARMY
(Brudermann)

Lemberg

XXX XI

Tarnopol

Tarnow

9–10 Sept: *renewed advance of Russian Fifth Army threatens flank of First and rear of Fourth armies*

Przemysl

Groddek-Jag

XXX IX

XXX X

Cracow

XX

XX

Brzeany

XXX VII

KUMMER GROUP

R. Dunajec

R. Dniester

XXX XII

Rohatyn

Neu Sandec

Gorlice

Sambol

26–30 Aug *(Battle of Gnila Lipa): Austrian Third Army decisively defeated*

XXX VIII

Ruczacz

11–26 Sept: *shattered and exhausted Austrian armies withdraw in confusion to Carpathian passes and R. Dunajec; fortress of Przemysl (garrison 100,000) holds out until March 1915*

Drohobycz

Stryi

XXX XXIV

Mariampol

EIGHTH ARMY
(Brusilov)

C a r p a t h i a n   M o u n t a i n s

Stanislau

XX

Horodenka

Złota Lipa

1500
1000
500
200
100
0 m

0   60 km
0   40 miles

A U S T R I A - H U N G A R Y

KÖVESS GROUP

Kolomea

SECOND ARMY
(Böhm-Ermolli)

1–6 Sept: *Second Army units arrive Serbian front; their attack northward in a pincer with Fourth Army is thrown back*

1/Galician campaign
23 August – 26 September

23 Aug – 1 Sept

→ Austrian advance

→ Russian advance

Austrian Third Army line, 26 Aug

⇢ Austrian retreat

⇢ Russian retreat

2 – 26 Sept

→ Austrian attack

→ Russian advance

⇢ Austrian retreat

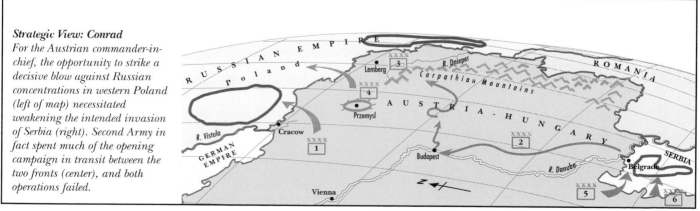

Strategic View: Conrad

For the Austrian commander-in-chief, the opportunity to strike a decisive blow against Russian concentrations in western Poland (left of map) necessitated weakening the intended invasion of Serbia (right). Second Army in fact spent much of the opening campaign in transit between the two fronts (center), and both operations failed.

R U S S I A N   E M P I R E

P o l a n d

R. Dnieper

R O M A N I A

Lemberg

XXXX 3

Carpathian Mountains

XXXX 4

Przemysl

A U S T R I A - H U N G A R Y

R. Vistula

GERMAN EMPIRE

Cracow

XXXX 1

XXXX 2

Budapest

R. Danube

SERBIA

Belgrade

Vienna

N

XXXX 5

XXXX 6

First Aisne and the 'Race to the Sea'

September – October 1914

The German armies, in retreat from the Marne (page 34), turned to face their pursuers on the River Aisne. This was an ideal defensive position; north of the river, high ground stretched westward for some 25 miles to Juvigny. The advancing Allies would be faced with the river and German guns in commanding positions on the opposite bank.

Battle of the Aisne

Units of the BEF and French Fifth Army forced their way across the river on 12 September (Map 1), but the possibility of a breakthrough was not grasped quickly enough. On the 13th the German Seventh Army sealed off the penetration, and repeated Allied attacks over the next four days failed to make progress on to the high ground.

Both sides then began to extend operations northward in what has misleadingly been termed 'The Race to the Sea' (Map 2). In fact, both Allies and Germans sought to recover lost momentum in the war of movement by striking around the open flank of the other. On the Allied side, first Castelnau's Second Army, then a detachment under Maud'huy (Tenth Army from 5 September), fought bloody and indecisive actions against similar German redeployments as the lines extended to Arras and beyond. The BEF was then withdrawn from the Aisne line and sent northward toward Armentières and Ypres.

The fall of Antwerp

The urgent need to secure the Channel ports now became evident to the German high command, for it was at Boulogne, Calais and Dunkirk that British troops and munitions were landing in growing numbers. In August the ports had been open for the taking: now they had to be fought for.

The newly appointed Chief of the German Great General Staff, Erich von Falkenhayn, who had replaced the discredited Moltke, resolved to launch Archduke Albrecht's Fourth Army in a direct drive for the ports; while Fourth Army was being redeployed, it was essential to reduce the fortress of Antwerp, where the Belgian Field Army of six divisions had taken refuge in August. The Belgians had made several sorties during the Allied retreat through France, and

clearly threatened any German attempt on the Channel ports.

From 28 September, the Belgian forts were pounded by German 42cm siege mortars and 30.5cm howitzers, while Beseler's reinforced III Reserve Corps mounted infantry assaults. Royal Navy marines assisted in the defense, and the British 7th Division was landed at Ostende to break the siege, but Antwerp was formally surrendered on 10 October. The Belgian and British garrison retreated westward.

The stabilized line

By the second week of October, the Belgian Army was stationed behind the Yser, holding the line from Nieuport to just north of Ypres. Here Albrecht's Fourth Army struck their line, and that of the BEF and French Territorials deploying around Armentières, with full force.

The Belgians, hard pressed, exhausted and becoming short of ammunition, struggled to halt the German attack. On 24 October, on King Albert's order, they opened the locks on the canalized river at Nieuport, allowing the sea to flood the low-lying fenland in the Germans' path of advance.

The flooding was, in essence, the opening phase of the First Battle of Ypres, for the Germans then had little choice but to turn the bulk of their northern force against the British salient running north, east and south of Ypres.

French officers monitoring the action during the 'Race to the Sea'. The cavalryman, left, wears a dragoon helmet, unchanged since Napoleonic times.

> *"We are marching in column... along a road which is under the observation of the enemy on hills in front. There are two Divisions marching on one road, shelled by enemy artillery. What a target we are for them!"*
>
> **Cpl. T. North, 1st Battalion, The Lincolnshire Regiment**

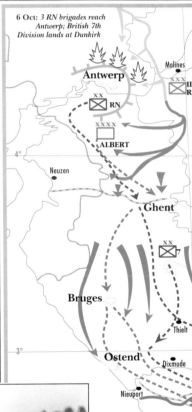

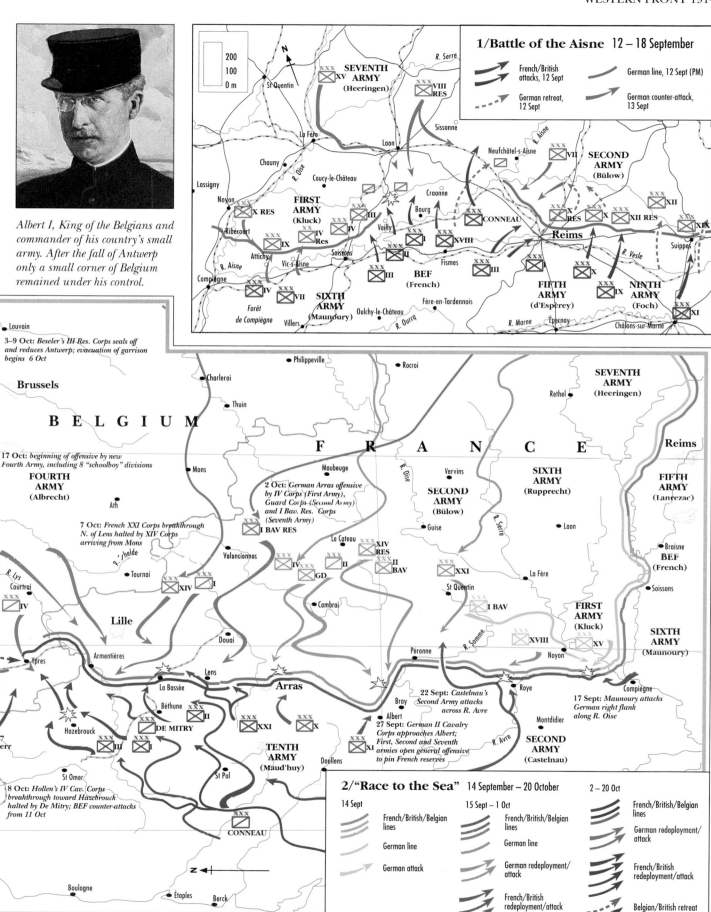

Albert I, King of the Belgians and commander of his country's small army. After the fall of Antwerp only a small corner of Belgium remained under his control.

Warsaw and Lodz   September – November 1914

Appointed chief of the German general staff on 14 September, Falkenhayn issued instructions on the 17th for German assistance to the Austrian armies still falling back in disorder after their Galician disaster (page 36). On the 22nd, German forces in East Prussia were formed into a new Ninth Army (Mackensen) and switched to southwest Poland, leaving only two corps in East Prussia. A combined German and Austrian Warsaw offensive began on 4 October.

Grand Duke Nicholas had anticipated such a move (see Strategic View). He regrouped his forces and counter-attacked, driving the German advance back from Warsaw on 20 October, and then making a strong thrust toward German Silesia. Third and Eighth armies resumed their advance on the Carpathian passes into Austria-Hungary.

Ninth Army retreated before the Russian advance, then was swiftly transferred northward toward Thorn by rail.

Battle of Lodz

On 11 November, the Ninth drove southeast against the Russian right flank (Map 1), taking 12,000 prisoners on the first day. Rennenkampf's badly-deployed First Army (it was caught astride the Vistula) was driven back toward Warsaw, and by the 18th some 150,000 men of Scheidemann's Second were encircled on three sides at Lodz by 250,000 Germans. A major Russian disaster was averted only by the resilience of Scheidemann's troops and by Plehve's forced march to his rescue. By the 23rd, Scheffer's XXV Reserve Corps was itself

in danger of encirclement, and exhaustion and shortage of ammunition had stalled any further German advance. In some of the most dramatic fighting of the war, XXV Reserve and Richthofen's cavalry cut their way out with over 16,000 prisoners.

Aftermath

Within a week, four additional German corps were transferred from the Western Front, and by 15 December the Russians were driven back to the River Bzura-Ravka before Warsaw. In the meantime, the Austrians at last recovered their poise at Limanowa (page 44), and stalled the Russian advance on Cracow. Lodz was a Russian tactical victory, but for the Germans it was a strategic success: Nicholas's Silesia offensive was called off and never resumed.

Siberian infantrymen in full service kit in Warsaw square, November 1914. The defeat at the V Siberian Corps was blamed upon the incompetence of the Russian divisional commanders.

"The situation demands the utmost from the men and their commanders, and you must forget about their tiredness."

Gen. Mackensen addressing XVII Corps on 14 November

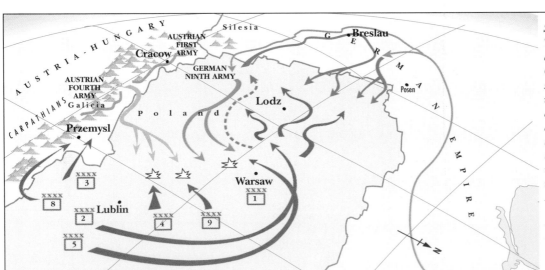

Strategic View: Nicholas
The Russian commander-in-chief was prepared for a Central Powers offensive into southern Poland; his plan was to withdraw before it and swing Second and Fifth armies north of Warsaw to trap his opponents against the Carpathians. The way would then be clear for an invasion of German Silesia. Ninth Army escaped his trap (dashed arrow), then redeployed by rail against his right wing from 9 November (darker tint).

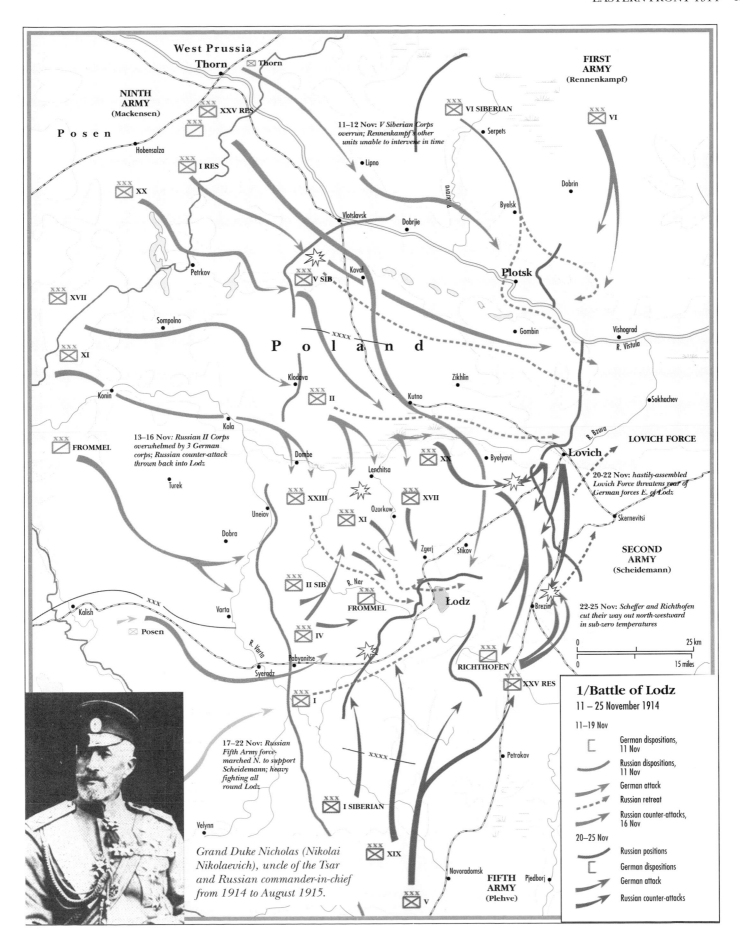

West Prussia

Thorn

☒ Thorn

**NINTH
ARMY**
(Mackensen)

P o s e n

☒☒☒ XXV RES

☒☒☒

Hobensalza

☒☒☒ I RES

☒☒☒ XX

Petrkov

☒☒☒ XVII

Sompolno

☒☒☒ XI

Konin

☒☒☒ FROMMEL

Turek

Kalish

Dobra

Uneiov

Varta

☒ Posen

R. Varta

Syeradz

*11–12 Nov: V Siberian Corps
overrun; Rennenkampf's other
units unable to intervene in time*

Lipno

Vlotslavsk

Dobrjie

✹
☒☒☒ V SIB

Koval

P o l a n d

xxxx

Klodava

☒☒☒ II

Kola

*13–16 Nov: Russian II Corps
overwhelmed by 3 German
corps; Russian counter-attack
thrown back into Lodz*

Dombe

Lenchitsa

☒☒☒ XXIII

✹

☒☒☒ XI

Ozorkow

R. Ner

☒☒☒ II SIB

☒☒☒
FROMMEL

☒☒☒ IV

xxx

Pabyanitse

☒☒☒ I

*17–22 Nov: Russian
Fifth Army force-
marched N. to support
Scheidemann; heavy
fighting all
round Lodz*

Velynn

☒☒☒ I SIBERIAN

✹

☒☒☒ XIX

☒☒☒ V

**FIRST
ARMY**
(Rennenkampf)

☒☒☒ VI SIBERIAN

Serpets

Byelsk

Dobrin

☒☒☒ VI

Vlotslavsk

Plotsk

Gombin

Zikhlin

Kutno

Vishograd

R. Vistula

Sokhachev

R. Bzura

LOVICH FORCE

Lovich

Byelyavi

☒☒☒ XX

✹

☒☒☒ XVII

Zgerj

Stikov

*20–22 Nov: hastily-assembled
Lovich Force threatens rear of
German forces E. of Lodz*

Skernevitsi

**SECOND
ARMY**
(Scheidemann)

Łodz

✹

Brezin

*22-25 Nov: Scheffer and Richthofen
cut their way out north-westward
in sub-zero temperatures*

☒☒☒
RICHTHOFEN

xxxx

Petrokov

☒☒☒ XXV RES

0 _____ 25 km

0 _____ 15 miles

Novoradomsk

Pjedborj

**FIFTH
ARMY**
(Plehve)

1/Battle of Lodz

11 – 25 November 1914

11–19 Nov

[German dispositions,
11 Nov

Russian dispositions,
11 Nov

German attack

Russian retreat

Russian counter-attacks,
16 Nov

20–25 Nov

Russian positions

[German dispositions

German attack

Russian counter-attacks

---

*Grand Duke Nicholas (Nikolai
Nikolaevich), uncle of the Tsar
and Russian commander-in-chief
from 1914 to August 1915.*

First Ypres October – November 1914

By the first week of October, a Belgian line had been established along the River Yser from Nieuport to Bixschoote, and the French line from the Aisne had extended as far north as Armentières. French territorial divisions, de Mitry's cavalry corps and the BEF now moved forward into the gap between the two lines, intent on finding and turning the right flank of the German main forces. These units arrived in position almost simultaneously with the beginning of the German Fourth Army's massive drive for the Channel ports (page 38). The British II Corps first clashed with the Germans on 10 October west of La Bassée; III Corps, despite heavy losses, reached Armentières, securing the bridges over the River Lys, while Allenby's Cavalry Corps came up on their left to support the proposed flanking attack. The German forces opposing them held their positions while Albrecht's Fourth Army struck the Belgian line, and all hopes of an Allied breakthrough swiftly evaporated.

The Ypres salient

As the Belgian and French units north of them were driven back, Haig's I Corps found itself exposed in a salient around Ypres. The Belgian decision to open the Yser flood barriers on 21 October forced Albrecht to redirect his efforts south of Dixmude, and from 22 October the full weight of the Fourth Army's attack fell against Haig's salient.

De Mitry's cavalry and the French IX Corps took over the defense of the northern half of the salient between 22 and 24 October as heavy German attacks by both Fourth and Sixth armies developed against the north and the south of the Allied position. From 24 October onward, fighting was continuous, both night and day, along the Ypres salient in conditions dominated by mud and wintry cold.

From 27 to 31 October six additional German divisions, (Group Fabeck) moved into the gap between Fourth and Sixth armies. Supported by a very heavy concentration of artillery and outnumbering the Allied troops south of the salient by 2 to 1, Fabeck's troops were thrown against the Allied line from 30 October to 4 November. In the heaviest fighting to date, Allenby's cavalry and the newly-arrived French XIV Corps were driven back beyond Wytschaete and Messines Ridge, and Haig's I Corps was

driven from Gheluvelt. The Allied position was only stabilized after a last-ditch counter-attack organized by Haig recovered Gheluvelt.

On 10 November the Germans launched another great attack, this time against the French lines around Dixmude, to the north. Next day, a renewed attack against British positions around Gheluvelt by Group Linsingen was spearheaded by Winckler's 4th Guards Division. The Germans broke through the line held by the British 1st Guards Brigade but were again repulsed by the last available Allied reserves. The failure of this attack ended the Allied crisis at Ypres; more and more French troops were transferred north to support the salient, and though minor attacks continued until 22 November, large-scale operations came to an end.

Consequences

Thus ended the last German attempt in 1914 to turn the Allied northern flank and take the Channel ports, and with it the war of movement in the west. Between 14 October and 30 November, the BEF lost some 58,000 men, many of them young officers and long-serving regular soldiers. The 7th Division alone lost all but 44 of its 400 officers, and all but 2336 of its 12,000 men. The BEF is said to have died at Ypres, leaving only a core to train new volunteers. The French lost nearly as many, an estimated 50,000.

German losses, totaling some 130,000 included many enthusiastic raw recruits and the battle soon became known as Kindermord: the Massacre of the Innocents

"The trenches themselves were quite different from anything I had imagined. They have been so often filled with water and rebuilt that nothing much was visable except seas of mud and holes full of water, and filthy but cheerful men standing about outside the bombproof shelters!"

**Capt. M. Mascall,
Royal Garrison Artillery
upon arrival at Ypres.**

British troops of the 2nd Battalion Scots Guards in a hastily-dug trench near Zandvoorde in October 1914. Such trenches were dug as a matter of course for self-protection – only later did they develop into a virtually continuous, complex line of defenses.

Sir John French, commander of the British Expeditionary Force. During the Ypres action his mood swung repeatedly between over-optimism and despair, in contrast to the calculated confidence of Foch, French commander in the immediate area.

"Time and time again... the men's nervousness manifested itself in alarms about Belgian snipers. The sight of a windmill was enough to start a rumour that the Belgians were transmitting messages by code by means of the position of the sails."

Herr Otto Hahn,
Offiziersstellvertreter
(deputy officer)

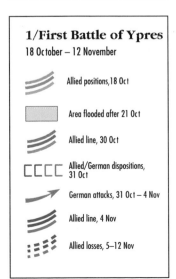

1/First Battle of Ypres

18 October – 12 November

Allied positions, 18 Oct

Area flooded after 21 Oct

Allied line, 30 Oct

Allied/German dispositions, 31 Oct

German attacks, 31 Oct – 4 Nov

Allied line, 4 Nov

Allied losses, 5–12 Nov

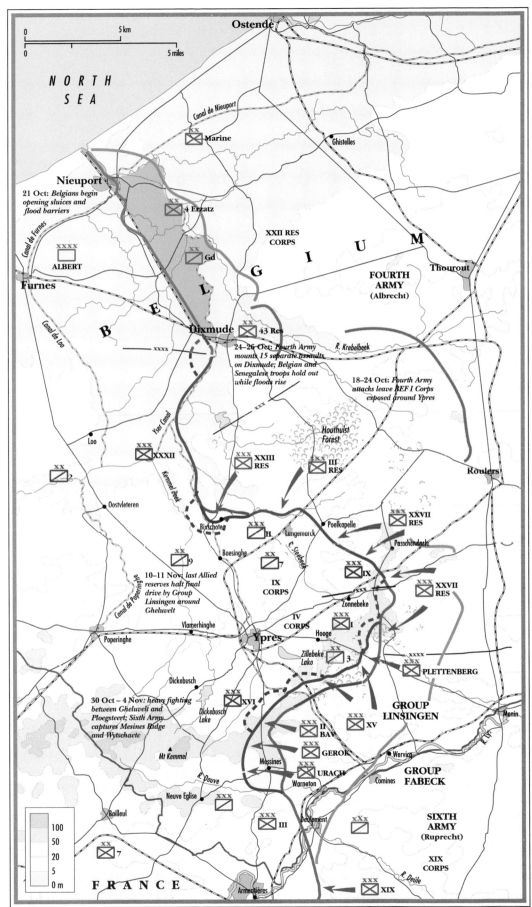

Ostende

NORTH SEA

Canal de Nieuport

Marine

Ghistelles

Nieuport

21 Oct: Belgians begin opening sluices and flood barriers

4 Erzatz

XXII RES CORPS

Gd

FOURTH ARMY (Albrecht)

Thourout

Canal de Furnes

ALBERT

Furnes

Canal de Loo

Dixmude

43 Res

R. Krebelbeek

24–26 Oct: Fourth Army mounts 15 separate assaults on Dixmude; Belgian and Senegalese troops hold out while floods rise

18–24 Oct: Fourth Army attacks leave BEF I Corps exposed around Ypres

Yser Canal

Loo

Houthulst Forest

XXXII

2

XXIII RES

III RES

Roulers

Kemmel Beek

Oostvleteren

Bixschote

H

Langemarck

Poelkapelle

XXVII RES

Passchendaele

9

Boesinghe

7

C. Steenbeek

IX

XXVII RES

Canal de Poperinghe

10–11 Nov: last Allied reserves halt final drive by Group Linsingen around Gheluvelt

IX CORPS

IV CORPS

Zonnebeke

Hooge

I

Vlamertinghe

Ypres

Zillebeke Lake

3

PLETTENBERG

Poperinghe

Dickebusch

30 Oct – 4 Nov: heavy fighting between Gheluvelt and Ploegsteert; Sixth Army captures Mesines Ridge and Wytschaete

XVI

Dickebusch Lake

GROUP LINSINGEN

Menin

R. Lys

II BAV

XV

Mt Kemmel

GEROK

Wervicq

GROUP FABECK

Messines

URACH

R. Douve

Warneton

Comines

Neuve Eglise

SIXTH ARMY (Ruprecht)

Bailleul

III

Deulemont

XIX CORPS

100
50
20
5
0 m

7

R. Deûle

FRANCE

Armentières

XIX

0   5 km
0   5 miles

Limanowa December 1914

At the beginning of December, the Russians remained in a favorable position on their southern front; the savage fighting around Łodz in November (page 40) had halted the German counter-offensive into Poland, and the simultaneous Austrian advance northeastward from Cracow had been pushed back. Austrian participation on the southern flank of the Łodz action had been possible only at the cost of transferring Böhm-Ermolli's Second Army northward from the Carpathians, and now Brusilov's Eighth Army was poised at the passes, ready to descend the southern slopes and advance on Budapest.

Conrad had left defense of the entire Carpathian front from the River Dunajec to Bukovina to Boroevic's weak Third Army (11 divisions) in the belief that victory could be achieved in Poland before the Russians could envelop the Austrian line in the southeast. Moreover, the Austrian commander-in-chief had left only weak formations immediately to the south of Cracow in order to strengthen his planned offensive to its north, and these were confronted by the advancing Russian Third Army under Radko-Dimitriev – clearly these units would be unable to support Boroevic's line. Conrad's immediate priority, therefore, was to reinforce the Austrian positions south of Cracow while preparing to transfer such extra troops as could be spared to the Carpathians.

New Russian plans

The Russian commander-in-chief, Grand Duke Nicholas, was confronted, as ever, with the conflicting demands of his two army group commanders, Ruzsky (Northwestern Front) facing the Germans in Poland, and Ivanov (Southwestern Front) facing the Austrians. In contrast to Ruzsky, whose forces had suffered heavy losses at Łodz, Ivanov was confident of victory. At a meeting at Siedlice on 29–30 November, he presented Nicholas with a proposal for a redirected offensive, brushing aside the weak forces opposing Radko-Dmitriev to take Cracow and threaten German Silesia from the southeast. This, he argued, would also restore the situation in Poland to Russia's favor. Nicholas gave his reluctant approval, also authorizing the transfer of two corps westward from Brusilov's army.

Conrad, however, had found a means of upsetting these plans. He transferred part of his Fourth Army well to the south of Cracow, and launched an attack under the command of one of his more effective commanders, Roth, against the southern flank of the advancing Russian Third Army. The ensuing battle fell into distinct, though often confused, phases. The Austrians successfully flanked the Russian advance on Cracow; then Brusilov's two Carpathian corps thrust westward to threaten Roth's position; finally, Boroevic seized the opportunity of a counter-offensive against the open Russian flank from the south.

At the same time, German forces in Poland, reinforced by units taken from the Western Front, launched a renewed offensive towards Łodz. Ruzsky was forced to evacuate the town on 6 December, and his battered forces withdrew to the line of the Bzura and Ravka rivers.

With Ruzsky's forces also in retreat, Ivanov had no choice but to retire from both the Carpathians and the Cracow front.

Consequences

Conrad's victory marked the turning point in the war between Russia and Austria-Hungary, and the high tide of Russian penetration into Austrian territory. The renewed German attack which captured Łodz in December played a part in forcing the Russians to retreat on Ivanov's front too, but the Austrian success at Limanowa could be said to have saved the Austro-Hungarian Empire, and to have ensured its continuing participation in the war.

"It appears that the Austrian forces are demoralised to a high degree and give no signs of active defence."

General Radko-Dimitriev reflecting the initial confidence enjoyed by many Russians immediately prior to Limanowa

Austrian troops near Uszok Pass in the Carpathians, at the end of the battle of Limanowa. The passes were captured by the Russian Eighth Army at the end of November, then recaptured in mid-December in the Austrian Third Army counter-offensive.

Russian artillery on the move in the Carpathian Mountains at the end of 1914. The action at Limanowa marked the maximum extent of Russian advance into the Austro-Hungarian Empire, and the point at which the campaign finally swung in Austrian's favor.

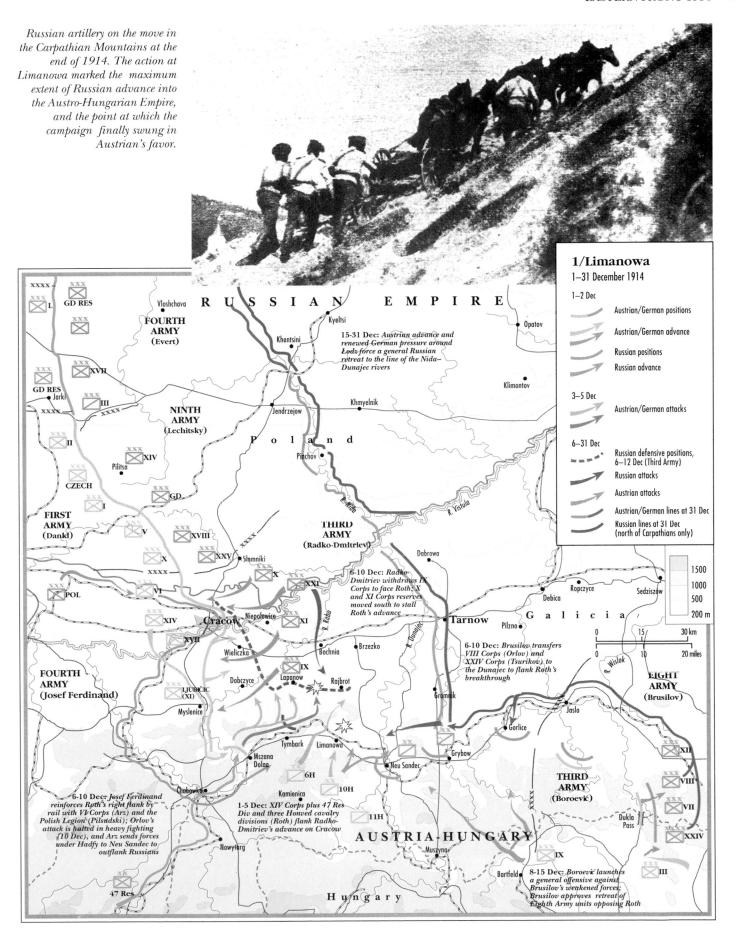

1/Limanowa
1–31 December 1914

1–2 Dec
- Austrian/German positions
- Austrian/German advance
- Russian positions
- Russian advance

3–5 Dec
- Austrian/German attacks

6–31 Dec
- Russian defensive positions, 6–12 Dec (Third Army)
- Russian attacks
- Austrian attacks
- Austrian/German lines at 31 Dec
- Russian lines at 31 Dec (north of Carpathians only)

RUSSIAN EMPIRE

FOURTH ARMY (Evert)

NINTH ARMY (Lechitsky)

Poland

THIRD ARMY (Radko-Dmitriev)

FIRST ARMY (Dankl)

FOURTH ARMY (Josef Ferdinand)

Galicia

EIGHTH ARMY (Brusilov)

THIRD ARMY (Boroević)

AUSTRIA-HUNGARY

Hungary

15-31 Dec: *Austrian advance and renewed German pressure around Łodz force a general Russian retreat to the line of the Nida–Dunajec rivers*

6-10 Dec: *Radko-Dmitriev withdraws IX Corps to face Roth; X and XI Corps reserves moved south to stall Roth's advance*

6-10 Dec: *Brusilov transfers VIII Corps (Orlov) and XXIV Corps (Tsurikov) to the Dunajec to flank Roth's breakthrough*

6-10 Dec: *Josef Ferdinand reinforces Roth's right flank by rail with VI Corps (Arz) and the Polish Legion (Pilsudski); Orlov's attack is halted in heavy fighting (10 Dec), and Arz sends forces under Hadfy to Neu Sandec to outflank Russians*

1-5 Dec: *XIV Corps plus 47 Res Div and three Honved cavalry divisions (Roth) flank Radko-Dmitriev's advance on Cracow*

8-15 Dec: *Boroević launches a general offensive against Brusilov's weakened forces; Brusilov approves retreat of Eighth Army units opposing Roth*

War at Sea 1914

The first year of the war brought no major clash between the world's two greatest naval powers, Britain and Germany. Instead, 1914 saw a number of small ensagements in the North and Mediterranean Seas, limited in scope but of considerable psychological effect. The German battlecruiser Goeben and the light cruiser Breslau were stationed in the Mediterranean, a threat to French troop convoys between her North African colony and the mainland. British naval forces hunted them but both ships managed to reach safety at Constantinople. This seemingly trivial chase had in fact momentous consequences, for to escape capture they were sold to Turkey for less than £4m, a transaction that proved a considerable inducement for Turkey shortly to enter the war on the side of the Central Powers.

On 28 August there was a clash between British and German cruisers at Heligoland Bight in the North Sea, in which the British proved superior. Twice German battlecruisers bombarded the east coast of England (Lowestoft, Scarborough and Hartlepool), killing a number of civilians. These limited assaults nevertheless brought home to the British public the hitherto unsuspected fact that the war would embrace civilians and servicemen alike.

The Atlantic and Pacific

Elsewhere in 1914 there were more significant naval engagements as the German overseas naval forces sought to disrupt Allied trade. The most powerful German flotilla was the East Asia Squadron, based at Tsingtao on the China coast (page 48). By the late Fall this flotilla (von Spee) of five ships had moved to the Juan Fernandez Islands, west of Chile. A British force (Cradock), based on the Falkland Islands and comprising two obsolescent armored cruisers, a modern cruiser and an armed merchantman, steamed around Cape Horn to engage the Germans. The two met in heavy seas off the port of Coronel on the evening of 1 November (Map 2). The result was a great shock to the British public, but perhaps hardly surprising: the British contingent, heavily out-gunned, was virtually destroyed, losing 1654 officers and men, the Germans a mere two men wounded.

British revenge, however, was swift. The Admiralty had already dispatched two battlecruisers and six light cruisers to the South

Atlantic. This flotilla reached the Falkland Islands on 7 December (Map 3). The following day, Spee attempted to destroy the Royal Navy coaling station at Port Stanley, was fired upon by the new British ships, and fled. In the ensuing battle, Spee lost four of his five ships.

Meanwhile, the menace of German raiders in the waters north of Australia, which delayed the sailing of the first convoy of ANZAC troops to Europe, was brought to an end when, on 9 November, the Australian warship Sydney sighted and fired upon the German light cruiser Emden, which had landed parties to destroy the Cocos Keeling wireless station. The Emden, during an extensive voyage through the Pacific since 14 August, had bombarded Madras, captured 19 British merchantmen and sunk two Allied warships.

Emden was forced aground on a coral reef and surrendered after losing 111 men. The landing party made good its escape in an old schooner and, after a fearful journey, managed to reach Arabia and finally made their way back to Germany.

" The lyddite would burst in the middle of a group and strip them of arms and legs – men would rush about with exposed bones, crazy from the effects of the shells – each explosion would account for about 40 men."

A survivor of the *Leipzig*

H.M.S. Goodhope, *the flagship of Admiral Cradock's squadron. At 2000hrs. on 1 November, 1914 the combined shelling of Scharnhorst and the Gneisenau resulted in a devastating explosion in Goodhope's magazine which tore the ship apart.*

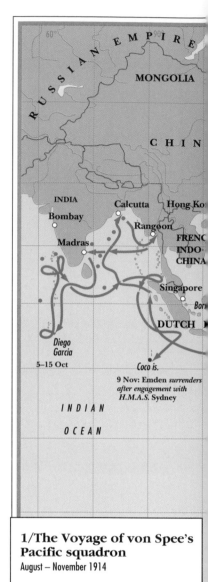

1/The Voyage of von Spee's Pacific squadron
August – November 1914

Track of S.M.S *Emden*
Track of S.M.S *Leipzig*
Track of S.M.S *Dresden*
Track of main German squadron
Track of S.M.S *Nurnberg*

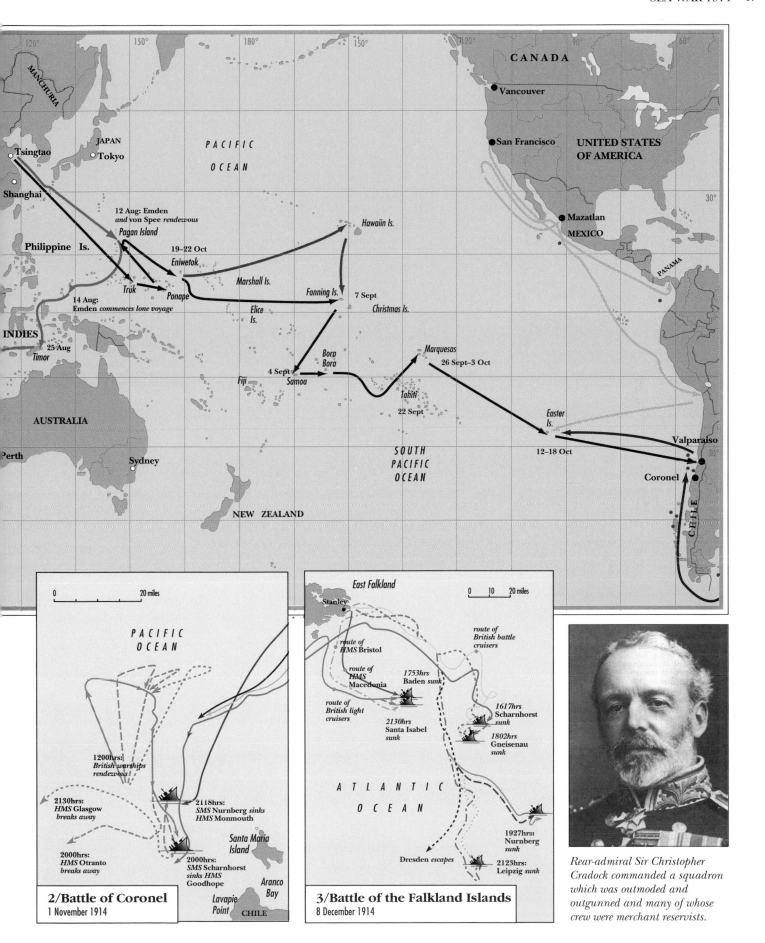

CANADA

Vancouver

San Francisco   UNITED STATES
                 OF AMERICA

Mazatlan
MEXICO

PANAMA

PACIFIC
OCEAN

Tsingtao

JAPAN
Tokyo

Shanghai

Philippine   Is.

12 Aug: Emden
and von Spee rendezvous

Pagan Island

19–22 Oct
Eniwetok

Hawaiin Is.

Truk

Ponape

14 Aug:
Emden commences lone voyage

Marshall Is.

Fanning Is.

7 Sept

Elice
Is.

Christmas Is.

INDIES

25 Aug

Timor

Fiji   Samoa   4 Sept

Bora
Bora

Marquesas
26 Sept–3 Oct

Tahiti
22 Sept

Easter
Is.

12–18 Oct

Valparaiso

Coronel

AUSTRALIA

Perth   Sydney

SOUTH
PACIFIC
OCEAN

CHILE

NEW ZEALAND

2/Battle of Coronel
1 November 1914

0   20 miles

PACIFIC
OCEAN

1200hrs:
British warships
rendezvous

2130hrs:
HMS Glasgow
breaks away

2118hrs:
SMS Nurnberg sinks
HMS Monmouth

2000hrs:
HMS Otranto
breaks away

2000hrs:
SMS Scharnhorst
sinks HMS
Goodhope

Santa Maria
Island

Aranco
Bay

Lavapie
Point   CHILE

3/Battle of the Falkland Islands
8 December 1914

East Falkland

Stanley

0   10   20 miles

route of
HMS Bristol

route of British
battle cruisers

route of
HMS
Macedonia

1753hrs
Baden sunk

1617hrs
Scharnhorst
sunk

route of
British light
cruisers

2130hrs
Santa Isabel
sunk

1802hrs
Gneisenau
sunk

ATLANTIC
OCEAN

1927hrs:
Nurnberg
sunk

Dresden escapes

2123hrs:
Leipzig sunk

Rear-admiral Sir Christopher
Cradock commanded a squadron
which was outmoded and
outgunned and many of whose
crew were merchant reservists.

The Widening War: Colonial Campaigns 1915

The conflict that erupted in August 1914 rapidly spread to the German colonies. In Africa, Germany's four possessions – Togoland, Cameroon, South West Africa and German East Africa – all adjoined those of Great Britain, France, Belgium or Portugal; the opening of military action was therefore almost simultaneous with the outbreak of war in Europe. Colonial mentality among the European inhabitants necessitated European command of all military units, but in the German colonies in particular, Africans formed the bulk of the fighting forces. In the British colonies, colonial fear of arming the African population resulted in longer reliance on British and South African troops, with the inevitable consequence of greatly reduced fighting efficiency in African conditions.

German African colonies

Togoland, hemmed in on three sides by British and French possessions (Map 1), fell easy prey. The Germans surrendered on 26 August.

Overrunning Cameroon posed a sterner

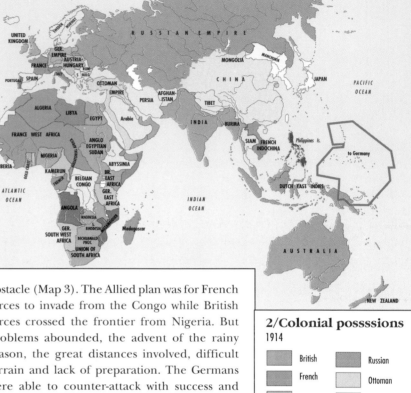

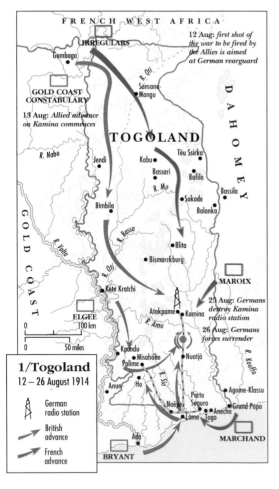

1/Togoland
12 – 26 August 1914

- German radio station
- British advance
- French advance

12 Aug: *first shot of the war to be fired by the Allies is aimed at German rearguard*

13 Aug: *Allied advance on Kamina commences*

25 Aug: *Germans destroy Kamina radio station*

26 Aug: *Germans forces surrender*

obstacle (Map 3). The Allied plan was for French forces to invade from the Congo while British forces crossed the frontier from Nigeria. But problems abounded, the advent of the rainy season, the great distances involved, difficult terrain and lack of preparation. The Germans were able to counter-attack with success and even temporarily to mount sorties into Nigeria. Converging columns of Allied troops slowly forced the German defenders back throughout 1915, but the campaign was not concluded until February 1916.

In South West Africa, German forces abandoned the coast on the outbreak of war and withdrew inland to Windhoek. Raiding parties into the Cape Province, however, only united most South Africans in their determination to repel the invaders. Louis Botha, the South African commander, organised an invasion which captured Windhoek by 20 May 1915 and overcame the last German resistance by 9 July. Botha had also put down a rebellion by disaffected Boers, on which the Germans had based great hopes for the survival of their colony.

German East Africa presented the Allies with the most difficult campaign of all, and German resistance continued throughout the entire war (page 162).

China and the Pacific

The small German possessions in the Pacific were quickly occupied by Australian and New Zealand forces (Samoa on 30 August, Kaiser Wilhelm's Land – now part of Papua New

2/Colonial posssssions 1914

British	Russian
French	Ottoman
German	Japanese
Deutch	Portuguese
Italian	American

Troops from the Union of South Africa move forward under fire in the desert country of German South West Africa.

Guinea – on 13 September, and the Solomon Islands on 15 September). Further north, Japanese troops occupied the Caroline, Marshall and Mariana Islands despite the misgivings of the US, Australia and New Zealand. The British need for Japanese naval help in finding German commerce raiders overrode the concerns of these other powers at Japanese expansion.

Meanwhile, in China, Japan embarked on the capture of the German colony of Kiaochow, protected by the fortress-city of Tsingtao (Map 2). 23,000 Japanese troops under Mitsuomi Kamio (with one British brigade) landed on the peninsula during September 1914 and advanced against the city and its garrison of 4000 German marines. The siege lasted over a month, in appalling weather conditions. After a heavy bombardment from both land and sea beginning on 31 October, the formidable final defenses of Tsingtao itself were breached on 6– 7 November, and the garrison surrendered on the 7th.

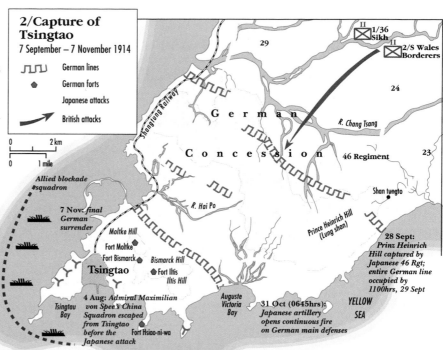

2/Capture of Tsingtao
7 September – 7 November 1914

- ⌐⌐⌐ German lines
- ⬠ German forts
- ▰ Japanese attacks
- ⬅ British attacks

Japanese soldiers inspect the massive German fortifications at Tsingtao after their capture of the colony.

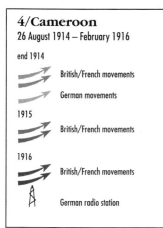

4/Cameroon
26 August 1914 – February 1916

end 1914
- → British/French movements
- → German movements

1915
- → British/French movements

1916
- → British/French movements
- ⚐ German radio station

Austrian soldiers engage a Russian aircraft with rifle fire.

PART II
1915

With unforeseen deadlock on the Western Front at the end of 1914, the swift victory which civilians and military alike on all sides had so confidently expected was plainly beyond reach. On land, the trench line ran in the west without interruption along the entire battle front – some 350 mls/563 km. At sea, the German High Seas Fleet lay potent but idle in harbors beyond the reach of the Royal Navy, not to be enticed by the British into battle. New mobilization of resources, new tactics, and indeed new strategies, were urgently required on both sides.

Resources

The initial clashes of 1914 had imposed unexpectedly severe demands upon the resources of all combatants, and new means had to be found to supply what was clearly now a long-term war effort. Quite apart from the severe and shocking manpower losses of the first phase of the war, demand for munitions was far outstripping supply by the end of 1914, even in Germany. The Prussian War Ministry's stock of artillery shells, for example, was all but expended in the first six weeks of the war, and orders to conserve artillery ammunition had been issued to German forces during the initial exchanges on the Aisne. Even more severe shortages facing the BEF became the subject of a newspaper campaign in Britain, and the problem was finally tackled by the establishment from 25 May of a Ministry of Munitions under Lloyd George. Production increased rapidly, but maximum supply was achieved only with time.

New tactics: the Western Front

The tactical problem on the Western Front was entirely new: until 1915 the possibility of defeating an enemy's main forces by maneuver had been a constant of warfare. Here, this option no longer obtained, yet it was manifestly in the west that the war had to be won. For the western Allies, German occupation of French territory made offensive action obligatory, and the realization during the first half of the year that substantial German forces were being transferred east made attack even more imperative. The task for 1915 was that of finding an effective (and economical in terms of casualties) means of breaking the German front, even as that front itself was progressively strengthened and developed. In Artois and the Champagne in the winter, at Neuve Chapelle, Festubert, Aubers Ridge and Artois again in the spring, and then at Loos, the Champagne again and Artois for the third attempt in the summer, new variations on the themes of artillery support, type of infantry assault and the placement and employment of reserves were attempted; all were defeated by the sheer impossibility of pushing infantry through a break in the enemy

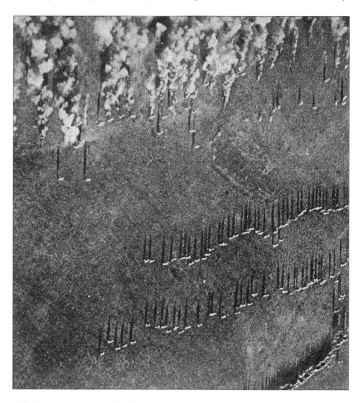

The commencement of a German gas attack on the Eastern Front, 1915. Of the weapons which were invented and used for the first time in World War I, it is poison gas which has perhaps the most potent and horrific associations

lines more quickly than enemy reinforcements could be brought up to seal the gap.

For the Germans, too, the problem of stalemate in the west remained intractable. Tactical innovation on the German side was largely in the field of defensive improvements (1915 saw the progressive development of second and even third trench lines behind the front line, the evolution of a more flexible approach to the deployment of troops in the lines – that is, holding most troops behind the front line in support trenches, from which they could be deployed to meet any attack – and the emergence of the concept of a "battle zone", actually behind the front line, in which enemy attacks were to be met and destroyed). The most significant development in German offensive tactics came at the Second Battle of Ypres (page 66), with the properly-organized use of gas for the first time on 22 April, where its effect, though dramatic, was nullified by absence of German reserves to exploit the gap created. The use of this new weapon had not yet been properly thought through; gas was subject to wind shifts and could therefore be swept back over the attackers themselves, and in any event, little thought had been given to the inevitable predicament of the attackers when they advanced into the saturated area.

For much of 1915, such tactical experimentation – despite its repeated, costly failure – helped to mask the real seriousness of the deadlock on the Western Front. For at least the first half of the year, in both Germany and the Allied powers, the belief persisted among civilians and in some military circles that a decisive military victory in the west could be achieved within the year.

New strategies: Germany

The development of new strategies on both sides for the prosecution of the war also helped to mask the seriousness of the deadlock in the east. For Germany, the strategic situation at the beginning of the year could not have been much less promising. The knockout blow in the west on which the Germans had relied had been denied them on the Marne, although Belgium and the industrial districts of north-eastern France had been overrun. In the east, despite the great victory at Tannenberg, limited German forces faced an enemy whose re-

serves of both manpower and military resilience were evidently still unplumbed; early 1915 found Russia again threatening both East Prussia and Galicia. Moreover, the suspected weakness of Austria-Hungary was now a proven fact to friend and foe alike. The famous complaint of the Austrian commander-in-chief, Conrad von Hötzendorff, in November ("We ... have been holding the door against half Asia") could not conceal the fact that German intervention in Poland at the end of 1914 had done nothing to shore up her ally's failing war effort against Russia. The weakness of Austria-Hungary, and the consequent threat that Italy or Romania or both (and perhaps also Bulgaria and Greece) might seize the opportunity to join the Allies was a major preoccupation of the German strategists at the turn of the year. The only strategic bright spot at the end of 1914 was the entry of Turkey into the war in October, which offered Germany the opportunity of stretching British, French and Russian resources over wide new fronts at the cost of relatively limited technical, advisory and material support to the new ally.

The failure of the Schlieffen Plan and of Austria-Hungary's initial offensives therefore demanded a redefinition of German priorities. For the new year, Germany had to stand on the defensive in the west while concentrating forces in the east for a decisive blow against Russia – a blow which would not only relieve Austria-Hungary, but also deter Italy and the Balkan neutrals from joining the Allies. Only in the first aim – deterring Italy – did the Germans fail; otherwise, 1915 brought Germany a succession of major victories in the war on land, unequalled in strategic importance until the events of 1917.

New strategies: the Allies

The Allies had also to rethink their strategy in 1915. Here at once arose a difference of opinion between what became termed the Westerners and the Easterners. The former (notably Joffre and the French High Command) argued that victory could be gained only in the west; the latter (among them Churchill and Kitchener) argued that Germany could more economically be defeated by the back door, that is by knocking the Turkish prop from beneath the Central Powers. The spuriousness of this reasoning (in fact, it was German support which

Prey to Turkish gunners, an Allied ship lands stores and evacuates wounded, Gallipoli, December 1915

"propped up" the other Central Powers, including Austria-Hungary, not vice-versa) did not detract from the appeal of such an operation to soldiers and politicians struggling to make sense of the deadlock in the West. From this was born the concept of an amphibious attack in the Dardanelles, with the object of capturing Constantinople (page 60).

The stated objectives of the plan were three: to provide British naval power with an offensive role; to avoid further costly commitments in France and Flanders; and to provide direct help to Russia which, in return, could export wheat to the western Allies. Perhaps none of these objectives was realistic; nevertheless, Turkey might have been knocked out of the war entirely if the expedition had been thrust with the surprise and energy that Churchill and others had envisaged. In the event, the entire operation was so mismanaged and inept as to equal the disastrous British incompetence of the Crimean War. Only the evacuation was planned and executed with precision, not one Allied life being lost.

Meanwhile, Allied hopes of breaking the strategic impasse in the west were bolstered by the decision of Italy to enter the war on the Allied side, in the hope of gaining territory from Austria and in the Balkans. Initially high Allied expectations turned sour, however, during the First to Fourth Battles of the Isonzo, in the course of which Italian forces made little progress for the loss of some 160,000 men and were left with no military option but to continue battering at the powerful Austrian defenses. A trench-bound stalemate as frustrating as that in France and Belgium was the only apparent Allied achievement on the new front.

In the Caucasus, Allied fears of a Turkish breakthrough against Russia proved groundless; the Turkish armies suffered terrible privations and loss, and were driven back, as they were in their badly-planned and executed advance on the Suez Canal and British Egypt. Hopes of further success against Turkey to compensate for the failure of the Gallipoli enterprise were dashed in Mesopotamia, however. A grandly-conceived advance up the River Tigris to Baghdad by a British army under Townshend was mishandled almost from the beginning; the expeditionary force was besieged at Kut, and forced to surrender in conditions which combined horror and farce (notably in the private offer of a ransom of one million pounds to the Turkish government for the release unharmed of Townshend and his troops). Both Turks and Germans made great propaganda capital out of the British humiliation, and confident Allied expectations of widespread revolt within the Turkish Empire came to nothing.

The Allied strategy of indirect approach against Germany and Austria-Hungary was not abandoned after the Gallipoli fiasco. On 5 October, an Anglo-French force of two divisions (including some troops from Gallipoli) was landed at Salonika in northern Greece in an attempt to support Serbia. These units also failed in their purpose, being repulsed by Bulgarian troops in an attempt to advance up the River Vardar. By the end of the year the Allied force was virtually interned in Salonika itself, while Britain and France applied heavy-handed political pressure on Greece to join the Allied cause.

U-boats
The German search for an answer to the strategic deadlock of 1915 extended to the war at sea, too. Early in the year, the German Government declared a blockade of the British Isles. German naval plan-

ners had estimated that a fleet of 200 U-boats would be sufficient to choke off all overseas trade to the British Isles, and that such an operation would literally starve Britain into withdrawing from the Allied war effort. This was a truly novel strategy, at least as regards the employment of U-boats in this role; hitherto, submarines had been seen as auxiliaries to fleets, useful as scouts and capable of damaging or even sinking individual enemy warships by torpedo, but little more. The short cruising range of U-boats and the fact that the Dover Straits were effectively closed to them by the Royal Navy suggested practical difficulties with the proposed blockade, but there were two more serious problems. First was the simple fact that in August 1914 only 28 U-boats had been in service, and creation of a fleet of 200 was a major, long-term undertaking. The second problem was that U-boat warfare posed a serious propaganda problem: submarines could not give warning of attack nor rescue the crews and passengers of ships that they had sunk. Their very success therefore gave further ammunition to the effective Allied propaganda image of German barbarism. Following the sinking of the *Lusitania,* which inflamed American indignation, these two considerations led to a temporary halt in U-boat activities.

The Eastern Fronts

Before the German offensive effort in the east was ready, the Russians renewed their thrusts in the

German troops advance across a newly constructed bridge after the capture of Grodeck, in Galicia, May – June 1915

Allied hopes of an Italian breakthrough were soon dashed as Italian troops were slaughtered during the Isonzo campaigns

spring both into East Prussia and toward the Carpathians. During the latter offensive they captured the great Austrian fortress of Przemysl on 22 March, but to the north they suffered a terrible defeat in the area of the Masurian Lakes and retired behind the frontier (page 58); Russian troops were not to threaten East Prussia again until 1944, in another war.

The success against the Austrians marked the high point of Russia's advance in 1915. Chronic shortages of weapons and munitions began significantly to reduce the effectiveness of the Tsarist armies at the very moment when Central Powers plans for massive thrusts eastward were implemented. The main blow (Mackensen) was delivered in Galicia, a subsidiary thrust (Below) in the north toward Riga. The German Eleventh Army's attack (with Austrian support) in Galicia at Gorlice, by the concentrated deployment of great numbers of artillery, achieved an immediate breakthrough, and swept the Russians eastward in disarray (page 70). This, in turn, exposed the flank of Russian troops in the Carpathians and they, too, were forced to withdraw. On 3 June the Germans retook the fortress of Przemysl. In the north, Below's advance from East Prussia took German forces to near the Gulf of Riga. Now a terrible threat was posed for Russia: massed German units attacked the Polish salient from the north, while Austro-German armies thrust up from the southeast. The overwhelming German superiority in artillery made the Russian position untenable: Warsaw was abandoned and the Russians retreated eastward to a line running almost straight, north to south, from Riga to Czernowitz, after massive losses of men and weaponry.

Austria-Hungary was thus able to transfer sufficient forces to the Italian front to contain any Italian advance on the Isonzo. An even more significant consequence was that Mackensen was freed to attack the north of Serbia at the end of the year; Bulgaria, inclining toward the Central Powers anyway after Allied failures at Gallipoli and in the Middle East, joined the Central Powers in September and simultaneously invaded Serbia from the east. Serbia was overrun, and the remnants of the Serb armies driven into exile in Corfu.

The year 1915, which had begun with such promise for the Allies, left them with nothing but foreboding and gloom. All their offensives on the Western Front had been frustrated with heavy loss; the Gallipoli campaign had ended in dismal and costly failure; stalemate prevailed along the Italian front on the Alps; and the Central Powers had achieved major strategic success against Russia while effectively knocking Serbia out of the war altogether.

Timeline 1915

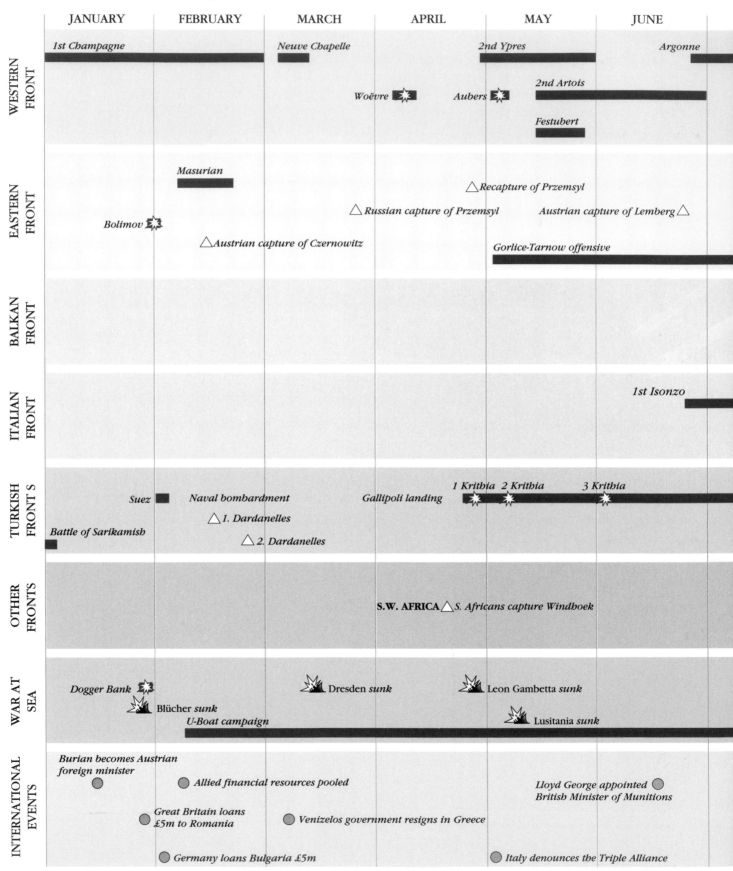

	JANUARY	FEBRUARY	MARCH	APRIL	MAY	JUNE

WESTERN FRONT

1st Champagne   Neuve Chapelle   2nd Ypres   Argonne

Woëvre ✦   Aubers ✦   2nd Artois

Festubert

EASTERN FRONT

Masurian

△ Recapture of Przemsyl

△ Russian capture of Przemsyl   Austrian capture of Lemberg △

Bolimov ✦

△ Austrian capture of Czernowitz

Gorlice-Tarnow offensive

BALKAN FRONT

ITALIAN FRONT

1st Isonzo

TURKISH FRONTS

1 Krithia 2 Krithia 3 Krithia

Suez ▪   Naval bombardment   Gallipoli landing   ✦ ✦ ✦

△ 1. Dardanelles

Battle of Sarikamish   △ 2. Dardanelles

OTHER FRONTS

S.W. AFRICA △ S. Africans capture Windhoek

WAR AT SEA

Dogger Bank ✦   ✦ Dresden sunk   ✦ Leon Gambetta sunk

✦ Blücher sunk   ✦ Lusitania sunk

U-Boat campaign

INTERNATIONAL EVENTS

Burian becomes Austrian foreign minister ●

● Allied financial resources pooled

Lloyd George appointed ●
British Minister of Munitions

Great Britain loans ● £5m to Romania

● Venizelos government resigns in Greece

● Germany loans Bulgaria £5m

● Italy denounces the Triple Alliance

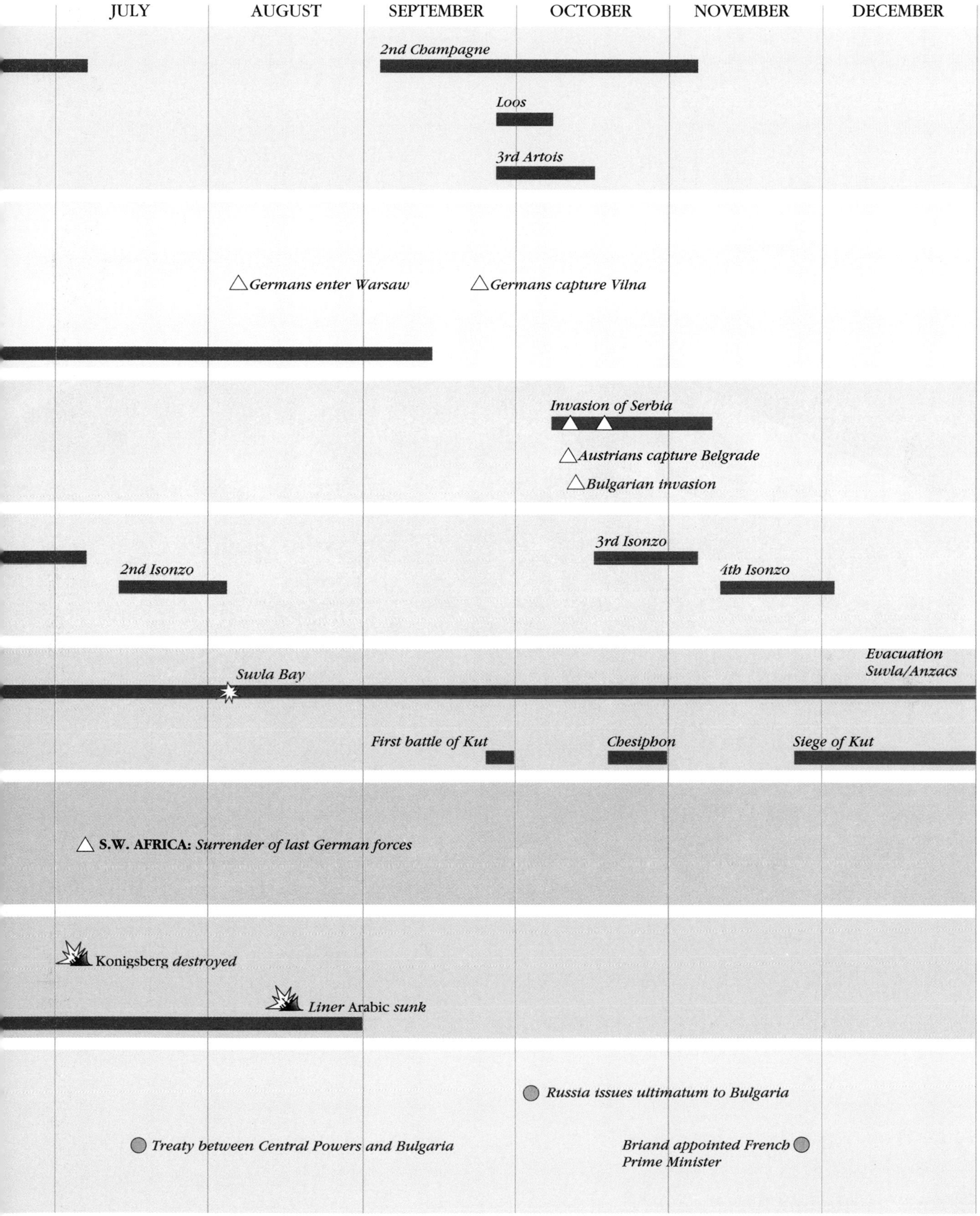

JULY	AUGUST	SEPTEMBER	OCTOBER	NOVEMBER	DECEMBER

2nd Champagne

Loos

3rd Artois

△*Germans enter Warsaw*   △*Germans capture Vilna*

Invasion of Serbia

△*Austrians capture Belgrade*

△*Bulgarian invasion*

3rd Isonzo

2nd Isonzo

4th Isonzo

Evacuation Suvla/Anzacs

Suvla Bay

First battle of Kut   *Chesiphon*   *Siege of Kut*

△ **S.W. AFRICA:** *Surrender of last German forces*

Konigsberg destroyed

Liner Arabic sunk

● *Russia issues ultimatum to Bulgaria*

● *Treaty between Central Powers and Bulgaria*   *Briand appointed French* ●
Prime Minister

Masuria February 1915

Hindenburg's winter offensive had its roots in German concern that a combined Italian-Romanian declaration of war in March would destroy Austria-Hungary. A decisive victory before the snows melted was needed as a deterrent, and to allow Austria to relieve Przemysl, in which 100,000 Austrian troops were besieged by the Russian Eleventh Army following the Central Powers's failed Warsaw offensive in November (page 40). The German plan involved a converging attack on the entire Russian front (see Strategic View).

The Russian high command was again hampered by the divergent aims of Ivanov (Southwestern Front), who proposed concentration against Austria, and Ruzsky (Northwestern Front), who argued that German strength in East Prussia was a constant threat to the front in Poland. Nicholas favored Ruzsky, and deployed the new Twelfth Army (Plehve) in northern Poland for an offensive into East Prussia timed for 20 February. Plehve's attack was pre-empted by the Germans.

The battle
The German blow was launched on 7 February, during a snowstorm, by the Eighth and Tenth armies (Map 2). Eighth Army hit the left flank of the Russian Tenth Army on that day and, on the following, the German Tenth, stationed to the north, rolled up the Russian right. Despite fierce resistance, the Russians were quickly driven back into Augustov Forest. There the Russian XX Corps (Bulgakov) fought with such heroism that the other three corps of the Tenth Army escaped encirclement eastward.

Consequences
Russians losses approached 200,000 (about 90,000 prisoners). The Germans had gained an

impressive tactical victory, but one whose strategic value was minimal, for Plehve was in position to counter-attack almost immediately, and the Germans had no reserves. Twelfth Army halted all further German advance. Meanwhile, the Austrian offensive, spearheaded by the German Südarmee, made no progress and failed to relieve Przemysl, which fell on 22 March.

The campaign represented the last German attempt to bolster Austria-Hungary indirectly, through action in the north: after Masuria the German high command recognized that their ally could be sustained only by the transfer south of significant German forces. These could only come from the Western Front. Falkenhayn reluctantly adopted such a policy from March onwards, and the attempt to knock Russia out of the war remained the overriding German preoccupation for the remainder of the year.

The Masurian Lakes region, East Prussia, under snow in the winter of 1914–15. Hindenburg had made a special study of the military topography of the area. His offensive in February ended any Russian threat to East Prussia, but failed to relieve the pressure on Austria-Hungary.

"very shaken, part of it altogether smashed and the rest falling back..."

Sievers describing the condition of the III Corps to Ruzsky on 12 February

---

Strategic View: Hindenburg
Hindenburg planned a massive pincer operation on the entire Russian front in Poland. While Ninth Army (Gallwitz) moved to keep the Russians occupied, Eighth Army and the new Tenth Army would break through from the north, to meet an Austrian/Südarmee attack from the south. Bolimow saw the first use of gas in the war.

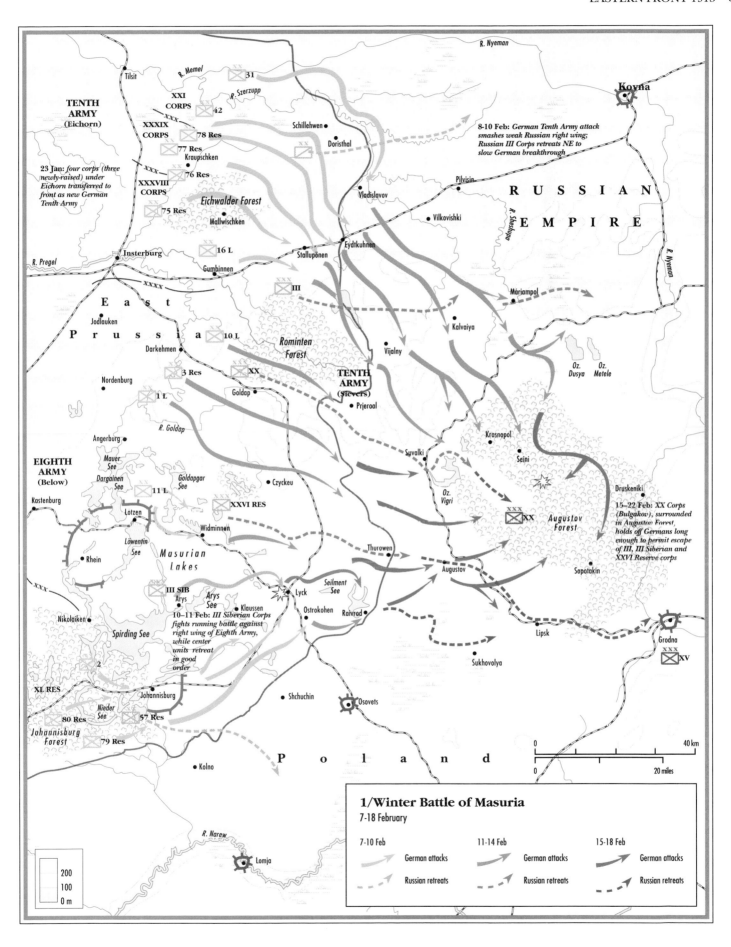

R. Nyeman

Tilsit
R. Memel
R. Szerzupp
31

**TENTH
ARMY**
(Eichorn)

**XXI
CORPS**   **42**

**XXXIX
CORPS**   **78 Res**

77 Res
Kraupschken

Schillehwen

Doristhal

Kovna

*8-10 Feb: German Tenth Army attack
smashes weak Russian right wing;
Russian III Corps retreats NE to
slow German breakthrough*

*23 Jan: four corps (three
newly-raised) under
Eichorn transferred to
front as new German
Tenth Army*

**XXXVIII
CORPS**   **76 Res**

75 Res

Eichwalder Forest

Mallwischken

Vladislavov

Pilvisin

R U S S I A N

E M P I R E

Vilkovishki

R. Sheshupa

R. Nyeman

R. Pregel

Insterburg

16 L

Gumbinnen

Stallupönen

Eydtkuhnen

Máriampol

E a s t

Jodlauken

XXXX

III

Kalvaiya

P r u s s i a

Darkehmen   **10 L**

Rominten
Forest

Vijalny

Oz.
Dusya
Oz.
Metele

3 Res

Nordenburg

1 L

Goldap

XX

**TENTH
ARMY**
(Sievers)

Prjeroal

Krasnopol

Seini

Druskeniki

R. Goldap

Angerburg

Suvalki

**EIGHTH
ARMY**
(Below)

Mauer
See
Dargainen
See

Goldapgar
See

Czyckeu

11 L

XXVI RES

Oz.
Vigri

XX

Augustov
Forest

*15–22 Feb: XX Corps
(Bulgakov), surrounded
in Augustov Forest,
holds off Germans long
enough to permit escape
of III, III Siberian and
XXVI Reserve corps*

Sopatakin

Kastenburg

Lotzen

Löwentin
See

Widminnen

Thurowen

Augustov

2

Rhein

Nikolaiken

XXXX

**Masurian
Lakes**

Spirding See

III SIB
Arys

Arys
See

Klaussen

Lyck

Seilment
See

Ostrokohen

Raivrod

Lipsk

Grodna

XV

*10-11 Feb: III Siberian Corps
fights running battle against
right wing of Eighth Army,
while center
units retreat
in good
order*

Sukhovolya

XL RES

Johannisburg

Nieder
See

80 Res   **57 Res**

Shchuchin

Osovets

79 Res

Johannisburg
Forest

Kolno

P o l a n d

0   40 km

0   20 miles

R. Narew

Lomja

1/Winter Battle of Masuria
7-18 February

7-10 Feb	11-14 Feb	15-18 Feb
German attacks	German attacks	German attacks
Russian retreats	Russian retreats	Russian retreats

200
100
0 m

Gallipoli The Allied Assault, February – May 1915

By the end of 1914 there was stalemate on both Western and Eastern fronts. The British War Council had toyed for some time with schemes for a direct assault on Turkey, and in early 1915 the possibility of a blow which would restore strategic mobility to the entire war began to grip the imagination of British planners. The original proposal was to use a number of older warships to force the Dardanelles, thus knocking Turkey out of the war at a stroke (see Strategic View). An extraordinary confusion soon took hold, however, over the ways in which this aim might be achieved.

Naval operations

The Allied naval attempt on the Dardanelles on 18 March came very close to success. The main Turkish batteries had been put out of action by about 1330hrs, and minesweepers led the fleet into the Dardanelles. As the warships passed through Erenkeui Bay, seven ships struck mines laid there on 8 March (Map 1).

Vice-Admiral Sir John de Robeck, commanding the operation, decided that the passage could not be forced by ships alone. A military expedition was only then finally resolved upon.

The landings

Kitchener agreed to the despatch of a Mediterranean Expeditionary Force from Egypt and the United Kingdom on 26 March. Commanded by General Sir Ian Hamilton, this force comprised some 78,000 men, largely Australians and New Zealanders (Anzacs), the British 29th Division and one French division. Matters went awry almost from the start, when incorrect stowage

of the expedition's transport ships necessitated an extra month's delay in Alexandria. By the time Hamilton made his first landings, the defenders were well prepared.

The landings at beaches X and Y were virtually unopposed, but as the commanders had been inadequately briefed, their forces made no attempt to intervene in the savage and bloody fighting which raged all day at beaches S, V and W. Here the defenders were severely punished by the opening naval bombardment, but remained in their trenches and inflicted sickeningly heavy casualties on the landing troops. A Turkish dusk counter-attack at Beach Y caused a panic evacuation during the night.

At Beach Z (Anzac Cove) the landing force, again largely unopposed, established a very cramped beachhead in the northern part of their intended landing zone, and sent patrols into the hinterland. Mustafa Kemal (later Kemal Attatürk), the one soldier of genius in the area, immediately occupied the commanding Sari Bair ridge with the entire Turkish 19th Division.

At both Anzac Cove and Cape Helles heavy Turkish counter-attacks were bloodily repulsed in the next few weeks, and the action then settled into a war of attrition, with enormous casualties on both sides, little territorial gain by either, and the added horrors of endemic dysentery and the blazing Turkish summer weather. All Allied hopes of a war of movement had been lost in the confusion of the first day.

French 155mm artillery in action on the heights of Sedd-el-Bahr, Cape Helles, with the destroyed Turkish fortifications in the background.

> " On land there was still a scene of indescribable confusion. On the narrow strip of sandy, stony beach, not more than about thirty to forty feet wide... men were moving in every direction. Troops landing, troops marching... men laden with rations, mules and horses packed with stores and water barrels and bearers coming down the cliffs with wounded and dying on stretchers. "
>
> **Father Eric Green, Army Chaplain's Dept.**

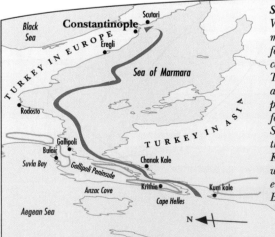

Strategic View: Churchill
Winston Churchill was a prime mover behind the British scheme for a direct strike at the Turkish capital via the Dardanelles. Turkish forces (green lines) were arrayed on the Gallipoli peninsula, but a fleet might force the Narrows and cross the Sea of Marmara without fear of the weak Turkish fleet. Knocking Turkey out of the war would aid Russia and encourage neutral Romania, Bulgaria and Greece to enter the war against the Central Powers.

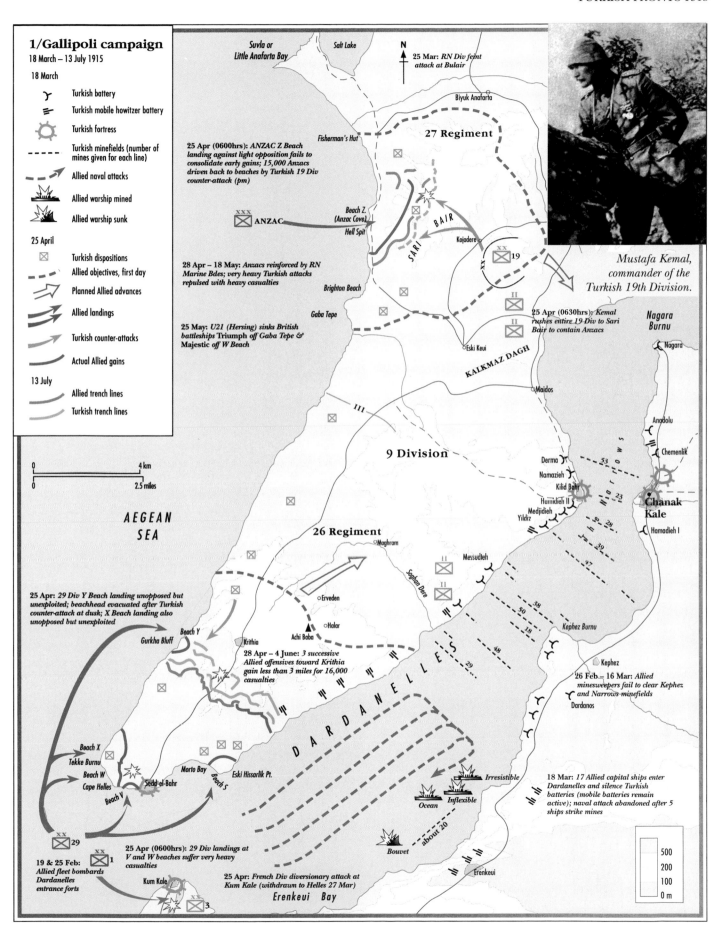

1/Gallipoli campaign
18 March – 13 July 1915

18 March

ᒋ Turkish battery

〰 Turkish mobile howitzer battery

⚙ Turkish fortress

┅┅ Turkish minefields (number of mines given for each line)

⇢ Allied naval attacks

💥 Allied warship mined

💥 Allied warship sunk

25 April

⊠ Turkish dispositions

┅┅ Allied objectives, first day

⇨ Planned Allied advances

➡ Allied landings

➡ Turkish counter-attacks

➡ Actual Allied gains

13 July

〰 Allied trench lines

〰 Turkish trench lines

Mustafa Kemal, commander of the Turkish 19th Division.

0 ———— 4 km
0 ———— 2.5 miles

Suvla or Little Anafarta Bay

Salt Lake

N

25 Mar: RN Div feint attack at Bulair

Biyuk Anafarta

27 Regiment

Fisherman's Hut

25 Apr (0600hrs): ANZAC Z Beach landing against light opposition fails to consolidate early gains; 15,000 Anzacs driven back to beaches by Turkish 19 Div counter-attack (pm)

ANZAC

Beach Z. (Anzac Cove)

Hell Spit

SARI BAIR

Kojadere

19

28 Apr – 18 May: Anzacs reinforced by RN Marine Bdes; very heavy Turkish attacks repulsed with heavy casualties

Brighton Beach

Gaba Tepe

25 Apr (0630hrs): Kemal rushes entire 19 Div to Sari Bair to contain Anzacs

Nagara Burnu

Nagara

25 May: U21 (Hersing) sinks British battleships Triumph off Gaba Tepe & Majestic off W Beach

Eski Keui

KALKMAZ DAGH

Maidos

Anadolu

Chemenlik

9 Division

Derma

Namazieh

53

Kilid Bahr

23

Hamidieh II

Medjidieh

Yildiz

Chanak Kale

28

26 Regiment

Maghram

Messudieh

39

Erveden

47

AEGEAN SEA

25 Apr: 29 Div Y Beach landing unopposed but unexploited; beachhead evacuated after Turkish counter-attack at dusk; X Beach landing also unopposed but unexploited

Beach Y

Gurkha Bluff

Krithia

Achi Baba

Halar

Soghun Dere

38

50

18

Kephez Burnu

28 Apr – 4 June: 3 successive Allied offensives toward Krithia gain less than 3 miles for 16,000 casualties

49

29

DARDANELLES

Kephez

26 Feb – 16 Mar: Allied minesweepers fail to clear Kephez and Narrows minefields

Dardanos

Beach X

Tekke Burnu

Beach W

Cape Helles

Beach V

Sedd-el-Bahr

Morto Bay

Beach S

Eski Hissarlik Pt.

Irresistible

Inflexible

Ocean

18 Mar: 17 Allied capital ships enter Dardanelles and silence Turkish batteries (mobile batteries remain active); naval attack abandoned after 5 ships strike mines

29

1

about 20

Bouvet

19 & 25 Feb: Allied fleet bombards Dardanelles entrance forts

25 Apr (0600hrs): 29 Div landings at V and W beaches suffer very heavy casualties

Kum Kale

25 Apr: French Div diversionary attack at Kum Kale (withdrawn to Helles 27 Mar)

3

Erenkeui

Erenkeui Bay

500
200
100
0 m

Neuve Chapelle March 1915

By the end of December 1914, Allied intelligence had detected the transfer of significant German forces from the quiescent West to the Eastern Front. In the first instance of what was to become a recurrent theme of 1915, French and Joffre agreed on the urgent need for an offensive to prevent the Germans stripping their line for a knock-out blow against Russia. Joffre was also keen to forestall moves to transfer French troops to the "minor" Balkan and Turkish theaters. The area selected was Artois, where Aubers Ridge was a tempting prize since existing British trenches were waterlogged.

The Neuve Chapelle salient

In October 1914 German forces in Artois had broken the British Smith-Dorrien trench line at Neuve Chapelle, seizing a salient which enabled them to fire on the British trenches to both flanks. Haig proposed, for early March, an offensive to recapture Neuve Chapelle, then to capture Aubers Ridge and threaten German communications between La Bassée and Lille.

The offensive was to be a British and Indian Army effort, the first major offensive of the war to be launched from a trench system. New artillery tactics had been developed: surprise was to be achieved by dispensing with a preliminary bombardment and shelling the enemy positions only while the infantry advanced. The artillery was then to concentrate on preventing enemy reserves from coming up. Some 340 guns were mustered – an unprecedented concentration. Four infantry brigades were to attack on a front of only 2000 yards.

German defenses consisted of a conventional single trench line, strongly held, supported by a line of strongpoints including machine guns some 1000 yards to the rear.

The offensive on 10 March achieved complete surprise, the German front line was overrun and the infantry advanced some 1200 yards. Thereafter, communications broke down at all levels, and no further exploitation was attempted. Moreover, German positions north and south of the assault had held firm, and Rawlinson (IV Corps) chose to hold 7 Division in reserve in case of a counter-attack. Already German reserves were being rushed up; during the night, they rapidly dug new trenches linking the strongpoints behind the main line.

Haig ordered a renewed offensive on 12 March, but the Germans launched a heavy assault that morning, in thick mist. All German attacks were held, but the ensuing British attacks also failed. At 2204hrs on 12 March Haig cancelled all offensives and ordered his troops to consolidate the ground they had taken.

Consequences

The Allies had taken and held an area some 4000yds wide and 1000yds deep, but had failed to achieve a breakout: the narrow front attacked and the collapse of communications had allowed German reserves to seal the breach more quickly than it could be exploited. The new artillery tactics were considered promising, but their success was attributed to the weight of fire rather than to the surprise achieved. On the German side, the narrow margin by which the line had held was recognized immediately, and preparation of a complete second trench line became a priority throughout the front. British casualties were 12,847, German about 12,000.

Sir Henry Rawlinson, commander of the British IV Corps at Neuve Chapelle. His concern about German strength at the Quadrilateral prompted him to hold 7 Division in reserve, rather than use it to exploit the initial breakthrough, and the opportunity for further advance was lost.

British gunners man a Mark 7 naval gun adapted for use on land. Such improvised heavy guns helped bring British artillery support at Neuve Chapelle to an unprecedented level, though far greater numbers of guns became the norm later in the war.

Right: Members of the Indian Corps in France at the end of 1914, carrying machine guns. The Garhwal and Bareilly Brigades of 7 (Meerut) Division formed the right wing of the Allied attack at Neuve Chapelle.

"The units of the Indian Corps may justly claim that they had the good fortune to arrive at the very moment when their services were most required to relieve a very desperate situation."

Lieutenant-Colonel
D.H. Drake Brookman
39th Garhwal Ritles

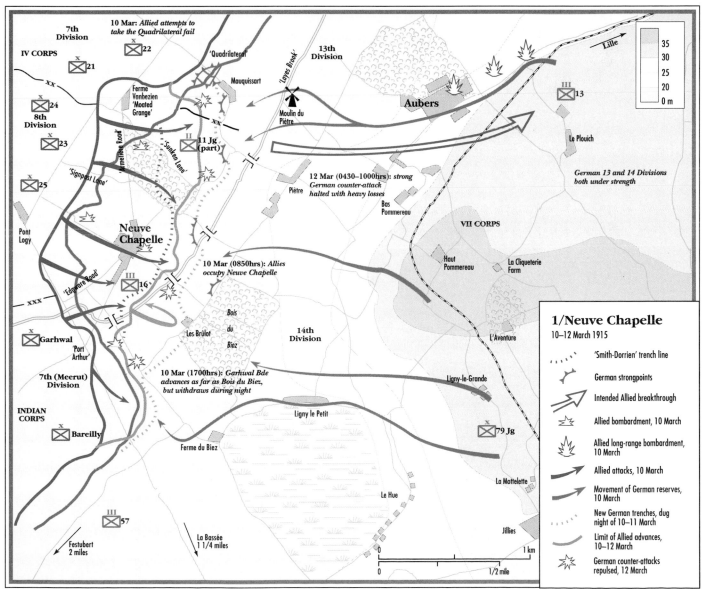

7th Division

IV CORPS

10 Mar: *Allied attempts to take the Quadrilateral fail*

22

21

'Quadrilateral'

13th Division

Mauquissart

'Layes Brook'

Lille

24

8th Division

Ferme Vanhezien 'Moated Grange'

Moulin du Piètre

Aubers

13

23

'Sunken Lane'

II 11 Jg (part)

Le Plouich

25

'Armentière Road'

'Signpost Lane'

Piètre

12 Mar (0430–1000hrs): *strong German counter-attack halted with heavy losses*

Bas Pommereau

German 13 and 14 Divisions both under strength

Pont Logy

Neuve Chapelle

VII CORPS

Haut Pommereau

La Cliqueterie Farm

'Edgware Road'

III 16

XXX

10 Mar (0850hrs): *Allies occupy Neuve Chapelle*

Bois du Biez

14th Division

L'Aventure

Garhwal

'Port Arthur'

Les Brûlot

7th (Meerut) Division

INDIAN CORPS

10 Mar (1700hrs): *Garhwal Bde advances as far as Bois du Biez, but withdraws during night*

Ligny-le-Grande

Bareilly

Ligny le Petit

79 Jg

Ferme du Biez

La Mottelette

Le Hue

III 57

Jillies

Festubert 2 miles

La Bassée 1 1/4 miles

0   1 km

0   1/2 mile

1/Neuve Chapelle
10–12 March 1915

'Smith-Dorrien' trench line

German strongpoints

Intended Allied breakthrough

Allied bombardment, 10 March

Allied long-range bombardment, 10 March

Allied attacks, 10 March

Movement of German reserves, 10 March

New German trenches, dug night of 10–11 March

Limit of Allied advances, 10–12 March

German counter-attacks repulsed, 12 March

35
30
25
20
0 m

The War at Sea 1915

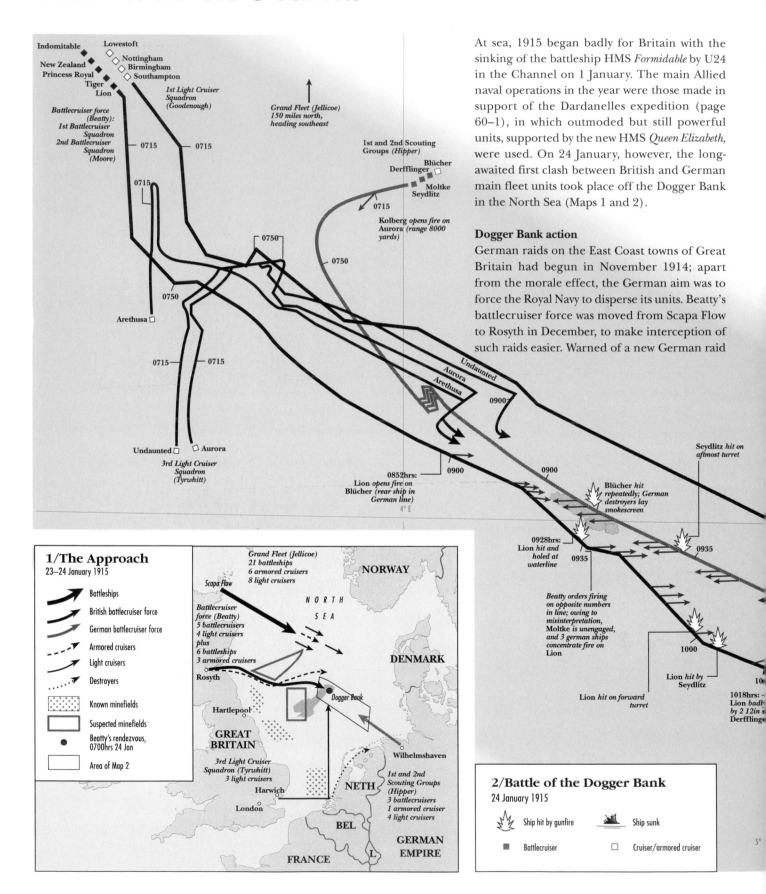

Indomitable
Lowestoft
New Zealand
Nottingham
Princess Royal
Birmingham
Tiger
Southampton
Lion

1st Light Cruiser
Squadron
(Goodenough)

Grand Fleet (Jellicoe)
150 miles north,
heading southeast

Battlecruiser force
(Beatty):
1st Battlecruiser
Squadron
2nd Battlecruiser
Squadron
(Moore)

1st and 2nd Scouting
Groups (Hipper)

Blücher

Derfflinger

Moltke
Seydlitz

0715

0715

0715

0715

0750

0750

0750

Kolberg *opens fire on*
Aurora (range 8000
yards)

Arethusa

0715   0715

Undaunted

Aurora

3rd Light Cruiser
Squadron
(Tyrwhitt)

Undaunted
Aurora
Arethusa

0900

0900

0900

Seydlitz *hit on*
aftmost turret

4° E

0852hrs:
Lion *opens fire on*
Blücher *(rear ship in*
German line)

Blücher *hit*
repeatedly; German
destroyers lay
smokescreen

0928hrs:
Lion *hit and*
holed at
waterline

0935

0935

1000

Beatty orders firing
on opposite numbers
in line; owing to
misinterpretation,
Moltke is unengaged,
and 3 german ships
concentrate fire on
Lion

Lion *hit by*
Seydlitz

Lion *hit on forward*
turret

1018hrs: -
Lion *badl*
by 2 12in s
Derffling

10

At sea, 1915 began badly for Britain with the sinking of the battleship HMS *Formidable* by U24 in the Channel on 1 January. The main Allied naval operations in the year were those made in support of the Dardanelles expedition (page 60–1), in which outmoded but still powerful units, supported by the new HMS *Queen Elizabeth*, were used. On 24 January, however, the long-awaited first clash between British and German main fleet units took place off the Dogger Bank in the North Sea (Maps 1 and 2).

Dogger Bank action

German raids on the East Coast towns of Great Britain had begun in November 1914; apart from the morale effect, the German aim was to force the Royal Navy to disperse its units. Beatty's battlecruiser force was moved from Scapa Flow to Rosyth in December, to make interception of such raids easier. Warned of a new German raid

1/The Approach
23–24 January 1915

➤	Battleships
➤	British battlecruiser force
➤	German battlecruiser force
⇢	Armored cruisers
→	Light cruisers
⋯→	Destroyers
▦	Known minefields
▭	Suspected minefields
●	Beatty's rendezvous, 0700hrs 24 Jan
▭	Area of Map 2

Grand Fleet (Jellicoe)
21 battleships
6 armored cruisers
8 light cruisers

NORWAY

Scapa Flow

Battlecruiser
force (Beatty)
5 battlecruisers
4 light cruisers
plus
6 battleships
3 armored cruisers

NORTH
SEA

Rosyth

DENMARK

Dogger Bank

Hartlepool

GREAT
BRITAIN

Wilhelmshaven

3rd Light Cruiser
Squadron (Tyrwhitt)
3 light cruisers

Harwich

NETH

London

1st and 2nd
Scouting Groups
(Hipper)
3 battlecruisers
1 armored cruiser
4 light cruisers

BEL

FRANCE

GERMAN
EMPIRE

L

2/Battle of the Dogger Bank
24 January 1915

✹	Ship hit by gunfire	⛴	Ship sunk
■	Battlecruiser	☐	Cruiser/armored cruiser

5°

Admiral Sir David Beatty received unanimous praise for his actions during the Dogger Bank engagement, though it might be argued that the failure of his subordinates to chase the defeated German flotilla was in part due to a lack of clarity in his signals.

"The spectacle of Moore and Co. yapping around the poor tortured Blücher, with beaten ships in sight to be sunk, is one of the most distressing episodes of the war."

Rear Admiral Keyes commenting on the decision of Rear Admiral Moore to concentrate fire upon the Blücher rather than give chase to the retreating German squadron.

---

on the night of 23–4 January by radio intercepts, Beatty's force made for a rendezvous off the Dogger Bank, supported by light cruisers (Tyrwhitt) from Harwich, armored cruisers and a squadron of battleships (Packenham and Bradford) from Rosyth, and the bulk of the Grand Fleet to the north (Map 1). The light cruisers sighted Hipper's force at 0715hrs, and the outnumbered Germans turned in flight.

In the running fight which followed (Map 2), the faster British battlecruisers failed to overhaul and destroy Hipper's force largely through a series of misunderstood orders. Hipper's flagship SMS *Seydlitz* was badly damaged, as was Beatty's flagship HMS *Lion*, which dropped out of action, but the only major British achievement was the sinking of the armored cruiser *Blücher*.

The severe damage caused to the *Seydlitz* by a cordite fire in the after turrets led to two important developments in the German High Seas Fleet. All capital-ship turrets were quickly fitted with anti-flash doors to prevent fire spreading from turret to magazine, thereby making them less vulnerable to massive explosions than British ships. Moreover, the Kaiser, now fearful of losing capital ships, ordered his navy to avoid all further risks.

The U-boat campaign

This in turn led, on 1 February, to Germany opening a U-boat campaign (page 118–19)

against merchantmen in waters around the British Isles, targeting even neutrals, with the object of starving Great Britain into surrender. U-boats, able to stay at sea for up to four weeks and armed with torpedoes and guns, were deployed particularly in the Western Approaches, on the transatlantic shipping routes.

The campaign met at first with considerable success, largely because few effective anti-submarine weapons had been developed by 1915: but the political cost was to be great. A U-boat sank a Norwegian vessel on 19 February and, on 1 May, the American tanker *Gulflight*, killing two of her crew. Then, on 7 May, the British liner *Lusitania* was sunk by U-20 off the coast of Ireland. Despite the fact that her cargo included ammunition and that prior to her departure from New York the German Embassy in Washington had warned Americans not to travel on her, the loss of 124 American lives (out of a total of 1198) caused such outrage in America that a strongly worded protest was issued.

When, on 19 August, the British liner *Arabic* was likewise sunk, with the loss of four American lives, American outrage was such that on 1 September Germany was obliged to discontinue unrestricted U-boat activity.

Nevertheless, in the eight months of the campaign, German U-boats had sunk almost one million tons of Allied shipping, offering an alluring prospect that Germany was later, in desperation, to re-embrace.

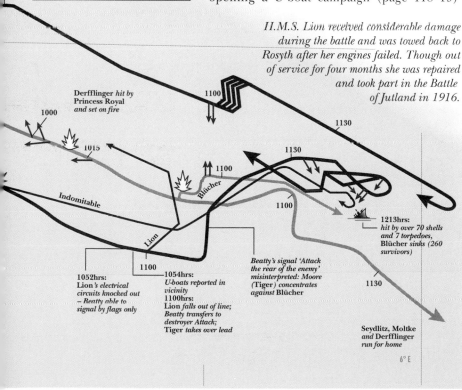

H.M.S. Lion received considerable damage during the battle and was towed back to Rosyth after her engines failed. Though out of service for four months she was repaired and took part in the Battle of Jutland in 1916.

1000

Derfflinger hit by Princess Royal and set on fire

1015

Indomitable

Lion

1100

1052hrs: Lion's electrical circuits knocked out – Beatty able to signal by flags only

1054hrs: U-boats reported in vicinity
1100hrs: Lion falls out of line; Beatty transfers to destroyer Attack; Tiger takes over lead

1100

Blücher

1100

1100

Beatty's signal 'Attack the rear of the enemy' misinterpreted: Moore (Tiger) concentrates against Blücher

1130

1130

1130

1100

1213hrs: hit by over 70 shells and 7 torpedoes, Blücher sinks (260 survivors)

1130

Seydlitz, Moltke and Derfflinger run for home

6° E

Second Ypres April – May 1915

The line of the Ypres salient had been established during November 1914. Behind the front line, comprising relatively shallow trenches - with few support positions, lay a more formidable second line of French construction, known to the British troops who had taken it over as "GHQ Line". This consisted of redoubts some 400 yards apart, with good fields of fire. In April 1915, despite grander ambitions in the East, the German high command planned to eliminate the salient once and for all, renewing their threat to the Channel ports and straightening a troop-consuming bulge in their line.

Gas

Archduke Albrecht agreed to the use of gas in Fourth Army's initial breakthrough attempt. By 8 April the cylinders of chlorine gas were in position in front of Ypres, but for 14 days the wind remained persistently in the wrong direction. Not until 22 April did conditions prove suitable. The gas was released at 1700hrs in the north of the salient toward Pilckem Ridge by two divisions of the XXVI Reserve Corps and one division of XXIII Corps on its right, while the other division of XXIII Corps, without the aid of gas, thrust at Steenstraat as a diversion, but made little progress. The greenish-yellow gas turned to a blue-white mist as it drifted into Allied positions. From both the 45th Algerian and 87th French Territorial division lines, a host of choking men poured backward, leaving a gap in the front nearly five miles wide. A German advance of four miles southward could now take Ypres.

The BEF Second Army commander, Horace Smith-Dorrien, ordered a counter-attack by units of Plumer's V Corps, supported by the 1st Canadian Brigade, at about 2000hrs. Meanwhile, Allied troops made hasty and improvised preparations against the next gas attack: they held wet cloths over their mouths and nostrils, for the gas had been identified as chlorine, which is soluble in water, and made primitive respirators out of lint and tape. The advancing Germans, overrunning areas saturated with gas, began digging in when they reached their first limited objectives, and Albrecht had insufficient reserves to exploit the breakthrough further.

Counter-attacking Canadian units penetrated the new German line and took Kitchener's Wood, but expected French support was not

forthcoming, and the Canadians had shortly to abandon their gains. The following day, the 23rd, limited British reserves mounted further small counter-attacks, which were beaten off with heavy losses. By that evening, however, the way to Ypres was almost plugged, though only 21 exhausted battalions (12 Canadian, 9 British) faced 42 German battalions with far greater numbers of artillery pieces. At 0400hrs on 24 April, Albrecht ordered a further gas attack, this time on the Canadian sector. By the afternoon German forces had reached beyond St Julien, but they were then driven back. The salient, however, had been compressed into an area six miles deep by only three miles across, and all British forces within it came under massed artillery fire.

Deadlock

Any further progress by either side became impossible, despite a month of attacks and counter - attacks. Smith-Dorrien recognized the futility of further Allied attacks, and recommended withdrawal to a straighter line nearer to Ypres. General French promptly dismissed him – thus losing perhaps his best commander – and appointed Plumer in his place.

On 1 May, Foch admitted to General French that Joffre, far from sending French support to Ypres, was planning an offensive near Arras. General French then ordered a withdrawal, by stages at night, to a line three miles east of Ypres, precisely what Smith-Dorrien had advocated. This still left a salient, albeit reduced (commanders at the front had urged a greater withdrawal to the straight line of defense formed by Ypres and the canal), dooming the British to further gas attacks and bombardment. Their relief came only at the end of May, when the Germans too had exhausted their supply of shells.

The German High Command defended its use of gas by stating that it had first been utilised by the French. The French had developed a rifle grenade which contained a small quantity of tear gas for use in attacking fortifications but this weapon had not been used in the war to date and the make-shift masks worn by these infantrymen reveal how little the French expected gas attacks.

"Of course, the chaps were all gasping and couldn't breathe. and it was ghastly, especially for chaps that were wounded – terrible for a wounded man to lie there! The gasping, the gasping!"

Sgt. Bill Hay, 9th Battalion, The Royal Scots.

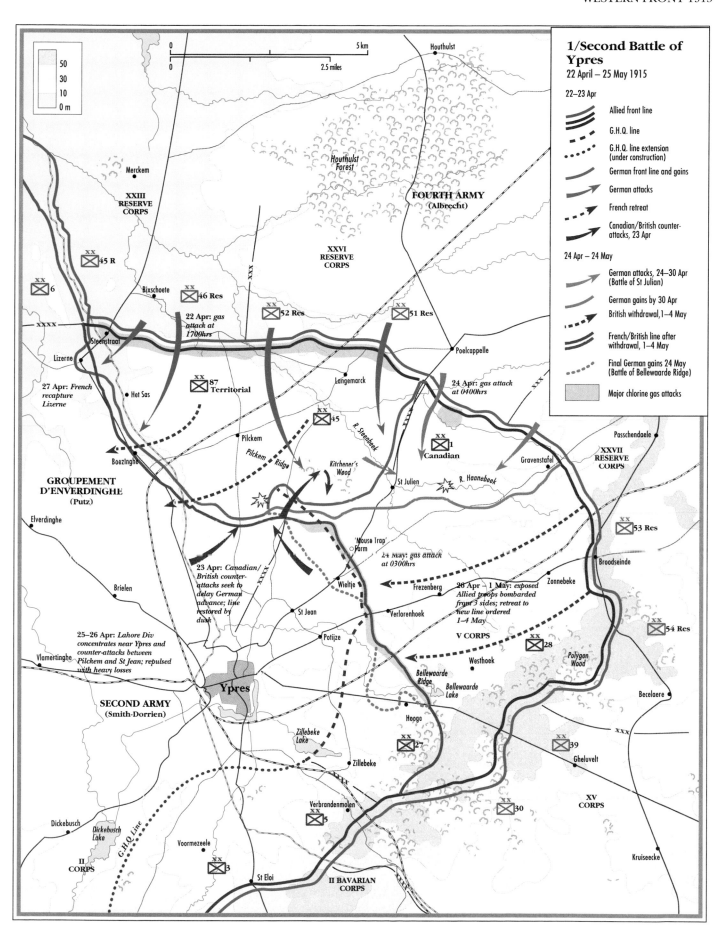

1/Second Battle of Ypres
22 April – 25 May 1915

22–23 Apr

Allied front line

G.H.Q. line

G.H.Q. line extension (under construction)

German front line and gains

German attacks

French retreat

Canadian/British counter-attacks, 23 Apr

24 Apr – 24 May

German attacks, 24–30 Apr (Battle of St Julian)

German gains by 30 Apr

British withdrawal, 1–4 May

French/British line after withdrawal, 1–4 May

Final German gains 24 May (Battle of Bellewaarde Ridge)

Major chlorine gas attacks

Houthulst

Merckem

XXIII RESERVE CORPS

45 R

6

Bixschoete

46 Res

Steenstraat

Lizerne

22 Apr: *gas attack at 1700hrs*

52 Res

XXVI RESERVE CORPS

FOURTH ARMY (Albrecht)

51 Res

Poelcappelle

27 Apr: *French recapture Lizerne*

Het Sas

87 Territorial

Langemarck

Pilckem

45

R. Steenbeek

24 Apr: *gas attack at 0400hrs*

Boezinghe

Pilckem Ridge

Kitchener's Wood

St Julien

1 Canadian

R. Haanebeek

Gravenstafel

Passchendaele

XXVII RESERVE CORPS

GROUPEMENT D'ENVERDINGHE (Putz)

Elverdinghe

'Mouse Trap' Farm

24 May: *gas attack at 0300hrs*

53 Res

Broodseinde

23 Apr: *Canadian/ British counter-attacks seek to delay German advance; line restored by dusk*

Brielen

Wieltje

Frezenberg

26 Apr – 1 May: *exposed Allied troops bombarded from 3 sides; retreat to new line ordered 1–4 May*

Zonnebeke

54 Res

St Jean

Verlorenhoek

25–26 Apr: *Lahore Div concentrates near Ypres and counter-attacks between Pilckem and St Jean; repulsed with heavy losses*

Potijze

V CORPS

28

Westhoek

Polygon Wood

Vlamertinghe

Ypres

Bellewaarde Ridge

Bellewaarde Lake

Becelaere

SECOND ARMY (Smith-Dorrien)

Zillebeke Lake

Hooge

27

39

Gheluvelt

Zillebeke

Dickebusch

Dickebusch Lake

G.H.Q. Line

Verbrandenmolen

5

30

XV CORPS

II CORPS

Voormezeele

3

St Eloi

II BAVARIAN CORPS

Kruiseecke

50
30
10
0 m

0   5 km
0   2.5 miles

Aubers Ridge and Festubert March – December 1915

Despite the failure of the 10 March attack at Neuve Chapelle (page 62) and the continuing action around Ypres (page 66), Haig was sufficiently confident by May 1915 to propose a renewed British offensive against Aubers Ridge. The new offensive was envisaged as a counterpart to a renewed French attack in Artois, where Joffre was determined to make amends for the costly failure of an attempt to seize Vimy Ridge during the winter. Strategically, the Allied aim was to force the withdrawal of German troops from the Russian front, where the German offensive in Masuria (page 58) had made Central Powers intentions obvious and where a further offensive was clearly in preparation.

The area chosen for the British attack was not promising. The ground in front of the ridge was flat, exposing advancing infantry to uninterrupted fire. The area had a high watertable, which made digging a trench more than two feet deep impossible (the Germans had created breastworks along their line, well supplied with fire points and supported by extensive communication trenches in the drier rear areas). Moreover, German machine guns in this sector were for the most part protected by bunkers which could only be destroyed by a direct hit. British guns were few in number, and the shortage of shells was reaching crisis point.

The BEF offensive was nevertheless scheduled for 9 May. The attack was preceded by a necessarily short but heavy artillery bombardment of some 30 minutes. At 0530hrs the British infantry moved forward.

The bombardment had neither neutralized the German front-line defenses nor blown adequate gaps in the wire. The German defenders, units of the German Sixth Army rested and reorganized after the Battle of Neuve Chapelle, staggered the advancing British troops with enfilade fire, and gains were minimal for enormous cost. Haig repeated the attack later in the day, but the renewed effort proved equally sanguinary. Early the following day (10 May), having lost 458 officers and 11,161 other ranks to little purpose, he cancelled the operation.

Artois and Festubert

The French attack on Vimy Ridge, known as the Second Battle of Artois, opened one week later,

and made initial gains of some three miles along the Lorette Spur and toward Souchez. Casualties were enormously high, however, and the German defensive line was never seriously threatened. Repeated French efforts up to 20 June had no other effect than to underline in blood the town of Souchez in French mental topography.

Haig mounted a further supporting attack on 15 May, aimed at the town of Festubert. As a result of British experiences at Aubers Ridge and in recognition of German defensive capacity, a more prolonged and accurate preliminary bombardment was employed, straining still further British shell resources. Again, the bombardment was only partially successful in cutting the German wire, and many shell fuzes failed.

The infantry assault, by 2nd Division and the Indian Corps' Meerut Division, was launched under cover of darkness, and resulted in utter confusion. Few attackers reached the German line, and those few penetrations that were made were quickly sealed off by the defenders. A subsequent attack to the south by 7th Division (Gough) was equally unsuccessful. Further attacks followed in the rain and mist, but German resistance and lack of visibility shortly brought activity to an end. The operation cost the Germans 5000 men and some 800 prisoners, the British 710 officers and almost 16,000 other ranks. Territorial gain was minimal. As at Neuve Chapelle, however, a disastrously false conclusion was drawn by British planners: given only a few more men and a few more guns, the breakthrough could have been won.

A German artillery post near Festubert. The Germans benefitted from a far better designed and constructed system of trenches than the British and they proved capable of withstanding even concentrated artillery fire.

"The distance to the front German trench was about 200 yards. For the first eighty the air was thick with smoke from smoke bombs, but as we emerged into view of the Hun, they let drive at us. I found my men dropping all around me, and when I reached the German wire I was practically alone."

Capt. W.G. Bagot Chester, 3rd Queens Alexandra's Own Gurka Rifles

The results of the attack. A field full of dead soldiers awaiting burial. The advancing British troops were mown down in their thousands as they advanced on the German defenses.

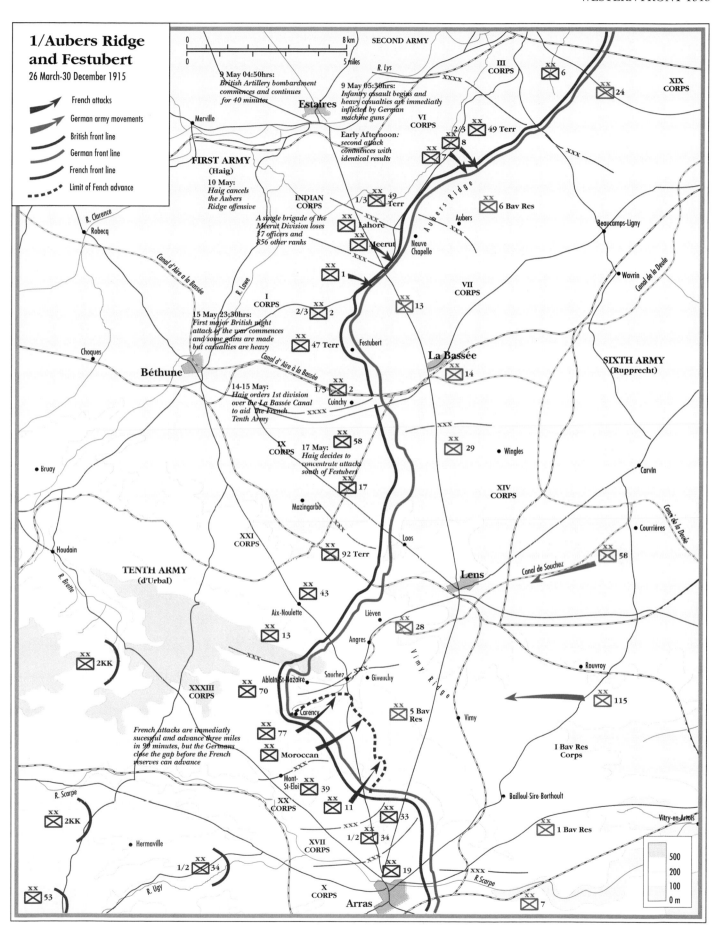

1/Aubers Ridge and Festubert

26 March-30 December 1915

French attacks
German army movements
British front line
German front line
French front line
Limit of French advance

SECOND ARMY

III CORPS

XIX CORPS

9 May 04:50hrs:
British Artillery bombardment
commences and continues
for 40 minutes

Estaires

Merville

9 May 05:30hrs:
Infantry assault begins and
heavy casualties are immediatly
inflicted by German
machine guns

VI CORPS

49 Terr

Early Afternoon:
second attack
commences with
identical results

FIRST ARMY
(Haig)

10 May:
Haig cancels
the Aubers
Ridge offensive

R. Clarence

Robecq

INDIAN CORPS

1/3 49 Terr

6 Bav Res

Aubers

Beaucamps-Ligny

A single brigade of the
Meerut Division loses
37 officers and
856 other ranks

Lahore

Meerut

Neuve Chapelle

VII CORPS

Wavrin

R. Lawe

I CORPS

1

2/3 2

13

15 May 23:30hrs:
First major British night
attack of the war commences
and some gains are made
but casualties are heavy

Choques

47 Terr

Festubert

La Bassée

SIXTH ARMY
(Rupprecht)

Béthune

Canal d' Aire a la Bassée

14-15 May:
Haig orders 1st division
over the La Bassée Canal
to aid the French
Tenth Army

1/3 2

Cuinchy

14

Bruay

IX CORPS

58

17 May:
Haig decides to
concentrate attacks
south of Festubert

17

29

Wingles

Carvin

XIV CORPS

Mazingarbe

XXI CORPS

92 Terr

Loos

Houdain

Lens

Courrières

43

Canal de Souchez

58

TENTH ARMY
(d'Urbal)

Aix-Noulette

Liéven

13

28

Angres

Rouvroy

2KK

Souchez

Givenchy

Vimy Ridge

115

XXXIII CORPS

70

Ablain-St-Nazaire

French attacks are immediatly
successful and advance three miles
in 90 minutes, but the Germans
close the gap before the French
reserves can advance

Carency

77

5 Bav Res

Vimy

I Bav Res Corps

Moroccan

Mont-St-Eloi

39

Bailleul-Sire-Berthoult

2KK

XX CORPS

11

33

Vitry-en-Artois

1 Bav Res

R. Scarpe

Hermaville

1/2 34

XVII CORPS

1/2 34

R. Ugy

19

R. Scarpe

53

X CORPS

Arras

7

500
200
100
0 m

Gorlice–Tarnow May 1915

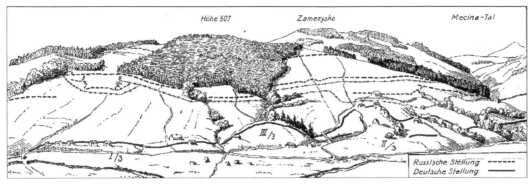

Höhe 507   Zamezysko   Mecina-Tal

Russische Stellung ——
Deutsche Stellung - - - -

A sketch of the Russian positions opposite the 11th Bavarian Infantry Division on 2 May, just southeast of Gorlice. The approximate location of the hill marked as "Zamezysko" (actually "Zamczysko") is marked on Map 1.

In February, Hindenburg's Masurian Lakes offensive (page 58) had resulted in tactical success in the north, but the comprehensive Russian defeat of the simultaneous offensive by Boroevic's Third Army and Linsingen's Südarmee towards the besieged Austrian fortress of Przemysl had weakened Austria's strategic position further. The fall of the fortress on 22 March and the loss of its garrison of 100,000 men left Falkenhayn with no option but direct and extensive intervention on the Austrian front, and German fears of an Italian declaration of war made a decisive (and deterrent) victory even more urgent. The transfer of troops from the West had begun at the end of 1914, and a major blow against Russia was the most important German objective for Spring 1915.

Mackensen's newly-formed Eleventh Army and the Austrian Fourth were given the task of breaking through the Russian Third Army between Gorlice and Tarnow, in Galicia. The initial aim of the operation was to roll back the Russian advance in the Carpathians to the east of the Lupkow Pass. Against Radko-Dmitriev's 14 infantry and 5 cavalry divisions, Mackensen and the Archduke Josef could muster 23 divisions and an overwhelming superiority in artillery. Mackensen's army took up its designated position at the end of April.

The breakthrough

During the night of 1/2 May, the advance German and Austrian troops moved across the extended no-man's land and dug in near the Russian front line. The next day, following four hours of heavy artillery fire, the attack was launched at 1000hrs. The Russian defenses, in many places virtually without artillery support at all due to the crippling shortage of ammunition, were overwhelmed, and Radko was reduced to bringing up reserves piecemeal to try to halt the enemy advance. Despite often heroic resistance, the entire Russian line along the Carpathians was rolled up. On 10 May, Radko reported that his army had "bled to death". By 14 May, the Austro-German advance had reached the River San, some 80 miles from its start line.

Przemysl was re-taken on 3 June, after heavy fighting, but the need to address Austrian problems in other theaters now intruded (Italy had declared war on 25 May). Parts of the Austrian Third Army were transferred to the Italian front, and Second, Fourth and a reinforced German Eleventh Army were regrouped into Army Group Mackensen, for an offensive against Lemberg (captured on 22 June). On 17 June, the Russian high command sanctioned a general fighting retreat.

The Central Powers achieved further spectacular results between June and September (see Strategic View). The new German Twelfth Army (Gallwitz) advanced into northern Poland toward Warsaw, which the Russians abandoned from 4 August; Brest Litovsk fell on 25 August, Grodno on 2 September and Vilna was occupied on 19 September. The battered Russians were able to halt the German advance, which by Fall had extended to some 300 miles, only with the aid of the worsening weather. But, by the end of 1915, the Eastern Front formed a line running from east of Riga on the Baltic to beyond the Dnieper in the south.

The Russian commanders had performed wonders in keeping their armies from disintegrating altogether, but the cost had been enormous – over one million casualties, making a total of nearly two million for the year as a whole. The strategic balance in the East had been transformed.

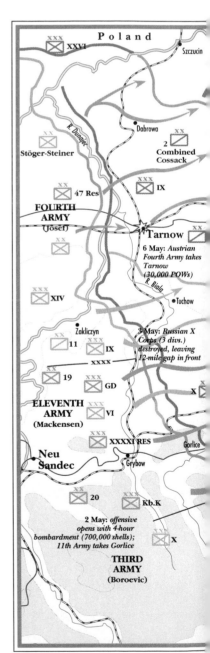

Poland

XXVI   Szczucin

R. Dunajec

Stöger-Steiner   Dabrowa   2 Combined Cossack

47 Res   IX

FOURTH ARMY (Jósef)   Tarnow

6 May: Austrian Fourth Army takes Tarnow (30,000 POWs)

R. Biala

XIV   Tuchow

Zakliczyn   *3 May: Russian X Corps (3 divs.) destroyed, leaving 12-mile gap in front*

11   IX

XXXX

19   GD   X

ELEVENTH ARMY (Mackensen)   VI

XXXXI RES   Gorlice

Neu Sandec   Grybow

20   Kb.K

2 May: offensive opens with 4-hour bombardment (700,000 shells); 11th Army takes Gorlice   X

THIRD ARMY (Boroevic)

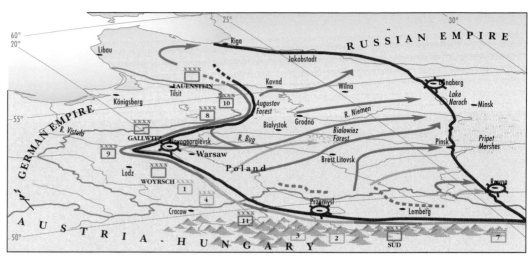

Strategic View: Falkenhayn
The success of Mackensen's Galicia offensive was such that Falkenhayn was able to contemplate the crippling of Russian offensive power altogether. By 13 July Mackensen's forces had advanced beyond the Galician border (dashed line); Lauenstein in the northeast and Gallwitz, Ninth and Eighth armies in Poland then joined the offensive. By the end of September the Russians had been forced back on Riga, Dunaberg and Pinsk in the greatest victory of the war so far.

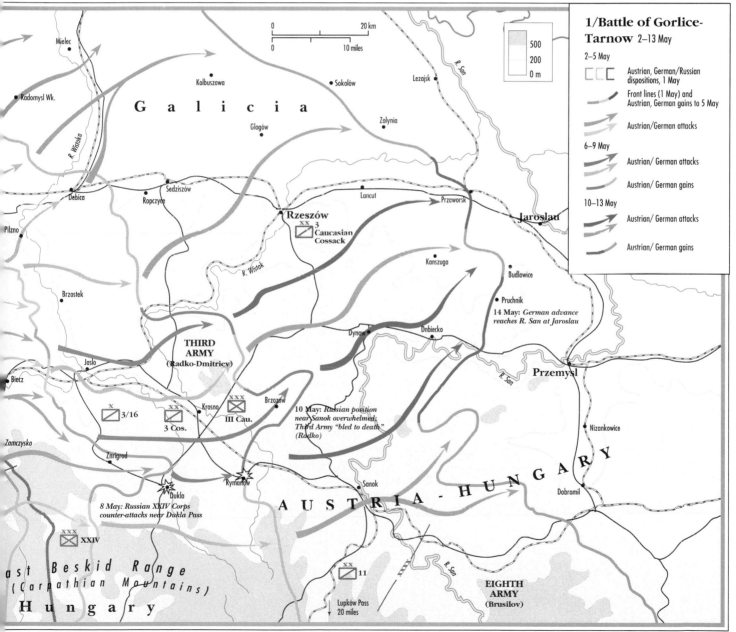

1/Battle of Gorlice-Tarnow 2–13 May

2–5 May
Austrian, German/Russian dispositions, 1 May
Front lines (1 May) and Austrian, German gains to 5 May
Austrian/German attacks

6–9 May
Austrian/ German attacks
Austrian/ German gains

10–13 May
Austrian/ German attacks
Austrian/ German gains

14 May: German advance reaches R. San at Jaroslau

10 May: Russian position near Sanok overwhelmed; Third Army "bled to death" (Radko)

8 May: Russian XXIV Corps counter-attacks near Dukla Pass

THIRD ARMY (Radko-Dmitriev)

EIGHTH ARMY (Brusilov)

Suez and Kut November 1914 – April 1916

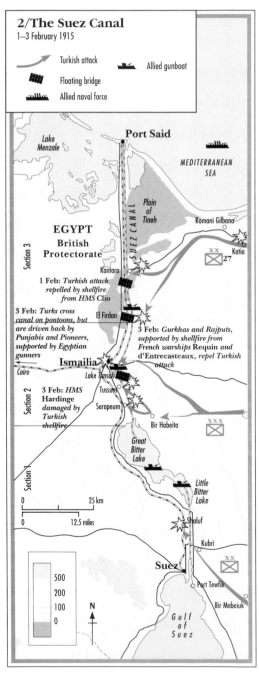

2/The Suez Canal
1–3 February 1915

→ Turkish attack
🚢 Allied gunboat
▮▮▮ Floating bridge
⚓ Allied naval force

Lake Menzale

Port Said

MEDITERRANEAN SEA

Plain of Tineh

Romani Gilbana

EGYPT
British Protectorate

SUEZ CANAL

Katia
XX 27

Kantara

Section 3

1 Feb: *Turkish attack repelled by shellfire from HMS Clio*

3 Feb: *Turks cross canal on pontoons, but are driven back by Punjabis and Pioneers, supported by Egyptian gunners*

El Firdan

3 Feb: *Gurkhas and Rajputs, supported by shellfire from French warships Requin and d'Entrecasteaux, repel Turkish attack*

Ismailia

Cairo

Lake Timsah

Tussum

Section 2

3 Feb: *HMS Hardinge damaged by Turkish shellfire*

Serapeum

Bir Habeita

XXX

Great Bitter Lake

Section 1

Little Bitter Lake

0   25 km
0   12.5 miles

Shaluf

Kubri

Suez
XX

500
200
100
0

N

Port Tewfik

Bir Mabeiuk

Gulf of Suez

An invasion of Egypt was one of the initial Turko-German aims in the Middle East. Djemal Kuçuk's VIII Corps left Beersheba in mid-January with a strength of about 20,000 men, crossing the Sinai Desert inland so as to avoid Allied naval domination of the coast road. Any hope of surprise was lost when British air patrols spotted the three Turkish columns, all Turkish attacks were broken up by shellfire and resolute defense by the Allied units along the Suez Canal (Map 2). Total Turkish casualties were nearly 2000, against 32 Allied dead and wounded.

Mesopotamia

The Allied expedition to Mesopotamia was mounted to protect the British-controlled Persian oil wells at Ahwaz. The area around Basra was quickly cleared and Ahwaz secured in April by a column under Major-General Sir George Gorringe.

On 11 May, Sir John Nixon ordered a reconnaissance in force up the Tigris by a reinforced division and a small naval flotilla under Major General Charles Townshend. Meanwhile, another column (Gorringe) advanced up the Euphrates to An Nasiriya.

Continuing his advance up the Tigris as the Turks withdrew before him, Townshend seized Al Amarah in June and Kut in September, but was halted by Turkish reinforcements at Ctesiphon. He had little option but to undertake a gruelling retreat to Kut to await support in the sweltering Mesopotamian summer.

Kut was soon invested by the Turks. Three relief forces tried successively to get through to Townshend; all failed, with a total loss of more than 10,000 men. Once casualties among the relief forces, which had attacked in vain against the Turkish lines covering the approaches to the city on either side of the Tigris, had risen to virtually twice the strength of the garrison, Kitchener concluded that further effort would be a fruitless waste of life and resources. Townshend, with his remaining troops starving and diseased, surrendered Kut on 29 April. The city was not to be retaken by the British until February 1917.

Consequences

A promising campaign, partly designed to enhance prestige in the area after the Gallipoli fiasco, had ended in disaster and lowered the Allies' standing throughout the Middle East.

Far left: This German propaganda postcard showing Turkish troops on the banks of the Suez Canal actually appeared at the end of 1914, several weeks before the unsuccessful Turkish assault. The inset portrait is of Enver Pasha, the Turkish Commander-in-Chief.

> *"I intend to defend Kut al Amara and not to retire any further. Reinforcements are being sent at once to relieve us... The way you have managed to retire under the very noses of the Turks is nothing short of splendid."*
>
> **Maj. Gen. C.V.F. Townshend, in a communiqué to his troops after the retreat to Kut.**

After the surrender of Kut, a British soldier from the garrison arrives back at Tigris Corps HQ in Basra in a pitifully emaciated condition.

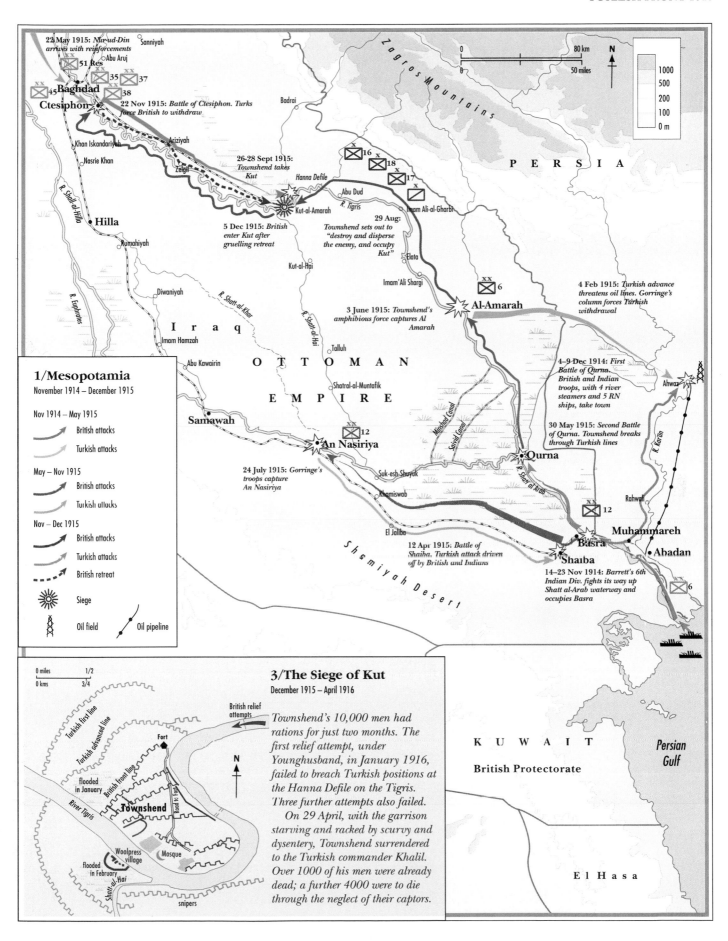

22 May 1915: *Nur-ud-Din arrives with reinforcements*

51 Res

35   37

45 **Baghdad**

38

Ctesiphon   22 Nov 1915: *Battle of Ctesiphon. Turks force British to withdraw*

Sanniyah

Abu Aruj

Badrai

Z a g r o s   M o u n t a i n s

P E R S I A

0 ___ 80 km
0 ___ 50 miles

N

	1000
	500
	200
	100
	0 m

Khan Iskandariyah

Nasrie Khan

Ariziyah

Zeigli

R. Shatt-al-Hilla

Hilla

Kumahiyah

R. Euphrates

26-28 Sept 1915: *Townshend takes Kut*

16

18

17

Hanna Defile

Abu Dud

R. Tigris

Kut-al-Amarah

Imam Ali-al-Gharbi

5 Dec 1915: *British enter Kut after gruelling retreat*

29 Aug: *Townshend sets out to "destroy and disperse the enemy, and occupy Kut"*

Kut-al-Hai

Imam'Ali Shargi

Elata

3 June 1915: *Townshend's amphibious force captures Al Amarah*

6

Al-Amarah

4 Feb 1915: *Turkish advance threatens oil lines. Gorringe's column forces Turkish withdrawal*

Diwaniyah

R. Shatt-al-Khar

R. Shatt-al-Hai

I r a q

Imam Hamzah

Talluh

O T T O M A N

E M P I R E

Ahwaz

R. Karun

4-9 Dec 1914: *First Battle of Qurna. British and Indian troops, with 4 river steamers and 5 RN ships, take town*

30 May 1915: *Second Battle of Qurna. Townshend breaks through Turkish lines*

Shatral-al-Muntafik

Samawah

12

An Nasiriya

24 July 1915: *Gorringe's troops capture An Nasiriya*

Minshad Canal

Saiyid Canal

R. Shatt al Arab

Qurna

12

Rahwali

Muhammareh

Suk-esh-Shuyuk

Khamiswab

El Jaliba

S h a m i y a h   D e s e r t

12 Apr 1915: *Battle of Shaiha. Turkish attack driven off by British and Indians*

Basra

Shaiba

14-23 Nov 1914: *Barrett's 6th Indian Div. fights its way up Shatt al-Arab waterway and occupies Basra*

6

Abadan

1/Mesopotamia

November 1914 – December 1915

Nov 1914 – May 1915

→ British attacks

→ Turkish attacks

May – Nov 1915

→ British attacks

→ Turkish attacks

Nov – Dec 1915

→ British attacks

→ Turkish attacks

--→ British retreat

✳ Siege

⚡ Oil field   ●—● Oil pipeline

K U W A I T

British Protectorate

Persian Gulf

E l   H a s a

3/The Siege of Kut

December 1915 – April 1916

0 miles ___ 1/2
0 kms ___ 3/4

Turkish first line

Turkish advanced line

Fort

British relief attempts

flooded in January

British front line

River Tigris

Townshend

Road to Fort

N

Woolpress village

Mosque

flooded in February

Shatt-al-Hai

snipers

Townshend's 10,000 men had rations for just two months. The first relief attempt, under Younghusband, in January 1916, failed to breach Turkish positions at the Hanna Defile on the Tigris. Three further attempts also failed.

On 29 April, with the garrison starving and racked by scurvy and dysentery, Townshend surrendered to the Turkish commander Khalil. Over 1000 of his men were already dead; a further 4000 were to die through the neglect of their captors.

Isonzo Battles 1915-1917

Despite obligations to Germany and Austria under the Triple Alliance, the Italian government resisted all Central Powers pressure to become involved in the war in 1914, and instead opened negotiations with both sides. Allied offers of territorial gains at Austria's expense after the war represented an inducement to Italy which the Central Powers were unable to match. From the end of 1914 German aims had been merely to conceal as far as possible the true extent of Austrian weakness from Italian observers, so as to prolong Italian neutrality while a decision was sought on other fronts. The strategic failure of the Masurian offensive in early 1915 and the fall of Przemysl (with its garrison of 100,000 Austrian troops) in March made even such limited Central Powers aims increasingly unsustainable.

In May 1915, just as the decisive Central Powers blow against Russia was taking shape, Italy entered the war on the Allied side, although at first declaring war on Austria alone.

The Italian Army, commanded by Luigi Cadorna, numbered some 875,000 men but it was short of ammunition reserves and lacked adequate artillery and transport. Moreover, all recent staff campaign studies had been solely defensive; no plans had been made for offensive action against Austria-Hungary.

Italian plans

The Italian frontier ran along the line of the Alps; Cadorna's strategic aim was to defend in the Trentino, where Austrian territory extended into Italy, while launching an attack over the River Isonzo, where Italian territory protruded into Austria. The latter sector, bordering on the Adriatic, was an area of relatively low ground, and had the political advantage of bordering on the main areas of Italian territorial ambition around Trieste; any advance eastward, however, necessarily risked an Austrian attack from the Trentino upon its rear.

Nevertheless, the northeastern front offered the prospect of success. The Italians could field two armies, the Second and Third, Austria only her Fifth Army, giving the Italians a considerable numerical superiority.

Italian attacks

The main Italian advance began at the end of May, but only seven of the 24 divisions were fully ready, and the offensive was badly disrupted by unexpected flooding on the Isonzo. Initial advances came rapidly to a halt. On the the other Austrian fronts, moreover, the Russians were reeling under Mackensen's blows (page 70) while Serbia was unable to make a demonstration; the Austrian high command was able to transfer five divisions from Serbia to the Isonzo, together with three divisions from the Galician front.

The Isonzo front was soon perilously close, as elsewhere, to a trench-bound stalemate. But shortly Italian mobilisation was complete and, on 23 June, Cadorna mounted a greater attack. This, the First Battle of the Isonzo, continued until 7 July, some 200,000 Italians and 200 guns battering against strong Austrian defenses.

On 18 July Cadorna, with more artillery, tried again the Second Isonzo, but the Austrians held and the Italians broke off the engagement when their artillery ammunition was exhausted by 3 August. In these two battles, the Italians lost some 60,000 men, the Austrians nearly 45,000. Little gain was made by either side.

Cadorna quickly made preparations for a bolder offensive in the Fall, by which time his forces held a 2:1 advantage in numbers and he had amassed some 1200 guns. Third Isonzo began on 18 October and lasted until 4 November; once more, the Austrian line held. A continuation of the third battle (Fourth Isonzo, 10 November – 2 December) likewise made insignificant gains.

Losses and consequences

This brought the Isonzo battles of 1915 to an end, actions which in six months had cost the Italians some 177,000 men, the Austrians 117,000. Italian civilian morale, high at the declaration of war, quickly plummeted with the evident inability of the army to make headway even against an Austria heavily committed on other fronts. The Isonzo battles would drag on.

Italian Bersaglieri cyclists advance toward the front. Still unrecovered from the North African war against Turkey in 1912, the Italian Army could muster no more than 300,000 effective troops in May 1915. full mobilization increased the number to 875,000.

An Austrian shell bursts in an Italian fire-trench, on the Isonzo front in late 1915.

Field Marshal Luigi Cadorna
was appointed chief-of-staff of the
Italian Army less than 12 months
before Italy's entry into the war.
Cadorna's primary function was
to modernize the army by
reorganizing its mobilisation
program, improving its
equipment and strenghthening
border defenses. The time allowed
him for the completion of these
tasks, however, proved to be
woefully inadequate and the
declaration of war found the
Italian Army in a condition of
unpreparedness. Cadorna would
command the Italian armies
throughout the Isonzo campaigns
but was finally replaced after the
crushing defeat of the Italian
Army at Caporetto, the twelfth
Battle of Isonzo (page 132).

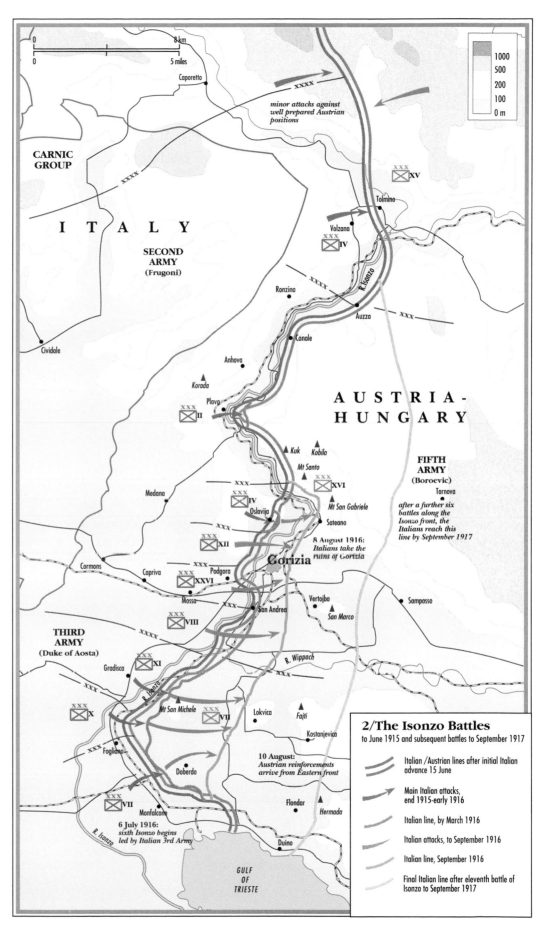

Artois and Champagne September – October 1915

Despite Allied reverses on the Western Front in May and June 1915, Joffre resolved to mount further attacks in the Fall. The Russian disaster at Gorlice–Tarnow (page 70) urged aggressive action in the west to relieve pressure on the ailing ally, and Joffre calculated that French strength (and, shortly, that of Britain too, with the "New Armies") was greater than at any point since the beginning of the war, for new forces, including colonial divisions, had at last replaced the losses of 1914. Conversely, German forces in the west had been pruned ruthlessly for the Russian operations.

Plans

Joffre planned a combined assault in Artois by the French Tenth Army (d'Urbal) and the British First Army (Haig), to pinch out the German salient around Vimy Ridge (Map 1). A convergent blow was to be delivered in the Champagne (Map 2) by the French Fourth and Second armies, aimed at cutting the railway from Sedan to Lille via Mezières and Douai upon which depended the German ability to reinforce any threatened point in their line.

Haig was against the offensive. He could muster only nine divisions, against the 36 he considered necessary. Moreover, despite the establishment in Britain of a Ministry of Munitions under Lloyd George, the supply of heavy artillery and shells was unlikely to reach adequate levels until 1916 (British factories were

producing only 22,000 shells a day, against some 100,000 in France and 250,000 in Germany and Austria). When Joffre and Foch remained adamant, Haig insisted at least on the use of gas to compensate for the shortage of artillery.

In the Champagne, Langle and Pétain were well supplied with artillery, and their hardened troops faced the weak formations of the German Liebert and Dittfürth divisions. On both fronts, however, German completion of a second line of defenses since the fighting in the Spring had

Champagne, 1915: French troops in a captured German trench.

2/Second Battle of the Champagne

25–30 September

25 Sept

⟶ French lines and maximum advance

⟶ German lines

➤ French attacks

26–30 Sept

➤ French attacks

➤ German counter-attacks

⟶ French gains by 30 Sept

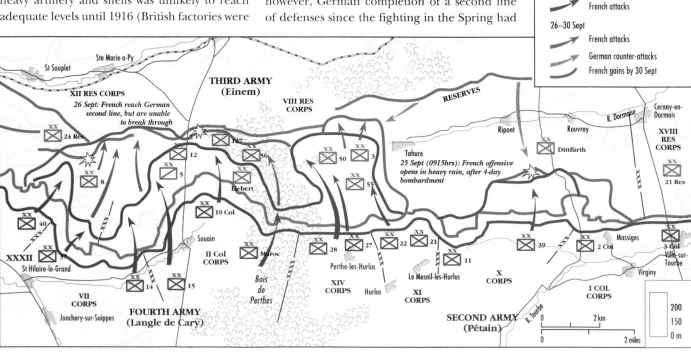

done much to compensate their shortage of manpower.

The battles

Allied attacks on both fronts began on 25 September. At Loos, the gas cloud drifted back over British trenches in the prevailing wind, poisoning many troops in the first wave. Inadequate bombardment left important parts of the German defenses intact, and Haig's tactical reserves were wasted trying to clear these. Furthermore, French held back the Army reserve (XI Corps) awaiting a breakthrough which never came; 21 and 24 Divisions were finally committed on the second day, and cut to pieces attacking the reinforced German second line. Britain's "New Armies" had suffered a disastrous baptism of fire.

Around Vimy Ridge, French gains were even smaller. Souchez and the area known as The Labyrinth were taken, but all attempts to advance further on to the Ridge itself were thrown back. In the Champagne, impressive gains on the first day to the west of Tahure still failed to clear the German second line (the redoubtable 10 Colonial Division was bombarded by misdirected French artillery in the German position), and repeated attacks up to October 6 brought no further advance as the German positions were reinforced.

Consequences

Attacks in Artois and Champagne cost the French some 191,797 officers and men; British losses at Loos were 60,000, German 65,000.

British recriminations over the mishandling of reserves led to French's removal and Haig's appointment as commander-in-chief in December. Foch's official comment on the French attacks – "We must abandon the brutal assault in masses more or less deep and dense... it has never reached its goal" – reflected the urgent need for a reappraisal of tactics in the face of manifest German superiority in all aspects of trench warfare.

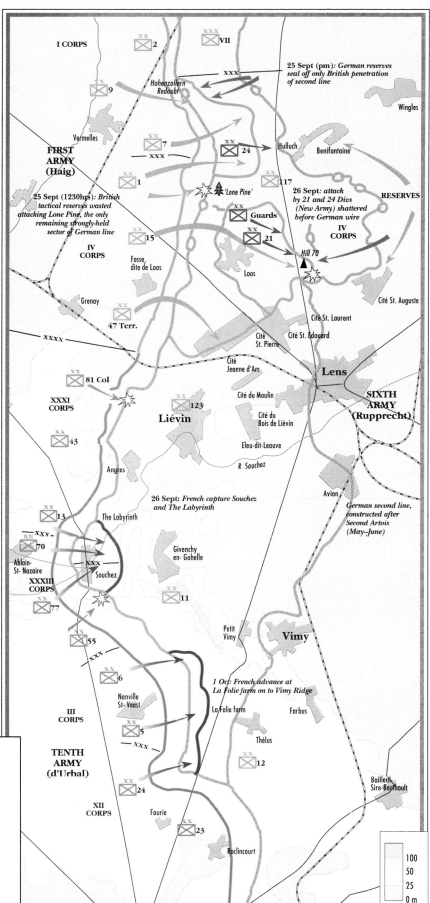

25 Sept (pm): German reserves seal off only British penetration of second line

25 Sept (1230hrs): British tactical reserves wasted attacking Lone Pine, the only remaining strongly-held sector of German line

26 Sept: attack by 21 and 24 Divs (New Army) shattered before German wire

26 Sept: French capture Souchez and The Labyrinth

German second line, constructed after Second Artois (May–June)

1 Oct: French advance at La Folie farm on to Vimy Ridge

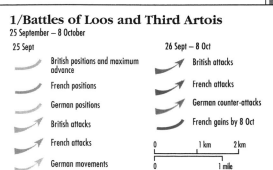

1/Battles of Loos and Third Artois

25 September – 8 October

25 Sept		26 Sept – 8 Oct	
	British positions and maximum advance		British attacks
	French positions		French attacks
	German positions		German counter-attacks
	British attacks		French gains by 8 Oct
	French attacks		
	German movements		

0   1 km   2 km

0   1 mile

Suvla Bay August – December 1915

In July 1915 the British Government sent a further three British divisions to the Gallipoli peninsula. Faced with the apparent impossibility of further advance against the well-prepared Turkish defenses on the Helles front, Hamilton resolved on a new plan: an attack on the Sari Bair range which dominated the Anzac position, accompanied by a landing of the new IX Corps at Suvla Bay, to its north. The plan was hampered from the outset by lack of communication between the two forces and lack of energetic leadership from the commander of the landing force, General Sir Frederick Stopford.

The battles

The main assault on Sari Bair was timed for the night of 6–7 August, preceded by a feint attack at Lone Pine. The feint swiftly escalated into some of the most savage hand-to-hand fighting in the entire war, while the troops from Anzac lost their bearings around Beauchop's Hill. The final push toward Chunuk Bair was launched three hours late. Turkish reinforcements made repeated counter-attacks in the following days, and Kemal personally directed the final attack toward the Farm on 10 August which forced the Allies to withdraw.

The Suvla landings, also on the night of 6–7 August, were safely made but not exploited. The troops, lacking both maps and orders, made no attempt to advance toward the lightly-held Anafarta Ridge, and remained all day on the waterless Suvla Plain while Turkish reinforcements were rushed from Bulair. Hamilton himself arrived on the 8th and instantly took matters in hand, but the IX Corps advance was

caught in the open by the arriving Turkish forces and driven back to its starting lines. The result, as at Anzac Cove, was deadlock.

Consequences

Allied losses at Anzac and Suvla approached 30,000; Turkish losses were fewer than half that total.

Hamilton was recalled on 15 October. His replacement, General Sir Charles Monro, advised immediate evacuation of the entire Gallipoli peninsula. Churchill subsequently commented scathingly, "He came, he saw, he capitulated."

The withdrawal proved the one successful operation of the campaign. The Anzac commander, General Sir William Birdwood, in

Troops of the Royal Navy Division launch an attack near Achi Baba (Cape Helles front) intended to prevent the transfer of Turkish troops to Suvla Bay.

Strategic View: Sanders and Kemal

For the Turkish commanders, the problem was that a new Allied offensive was expected, but Royal Navy control of the seas meant that a landing could be made at any point. The instant transfer of reserves to the threatened position was therefore essential: this Kemal managed with great skill, and the courage of his men doomed the Anzac–Suvla operation.

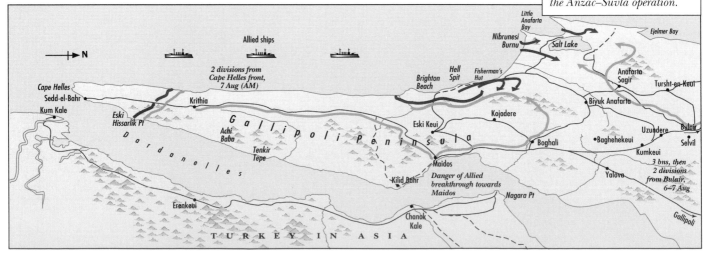

command of the whole operation, planned and executed a highly skilled evacuation of the Anzac and Suvla positions on the nights of 18-19 and 19-20 December, and Cape Helles on 8-9 January 1916. Numerous subterfuges were devised to maintain the illusion of continued occupation, and every surviving Allied soldier was evacuated safely.

The campaign had been a disaster for the Allies. The attempted knockout blow against Turkey had failed, though Turkish reserves had been tested to the limit; no supply route was opened to Russia. Furthermore, the consequences of Allied failure were not lost on Bulgaria, which joined the Central Powers one month after the Suvla landings, with catastrophic consequences for Serbia (page 80).

West Beach
Little West Beach
Kangaroo Beach

Suvla Burnu

Karakol Dagh

7 Aug: IX Corps patrols probe Karakol Dagh ridge (virtually undefended), but make no advance

R. Azmak

Suvla or Little Anafarta Bay

A Beach

Suvla Plain

6-7 Aug: 34 Brigade (11 Division) lands south of its intended beaching point

XX 10

Nibrunesi Burnu   South Pier   Lala Baba

IX CORPS

6-7 Aug: total Turkish strength at Suvla is 1,500 men before reinforcements are brought forward

Salt Lake (dry in summer)

7 Aug: shell fire from a British destroyer proves the impossibility of an infantry advance across the dry lake bed

Anafarta Ridge

Anafarta Sagir

C Beach

B Beach

XX 11

Chocolate Hill

Scimitar Hill

Green Hill

Hill 100

8 Aug: IX Corps attempts to take Chocolate Hill repulsed

W Hills

Tekke

Biyuk Anafarta

Demakjelik Bair

Agghyl Dere

Beauchop's hill

Between 10-20 Dec. 1915 83,048 troops were evacuated from Suvla and Anzac, with no casualties

6 Aug (2300hrs): main attack leaves Anzac positions

Chailuk Dere

Table Top

Abdel Rahman Bair

8 Aug: summit of Chunuk Bair briefly held by NZ/British forces; constant artillery fire and counter-attacks cause up to 90 percent casualties (position evacuated night 9-10 Aug)

Koja Chemen Tepe

The Farm

Hill Q

Chunuk Bair

Fisherman's Hut

7 Aug (0700hrs): Anzac attacks at Pope's Post and The Nek repulsed owing to lack of expected flank support from Sari Rair

XX A/NZ

XX 13

Rhododendron Spur

Sari Bair

XX 7

8 Pier
Pier William's
Milo Pier

Ari Burnu

Watson Pier

ANZAC

Nek

XX 2 Aus

Pope's

Battleship Hill

XX 9

XX 4

Anzac Cove (Z Beach)

Monash gully

Quinn's

Hell Spit   Drighton Pier   XX 1 Aus

3-5 Aug (nights): Allied reinforcements totaling 20,000 men arrive at Anzac

6 Aug (0530hrs): feint attack by 2 and 4 Bns, 1 Australian Div – savage hand-to-hand fighting

Lone Pine

Brighton Beach

XX 19

Kojadere

N

5 Aug: strong Turkish attack on Lean's trench repulsed

1/Suvla Bay and Anzac Cove
6 August – 30 December 1915

Allied lines, 6 Aug

Turkish lines, 6 Aug

Allied main attack objective by 0700hrs, 7 Aug

Allied movements and attacks, 6-7 Aug

Turkish movements and attacks, 6-7 Aug

Allied attacks, 8-10 Aug

Turkish attacks, 8-10 Aug

Embarkation points, Dec 1915

Serbia October – November 1915

Serbia's comprehensive defeat of two Austrian invasions in 1914 (page 36) had caused losses which were virtually irreplaceable in the Serbian Army. By the end of 1915 Serbia's military situation had become even more perilous due to a a serious typhoid epidemic which had further weakened both military and civilian populations. With the evident failure of the Allied Gallipoli operation (pages 60 and 78), the major Central Powers successes against Russia between May and September (page 70) and the Austrian success in stalemating the Italian offensives along the Isonzo (page 74), the Central Powers were once more free to focus their attention on Serbia. Even more serious, Germany had succeeded in drawing Bulgaria into an alliance (signed 6 September), and their bitter rivalry since the second Balkan War left the Serbs with no illusions as to Bulgarian aims.

Austrian and German interpretations of the proposed expedition against Serbia differed markedly, however. Austria sought the opportunity to make amends for the failures of 1914. Germany, on the other hand, sought first the restoration of direct communication with Turkey, and second the establishment of a quiescent Balkans without either extensive military commitment or disturbance of Greek neutrality. Austrian hopes of a significant role in the operation were hampered by a sharp reverse inflicted by the Russians at Rovno during September.

The Western Allies had failed to grasp the strategic advantage of reinforcing Serbia, and were unable or unwilling to supply the sorely-needed technical assistance, heavy artillery and munitions which might have helped redress the military imbalance. The only strategic advantage gained by the Serbs was an alliance with Greece guaranteeing Greek assistance in the event of Bulgarian invasion. Greek appeals for Allied support in this eventuality were met by the landing of an Anglo-French force under Maurice Sarrail at Salonika in northern Greece in October, but the role of this force and the possibility of Greek aid to Serbia were both rendered uncertain by the dismissal of the pro-Allied Greek premier, Eleutherios Venizelos, at the same time and the announcement of strict Greek neutrality.

The campaign

Falkenhayn had begun withdrawing Gallwitz's Eleventh Army from the Russian front in August to support the Austrian Third Army opposite Belgrade (Map 1). Mackensen, given overall command of the operation, planned a direct advance up the Morava valley (thus avoiding the supply difficulties which had proved fatal to Austrian offensives from the west), supported by a Bulgarian invasion from the east to cut off Serbian retreat southward. On 6 October the Austrian and German armies attacked. Their progress was checked by fierce Serbian resistance south of Belgrade, but then the First and Second Bulgarian armies attacked westward across the rear of the Serbian armies, brushing aside the weak Serbian units which were all that could be spared to face them. British and French forces made little progress against the Bulgarians. Putnik, the Serbian commander-chief organized a desperate counter-attack southward across the historic Plain of Blackbirds (to the east of Pristina); when this was halted by the Bulgarians, the Serbs were left with no option but retreat across the mountains into Montenegro and Albania to meet up with the Western Allies in their Adriatic ports.

Consequences

The retreat across wintry mountains cost many lives. Serbian losses during the campaign were about 100,000 killed or wounded, 160,000 taken prisoner and 900 guns lost. An Allied evacuation of Salonika seemed prudent, but was discounted largely for political reasons in view of the Dardanelles debacle. Instead, the Salonika force was further increased, not only by the Serbian remnants (evacuated from Albania by sea, and still a tough fighting force), but by fresh British and French formations and troops from Italy and Russia.

This force, ultimately of half a million men, was intended to moderate German influence on Greece and provide a base of operations for possible support of Romania, which was expected shortly to enter the war. In fact, however, the garrison made no significant contribution to the war until late 1918. The Germans, for their part, were content to barricade these troops under Bulgarian guard, while moving their own troops (over Austrian protests) to more promising theaters.

Radomir Putnik, veteran commander in the Balkan Wars, modernized and reorganized the Serbian Army during his three terms as War Minister. He was probably the most gifted of all the supreme commanders at the beginning of the war, and in 1915 he fought a skilled and vigorous series of holding actions against overwhelming opposition, but the expected Allied aid failed to materialize.

The survivors of the Serbian army trek into exile. Their rear defended against Austrian assault by two or three relatively strong divisions, the remaining Serbs, frozen, disillusioned and exhausted, retreated as rapidly as possible. The Serbs felt that they had been betrayed by the Allies and were bitter in their recriminations.

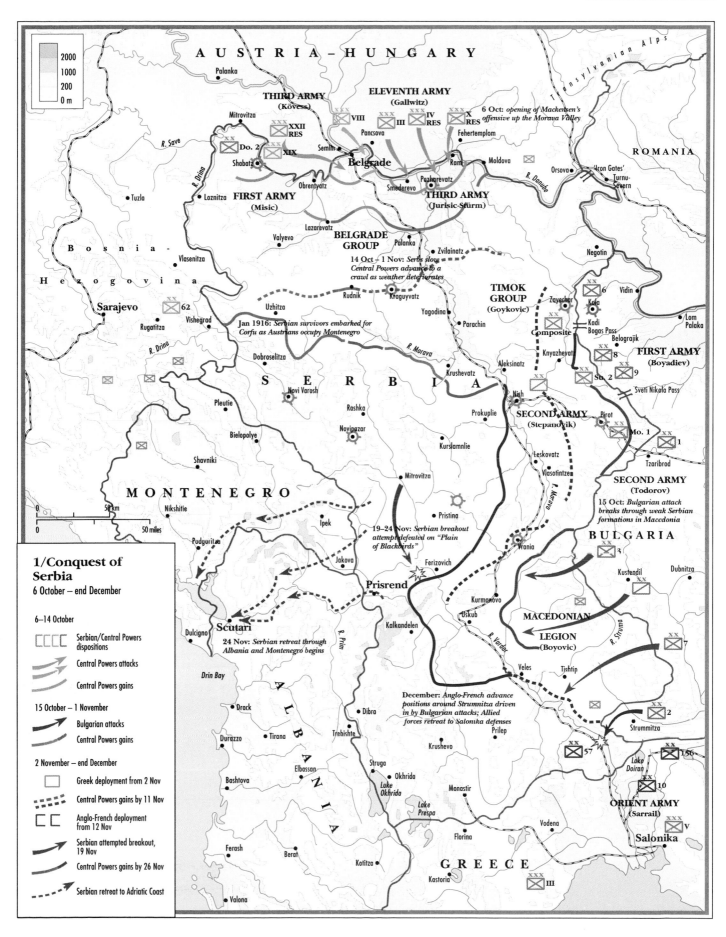

AUSTRIA-HUNGARY

Palanka

THIRD ARMY
(Kövess)

ELEVENTH ARMY
(Gallwitz)

Mitrovitza

VIII

III

IV
RES

X
RES

6 Oct: opening of Mackensen's
offensive up the Morava Valley

XXII
RES

Pancsova

Fehertemplom

Transylvanian Alps

R. Save

XIX

Do. 2

Semlin

ROMANIA

Shabatz

Belgrade

Ram

Moldova

Orsova

'Iron Gates'
Turnu-
Severn

Tuzla

Loznitza

Obrentyatz

Smederevo

Pazharevatz

R. Danube

R. Drina

FIRST ARMY
(Misic)

Valyevo

Lazarevatz

THIRD ARMY
(Jurisic-Stürm)

B o s n i a -

Vlasenitza

**BELGRADE
GROUP**

Palanka

Zvilainatz

Negotin

14 Oct – 1 Nov: Serbs slow
Central Powers advance to a
crawl as weather deteriorates

**TIMOK
GROUP**
(Goykovic)

Zayechar

Kula

Vidin

H e z o g o v i n a

Sarajevo

62

Uzhitza

Rudnik

Kraguyvatz

Yagodina

Parachin

Kadi
Bogas Pass

6

Lom
Palaka

Belgrajik

Rugatitza

Vishegrad

Jan 1916: Serbian survivors embarked for
Corfu as Austrans occupy Montenegro

R. Morava

Knyazhevat

Aleksinatz

Composite

8

FIRST ARMY
(Boyadiev)

R. Drina

Dobroselitza

Krushevatz

Str. 2

9

Sveti Nikola Pass

Pleutie

S E R B I A

Nish

SECOND ARMY
(Stepanovik)

Novi Varosh

Rashka

Prokuplie

Pirot

Mo. 1

1

Bielopolye

Novipazar

Kurslamnlie

Leskovatz

Tzaribrod

Shavniki

Vlasotintzen

R. Morava

SECOND ARMY
(Todorov)

Mitrovitza

15 Oct: Bulgarian attack
breaks through weak Serbian
formations in Macedonia

M O N T E N E G R O

Nikshitie

Pristina

B U L G A R I A

Ipek

19–24 Nov: Serbian breakout
attempt defeated on "Plain
of Blackbirds"

Vrania

3

Podgoritza

Jakova

Ferizovich

Kustendil

Dubnitza

Prisrend

Kumanovo

Uskub

MACEDONIAN

**1/Conquest of
Serbia**
6 October – end December

Scutari

Kalkandelen

Kurmanovo

LEGION
(Boyovic)

R. Struma

7

Dulcigno

24 Nov: Serbian retreat through
Albania and Montenegro begins

R. Prim

Veles

Tjshtip

R. Vardar

6–14 October

CCCC Serbian/Central Powers
dispositions

Central Powers attacks

Central Powers gains

December: Anglo-French advance
positions around Strumnitza driven
in by Bulgarian attacks; Allied
forces retreat to Salonika defenses

2

15 October – 1 November

Bulgarian attacks

Central Powers gains

Drin Bay

Drack

Dibra

Trebishte

Prilep

57

Strummitza

2 November – end December

Greek deployment from 2 Nov

Central Powers gains by 11 Nov

Durazzo

Tirana

Krushevo

Lake
Doiran

156

Anglo-French deployment
from 12 Nov

Bashtova

Struga

Okhrida

Monastir

10

Serbian attempted breakout,
19 Nov

Elbassan

Lake
Okhrida

Lake
Prespa

Florina

Vodena

ORIENT ARMY
(Sarrail)

Central Powers gains by 26 Nov

Ferash

Berat

Kotitza

V

Serbian retreat to Adriatic Coast

Valona

G R E E C E

Kastoria

Salonika

III

A L B A N I A

By 1916 the struggle to control the airspace over the front line had become more scientific and organized.

PART III
1916

The critical theater of military operations in 1914 had been in the west, and that of 1915 in the east; in 1916 the Western Front once more occupied center stage for Allied and Central Powers planners alike.

On the Allied side, the growing strength of Great Britain's new armies (by the end of 1915 British forces in France had risen to 38 divisions), and the great improvement in quantity (if not quality) of British munition supplies during the past year, seemed to offer some prospect of breaking the trench deadlock by sheer weight of numbers; for the French High Command, the increased British war effort at the very least offered some relief to a France reaching the end of its ability to bear the brunt of the war on the Western Front. On 5 December 1915, therefore, Joffre called an Allied conference to co-ordinate plans at his Chantilly headquarters, the first attempt of the war to obtain Allied unity of action on all fronts. The agreement reached, in necessarily imprecise terms, was for simultaneous Allied attacks on the Western, Eastern and Italian Fronts in the summer of 1916. The delay until summer was necessary because neither the level of training among new British troops nor the supply of munitions from British factories could be expected to be satisfactory earlier, and because every extra month was vital in the huge effort being made in Russia to make good the shortages and losses of 1915. Meanwhile, limited attacks only were to be made in the west.

At the Chantilly conference, the British High Command, under the direction of Haig, favored an attack in Flanders supported by an amphibious landing behind the German flank; the French – the dominant military voice – demanded a joint attack astride the River Somme. The reason advanced by the French planners was the more favorable nature of the terrain there than in Flanders. The facts that the Somme area lacked any major railroad close to the front, that no strategic prize could be gained there even if a great advance proved possible, and

that in any event the Germans held naturally strong defensive positions, which they had greatly fortified, in the area, were brushed aside. Joffre's main reason for choosing the Somme for a joint Anglo-French attack was unacknowledged: it was here that the British and French armies met, so that the British would be obliged to play their full part in the offensive without the French relinquishing overall direction of the operation.

By early February the outline of the Anglo-French campaign for 1916 had been settled: the French were to mount an assault with 39 divisions south of the Somme, the British with nearly 30 divisions north of the river. Simultaneous Russian and Italian offensives scheduled for July would ensure that

A lull in the fighting around Verdun. The opening German bombardment lasted for 21 hours and caused enormous casualties among the helpless French infantry. During the longest battle of the war the French suffered 542,000 casualties and the Germans 434,000

German reserves could not be transferred from other fronts to meet the threat. The British and French were divided on one question only: that of preliminary attacks, intended to divert German attention from the scene of the main effort. The French insisted that the British stage these attacks, while the British, conscious of the inexperience of their new divisions coming into the line, resisted the demand.

The Germans, however, under the guiding hand of the arch-Westerner Falkenhayn, were poised to pre-empt these plans.

German plans

Falkenhayn's objective for 1916 was to realize his long-cherished plan for an offensive in the west. He regarded Britain as Germany's most important enemy, but recognized that a direct and fatal blow against Britain was impossible. Russia was reeling and could be dealt with later, for further German victories in the east would simply draw German armies further and further into Russian territory without prospect, still less certainty, of destroying the Russian armies. But France, he calculated (not incorrectly), was nearing the end of its ability to sustain the war effort: a blow against France might therefore effectively end the war at a stroke.

He planned an offensive of no great strategic imagination, but based on a shrewd insight into the well-springs of French national consciousness and a certain tactical subtlety. The target of this offensive was to be the fortress-city of Verdun. Verdun's fortifications had been stripped of their heavy guns for the Champagne offensive of the previous September, and Verdun was, in any event, of no great strategic value to France. But it was a symbol of French national pride. Verdun had a long history: it had been an important city in Roman times, and Vauban, the great fortress-builder of Louis XIV's reign, had fortified it with elaborate entrenchments and bastions as a key point in French eastern defenses. In the Franco-Prussian War of 1870–71, Verdun had withstood a siege of 10 weeks, finally falling only through lack of supplies. Symbolically, Verdun stood in defiant opposition to the great German citadel of Metz, and this symbolism was powerful enough in French minds to demand the city's defense by all means possible. Perhaps the

most important of all reasons for its defense lay in the fact that its fall would inevitably entail the fall also of Briand's government in France. Falkenhayn predicted, that the French would be prepared to defend Verdun to the death.

Tactically, Falkenhayn's much-quoted intention of "bleeding the French Army white" requires some explanation. The evidence of the war so far had been that no attacker could hope to inflict heavy casualties on defenders in trenches without suffering equal or greater casualties in the attempt; in most cases, offensives had involved bombardments and counter-bombardments, attacks and counter-attacks on both sides, so that casualties had remained roughly equal. The corollary of Falkenhayn's choice of Verdun for his offensive operation, therefore, was a tactical approach designed to ensure that French casualties would exceed German. He planned an intense and very heavy bombardment, followed by an immediate attack by relatively light forces, aimed at achieving a shallow penetration of the French defenses only. The attackers would then dig in, forcing the French to counter-attack into the teeth of massed German artillery and machine guns, and thus to take very heavy casualties. The German artillery would then be moved forward, and the whole process repeated, and repeated again and again until the French army had been destroyed.

The offensive opened on 21 February, and lasted virtually the entire year; by June German forces had taken Fort Vaux and the French commander, Pétain, was recommending withdrawal, but German forces had to be transferred to the Eastern Front and to the Somme after July, and Falkenhayn himself was relieved of command on 29 August in a tacit German acknowledgement that the offensive was failing.

The Somme

As the slaughter at Verdun increased, the proposed Allied offensive on the Somme acquired a new significance. Responsibility for the offensive necessarily now fell largely on the British, and its purpose came to be no more than to relieve pressure on the French at Verdun. On 1 July Rawlinson's Fourth Army made the principal effort, with Allenby's Third Army to the north and the French Northern Army Group to the south in support. By nightfall,

British infantrymen man a Vickers machine gun during the Battle of the Somme. The Vickers was a variation of the original Maxim. Adopted by the British Army in 1912, it remained in constant service for over 50 years

the British had lost 19,000 dead (some 60,000 casualties in all) for little territorial and no tactical gain. 1 July proved to be the most bloody day in the British Army's history, and the bloodiest single day for any protagonist in the entire war.

This was, however, the offensive for which Britain had been preparing since 1914. Haig resolved to continue his attacks, though in less concentrated form, until they simply ran out in the mud and rain of November, all to little purpose. British idealism died on the Somme: young men, who had enlisted with patriotic fervor, convinced, as they had been assured, that the Somme Offensive would be the "big push" leading to victory, became disillusioned and their remaining loyalty was given no longer to their commanders or to ideals, but merely to the comrades with whom they sought to survive the horror of the trenches. The brutal truth of the Somme was that the hard professionalism of the BEF in 1914 had been squandered in the first months of the war, that the bravery of the New Army troops in 1916 could not compensate for their lack of training and experience, and that without training and experience huge numbers simply did not last long enough at the front to learn how to survive.

The lasting scar in British national consciousness that the Somme caused was paralleled in Germany, however, and German losses over the whole battle equalled those of Britain. It could be argued that after Verdun and the Somme neither the French, British nor German armies were ever the same again.

Brusilov offensive

Russian offensive strategy for 1916 had been designed to coincide with Anglo-French attacks in the west and Italian thrusts from the south. The main Russian plan called for an attack by 26 divisions in July toward Vilna. Meanwhile, to ensure that Germany did not rush reinforcements by rail to the threatened area, Brusilov, commanding the Southwestern Front, was ordered to make diversionary attacks throughout his sector.

But pressure in the west (Falkenhayn's assault on Verdun and Austrian attacks in the Trentino) prompted appeals from both France and Italy for Russia to bring forward the offensive. Despite the obvious dangers of launching in March an offensive planned for July, Russia for the second time went at once and without hesitation to the aid of the western Allies.

The attack, near Lake Naroch, was well planned and involved masses of men and large quantities of munitions painstakingly stockpiled since the previous year. Unfortunately, the Germans were aware of Russian intentions through the capture of documents, and were able to inflict a costly defeat on their enemies. A further appeal to Russia for help then came from Italy. Brusilov, commanding four armies in the south between Kovel and the Romanian border, was willing to attack without any further preparation. His forces arose from their defensive positions in June and advanced along his entire front, preceded by an expertly-planned and co-ordinated bombardment. The Austrians, who held most of the front opposite Brusilov, were taken wholly by surprise and overwhelmed; the Russians had recovered vast areas south of the Pripet Marshes by September, when German reinforcements, supply problems and the imminent advent of winter brought the over-prolonged offensive to a halt. Brusilov's achievement was the greatest Russian success of the war, but the cost - more than one million casualties – brought disillusionment to

Russian soldiers and civilians alike. In reality, 1916 represented the last chance for Russia to win the war, and the failure of the Stavka (Russian High Command) to grasp the opportunity presented by Brusilov's initial, spectacular breakthrough meant that the chance was lost. The offensive was thus instrumental in Russia's collapse and revolution of the following year.

Other fronts

On the Italian Front, the insignificant gains at great cost to the Italians of the first four Battles of the Isonzo were repeated in the fifth battle in March, and the projected Italian summer offensive was preempted by the Austrian Trentino Offensive from mid-May (made possible by the defeat of Serbia at the end of 1915). Austrian progress was halted by the need to transfer units to the Eastern Front when the Brusilov Offensive opened, but three further Italian attempts along the Isonzo in the remainder of the year were unsuccessful despite the capture of Gorizia (Görz) in the sixth battle.

Romania entered the war on the Allied side against Austria on 28 August, when Brusilov's offensive appeared irresistible. Seldom has a military miscalculation been so gross or its punishment so swift, for the German High Command was prepared for such an eventuality despite commitments elsewhere. Units from other fronts under the freshly-demoted Falkenhayn and a largely Bulgarian army withdrawn from Serbia and Salonika and commanded by

Austrian storm-troopers launch an attack during the Trentino Offensive, May 1916

Mackensen were thrown against the Romanians. After three months of savage fighting, Romanian troops were routed and most of the country occupied by the Central Powers, remaining Romanian troops fleeing to the northern province of Moldavia to seek protection from their Russian ally. More significantly for the Allies, Romania's great reserves of oil and wheat, though extensively sabotaged by British agents, were lost to the Central Powers.

During 1916 fighting between Russia and Turkey continued in the Caucasus, and was marked by spectacular if ultimately indecisive Russian successes, including an amphibious offensive along the Black Sea coast which contrasted markedly in both planning and execution with the British fiasco at Gallipoli the year before. In Salonika the Allied Expeditionary Force was expanded by Anglo-French units and the arrival of the earlier defeated but now reformed Serbian Army. Late in August, Bulgarian and German forces mounted a limited offensive to drive back Allied forward positions in the Battle of Florina, but the ground was retaken by Allied counter-attacks after the withdrawal of Bulgarian units to Romania. Despite this, and despite the intervention of Italian troops against the Austrians in Albania, the Allied force remained in virtual blockade, impotent to affect events elsewhere.

At sea, Germany resumed the U-boat war in February, but halted operations again in May after further American protests, and the long-awaited main fleet action – the only such encounter in the entire war – occurred at Jutland on 31 May – 1 June. The battle was inconclusive despite being the largest sea battle in history; the British Grand Fleet suffered slightly greater damage than the German High Seas Fleet, but retained the initiative. Despite German claims of victory, Jutland confirmed that the German Navy could not operate in the North Sea without risking destruction; it remained in port for the remainder of the war.

Attitudes

The idealistic belief of soldiers of all sides in the justness of their cause, the ability of their commanders and the certainty of ultimate victory could be said to have perished in 1916, in Great Britain, France, Austria, Russia, and even Germany.

The impasse, with victory continuing to elude

Field Marshal Sir Douglas Haig with General Sir Henry Rawlinson at 4th Army Headquarters, July 1916

both sides despite unprecedented effort during the year, led to a number of changes in command. French enthusiasm for Joffre's policy of offensives was exhausted; he was removed from command in December and replaced by Robert Nivelle. Tsar Nicholas II, despite advice from his ministers, assumed personal command of all Russian forces, Grand Duke Nicholas being sent to command in the Caucasus. Falkenhayn was given, as a consolation, executive command in the Balkans after his replacement in supreme command by Hindenburg and, effectively, Ludendorff. Conrad was shortly (1917) to be replaced and sent to command on the Italian front. Only Haig, who had succeeded French after the Battle of Loos in 1915, survived the disaster on the Somme.

For civilians, the war was drawing ever closer. The privations of wartime (even in Germany, in which 1916 ended in the "Turnip Winter" – so called because widespread failure of the harvest resulted in a period of severe hardship in which turnips were the only foodstuff in ready supply) could be tolerated, but the mounting military losses were near unbearable. In Britain, where conscription was at last introduced in January 1916 (this itself was a profound acknowledgement of the extent to which the war had changed pre-war liberal sensibilities) many men had enlisted in locally-raised units which bore with pride their unofficial, local names: in the course of the Battle of the Somme, therefore, whole communities up and down Britain were deprived of their menfolk in a single offensive. Similar experiences were common in France, in Russia, in Austria, in Italy and in Germany.

The great battles of 1916 brought the war home with a new intensity throughout Europe; some 60 percent of infantry units in the French Army, for instance, were employed at Verdun at some stage of the battle, which brought the horror of Falkenhayn's "mincing machine" into the personal consciousness of a very high proportion of French households.

Civilian workers on both sides began for the first time since 1914 to query the war's purpose: was it patriotic endeavor in a just cause or simply madness? For still no one had found the key to victory. The outlook for 1917, after two full years of war, was ominous for all.

Timeline 1916

	JANUARY	FEBRUARY	MARCH	APRIL	MAY	JUNE

WESTERN FRONT

Battle of Verdun
Douaumont
Vaux

EASTERN FRONT

1st battle, Lake Naroch

Brusilov Offensive

BALKAN FRONT

△ *Serbs evacuate to Corfu*

ITALIAN FRONT

5th Isonzo

Trentino offensive

Italian counter-offensive

TURKISH FRONTS

⬤ *Gallipoli evacuation complete*

Erzerum

△ *Bitlis captured*

△ *Trebizond captured*

△ *Capture of Mecca by arab revolt*

⬤ *1st attempt to relieve Kut*

⬤ *2nd attempt to relieve Kut*

⬤ *3rd attempt to relieve Kut*

△ *Kut surrenders*

OTHER FRONTS

△ *Capture of YAUNDE (Cameroon)*

△ *MORA surrenders (Cameroon)*

△ *Derenter occupies Moshi*

WAR AT SEA

💥 *1st depth charge Submarine kill*

Jutland

INTERNATIONAL EVENTS

⬤ *Stürmer appointed Russian Prime Minister*

⬤ *Limited but compulsory military service introduced in Great Britain*

⬤ *1st Russian troops land at Marseilles*

⬤ *Beginning of Irish Uprising (ends 1 May)*

⬤ *Anglo-French 'Pacific' blockade of Greece*

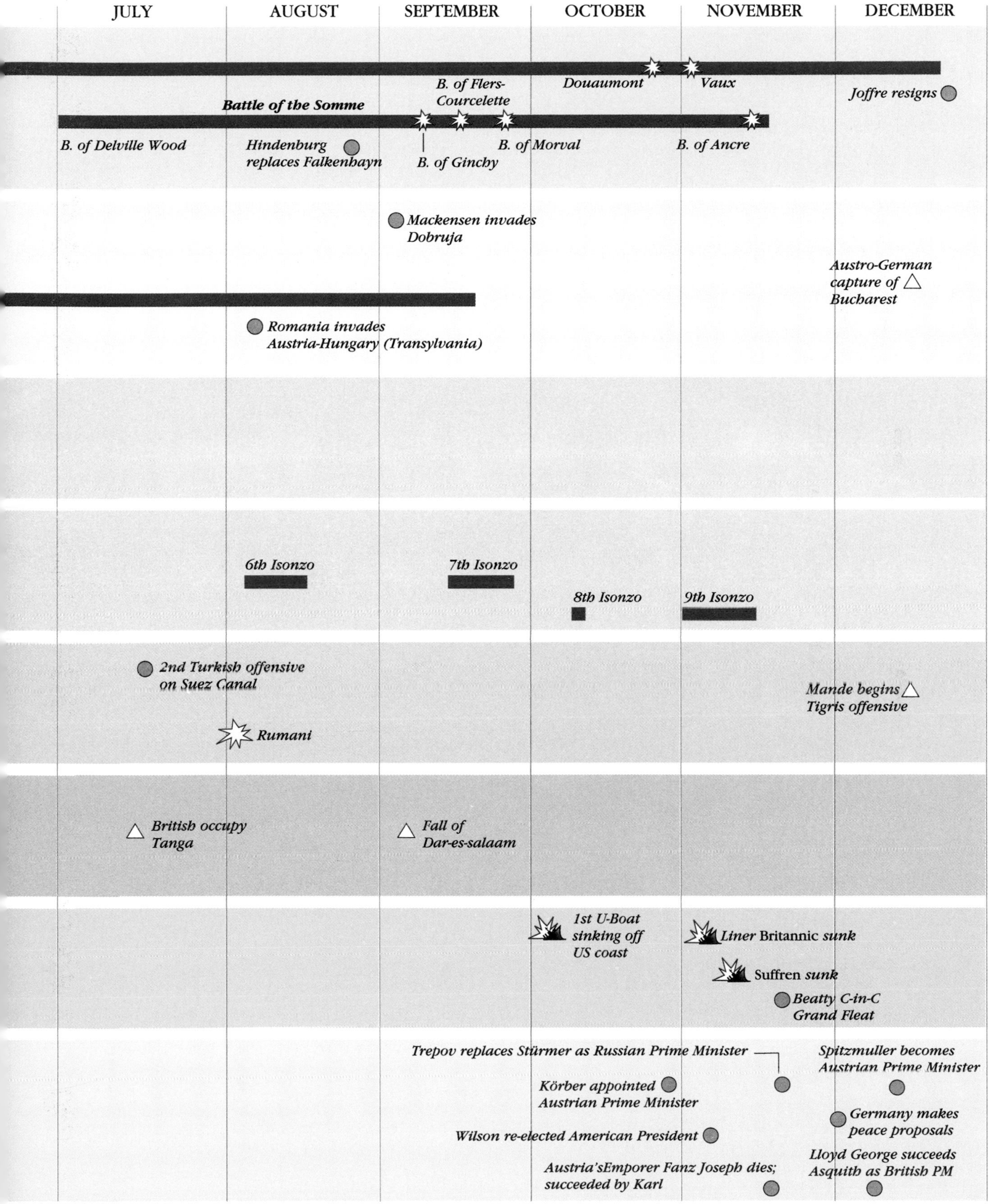

JULY	AUGUST	SEPTEMBER	OCTOBER	NOVEMBER	DECEMBER

Douaumont

Vaux

Joffre resigns

B. of Flers-Courcelette

Battle of the Somme

B. of Delville Wood

Hindenburg replaces Falkenhayn

B. of Ginchy

B. of Morval

B. of Ancre

Mackensen invades Dobruja

Austro-German capture of △ Bucharest

Romania invades Austria-Hungary (Transylvania)

6th Isonzo

7th Isonzo

8th Isonzo

9th Isonzo

2nd Turkish offensive on Suez Canal

Mande begins △ Tigris offensive

Rumani

British occupy △ Tanga

Fall of △ Dar-es-salaam

1st U-Boat sinking off US coast

Liner Britannic *sunk*

Suffren sunk

Beatty C-in-C Grand Fleat

Trepov replaces Stürmer as Russian Prime Minister

Spitzmuller becomes Austrian Prime Minister

Körber appointed Austrian Prime Minister

Germany makes peace proposals

Wilson re-elected American President

Lloyd George succeeds Asquith as British PM

Austria's Emporer Fanz Joseph dies; succeeded by Karl

Armenia 1914–1916

Commitments on other fronts for both Russia and Turkey, and the lateness of the year, should have ensured that the Caucasus front remained quiet at least until spring 1915. The easy repulse of a local Russian offensive at Koprukeui in early November, however, encouraged the ambitious Enver Pasha, proponent of grandiose though ill-defined Pan-Islamic and Pan-Turan Turkish ambitions in the region, to launch an improvident advance on Kars in December.

Enver's Third Army advanced through rugged mountain terrain rendered doubly inhospitable by temperatures as severe as -20C (-36F). The Turkish X Corps had lost over one-third of its strength before action was joined.

Enver's forces were unable to take Sarikamish, and IX Corps was virtually annihilated by Russian reserves brought up from Kars. In all, some 75,000 Turks perished, out of a total of 95,000. The Russians sustained 16,000 killed and wounded, together with some 12,000 cases of frostbite and disease.

With the destruction of much of the Turkish army (and Enver's removal from command), initiative on the front passed to Russia. Events on the Eastern Front in 1915 ensured, however, that no major Russian offensive was possible during the summer. Both sides spent much of the year engaged in intrigue and small-scale but vigorous military action in northern Persia, culminating in the Russian occupation of Tehran, Hamadan and Qom by the end of 1915.

Armenian massacres

From February 1915, however, the Turkish government seized the opportunity to instigate a policy of virtual genocide against the substantial Armenian minority in eastern Turkey, on the charge that the Armenians were aiding Russia. More than one million Armenians were either murdered or deported to die in the wastes of Syria or Mesopotamia in 1915 alone. The Armenians rose in revolt in the area around Van in April, occupying the city itself and then retreating with the Russians when the Turks briefly regained control of the area in early August.

The 1916 campaign

At the end of 1915, Yudenich, one of the most able Russian commanders, planned a large offensive aimed at breaking the Turkish front before reinforcements released by the Allied failure at Gallipoli became available. Thus the Russians advanced toward Erzerum on a wide front from 10 January. The Turkish Third Army was forced back, with losses of some 25,000 men in the second Battle of Koprukeui, on its defenses at Erzerum itself. Yudenich's troops stormed through the city's ring of forts via the 10,000 foot Kargapazar Range (Map 2). Simultaneously, the well-coordinated Russian army and naval offensive along the Black Sea coast captured Trebizond on 18 April.

Enver, now directing Turkish strategy, planned a counter-stroke by the Third Army (now Vehib Pasha) with a newly–positioned Second Army to advance on Bitlis against Yudenich's left flank. Yudenich, however, smashed the Third Army at Erzingan on 25 July and virtually destroyed it, the Turks sustaining 34,000 casualties. Despite minor successes won by Mustafa Kemal, now in command of a corps, Second Army could make little progress. Both sides, mindful of earlier experience, went into winter quarters in the fall, bringing activity on the front almost to an end.

Gen. Nicolai Yudenich above ensured that his troops were fully prepared for fighting in sub-zero temperatures and his daring plans recieved full support from the equally competant Grand-Duke Nicolas.

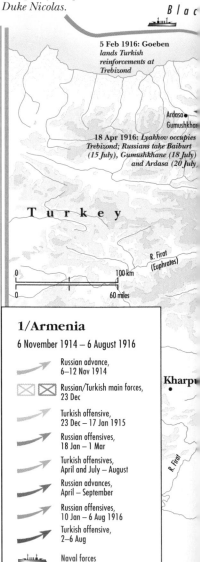

5 Feb 1916: Goeben lands Turkish reinforcements at Trebizond

18 Apr 1916: Lyakhov occupies Trebizond; Russians take Baiburt (15 July), Gumushkhane (18 July) and Ardasa (20 July)

Turkey

Ardasa•
Gumushkhan

R. Firat
(Euphrates)

0   100 km
0   60 miles

B l a c

Kharp

R. Firat

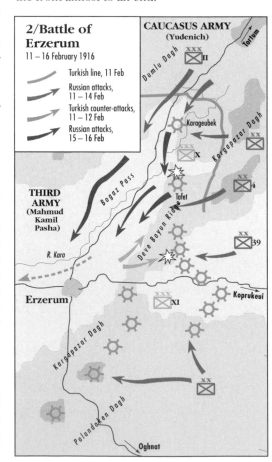

2/Battle of Erzerum
11 – 16 February 1916

→ Turkish line, 11 Feb
→ Russian attacks, 11 – 14 Feb
→ Turkish counter-attacks, 11 – 12 Feb
→ Russian attacks, 15 – 16 Feb

CAUCASUS ARMY (Yudenich)

Tortum

Dumlu Dagh

II

Karageubek

Kargapazar Dagh

X

4

Tafet

Bogaz Pass

39

THIRD ARMY (Mahmud Kamil Pasha)

Deve Boyun Ridge

R. Kara

Erzerum

XI

Koprukeui

Kargapazar Dagh

Palandoken Dagh

Oghnat

1/Armenia
6 November 1914 – 6 August 1916

→ Russian advance, 6–12 Nov 1914
⊠ ⊠ Russian/Turkish main forces, 23 Dec
→ Turkish offensive, 23 Dec – 17 Jan 1915
→ Russian offensives, 18 Jan – 1 Mar
→ Turkish offensives, April and July – August
→ Russian advances, April – September
→ Russian offensives, 10 Jan – 6 Aug 1916
→ Turkish offensive, 2–6 Aug
⚓ Naval forces

Russian troops pose with a Turkish gun after the capture of the fortress of Erzerum on 16 February 1916. The surrounding forts mounted about 300 guns, but over 200 of these, including this weapon, were outmoded. Erzerum was a naturally strong position, but the attack by Yudenich's 4th Division via the 10,000 foot Kargapazar Ridge took the defenders by surprise (Map 2). The Russian capture of Erzerum opened the way to Baiburt, Oghnat and Erzingan (Map 1) and effectively broke the Turkish Third Army for the second time in little over a year.

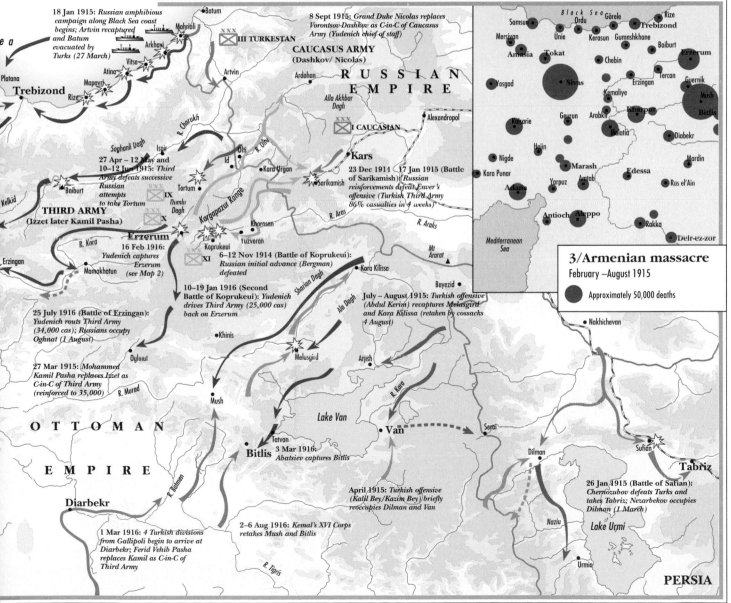

18 Jan 1915: *Russian amphibious campaign along Black Sea coast begins; Artvin recaptured and Batum evacuated by Turks (27 March)*

8 Sept 1915: *Grand Duke Nicolas replaces Vorontsov-Dashkov as C-in-C of Caucasus Army (Yudenich chief of staff)*

XXX
III TURKESTAN

CAUCASUS ARMY
(Dashkov/ Nicolas)

R U S S I A N   E M P I R E

Alla Akhbar Dagh

XXX
I CAUCASIAN

Kars

23 Dec 1911 / 17 Jan 1915 (Battle of Sarikamish): *Russian reinforcements defeat Enver's offensive (Turkish Third Army 86% casualties in 4 weeks)*

27 Apr – 12 May and 10–12 Jun 1915: *Third Army defeats successive Russian attempts to take Tortum*

XXX
IX

Dumlu Dagh

Kargapazar Range

THIRD ARMY
(Izzet later Kamil Pasha)

XXX
X

Erzerum

16 Feb 1916: *Yudenich captures Erzerum (see Map 2)*

XXX
XI

6–12 Nov 1914 (Battle of Koprukeui): *Russian initial advance (Bergman) defeated*

10–19 Jan 1916 (Second Battle of Koprukeui): *Yudenich drives Third Army (25,000 cas) back on Erzerum*

25 July 1916 (Battle of Erzingan): *Yudenich routs Third Army (34,000 cas); Russians occupy Oghnat (1 August)*

27 Mar 1915: *Mohammed Kamil Pasha replaces Izzet as C-in-C of Third Army (reinforced to 35,000)*

July – August 1915: *Turkish offensive (Abdul Kerim) recaptures Melasgird and Kara Kilissa (retaken by cossacks 4 August)*

Mt Ararat ▲

O T T O M A N   E M P I R E

3 Mar 1916: *Abatsiev captures Bitlis*

April 1915: *Turkish offensive (Kalil Bey/Kazim Bey) briefly reoccupies Dilman and Van*

26 Jan 1915 (Battle of Safian): *Cherniozubov defeats Turks and takes Tabriz; Nezarbekov occupies Dilman (1 March)*

2–6 Aug 1916: *Kemal's XVI Corps retakes Mush and Bitlis*

1 Mar 1916: *4 Turkish divisions from Gallipoli begin to arrive at Diarbekr; Ferid Vehib Pasha replaces Kamil as C-in-C of Third Army*

Lake Van

Lake Urmi

PERSIA

3/Armenian massacre
February –August 1915
● Approximately 50,000 deaths

Black Sea
Samsun, Ordu, Görele, Rize, Trebizond, Mersivan, Unie, Kerasun, Gumushkhane, Amasia, Tokat, Chebin, Baiburt, Yosgad, Sivas, Erzingan, Tercan, Guernik, Kemaliye, Mush, Katsarie, Geurun, Arabkir, Kharpm, Bitlis, Nigde, Hajin, Malatia, Diabekr, Kara Punar, Marash, Mardin, Yarpuz, Amtab, Edessa, Adana, Ras el'Ain, Antioch, Aleppo, Rakka, Mediterranean Sea, Deir-ez-zor

Batum, Mahriali, Arkhavi, Vitse, Atina, Mapavri, Rize, Platana, Trebizond, Artvin, Ardahan, Alexandropol, Ispir, Olti, Id, Kara Urgan, Sarikamish, Soghanli Dagh, Tortum, Baiburt, Kelkid, Khorasan, R. Kara, R. Aras, R. Araks, Erzingan, Mamakhatun, Koprukeui, Yuzveran, Khinis, Oghnut, R. Murad, Melasgird, Arjish, Kara Kilissa, Bayezid, Nakhichevan, Mush, Tatvan, Bitlis, Van, Serai, Dilman, Sufian, Tabriz, Naziu, Urmia, Diarbekr, R. Botman, R. Tigris

Verdun: the German offensive
February – May 1916

The fortress-city of Verdun and its double ring of forts were situated on the River Meuse in a French salient cut off from the south by the German-held salient around St Mihiel. Strategically, Verdun was of little importance – indeed, by abandoning it, the French would have shortened, straightened and strengthened their line. Moreover, the fortress had recently been stripped of its guns for service elsewhere and was guarded by a single line of trenches .

Falkenhayn's plan

Falkenhayn's offensive was almost without any strategic aim: instead, the political and symbolic importance of Verdun to the French and a further refinement of the trench warfare tactics developed during 1915 (see Introduction) were to be harnessed in a major operation with no other aim than to cause the French Army such heavy casualties as to destroy France's will to continue the war. The instrument chosen for this operation was Crown Prince Wilhelm's Fifth Army, backed by the heaviest concentration of artillery ever assembled.

The assault

The opening barrage had been timed for 12 February, but sudden deterioration in the weather demanded postponement first by 24 hours, then repeatedly, until conditions improved on 21 February. On that day, for nine uninterrupted hours, the bombardment raged, steadily intensifying in its ferocity. The devastation caused was soon intolerable. Many surviving French soldiers were splattered as much by the blood of their comrades as by mud.

At about 1645hrs the bombardment abruptly ceased, and German infantry – some armed with a new weapon, the flame thrower, advanced through an eerie silence between Bois de Haumont and Herbevois on the east bank of the Meuse. The French line had been pulverized but, incredibly, those French infantry who survived stood firm: heavy casualties ensued on both sides until the advent of darkness.

For four further days, the German tactics of relatively shallow penetration, immediate refortification of French positions taken and the concentration of overwhelming artillery fire upon French counter-attacks brought significant results; on the 25th Douaumont, the greatest of

"Like a vision in hell – for days I have seen nothing but the most terrible things human mind can depict."

The painter Franz Marc in a letter home from the Verdun front, 3 March. Killed in French artillery bombardment, 4 March 1916.

the Verdun forts, was overrun, and the fall of Verdun itself seemed imminent.

The second phase

Even the sanguine Joffre now recognized the seriousness of the situation. Henri Pétain's Second Army was ordered to reinforce the Third, all available artillery and aircraft were rushed to the front and Pétain was given overall command. Heavy enfilading fire from French artillery positions on the west bank of the Meuse was poured into the German gains, and a supply route for trucks (the Voie Sacrée) organized into the city. French positions in the Woevre were given up, and the troops rushed to the defense of the main Verdun positions. By the end of February the initial German advance had been stemmed.

The Germans were also reinforcing their positions, by bringing up three flanking corps – the VI Reserve on the right and the XV and V Reserve on the left. Throughout March and April these formations mounted heavy attacks aimed at rectifying the initial mistake of failing to clear the west bank of the Meuse. By 9 April part of the key hill known as Le Mort Homme had fallen (though French counter-attacks were temporarily to recapture lost ground shortly afterwards) and by 6 May the Fifth Army had advanced almost to Avocourt and Chattancourt.

"I have returned from the toughest trial that I have ever seen - four days and four nights - ninety-six hours - the last two days soaked in icy mud - under terrible bombardment, without any shelter other than the narrowness of the trench, which even seemed to be too wide; not a hole, not a dugout, nothing, nothing... I arrived there with 175 men. I returned with 34, several half mad."

Captain Augustin Cochin,146th Regiment, in a letter home from le Mort Homme, 14 April 1916

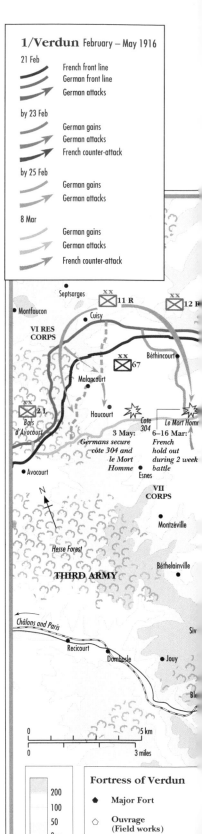

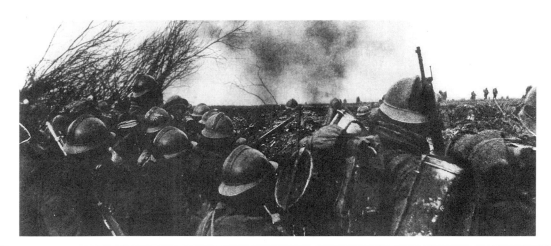

A French division counter-attacks ahead of Louvemont, northwest of Douaumont. The pentagonal fort of Douaumont was the largest and strongest in the region and was therefore an important German objective. The snow storms of 11 February had given the French commanders the necessary time to effectively position their forces in such strategically important areas.

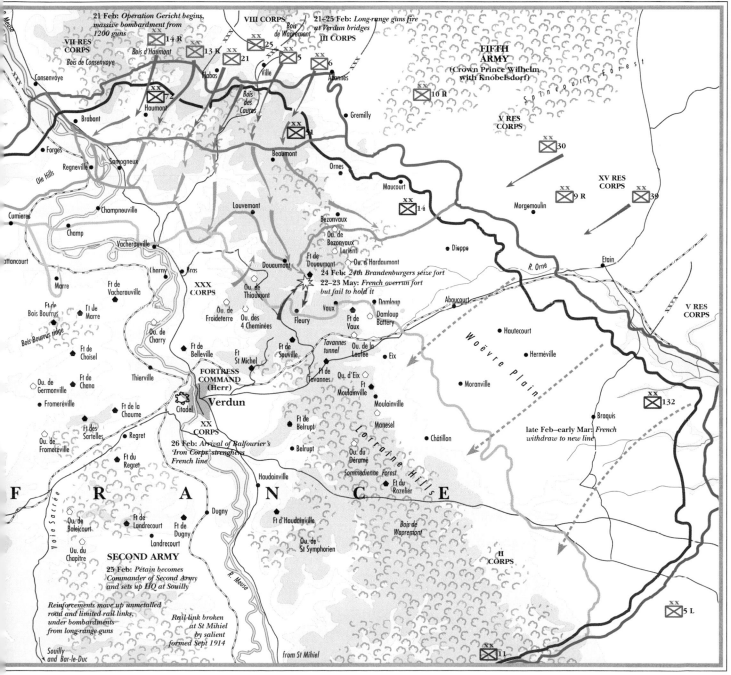

21 Feb: Operation Gericht begins, massive bombardment from 1200 guns

VII RES CORPS

21–25 Feb: Long-range guns fire at Verdun bridges

VIII CORPS

III CORPS

FIFTH ARMY
(Crown Prince Wilhelm with Knobelsdorf)

V RES CORPS

XV RES CORPS

24 Feb: 24th Brandenburgers seize fort
22–23 May: French overrun fort but fail to hold it

XXX CORPS

FORTRESS COMMAND (Herr)

Verdun

XX CORPS

26 Feb: Arrival of Balfourier's 'Iron Corps' strengthens French line

late Feb–early Mar: French withdraw to new line

V RES CORPS

Woëvre Plain

Lorraine Hills

II CORPS

SECOND ARMY

25 Feb: Pétain becomes Commander of Second Army and sets up HQ at Souilly

Reinforcements move up unmetalled road and limited rail links, under bombardments from long-range guns

Rail link broken at St Mihiel by salient formed Sept 1914

F R A N C E

Souilly and Bar-le-Duc

from St Mihiel

The Trentino Offensive May–June 1916

Cadorna's plans for a renewed offensive on the Isonzo were interrupted in May when Conrad von Hötzendorf launched a heavy attack in the Trentino. Conrad had long sought an opportunity for an offensive against Italy, but had hitherto been restrained by Falkenhayn, who virtually ordered Austria to remain on the defensive in the Alpine region.

Austrian plans

In 1916, seeking a tonic for Austrian servicemen and civilians alike, Conrad drew up plans, to be executed in conjunction with German forces, to move out of the strongly fortified Austrian positions and cut deep into the left flank of the Italian Army. Austrian forces could then, in theory, reach Venice itself, cutting off the Italian forces on the Isonzo and forcing Italy to conclude a separate peace with the Central Powers.

Conrad therefore suggested to Falkenhayn a joint endeavor along a front of 25 miles, comprising 16 divisions, formed into two armies. The Austrians, by withdrawing formations from unthreatened theaters, could field eight divisions; the other eight, for the supporting army, would have to be supplied by the Germans.

Falkenhayn, already preoccupied with the attack at Verdun (page 92) refused point blank to make such a commitment. Conrad therefore reconceived the attack as a purely Austrian venture, withdrawing further units from the quiescent Russian front. Largely for political reasons, he appointed Archduke Eugen as commander-in-chief for the attack, and was able to raise 14 divisions and 60 heavy artillery batteries, formed into two armies – the Eleventh (Dankl) and the Third (Kövess).

The mountainous region chosen for the attack presented formidable problems, compounded by snow and intense cold in winter and early spring. Conrad's planned offensive in April had to be delayed until May.

The attack

On 15 May, the Austrian offensive opened against the Italian First Army (Pecori-Giraldi), a force of 176 battalions, many inexperienced, supported by some 850 guns.

Conrad's plans for a swift and decisive victory soon came to grief. Pecori-Giraldi's front lines had been savaged by a barrage which com-

menced at 06:00hrs, and they were quickly over-run, but in other areas the Austrian forces were able to make little headway against dogged, heroic Italian resistance. At Piazza the Roma Brigade withstood Austrian assaults for three days, and suffered almost complete annihilation as a result. The Austrians also suffered, and severe punishment was inflicted on the Kaisershutz Division west of Valsara, where the difficult terrain aided the defenders and hampered the assailants. Poor communications and subsequent confusion resulted in Archduke Eugen ordering his forces to regroup on May 20. This further delay added to the problems which were becoming increasingly difficult to summount; Austrian supply lines were stretched to their limit and the artillery could no longer offer the kind of support which had greatly contributed to earlier sucesses. The Italian Army was being forced into retreat, but only after tenacious resistance and its withdrawal was always marked by the destruction of its defenses. Moreover, urgent Italian appeals for help to the other Allies were answered on 4 June by the launching of the Brusilov offensive (page 98) on the Russian Front. The weakness of Austrian formations in Galicia and the scale of the Russian break-through gave Conrad little option but to rush formations to the east, which in turn dictated an immediate retirement to defensive positions on the Trentino front.

Consequences and losses

Once again Conrad had exhibited an inability to execute his imaginative ideas, and his success in preventing extensive Italian incursions into Austrian territory could do little to save him. Falkenhayn's resentment at Conrad's disregard of his views was greatly increased by the disaster in Galicia in face of Brusilov, and he intervened to secure Conrad's dismissal. Further Austrian withdrawal in the Trentino allowed Cadorna to reoccupy some of the territory lost and to transfer formations to the Isonzo, there to resume his own offensive operations.

Italian losses in the Trentino campaign amounted to more than 147,000, of whom 40,000 were prisoners; 300 guns were taken and vast quantities of supplies. Austrian losses, including 26,000 prisoners, amounted to 81,000. Activity on the Italian front now returned to the Isonzo theater.

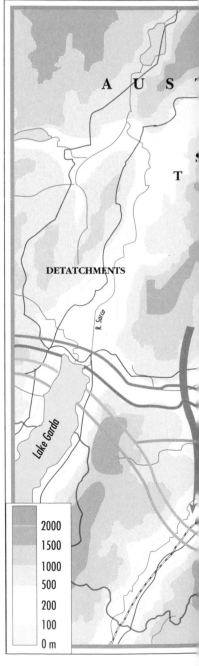

AUST

T

DETATCHMENTS

R. Sarca

Lake Garda

2000
1500
1000
500
200
100
0 m

Below left: Austrian troops advance with the aid of flamethrowers. German forces were the first to use flame-throwers in 1914, but they quickly shared such technological advances with their weaker alllies. Though capable of instilling great fear in the enemy, early models had only limited use since their effective range did not exceed 40 yards.

Right :Italian troops man an A.13 heavy artillery piece, 1915.

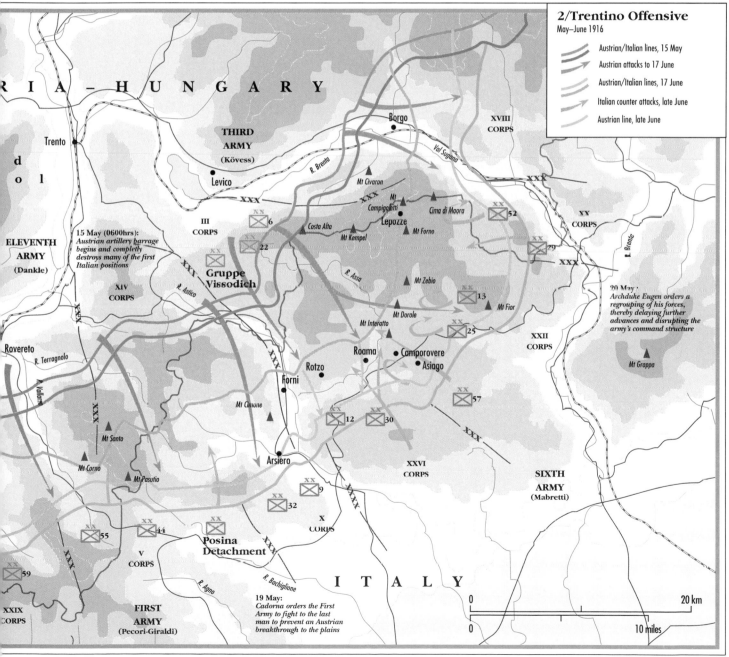

2/Trentino Offensive
May–June 1916

Austrian/Italian lines, 15 May

Austrian attacks to 17 June

Austrian/Italian lines, 17 June

Italian counter attacks, late June

Austrian line, late June

AUSTRIA–HUNGARY

Trento

THIRD ARMY (Kövess)

Borgo

XVIII CORPS

Val Sugana

ELEVENTH ARMY (Dankle)

Levico

R. Brenta

Mt Civaron

Mt Campigoletti

Cima di Maora

52

XX CORPS

III CORPS

6

Costa Alta

Lepozze

Mt Forno

79

R. Brenta

15 May (0600hrs): *Austrian artillery barrage begins and completly destroys many of the first Italian positions*

22

Mt Kempel

XIV CORPS

Gruppe Vissodich

R. Astico

R. Assa

Mt Zebio

13

Mt Fior

20 May : *Archduke Eugen orders a regrouping of his forces, thereby delaying further advances and disrupting the army's command structure*

Rovereto

R. Terragnolo

R. Vallarsa

Mt Dorole

Mt Interotto

25

XXII CORPS

Mt Grappa

Roama

Camporovere

Rotzo

Asiago

Forni

Mt Cimone

57

Mt Santo

12

30

Mt Corno

Mt Pasutio

Arsiero

XXVI CORPS

SIXTH ARMY (Mabretti)

9

55

32

X CORPS

44

59

V CORPS

Posina Detachment

R. Bachiglione

19 May: *Cadorna orders the First Army to fight to the last man to prevent an Austrian breakthrough to the plains*

I T A L Y

XXIX CORPS

FIRST ARMY (Pecori-Giraldi)

R. Agno

0   20 km

0   10 miles

Jutland May 1916

A major naval action between the British Grand Fleet and the German High Seas Fleet had been expected from the beginning of the war. In the event, the two great fleets were not to engage until 31 May 1916.

German plans

The German plan was to entice Beatty's force from Rosyth, then to overwhelm the British battlecruisers with Scheer's entire High Seas Fleet before Jellicoe could intervene. The German fleet left harbor early on 31 May. Hipper's battlecruisers steamed northward along the Danish coast to attack merchantmen off Norway and lure Beatty to the scene (Map 1).

Unknown to Scheer, however, the British possessed a German naval codebook captured by the Russian Navy in the Baltic, and were monitoring all German movements. Beatty and Jellicoe both left port at about 2130hrs.

The battle

The complex battle fell into two main parts: a fight between Beatty's and Hipper's battlecruisers (Map 2), followed by a massive and confused clash of dreadnoughts (Map 3).

Hipper sighted Beatty at about 1520hrs and turned south, hoping to draw the British on to Scheer's guns. A long-range gunnery duel between the rival battlecruisers began some twenty minutes later, in which Beatty quickly and disastrously lost two major ships, *Indefatigable* and *Queen Mary*, both casualties of the British lack of anti-flash doors. Evan-Thomas's 5th

> *"I laughed grimly and now I began to engage our enemy with complete calm...and with continually increasing accuracy. All thoughts of death or sinking vanished. The true sporting joy of battle woke in me and all my thoughts concentrated on one desire, to hit, to hit rapidly and true, to go on hitting."*
>
> Cdr. G. Von Hase, Control Officer, S.M.S. Derfflinger

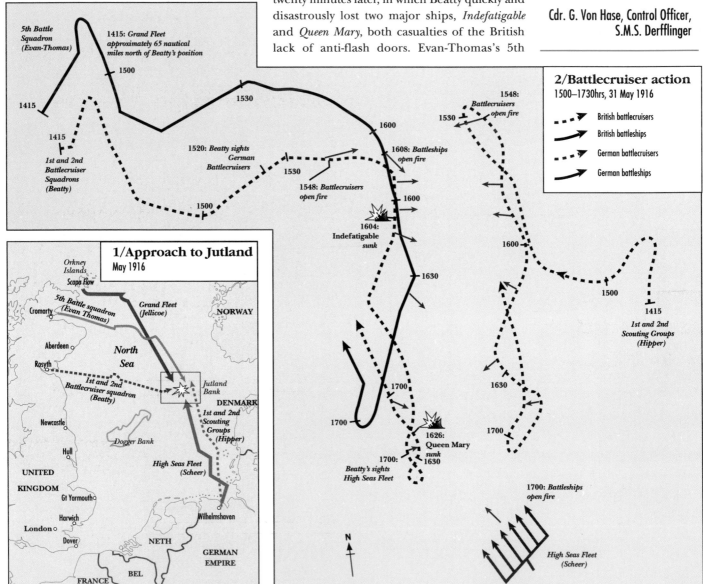

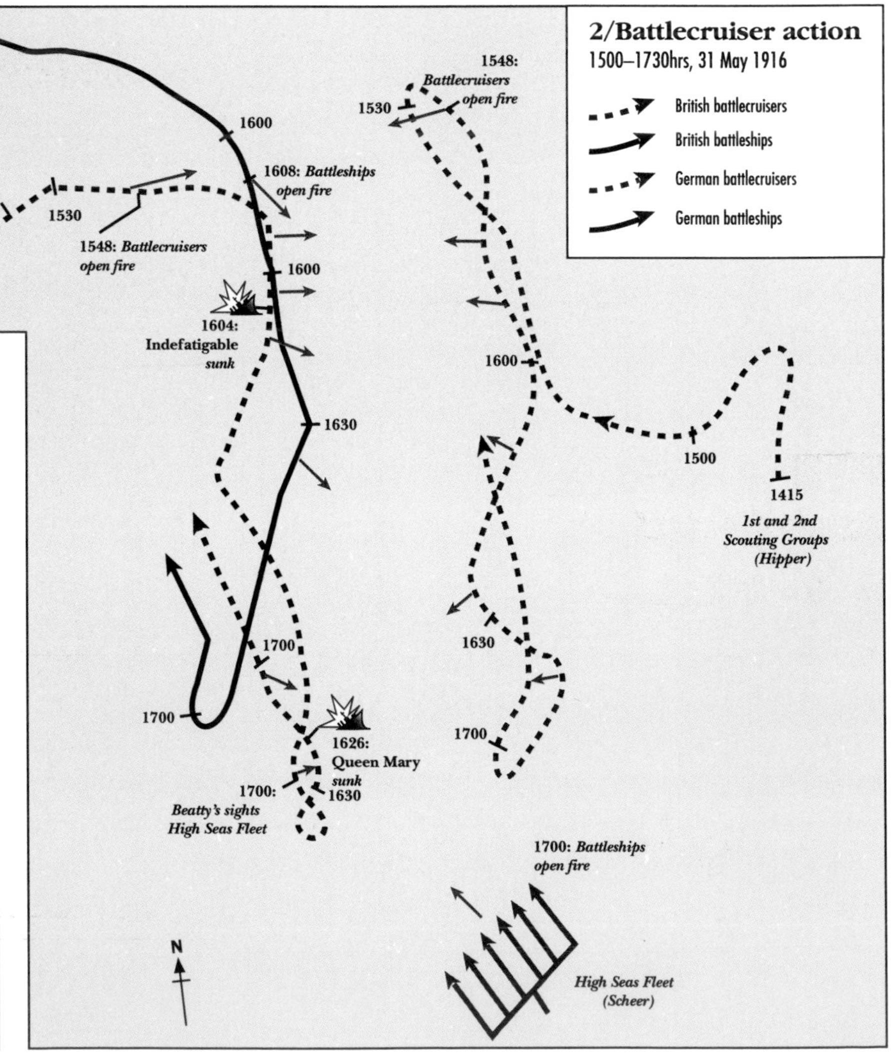
2/Battlecruiser action
1500–1730hrs, 31 May 1916
British battlecruisers
British battleships
German battlecruisers
German battleships
5th Battle Squadron (Evan-Thomas)
1415: Grand Fleet approximately 65 nautical miles north of Beatty's position
1500
1415
1530
1415
1st and 2nd Battlecruiser Squadrons (Beatty)
1520: Beatty sights German Battlecruisers
1500
1530
1548: Battlecruisers open fire
1600
1608: Battleships open fire
1600
1604: Indefatigable sunk
1630
1700
1700
1626: Queen Mary sunk
1700: Beatty's sights High Seas Fleet
1630
1548: Battlecruisers open fire
1530
1600
1500
1415
1st and 2nd Scouting Groups (Hipper)
1630
1700
1700: Battleships open fire
High Seas Fleet (Scheer)
N

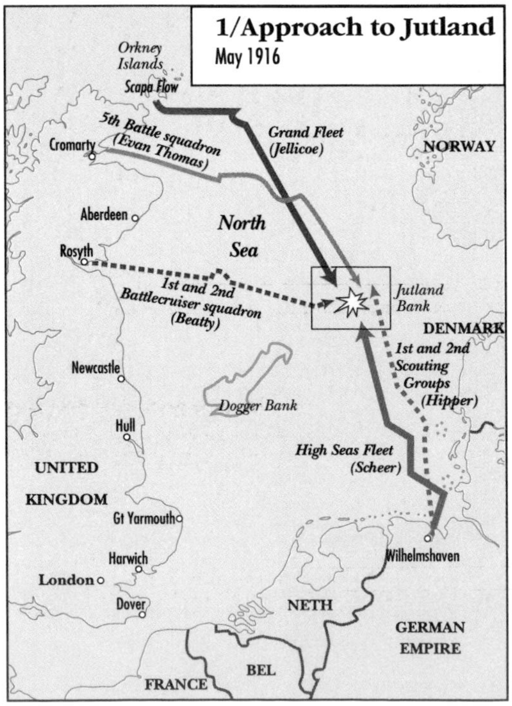
1/Approach to Jutland
May 1916
Orkney Islands
Scapa Flow
5th Battle squadron (Evan Thomas)
Cromarty
Grand Fleet (Jellicoe)
NORWAY
Aberdeen
North Sea
Rosyth
1st and 2nd Battlecruiser squadron (Beatty)
Jutland Bank
DENMARK
1st and 2nd Scouting Groups (Hipper)
Newcastle
Dogger Bank
Hull
High Seas Fleet (Scheer)
UNITED KINGDOM
Gt Yarmouth
Harwich
London
Wilhelmshaven
Dover
NETH
GERMAN EMPIRE
BEL
FRANCE

Battle Squadron now appeared within range, and Scheer had to go to Hipper's assistance. Beatty sighted Scheer's fleet at about 1640hrs and turned north toward Jellicoe.

The second engagement

The two main fleets were now rapidly closing. Jellicoe's fleet was deployed in six columns, over a width of 4mls/6km. On sighting the German fleet, he ordered a turn to port across the German line, to "cross the T" (thus enabling all the British ships to pour fire into the leading Germans ships).

Scheer at once turned about, heading westward, away from his base. Jellicoe seized the opportunity to place his fleet between the Germans and their harbors, but the combination of fog, dense smoke and fading light was already making visibility increasingly unfavorable.

Scheer inexplicably turned eastward again, bringing his fleet soon after 1900hrs opposite the center of Jellicoe's line, no more than 5mls/8km distant. A general engagement now began, in which British numerical superiority and heavier guns threatened to prove decisive despite the further loss of the battlecruiser *Invincible*. Scheer quickly executed a second battle turn westward, while Hipper's battlecruisers took heavy punishment covering his withdrawal. Nightfall came at about 2100hrs, and Scheer was able to escape eastward across the rear of Jellicoe's line in the darkness, losing the old battleship *Pommern* but reaching the safety of Wilhelmshaven.

At 1315hrs the next day, having searched for stragglers and seamen in lifeboats, Jellicoe ordered his ships to return to their harbors.

Consequences

The Royal Navy suffered the more serious losses – three battle-cruisers, three armored cruisers and eight destroyers to Germany's one battleship, five cruisers and five destroyers, and 6097 sailors to Germany's 2545. Despite some criticism of Jellicoe at the time and since, Jutland confirmed the Royal Navy's dominance of the

North Sea. Though the Germans were to make further raids on the British coast, the High Seas Fleet never again put to sea to confront the Grand Fleet.

Reinhard Scheer, commander of the High Seas Fleet, was a decisive and capable admiral, but risked the destruction of his fleet at Jutland. Of the four main commanders involved, only his battlecruiser commander 'Hipper' cannot be faulted for his actions in the battle.

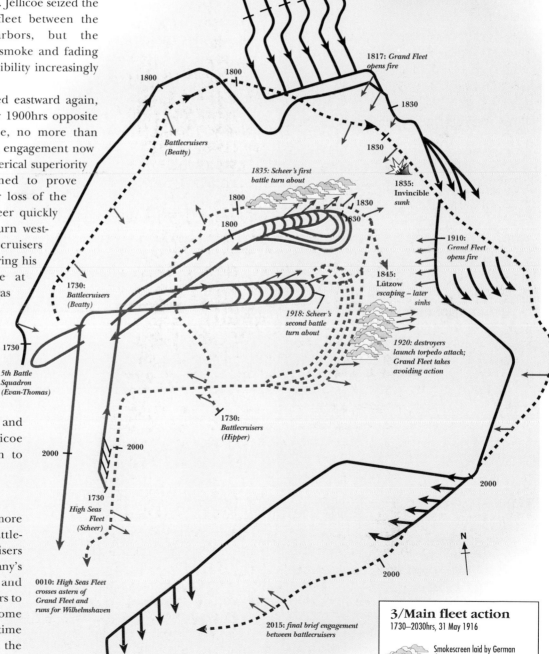

The Brusilov Offensive Russian Breakthrough, June 1916

In early 1916 Russia again went precipitately to the aid of the western Allies. After an astonishing recovery since the disasters of 1915, Russian industry was producing 100,000 rifles a month, and hundreds of thousands of new recruits had been enlisted. An offensive to coincide with planned French and British summer offensives on the Western Front was therefore prepared, but after the German attack at Verdun the Russian High Command bowed to French pressure to attack in the spring.

Lake Naroch

On 18 March Ragoza's Second Army launched a major two-pronged offensive around Lake Naroch (Map 1). Despite a two-day bombardment, the attack made little progress in the spring thaw, and losses were heavy – between 70,000 and 100,000, against 20,000 Germans.

The Brusilov offensive

After the failure at Lake Naroch, the Russian High Command resumed planning a July offensive, again in the genaral direction of Vilna. Once more an enemy offensive disrupted preparations – this time in May in the Trentino (page 94). Only the commander of the South Western Front, Alexei Brusilov, was prepared to bring his plans forward. With only 38 divisions to Austria's 37 on his front, Brusilov resolved on a novel method of attack. His plan was to launch all four of his armies simultaneously, with careful preparation and maximum surprise, along the entire front of 300 miles, thus making it impossible for Austrian reserves to be switched to danger points. He ordered a short and intense preliminary bombardment to take out selected points rather than to pound the whole Austrian front line.

The Austrians believed their front-line defenses virtually impregnable. In many sectors they had dug up to five lines of trenches, many 20ft/8m deep, covered with timber and stocked with food and weapons. Many troops had settled into an almost comfortable existence, with bakeries, and other amenities just behind the front line.

The campaign

Brusilov opened his general offensive on 4 June. As the Russians advanced, their artillery employed curtain fire to trap the Austrians in their deep shelters, which quickly became prisons in which death or surrender were the only options. In the north, the cautious Kaledin made rapid progress until halted by German reinforcements rushed from other fronts, while Letchitsky's slightly later offensive in the south virtually destroyed the Austrian Seventh Army. Within the month Brusilov had penetrated nearly 60mls/96km along the entire front, capturing almost the whole of the Bukovina and the strategically important towns of Dubno, Lutsk and Czernowitz. Some 350,000 prisoners were taken, together with 400 artillery pieces. The situation in the east, it seemed, had been transformed.

Above right: Alexei Alexeevich Brusilov, masterminded Russia's greatest success. In his June 1916 offensive, secrecy was strictly enforced, enemy positions studied in detail, artillery ammunition amassed and divisional commanders thoroughly briefed; the scale of his breakthrough overwhelmed the Austrian armies.

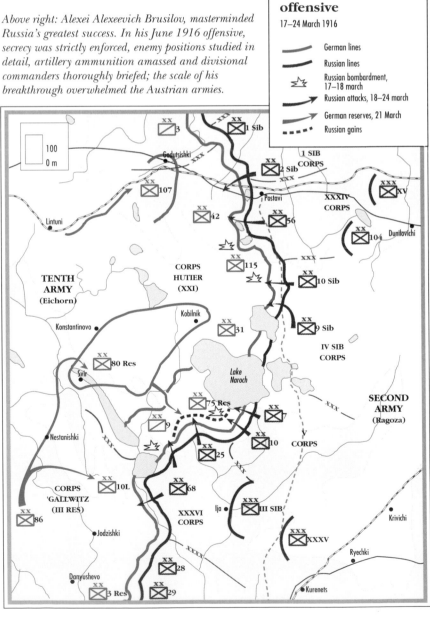

1/Lake Naroch offensive
17–24 March 1916

- German lines
- Russian lines
- Russian bombardment, 17–18 march
- Russian attacks, 18–24 march
- German reserves, 21 March
- Russian gains

2/Brusilov offensive
4–23 June 1916

4–6 June

Russian lines and gains by 7 June
Austrian /German lines
Russian attacks
Russian gains, 5 June (pm)

7–10 June

Russian attacks
Russian gains

11–23 June

Russian attacks
German/Austrian counter-attacks
Russian gains

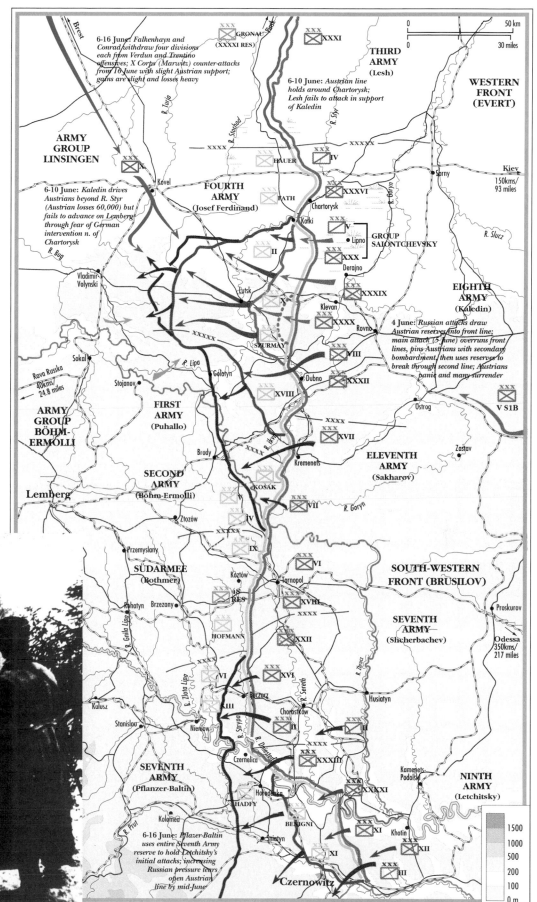

6-16 June: Falkenhayn and Conrad withdraw four divisions each from Verdun and Trentino offensives; X Corps (Marwitz) counter-attacks from 16 June with slight Austrian support; gains are slight and losses heavy

6-10 June: Austrian line holds around Chartorysk; Lesh fails to attack in support of Kaledin

6-10 June: Kaledin drives Austrians beyond R. Styr (Austrian losses 60,000) but fails to advance on Lemberg through fear of German intervention n. of Chartorysk

4 June: Russian attacks draw Austrian reserves into front line; main attack (5 June) overruns front lines, pins Austrians with secondary bombardment, then uses reserves to break through second line; Austrians panic and many surrender

6-16 June: Pflazer-Baltin uses entire Seventh Army reserve to hold Letchitsky's initial attacks; increasing Russian pressure tears open Austrian line by mid-June

Russian heavy artillery in action in a wood near Lake Naroch in March 1916. Huge quantities of ammunition were expended to little effect in the attempt to break the German lines. In June, Brusilov's artillery bombardment, planned in minute detail, was devastatingly effective against the Austrians.

The Somme The Allied offensive, July 1916

Allied plans for a major offensive astride the River Somme in the summer of 1916 were disrupted by Falkenhayn's attack at Verdun in February. German pressure on the French, the Austrian Trentino offensive in Italy (page 94) and the failure of the Russian Lake Naroch offensive (page 98) gave Haig little choice but to reorganize the attack as a largely British effort, despite concerns over the battle-readiness of the British "New Armies".

The first day

To compensate as far as possible for the lack of experience of many of the troops involved, British planners developed a tactical timetable for the assault, minimizing the need for local initiative. Artillery preparation was very detailed, involving five days of intensive bombardment: in the final 65 minutes before zero hour, no fewer than 224,221 shells were fired and ten huge mines detonated on a 25-mile front.

Fourth Army's detailed orders stipulated an advance across no-man's land at a pace of 100yds/91m a minute, with a one-minute interval between successive battalions, and in close formation. Much of the German front remained unbroken by the bombardment and, as it ceased, troops rushed out of their deep shelters to re-man their machine guns. They were astonished to find themselves confronted with so easy and steady a target.

Haig's plans had called, on the first day, for the penetration of the German front from Serre in the north to Maricourt in the south. In the second phase, he planned to take the high ground between Bapaume and Guinchy, followed by a breakthrough toward Arras and a general advance eastward in the direction of Cambrai.

Instead, the attacking troops were cut down in their thousands, many not even getting past their own wire. British losses, an hour after the attack began, were in the region of 30,000. By nightfall the British Army had lost some 60,000 men, the greatest loss in one day in its history.

Gains were insignificant. The headway made by the French and by right wing British units (Map 1) were more than offset to the north, where all reports were of failure. With six divisions, the Germans had held off a heroic but grotesquely wasteful attack by a total of 18 Allied divisions. Thus enabling the Germans to bring

up further divisions to strenghen the front.

The follow-up phase

Despite the losses of the first day, Haig remained confident and determined on continued attack. As German reinforcements rushed to the front (Falkenhayn cancelled all further offensives at Verdun on 2 July), Fourth Army and the French Sixth Army made a succession of further costly pushes. On 13–14 July the German second line was finally broken around Bezantin Ridge, but the South African Brigade was forced back from Delville Wood by the 20th, and German counter-attacks limited any further advance. The Anzac Corps forced their way into Pozières village on the 23rd as Haig launched his second major offensive, aimed at clearing Pozières Ridge.

The lull before the storm: General de Lisle, divisional commander addressing the 1st Lancashire Fusiliers, before the opening of the Somme offensive on 1 July. Soldiers like these would advance carrying 66 pounds of equipment, within 12 hours of the offensive beginning typically of the infantry battalions involved 60% of the officers and 40% of the men would become casualties.

Tunnels were dug beneath ten strongpoints in the German front line before the attack. This picture, taken at Hawthorn Ridge, Beaumont Hamel, shows the detonation of 18 tons of explosive beneath a German redoubt some 500 yds/460m in front of the British line 10 minutes before zero hour.

" There came an order that you must not stop to help a wounded comrade during an attack. Those that did were sitting targets for enemy machine-gunners and consequently nobody reached the objective. Nobody knew what was happening or was supposed to happen."

Corporal H. Diffey, 15th Battalion, Royal Welsh Fusiliers

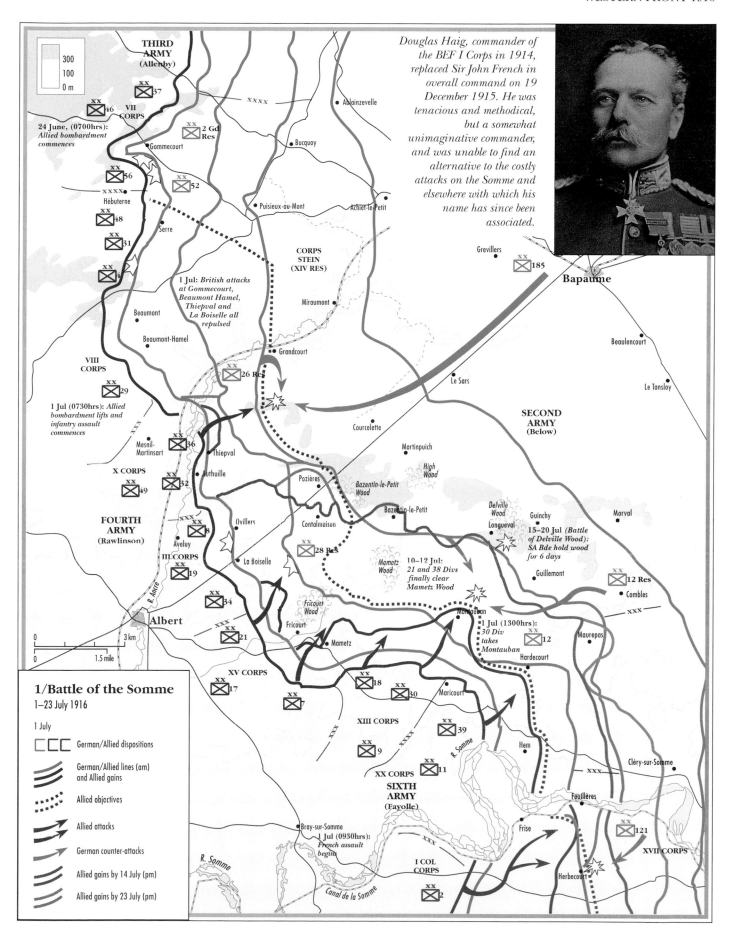

THIRD ARMY (Allenby)

300
100
0 m

XX 37

XX 46 **VII CORPS**

24 June, (0700hrs): *Allied bombardment commences*

XX 2 Gd Res

Gommecourt

Ablainzevelle

Bucquoy

XX 56

XXXX

Hébuterne

XX 52

Puisieux-au-Mont

Achiet-le-Petit

XX 48

Serre

XX 31

CORPS STEIN (XIV RES)

XX 4

1 Jul: *British attacks at Gommecourt, Beaumont Hamel, Thiepval and La Boiselle all repulsed*

Miraumont

Grevillers

XX 185

Bapaume

Beaumont

Beaumont-Hamel

Grandcourt

Beaulencourt

VIII CORPS

XX 26 Res

Le Sars

Le Tansloy

XX 29

1 Jul (0730hrs): *Allied bombardment lifts and infantry assault commences*

XXX

Mesnil-Martinsart

XX 36

Thiepval

Courcelette

SECOND ARMY (Below)

Martinpuich

X CORPS

XX 49

XX 32

Authuille

Pozières

High Wood

Bazentin-le-Petit Wood

Bazentin-le-Petit

Delville Wood

Guinchy

Morval

15–20 Jul *(Battle of Delville Wood): SA Bde hold wood for 6 days*

Longueval

FOURTH ARMY (Rawlinson)

XXX

XX 8

Ovillers

Contalmaison

XX 28 Res

Mametz Wood

10–12 Jul: *21 and 38 Divs finally clear Mametz Wood*

Guillemont

XX 12 Res

Combles

Aveluy

II CORPS

XX 19

La Boiselle

XX 34

Fricourt Wood

Montauban

1 Jul (1300hrs): *30 Div takes Montauban*

Maurepas

Albert

0   3 km

0   1.5 mile

Fricourt

Mametz

XX 21

XV CORPS

XX 17

XX 7

XX 18

XX 30

Maricourt

XX 12

Hardecourt

Hem

Cléry-sur-Somme

1/Battle of the Somme
1–23 July 1916

1 July

⊏⊏⊏ German/Allied dispositions

German/Allied lines (am) and Allied gains

Allied objectives

Allied attacks

German counter-attacks

Allied gains by 14 July (pm)

Allied gains by 23 July (pm)

XIII CORPS

XX 39

XX 9

XX CORPS

XX 11

SIXTH ARMY (Fayolle)

R. Somme

Feuillères

Frise

XX 121

Bray-sur-Somme

1 Jul (0930hrs): *French assault begins*

R. Somme

I COL CORPS

XX 2

XVII CORPS

Herbecourt

Canal de la Somme

Douglas Haig, commander of the BEF I Corps in 1914, replaced Sir John French in overall command on 19 December 1915. He was tenacious and methodical, but a somewhat unimaginative commander, and was unable to find an alternative to the costly attacks on the Somme and elsewhere with which his name has since been associated.

Brusilov The Offensive Collapses June – September 1916

The Stavka, Russia's allies and the Central Powers were alike astonished by Brusilov's seemingly unstoppable advance (pages 98–9). The proposed main Russian offensive towards Vilna now became of secondary importance, and reinforcements, weaponry and supplies were hastened to Brusilov's front. Here again Russian objectives were to be inhibited by the inadequate railway system, so that troops and supplies, though available, could not be transported in sufficient numbers to provide the support necessary to maintain the impetus of Brusilov's attack or affect its outcome.

The offensive falters

Early in July, an ominous sign emerged. Though the Austrians were falling back in disarray, German formations were retreating with discipline. Bothmer's Südarmee, sited between the Russian Eleventh and Seventh armies, and Linsingen's forces opposite the Russian right near Kovel both held up Brusilov's advance. The situation for the Central Powers nevertheless remained perilous. Falkenhayn was obliged to gather reinforcements from wherever he could, including four divisions from the west, where they were sorely needed, while Conrad had no option but to call off his offensive in the Trentino and return to the Eastern Front troops he had earlier withdrawn.

By mid-July , therefore,the balance of forces on Brusilov's front had changed. The efficient German and Austrian railroad network had enabled reinforcements to be brought up rapidly, and some were used to counter-attack on the northern flank of Brusilov's advance. This clearly was the moment for the Russian commander to call a halt, but he was urged on by the Russian high command. Throughout July and into August he pressed forward, while other Russian attacks were made to the north of his armies. In the south, Letchitsky's troops reached the Carpathian Mountains by the end of August, but had advanced so far that replenishment of men and material became almost impossible. The advance by Kaledin and Sakharov to the north had stalled in the face of enemy rein-forcements. By September all further Russian progress was impossible.

Consequences

The Brusilov offensive, at first brilliantly and

Russian troops in a captured German trench; the Brusilov offensive saw their greatest success against Germans and Austrians alike. Russian infantrymen were equipped with two 30-round ammunition pouches worn either side of the belt buckle, an entrenching tool, a haversack and canteen worn over the right shoulder and an ammunition bandolier over the left, over which a greatcoat containing a spare pair of boots and a section of tent was rolled. The standard rifle, with a sword bayonet fixed at all times on active service, was the 7.62mm 1891 Moisin-Nagant, with a 5-round magazine, weighing almost nine pounds. The Russian supply organization was stretched to breaking point and its ability to deliver food and equipment to the troops on the front line was instrumental in lowering their moral.

unexpectedly successful, in fact marked a fatal reverse. The offensive was the most competent Russian operation of the war and strategically it weakened the offensives of the Central Powers at Verdun and in the Trentino; it contributed to the downfall of Falkenhayn and of Conrad, and effectively eliminated Austria as a major military power (after the offensive, Austria was left with no option but to comply with German strategic direction). Austrian losses were greater, but the Russians lost a million men, a sacrifice without lasting reward that was ultimately beyond the endurance even of Russian soldiers. Romania's entry into the war at the end of August (pages 104–5) served only to saddle the Russian high command with an unwanted extra responsibility, which further reduced the resources available for Brusilov. These factors, and the growing difficulties in obtaining weapons and supplies, sapped the will of Russian troops to attack. Even before the offensive opened, the Russian Army had sustained more than five million casualties, and the additional losses led to unrest and indiscipline. Soon the majority of troops were no longer prepared to support the war. The Brusilov offensive did not cause the Russian Revolution, but it may be argued that the failure of the offensive made the Revolution possible.

"The German people exhibited such astounding energy, doggedness, sturdy patriotism, courage, endurance, discipline, and readiness to die for their country that, as a soldier, I cannot but salute them. They fought with lion -like bravery and an amazing tenacity against the whole world."

**Gen. Aleksi Brusilov,
" A Soldier's Notebook"**

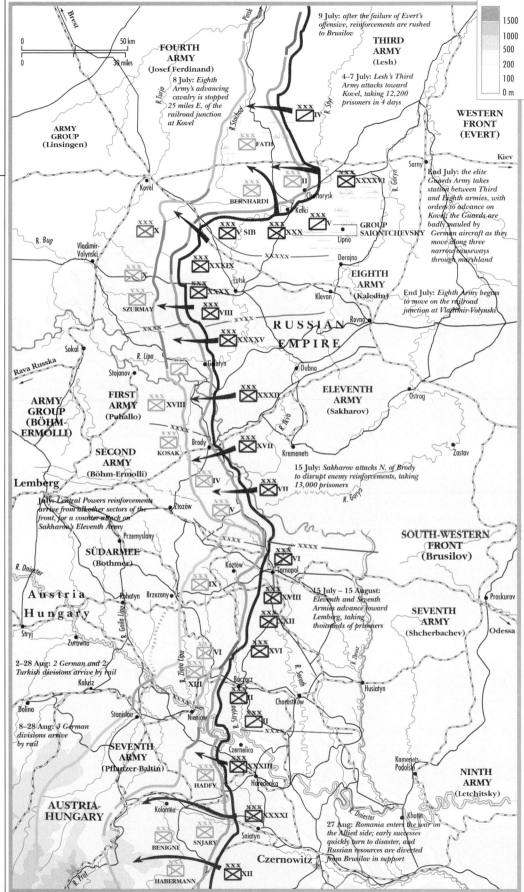

1/Brusilov II
23 June – 15 September 1916

Russian lines, 23 June

Austrian /German lines, 23 June

Austrian /German lines, 30 July

Austrian /German lines, 31 Aug

Austrian/German lines, 15 Sept

Russian attacks,
23 June – 30 july

Between June and September
1916 bitter criticism was levelled
at the Tsar and his government
for their incompetance in the
handling of the war. Increasing
political instability was neglected
in the rapid rise and fall of the
Tsar's ministers. General
Polivanov, Minister of War, was
one of the Russian army's most
able administrators but his efforts
to reorganise the army and his
opposition to the ascending of
Rasputin brought about his
dismissal in early 1916.

Romania September 1915 – January 1917

Romania had remained neutral since the beginning of the war, but had gradually moved toward intervention on the Allied side, largely in the hope of territorial gain in Transylvania.

In the summer of 1916 the moment seemed auspicious. The Germans had failed at Verdun (page 92) and were sorely stretched on the Somme (page 100); in the east, Italy had won the sixth Battle of the Isonzo (page 74) and the Brusilov Offensive (page 98) had come close to knocking Austria out of the war altogether. Russian help, it seemed, would be available if needed, and any response by the Central Powers limited. Moreover, the Romanian army had recently been doubled in size: in 1916 it numbered some 564,000 men, though both equipment and training were poor. War was declared on 27 August, and Transylvania was invaded immediately, against weak Austrian defenses.

The campaign
The Germans had long foreseen Romanian intervention, and now prepared a powerful response, stripping all other fronts of reserves. The Austrian First and German–Austrian Ninth armies, under the overall command of Falkenhayn (demoted from chief of staff after his failure at Verdun) threw back the invaders with a sharp counter-offensive at Hermannstadt and Kronstadt. Meanwhile the German-reinforced Bulgarian Danube Army Group, under Mackensen, invaded Dobruja and drove the Romanian, Russian and Serbian defenders northward.

Falkenhayn's offensive toward Bucharest was stopped at the passes, but Averescu bungled a counter-blow at Mackensen. German reinforcements under Kühne then swept into Walachia, while Mackensen sent Kosch's troops across the Danube in Culcer's rear. The German-led armies routed Culcer, then defeated Averescu at the Arges River. Bucharest fell on 6 December. Russian assistance to Romania throughout the campaign had been grudging and ineffective.

Consequences
By January, Romanian forces had retreated, with losses of 350,000, into Moldavia, where they were to some extent protected by their Russian ally. A British-organized sabotage operation denied much of Romania's oil and grain to the Central Powers, but a major threat to Austria-Hungary had been neutralized within three months.

A column of Romanian infantry advances up a hillside in late 1916. Their courage was no match for the experience and superior equipment of the Germans and Austrians.

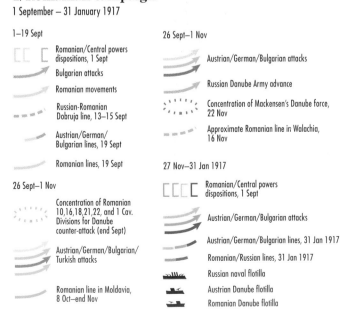

1/Romanian campaign
1 September – 31 January 1917

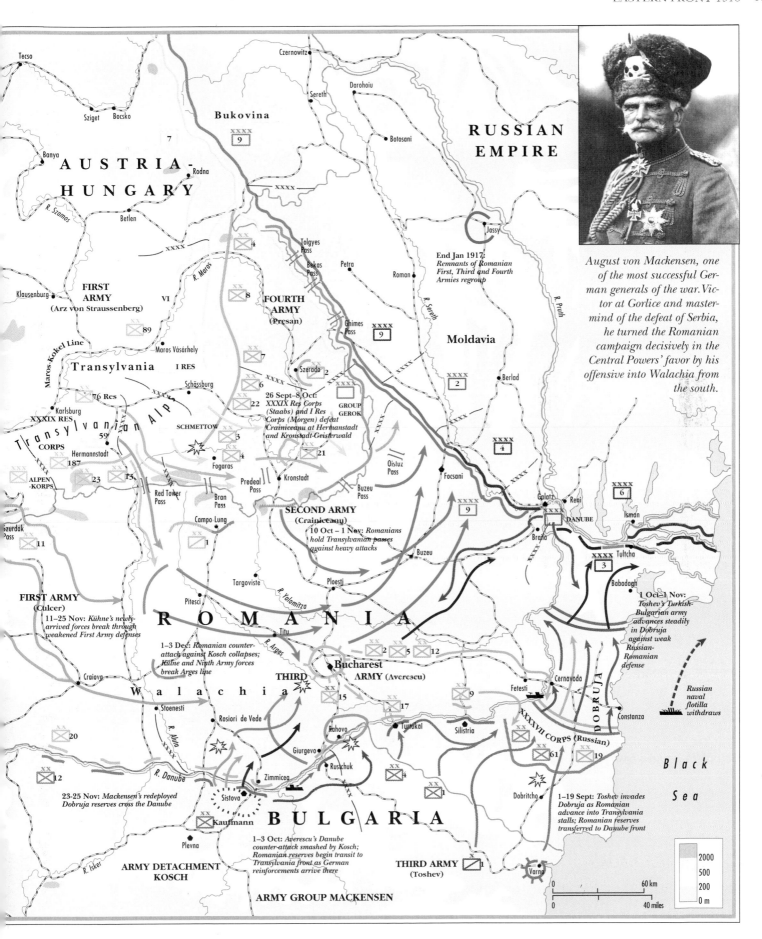

Tecso
Sziget • Bocsko
Banya
Rodna
Betlen
R. Szamos

AUSTRIA-HUNGARY

Bukovina
XXXX 9
7
Czernowitz
Sereth
Darohoiu
Botosani
Roman
Petra
R. Sereth

RUSSIAN EMPIRE

Jassy

End Jan 1917:
Remnants of Romanian First, Third and Fourth Armies regroup

August von Mackensen, one of the most successful German generals of the war. Victor at Gorlice and mastermind of the defeat of Serbia, he turned the Romanian campaign decisively in the Central Powers' favor by his offensive into Walachia from the south.

Klausenburg
FIRST ARMY
(Arz von Straussenberg)
VI
XXXX
XX 4
Tolgyes Pass
Bekas Pass
XX 8
FOURTH ARMY
(Presan)
XXXX 9
Ghimes Pass
Moldavia
Berlad
XXXX 2
R. Pruth

Maros-Kokel Line
XX 89
Maros Vásárhely
Transylvania
I RES
XX 7
Szereda
XX 6
XX 22
Schässburg
76 Res
XXXIX RES
Karlsburg
CORPS
59
SCHMETTOW XX 3
26 Sept–8 Oct: *XXXIX Res Corps (Staabs) and I Res Corps (Morgen) defeat Crainiceanu at Hermannstadt and Kronstadt-Geisterwald*
XX 4
XX 21
GROUP GEROK
XXXX 4
XXXX 9

Hermannstadt
187
ALPEN-KORPS
XX 23
XX 13
Red Tower Pass
Fogaras
XX 4
Predeal Pass
Kronstadt
Oisluz Pass
Focsani
Galatz
Reni
Isman
XXXX 6

szurdak Pass
XX 11
Bran Pass
Campo-Lung
XX 1
SECOND ARMY
(Crainiceanu)
10 Oct–1 Nov: *Romanians hold Transylvanian passes against heavy attacks*
Buzeu Pass
Buzeu
DANUBE
Braila
Tultcha
XXXX 3
Babadagh

FIRST ARMY
(Culcer)
11–25 Nov: *Kühne's newly-arrived forces break through weakened First Army defenses*
Targoviste
Pitesci
ROMANIA
Titu
R. Valamitza
Ploesti
Cernavoda
Fetesti

1 Oct–1 Nov: *Toshev's Turkish-Bulgarian army advances steadily in Dobruja against weak Russian-Romanian defense*

Craiova
1–3 Dec: *Romanian counter-attack against Kosch collapses; Kühne and Ninth Army forces break Arges line*
R. Arges
Bucharest
THIRD ARMY (Averescu)
XX 2 XX 5 XX 12
XX 15
XX 17
XX 9
XXXVII CORPS (Russian)
XX 61 XX 19
Constanza
DOBRUJA

Russian naval flotilla withdraws

Walachia
Stoenesti
Rosiori de Vede
Rahova
Giurgevo
Turtukal
Silistria
Zimnicea
XX 20
XX 12
R. Aluta
R. Danube
Ruschuk
XX 4
XX 1
Dobritcha

1–19 Sept: *Toshev invades Dobruja as Romanian advance into Transylvania stalls; Romanian reserves transferred to Danube front*

Black Sea

23–25 Nov: *Mackensen's redeployed Dobruja reserves cross the Danube*
Sistova
XX Kaufmann
BULGARIA
Plevna
R. Isker
ARMY DETACHMENT KOSCH
1–3 Oct: *Averescu's Danube counter-attack smashed by Kosch; Romanian reserves begin transit to Transylvania front as German reinforcements arrive there*
THIRD ARMY (Toshev)
XX 1
Varna

ARMY GROUP MACKENSEN

2000
500
200
0 m

0   60 km
0   40 miles

The Somme: War of Attrition July – November 1916

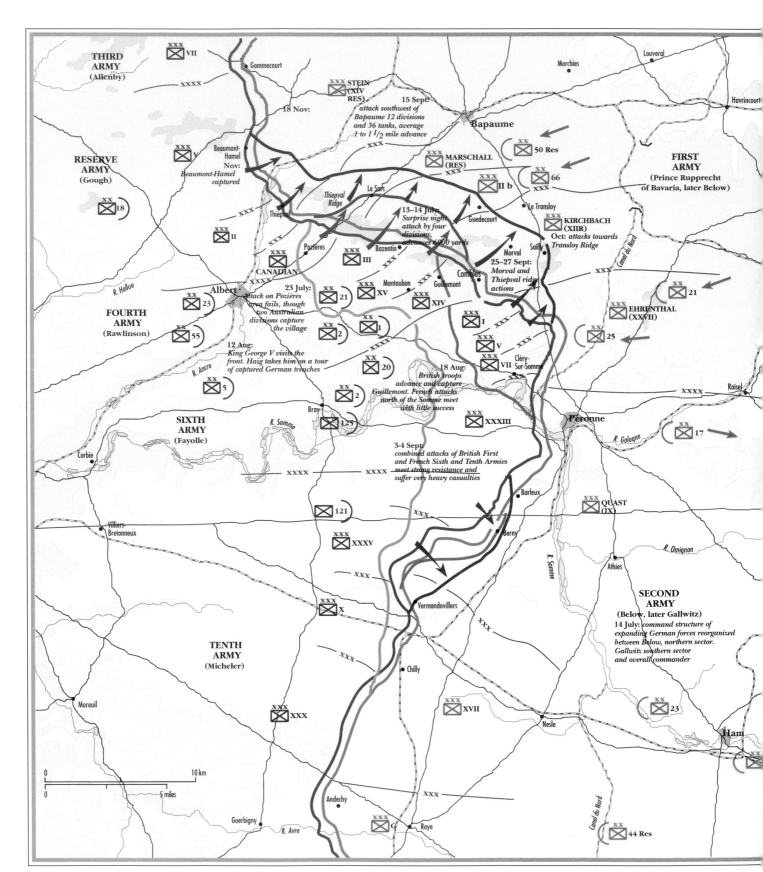

THIRD ARMY
(Allenby)

Gommecourt

18 Nov:

RESERVE ARMY
(Gough)

Beaumont-Hamel
Nov:
Beaumont-Hamel captured

XXX V

XX 18

XXX II

STEIN (XIV RES)
15 Sept:
attack southwest of Bapaume 12 divisions and 36 tanks, average 1 to 1½ mile advance

Bapaume

MARSCHALL (RES)

Thiepval Ridge

Le Sars

II b

50 Res

66

FIRST ARMY
(Prince Rupprecht of Bavaria, later Below)

Thiepval

13–14 July:
Surprise night attack by four divisions, advances 6000 yards

Guedecourt

Le Transloy

KIRCHBACH (XIIR)
Oct: *attacks towards Transloy Ridge*

Pozières

Bazentin

Morval

Sailly

21

Albert
23 July:
Attack on Pozières area fails, though two Australian divisions capture the village

XXX II

III

Montauban

Guillemont

Combles

25–27 Sept:
Morval and Thiepval ridge actions

EHRENTHAL (XXVII)

XX 21

FOURTH ARMY
(Rawlinson)

XX 23

XX 55

XX 21

XV

XIV

I

V

25

R. Hallue

12 Aug:
King George V visits the front. Haig takes him on a tour of captured German trenches

XX 2

XX 1

VII

Cléry-Sur-Somme

CANADIAN

R. Ancre

XX 5

XX 20

18 Aug:
British troops advance and capture Guillemont. French attacks north of the Somme meet with little success

Péronne

XX 17

Bray

XX 2

XXXIII

R. Gologne

Corbie

R. Somme

XX 125

3–4 Sept:
combined attacks of British First and French Sixth and Tenth Armies meet strong resistance and suffer very heavy casualties

Roisel

SIXTH ARMY
(Fayolle)

Barleux

QUAST (IX)

R. Omignon

Athies

Villiers-Bretonneux

121

Berny

XXXV

Vermandovillers

R. Somme

SECOND ARMY
(Below, later Gallwitz)
14 July: *command structure of expanding German forces reorganized between Below, northern sector. Gallwitz southern sector and overall commander*

TENTH ARMY
(Micheler)

X

Chilly

Moreuil

XVII

Nesle

23

XXX

Ham

10 km

5 miles

Guerbigny

R. Avre

Andechy

G

Roye

Canal du Nord

44 Res

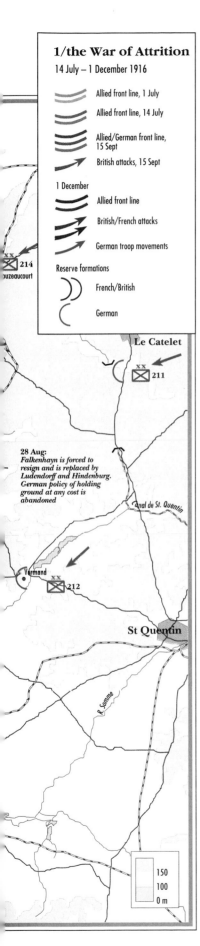

1/the War of Attrition
14 July – 1 December 1916

Allied front line, 1 July

Allied front line, 14 July

Allied/German front line, 15 Sept

British attacks, 15 Sept

1 December

Allied front line

British/French attacks

German troop movements

Reserve formations

French/British

German

⊠ 214
ouzeaucourt

Le Catelet

⊠ 211

28 Aug:
Falkenhayn is forced to resign and is replaced by Ludendorff and Hindenburg. German policy of holding ground at any cost is abandoned

Canal de St. Quentin

Vermand

⊠ 212

St Quentin

R. Somme

150
100
0 m

Despite the dreadful losses on 1 July, Haig still continued to press forward with limited attacks. Falkenhayn, determined to halt any British advance, began moving up troops from the Verdun sector. To this extent, and this only, Haig quickly accomplished at least one objective of his offensive.

The continuing battle

A British night attack on 13 July broke the German second line. Cavalry were thrown into the gap – the last time horse cavalry was used en-masse in western Europe – but were savaged by machine gun fire. Other reserves were slow to come up and the cavalry became swamped by a German counter-attack. On 20 July a new offensive by 17 British and French divisions was launched on the line Pozières-Foucaucourt. A few hundred yards were taken but at heavy cost in life. By the end of July an advance by the British of about two and a half miles had been made on a front less than two miles wide.

The battle, never dormant, erupted again on a great scale on 15 September, when Haig attacked southwest of Bapaume. By now, reports from senior commanders, hitherto confident, were becoming less sanguine, for it was evident to all that the British, despite pushing forward with undiminished courage, were suffering a disaster of gruesome proportions, with hundreds of thousands of men dying for little territorial, and no strategic, gain.

Tanks

Faced with the prospect of disaster, Haig decided to employ a new British invention for the first time - the tank. When Haig made this decision, only 60 of the original 150 machines had been secretly shipped to France. Of that number, only 49 were actually employed. Mechanical failings in this early model reduced the total further, so that a mere 32 reached the starting line. Of these, nine broke down during the action and five became immobilized in battlefield craters. The 18 effective tanks rendered useful aid, notably in capturing Flers, but the greater prize of a breakthrough eluded them. The territorial gains and hundreds of prisoners taken hardly offset the premature revelation to the Germans of the new weapon.

Throughout what remained of the autumn, bad weather hampered Haig's aggressive operations, but the Somme offensive dragged on until, with the advent of winter rain in mid-November, exhausted and hungry men could no longer drag themselves through the deepening mud. The campaign died away, leaving only disappointment and despair.

Consequences and losses

When the battle petered out in mid-November, after four and a half months of continuous attack, the Allies had advanced only a little more than eight miles on a 20-mile front. By then the BEF was astride the ridge originally occupied by the Germans.

For these gains the British lost some 420,000 men, the French 195,000 and the Germans a shocking total of 650,000, of whom a high proportion were pre-war officers and noncommissioned officers.

In the opinion of the German High Command, the Somme was the bloody graveyard of the German Army. Haig was more sanguine, for Allies and Germans alike, idealism perished on the Somme. Men in the trenches on both sides began to lose faith in their leaders, many even in the cause for which they fought; only one loyalty remained undiminished – that due to their comrades.

"We were in the parapets, waiting to go over and waiting for the tank. We heard the chunk, chunk, chunk, chunk, *then silence! The tank never came."*

Private Charles Cole,
1st Battalion, Coldstream Guards

A British army chaplain takes the names of both British and German wounded after the attack on Pozières Ridge, 30 July 1916.

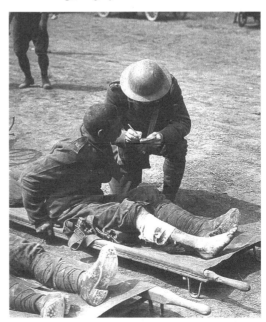

Verdun: The French Counter-attack June – December 1916

The need to clear the west bank of the Meuse and to defeat a French counter-attack around Douaumont on 22–3 May prevented Crown Prince Wilhelm's Fifth Army from renewing its offensive on the east bank until the beginning of June. Within another week, however, the almost flattened Fort Vaux, smallest of the forts ringing Verdun, had fallen, and Fifth Army had advanced to Thiaumont, almost to Pétain's designated last line of defense.

By now, however, the German commanders, other than Falkenhayn himself, were beginning to lose their nerve. The opening of the Brusilov Offensive (page 98) forced a suspension of German offensive operations, and on 11 June, four days after the fall of Fort Vaux, Pétain had asked Joffre to bring forward the Allied offensive (now to be largely British, for French forces had be re-routed to Verdun) on the Somme. Despite German use on 20 June of a new form of Diphosgene gas shell, which temporarily paralyzed French artillery support and allowed the Germans to come within attacking distance of Verdun itself, the crisis point had now passed.

The counter-offensive

On 24 June, learning of the opening British barrage on the Somme, Falkenhayn ceased ammunition and troop reinforcements to Verdun. The summer was to pass with a series of local attacks and counter-attacks which saw Thiaumont change hands sixteen times, but from mid-July Verdun was safe. From the end of August, the German high command (dominated by Hindenburg and Ludendorff, following Falkenhayn's demotion on the 28th) sought only to limit German defensive commitments, while French pressure slowly intensified.

During the Fall, the French regained all the territory they had earlier lost, making extensive

---

"I was now convinced, after the stubborn to-and-fro contest for every foot of ground… that although we had more than once changed our methods of attack, a decisive success at Verdun could only be assured at the price of heavy sacrifices, out of all proportion to the desired gains."

**Crown Prince Wilhelm,
Commander of the German Fifth Army**

"Every sign of humanity has been swept away. The woods and roads have vanished like chalk wiped from a blackboard; of the villages nothing remains but grey smears. During heavy bombardments and attacks I have seen shells falling like rain."

**An unknown Allied airman
commenting on the aerial view of Verdun**

---

use of a new scheme of co-operation between artillery and infantry based on a creeping barrage designed to keep the German defenders under cover almost to the moment at which French infantry overran their positions. On one day alone, 24 October, a dashing attack retook not only Fort Douaumont but also ground that the Germans had taken four months to capture. Fort Vaux was recaptured on 2 November, and the final French offensive on 15 December pushed the front lines back virtually to their positions of the preceding February.

Consequences and losses

In 10 months of fighting, some 37 million shells, German and French, were fired. A reasonable estimate of human loss is some 377,000 French and 337,000 Germans. Up to 40 German divisions and up to two-thirds of the entire French Army's infantry were employed at some time at Verdun, with the result that almost nobody in France – and few in Germany – escaped some sort of exposure to the horror of the battle. Falkenhayn himself was the most significant casualty on the German side; on the French side, Joffre's removal for political reasons in December 1916 resulted in the elevation of Robert Nivelle, hero of the recapture of Douaumont and obsessive proponent of the creeping artillery barrage, to supreme command.

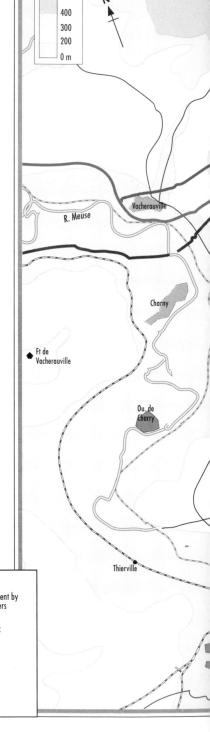

1/Verdun
1 September – 16 December 1916

- •••••• German front line, 1 June
- ⌒ German front line, 24 Oct
- ⌒ French front line, 24 Oct (AM) and gains by PM
- ➤ French attacks, 24 Oct

- ✻ Long-range bombardment by French 400mm howitzers
- ⌒ French gains by 16 Dec
- ⬢ Major fort/ Major ouvrage
- ⬟ fort
- ⬠ Ouvrage

Map labels: Samogneux, Vacherauville, R. Meuse, Charny, Ft de Vacherauville, Ou. de Charny, Thierville; elevation scale 400 / 300 / 200 / 0 m; N (north arrow)

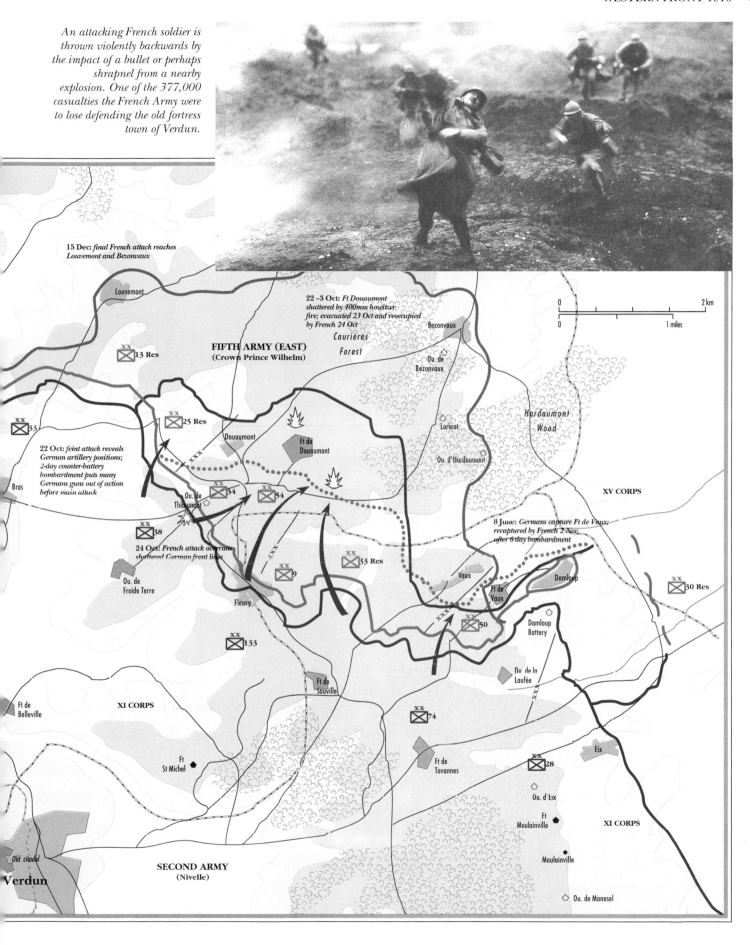

An attacking French soldier is thrown violently backwards by the impact of a bullet or perhaps shrapnel from a nearby explosion. One of the 377,000 casualties the French Army were to lose defending the old fortress town of Verdun.

15 Dec: *final French attack reaches Louvemont and Bezonvaux*

Louvemont

22–3 Oct: *Ft Douaumont shattered by 400mm howitzer fire; evacuated 23 Oct and reoccupied by French 24 Oct*

Bezonvaux

0   2 km
0   1 miles

XX 13 Res

FIFTH ARMY (EAST)
(Crown Prince Wilhelm)

Caurières Forest

Ou. de Bézonvaux

XX 33

XX 25 Res

Douaumont

Ft de Douaumont

Lorient

Hardaumont Wood

22 Oct: *feint attack reveals German artillery positions; 2-day counter-battery bombardment puts many Germans guns out of action before main attack*

Bras

Ou. de Thiaumont

XX 54

XX 54

Ou. d'Hardaumont

XV CORPS

XX 38

24 Oct: *French attack overruns shattered German front lines*

8 June: *Germans capture Ft de Vaux; recaptured by French 2 Nov after 6 day bombardment*

Ou. de Froide Terre

XX 9

XX 33 Res

Vaux

Damloup

XX 30 Res

Fleury

Ft de Vaux

Damloup Battery

XX 50

XX 133

Ou. de la Laufée

Ft de Souville

Ft de Belleville

XI CORPS

XX 74

Ft St Michel

Eix

XX 28

Ft de Tavannes

Ou. d'Eix

Old citadel

Verdun

SECOND ARMY
(Nivelle)

Ft Moulainville

XI CORPS

Moulainville

Ou. de Manesel

One of over a million American soldiers to arrive in Europe.

PART IV
1917

Nineteen-seventeen was a watershed in military history, in the history of Europe and of the World. At its outset any earlier commander would have recognized the scene: great states, motivated by ambitions and fears, forming coalitions, not for the destruction of other states but for supremacy or at least safety. At the year's end all would be changed and foreign to such a commander. In the east, Bolshevism, an entirely new concept, would have arisen, while westward a new, non-European nation – the United States – industrially and numerically growing toward a strength equal to that of all industrialized European nations combined, was able, and ultimately prepared, to intervene in European affairs. Further, the commander would have been astonished by the advent of new weaponry springing from industrial technology – notably, massed production of submarines and tanks.

Political and military changes in leadership greatly affected strategy in the west. Ludendorff, with the support of Hindenburg and with the Kaiser's approval, advocated inactivity in the west while mounting a great blow against Italy, to knock her out of the war. To this end methodically and in secret, a new defensive position, called by the Allies the "Hindenburg Line" and by the Germans the "Siegfried Line", had been constructed some 20 miles to the rear of the front line to shorten the over-stretched German front. This was built to great strength across the line Lens-Noyon-Reims, to which German forces retreated in good order, the operation being completed by early April. In the process, German forces virtually denuded the area of life – yet a further example in Allied eyes and propaganda, of German ruthlessness.

Unrestricted U-boat warfare
Despite provocation over two years, since the sinking by a U-boat of the *Lusitania* in May 1915, the American president, Woodrow Wilson, had continually made peace overtures, of which he envisaged himself the arbiter – without, it would seem, under-

standing the psychology of the peoples at war, now no longer thinking in terms of governmental policies but driven by an almost primitive group, and national, instinct. Thus in Great Britain, Lord Lansdowne, once Foreign Secretary, incurred national opprobrium when he advocated a negotiated peace in a letter in the *Daily Telegraph* (*The Times* had earlier refused to publish it). Tentative German peace feelers, seen by the Allies, with some justification, as devious, mere subterfuges to retain at least some of their seized land, were likewise abruptly dismissed. The time for negotiations had passed, for Lloyd George had achieved the Premiership on the assumption that he would prosecute the war with more vigor and efficiency than Asquith; in France,

British and French troops man a trench on the Western Front, 1917. Living in conditions of appalling hardship and infested with lice their disillusionment was increased by the failures at Passchendaele and the Nivelle Offensive

Neville proclaimed himself confident of victory, while in Germany Ludendorff's growing ascendency likewise precluded compromise.

The German High Command was now faced with an awesome decision, over which heated debates erupted. Their U-boat fleet had expanded greatly since operations were abated in 1915 for fear of inducing American intervention. In 1917, however, Germany had at hand a weapon that could, if used with ruthlessness, sink so much Allied shipping as to starve Great Britain into submission and thereby cause Allied collapse. But unrestricted U-boat activity would assuredly bring America into the war. It was a gamble for the highest stakes: Germany took it when on 31 January 1917, she proclaimed unrestricted U-boat warfare while conducting covert negotiations for a German–Mexican (and possibly Japanese) alliance. On 3 February the inevitable happened: the U.S.A. severed relations with Germany, as shortly did some Latin American nations (Brazil, Bolivia, Peru and others), followed by China on 11 March. The "Zimmermann Note" further inflamed American opinion. On 13 March President Wilson authorized the arming in self-defense of all vessels passing through war zones. Following the sinking of a number of American ships by German U-boats, Wilson, having secured the authority of Congress, declared war on Germany on 6 April. Germany now had time only, and limited time, to resolve matters in Europe before the might of American munitions and manpower were thrown into the conflict against her.

Western Front

By 5 April German armies in the west were safely ensconced in and behind their Hindenburg Line, in readiness for any Allied frontal attacks. The first came on 9 April at Arras, when the British First (Horne) and Third (Allenby) armies, following an intense bombardment after gaining air superiority struck at the German Sixth Army (von Falkenhausen) as a preliminary to the Nivelle Offensive. Canadian troops took Vimy Ridge (page 124) but the British Fifth Army (Gough) to the south made only limited progress. Although the British won a tactical success no breakthrough was achieved. By 15 April, when the advance had been halted, the British had lost some 84,000 men, the Germans about 10,000 fewer.

Nivelle's offensive (page 122), opening on 16 April on a front of 40 miles between Soissons and Reims with the object of taking the ridges of the Chemin des Dames, comprised some 1,200,000 men and 7,000 guns. The Germans, forewarned by Nivelle's boasts, were ready for them. Immediately before the attack, the Germans gained air superiority and then destroyed French tanks moving into position. The failure, one of the war's most avoidable, cost the French some 120,000 casualties in five days without achieving Nivelle's promise of a breakthrough and victory. From this pointless expenditure of life arose the outbreak of mutinies in the French Army, which were quelled by Pétain (who replaced the discredited Nivelle on 15 May) by the end of the month.

In June, Haig launched a further attack in Flanders to remove German pressure on the French. As a preliminary to this offensive in the Ypres salient, Plumer and his Second Army were ordered to take Messines Ridge, which was achieved in masterly fashion (page 126). This victory gave Haig room to launch his long cherished offensive on 31 July in Flanders, in the Third Battle of Ypres or Passchendaele (page 128). The attacks, which continued into November, petered out in the rain and mud, made more impassable by heavy and prolonged bombardment. During these operations, the Germans used mustard gas for the first time. By the end of the first week of November, Haig had deepened the Ypres salient by about five miles; for this negligible achievement, the British sustained some 300,000 casualties, the supporting French some 8,500.

Haig undaunted, resolved to attack elsewhere to give the French armies further time to recover from the mutinies. On 20 November, the British Third Army (Byng) struck the German Second Army (Marwitz) at Cambrai, achieving complete surprise by the use of tanks in mass for the first time (page 138). Reserves, both of men and, crucially, tanks were inadequate and the breakthrough on a six-mile front could not be exploited.

Eastern Front

Russian disintegration, following the losses sustained in the Brusilov Offensive (page 102), began on 12 March with the mutiny of the Petrograd gar-

During the last of General Brusilov's offensives Russian troops collect in the town of Chernowitz in Galicia

rison. It quickly gathered pace. A Provisional Government was established, Nicholas II abdicated, military discipline began to break down. Mutinous soldiers and sailors murdered their officers or deprived them of their authority. Bolshevik agitators fanned the flames. Germany temporarily ceased all aggressive moves to prevent Russians reuniting in defense of their homeland.

Alexander Kerensky, appointed War Minister on 16 May, and later Prime Minister, tried to stage an offensive on the Galician Front, led again by Brusilov. Despite achieving early, limited gains, the attacks quickly succumbed as German resistance stiffened. Following German counter-attacks and in the north, their capture of Riga, the Russian Army disintegrated. Chaos ensued and, following the Bolshevik Revolution on 7 November, Lenin and Trotsky seized power and began negotiating peace terms with Germany. Russia was effectively out of the war.

Italian Front

The Italians, fearing an Austrian attack following growing Russian turbulence, sought from Great Britain and France assurance of their aid in such an eventuality. This was agreed to and given. Mean-

while, the Italians again attempted to smash their way through mountainous terrain during the Tenth and Eleventh Battles of the Isonzo, the results of which were heavy losses and an Austrian appeal to Germany for assistance.

This was given, and on 24 October a new Austro-German Army struck, destroying the Italian Second Army and forcing a general withdrawal, which was halted only on the Piave with the assistance of British and French reinforcements – 11 divisions in all – sent in support, as earlier promised.

For the Allies there was but one favorable result in the west during 1917: on 5 November, a conference at Rapallo at last established a Supreme War Council to co-ordinate strategy.

Other fronts

Russian collapse removed pressure on Turkey and allowed her to move troops to other theaters. But Turkey was herself now approaching collapse. Earlier clashes with the British had not all been one-sided in 1917, but the arrival of Allenby heralded British supremacy in the Palestinian area. He scored a crucial victory at Beersheba (31 October), then forced the Turks to abandon Gaza and, on 9 December, took Jerusalem (page 140). These Turkish reverses led them to withdraw troops from Mesopotamia, where British troops were able to advance and take Baghdad on 11 March.

Prospects

By the end of 1917, Russia had stopped fighting, nor did her army any longer exist even if the will to fight had been there. Austria, though her troops continued to fight doggedly, was tired of, and anxious to escape, the war which she had herself instigated. Great Britain, for her part, had subdued the U-boat menace and avoided starvation by the convoy system, but had little hope of a decisive victory on the Western Front. Italy, reunited by patriotism after her calamitous defeat at Caparetto (page 132), remained a threatening, though containable, adversary on the Allied side.

Thus the Allies entered the New Year, though buoyed by the capture of Jerusalem, a propaganda rather than strategic victory, with a sense of frustration. None of 1917's spring buds had flowered. Allied offensives in the west had bogged down at terrible cost, largely through disunity of command. Hunger and fatigue prevailed among all the civilian populations. France was near to her limits, her ability to raise troops of serviceable age exhausted. One hope alone glimmered: the ever increasing number of Americans reaching the Western Front with their abundance of weaponry.

The Central Powers, for their part had been more successful than they could have hoped; nevertheless, they now felt the strangulation imposed by Allied naval blockade. Turkey and Bulgaria were reaching the end of their resources, and to Germany herself fell more and more the burden of the war.

One view prevailed: both Allies and Central Powers believed that they must win before their countries, and all Europe, fell into exhausted chaos and succumbed to Bolshevik dictatorship and ruin. That was the bleak and awesome prospect all faced in 1918.

British infantry advance from their trenches near Arras, March 1917

No power other than Britain developed a truly successful tank or "landship" during the war. The success of the tank was as much of a surprise to the Allies as it was to the Germans and initial advances were frequently denied essential support. Tanks were also placed at a disadvantage by being called upon to attack in unsuitable conditions. At Passchendaele, for instance, the region's terrain, ploughed by a combination of shells and rain rendered advance impossible

Timeline 1917

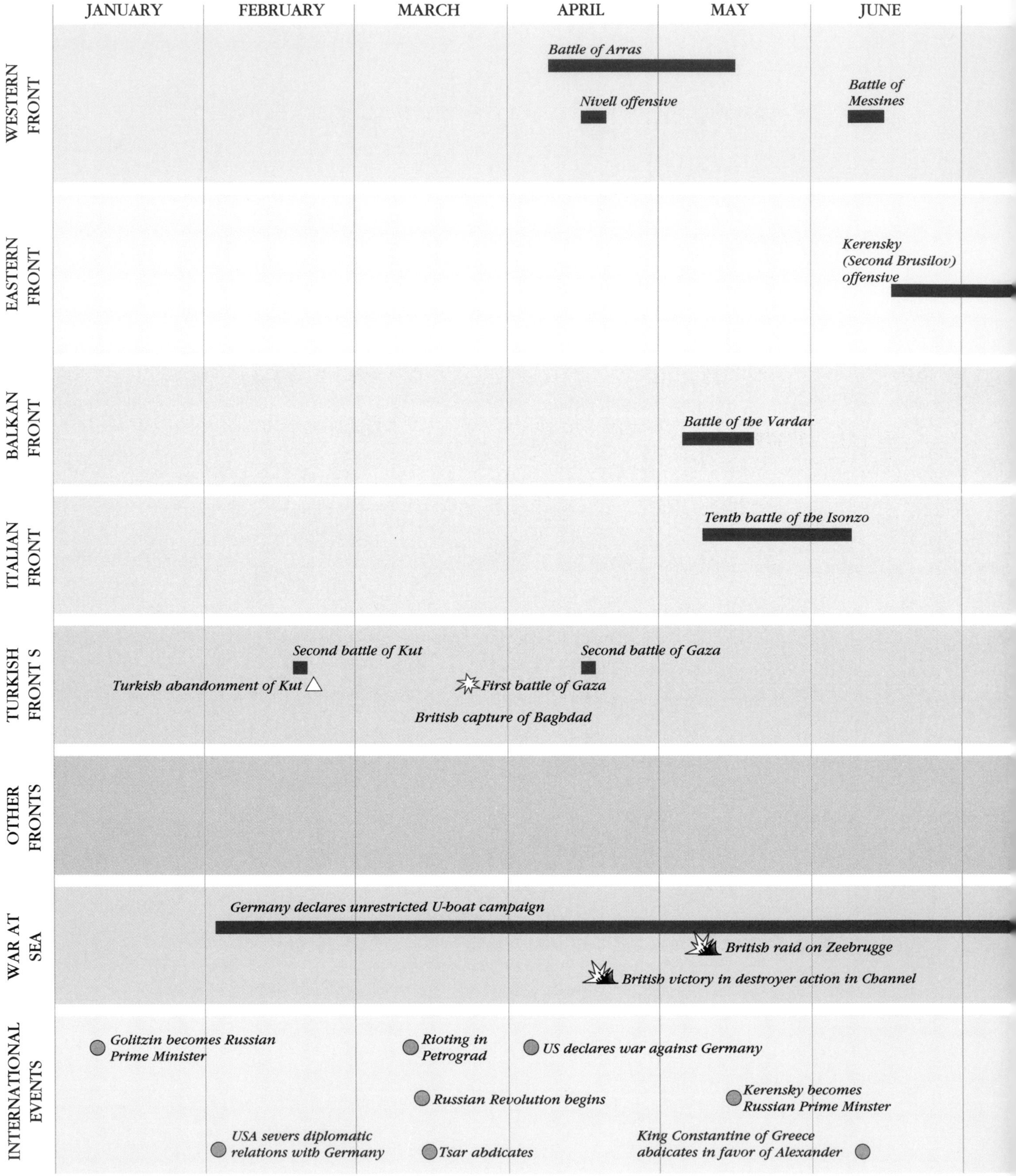

	JANUARY	FEBRUARY	MARCH	APRIL	MAY	JUNE
WESTERN FRONT				*Battle of Arras* ▬▬▬▬▬▬		*Battle of Messines* ▬
				Nivell offensive ▬		
EASTERN FRONT						*Kerensky (Second Brusilov) offensive* ▬▬▬
BALKAN FRONT					*Battle of the Vardar* ▬▬	
ITALIAN FRONT					*Tenth battle of the Isonzo* ▬▬▬▬	
TURKISH FRONT S	Turkish abandonment of Kut △	*Second battle of Kut* ■	*First battle of Gaza* ✸ British capture of Baghdad	*Second battle of Gaza* ■		
OTHER FRONTS						
WAR AT SEA	*Germany declares unrestricted U-boat campaign* ▬▬▬▬▬▬▬▬▬▬▬▬▬			✸ *British raid on Zeebrugge* ✸ *British victory in destroyer action in Channel*		
INTERNATIONAL EVENTS	● *Golitzin becomes Russian Prime Minister*	● *USA severs diplomatic relations with Germany*	● *Rioting in Petrograd* ● *Russian Revolution begins* ● *Tsar abdicates*	● *US declares war against Germany*	● *Kerensky becomes Russian Prime Minster* *King Constantine of Greece abdicates in favor of Alexander* ●	

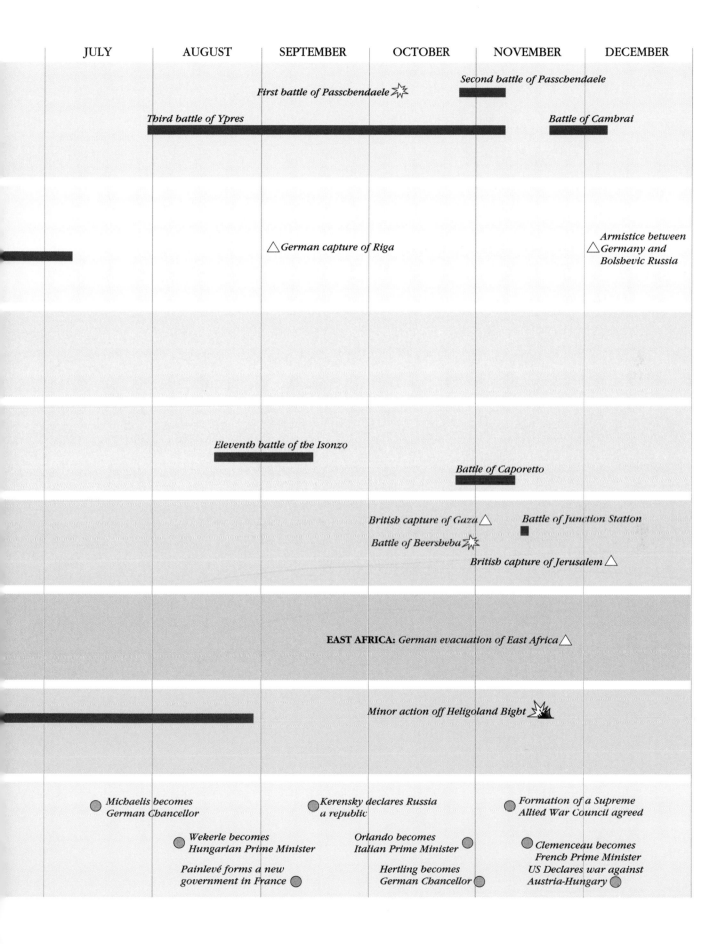

JULY	AUGUST	SEPTEMBER	OCTOBER	NOVEMBER	DECEMBER

First battle of Passchendaele

Second battle of Passchendaele

Third battle of Ypres

Battle of Cambrai

△ German capture of Riga

Armistice between
△ Germany and
Bolshevic Russia

Eleventh battle of the Isonzo

Battle of Caporetto

British capture of Gaza △

Battle of Junction Station

Battle of Beersheba

British capture of Jerusalem △

EAST AFRICA: German evacuation of East Africa △

Minor action off Heligoland Bight

Michaelis becomes
German Chancellor

Kerensky declares Russia
a republic

Formation of a Supreme
Allied War Council agreed

Wekerle becomes
Hungarian Prime Minister

Orlando becomes
Italian Prime Minister

Clemenceau becomes
French Prime Minister

Painlevé forms a new
government in France

Hertling becomes
German Chancellor

US Declares war against
Austria-Hungary

The U-boat war 1917–1918

In February 1917, when the German naval command took the momentous decision to resume unrestricted U-boat warfare against all ships in British waters or bound for Britain. German naval planners had calculated that the political risk of bringing America into the war on the Allied side was outweighed by the prospect that the choking-off of British trade would cause such hardship – and even starvation – in Britain as to force the British government to sue for peace. American intervention, it was calculated, would not be fully felt for some two years, while Great Britain could be starved into submission within five months.

The campaign

The opening weeks of renewed unrestricted U-boat operations came near to success. In the whole of 1915, including the previous period of unrestricted submarine warfare, 227 British merchant ships (855,721 gross tons) had been sunk by U-boats; in April alone, the most successful month of the 1917 campaign, 155 ships, totaling over half a million tons gross, were sunk. There were, however, always too few U-boats available (148 in all) to achieve the predicted results.

Despite this, Allied shipping losses mounted alarmingly. Nearly a million tons of Allied shipping, some two-thirds of it British, had been lost by the end of April, raising the prospect not only of civilian starvation but of denuding British armies of supplies.

The convoy system

The most obvious defensive measure, a revival of the escorted merchant-ship convoys of the age of sail, was at once rejected by the Admiralty as too dangerous because it would require the stripping of virtually all light cruisers and destroyers from the Grand Fleet.

Despite Jellicoe's objections, the prime minister, Lloyd George, on the recommendation of more junior officers, Beatty and the Americans, instituted the system on 10 May. Each convoy comprised 40 or more merchantmen, with destroyer escort ships equipped with depth charges, stationed on either side. The effect was dramatic; by the end of October, of more than 1,500 homeward-bound vessels, a mere 24 were lost. At the same time, more U-boats were sunk, since they no longer faced lone merchantmen but grouped destroyers. Allied shipping losses by the end of 1917 exceeded eight million tons, but Allied shipbuilding more than offset these losses.

Other naval actions

Between February and April Germany made destroyer raids in the Channel, in one of which two British destroyers were sunk, another in which two German destroyers were sent to the bottom by HMS Broke. In December German raids on British Scandinavian convoys caused heavy losses of merchantmen, inducing Beatty thereafter to use a squadron of battleships as escort for all North Sea convoys.

"The lone U-boat might well sink one or two of the ships, or even several, but that was but a poor percentage of the whole. The convoy would steam on… and it would reach Britain, bringing a rich cargo of foodstuffs and raw materials safely to port."

Capt. Karl Dönitz, U-boat commander

Claus von Bergens 1917 impression of U53 sinking an Allied fishing vessel.

Ships sunk by U-boats

1	September 1916 – April 1916
2	May 1917 – January 1918
3	February 1918 – October 1918
•	Ship sunk

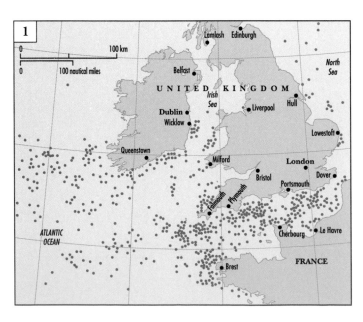

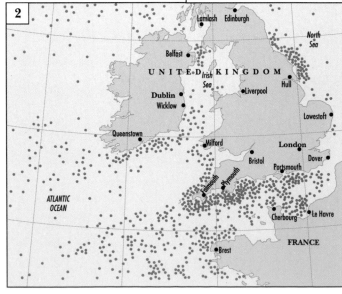

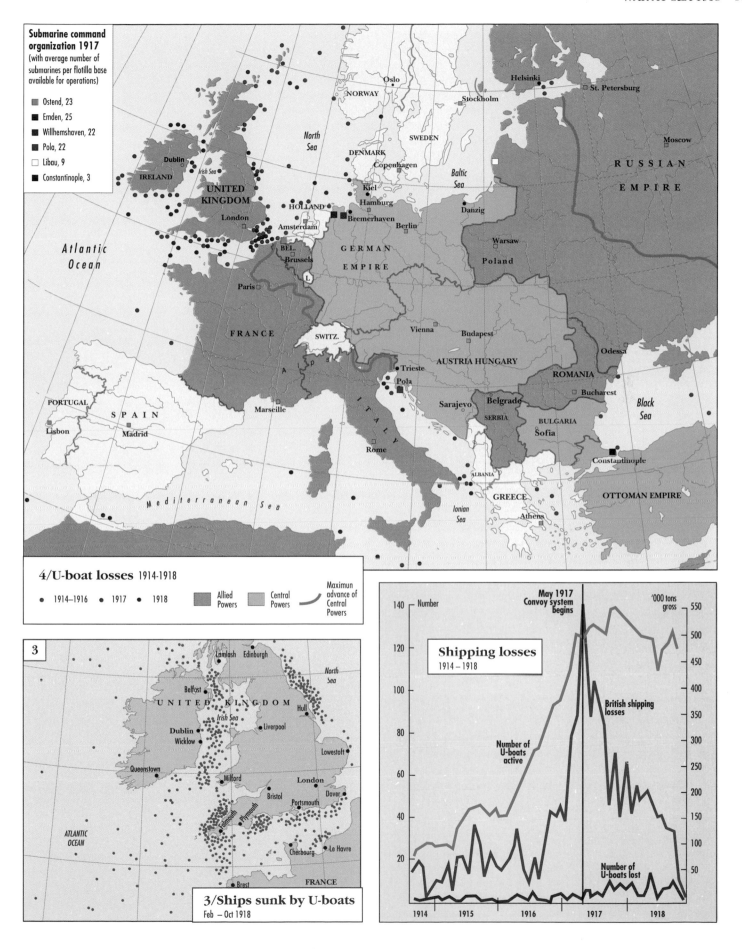

Submarine command organization 1917
(with average number of submarines per flotilla base available for operations)

- Ostend, 23
- Emden, 25
- Willhemshaven, 22
- Pola, 22
- Libau, 9
- Constantinople, 3

4/U-boat losses 1914-1918

- 1914–1916
- 1917
- 1918

Allied Powers

Central Powers

Maximun advance of Central Powers

3/Ships sunk by U-boats
Feb – Oct 1918

Shipping losses
1914 – 1918

May 1917 Convoy system begins

'000 tons gross

Number of U-boats active

British shipping losses

Number of U-boats lost

The Hindenburg Line March-April 1917

German success in disrupting Allied plans for a war-winning offensive in Summer 1916 was bought only at the cost of murderous losses both at Verdun and in the reduced Somme offensive, while the huge early success of the Brusilov Offensive had further weakened Falkenhayn's hold on the direction of the war. His replacement by Hindenburg and Ludendorff heralded a new approach to the war in the West; for 1917, as for 1915, the German strategy was to be defense on the Western Front while the final, knockout blow was delivered at Russia; meanwhile the proposed unrestricted U-boat campaign was to be directed at forcing Britain out of the war.

At Verdun, the exhausted German Fifth Army still held strong positions, and the French were equally worn out by their exertions. On the Somme, however, Ludendorff rightly expected a renewed British offensive in the new year, and the grinding, costly Allied attacks of the previous year had left German forces around Bapaume and between Peronne and Soissons holding lengthy and exposed salients (Map 1). In the Winter of 1916–17, German engineers had begun creating a powerfully fortified rear line (the Siegfried Line – known to the Allies as the Hindenburg Line through misinterpretation of information from a prisoner) from Arras to Rheims; this line's impregnability was much trumpeted to an increasingly war-weary German public, and from the beginning of February Ludendorff began preparing an audacious withdrawal to it, shortening the front by 25 miles and releasing 13 divisions to a general reserve. The operation was codenamed Alberich.

The withdrawal

The main withdrawal began on 16 March, and was not detected by the Allies until the 25th. The retreat was accompanied by a ruthless "scorched earth" policy (Crown Prince Rupprecht in fact threatened resignation over what he saw as excessive savagery) – the entire area was laid waste, villages razed, trees cut down, water wells contaminated and the ensuing wreckage littered with explosive booby-traps.

The Allied pursuit was slow and cautious, and British offensive plans were again disrupted: the supporting attacks requested by Nivelle, the new French commander-in-chief could now be delivered only around Arras, where the German line was unchanged (page 122).

The Hindenburg Line was novel in several respects. The defensive line was sited on the reverse, rather than the forward, slopes of hills. Defensive positions on the forward slopes, with artillery observation posts on the crest, had the clear advantage of uninterrupted view of the enemy's lines but the disadvantage of exposing defenders to the full weight of enemy artillery bombardment. From the reverse slope, with artillery observers sited near their batteries to the rear, guns, in greater safety, could sweep the enemy lines as they attacked over a crest.

Second, the new defenses represented the most sophisticated development to date of the concept of a flexible defensive zone rather than a firm line. To the rear of the lightly-held front line lay two heavily fortified defensive positions, with massed machine guns. Behind these were stationed German reserves, concentrated for counter-attack. Each defensive line, some providing sleeping quarters, was spaced in depth, so that if one were taken the enemy's artillery would have to be moved forward prior to bombarding the next.

So strong and effective were the Hindenburg Line's defences that it was not until the last weeks of the war that the Allies finally broke through.

A cut-away view of the Hindenburg line defences reveals the network of tunnels and chambers behind the trenches. Many of the new ideas for strategic defence were the work of Colonel Von Lossberg, chief of staff to General Von Below's 2nd Army.

"The decision to retreat was not reached without a painful struggle... but it was necessary for war reasons, we had no choice."

Gen. Ludendorff, 'My War Memories'

Inhabitants of the devastated village of Mons-en-Chausée welcoming British troops on 21 March 1917. Much of the territory abandoned by the Germans was heavily damaged by three years of war; the Allied advance was slow and cautious.

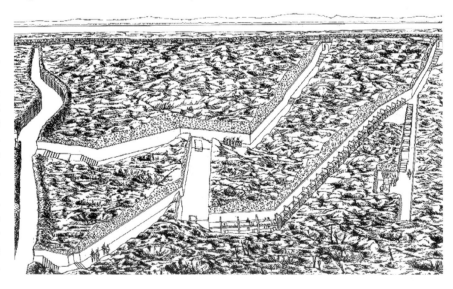

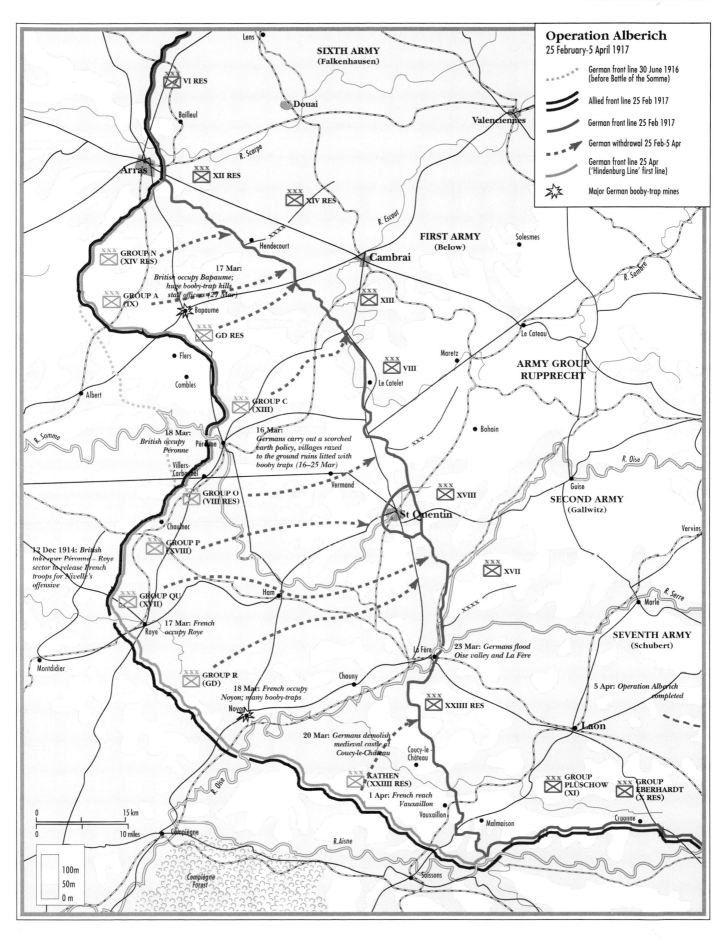

Operation Alberich
25 February–5 April 1917

- ⋯⋯ German front line 30 June 1916 (before Battle of the Somme)
- ━━ Allied front line 25 Feb 1917
- ━━ German front line 25 Feb 1917
- ┅┅▶ German withdrawal 25 Feb–5 Apr
- ━━ German front line 25 Apr ('Hindenburg Line' first line)
- ✸ Major German booby-trap mines

SIXTH ARMY
(Falkenhausen)

Lens

Douai

Valenciennes

VI RES

Bailleul

R. Scarpe

Arras

XII RES

XIV RES

R. Escaut

FIRST ARMY
(Below)

Hendecourt

Cambrai

Solesmes

R. Sambre

GROUP N
(XIV RES)

17 Mar:
British occupy Bapaume;
huge booby-trap kills
staff officers (27 Mar)

GROUP A
(IX)

Bapaume

XIII

Le Cateau

GD RES

ARMY GROUP
RUPPRECHT

Flers

VIII

Maretz

Combles

Le Catelet

Albert

GROUP C
(XIII)

16 Mar:
Germans carry out a scorched
earth policy, villages razed
to the ground ruins litted with
booby traps (16–25 Mar)

Bohain

R. Somme

18 Mar:
British occupy Péronne

Péronne

R. Oise

Villers-
Carbonnel

Vermand

XVIII

Guise

SECOND ARMY
(Gallwitz)

GROUP O
(VIII RES)

St Quentin

Vervins

Chaulnec

GROUP P
(XVIII)

Ham

XVII

R. Serre

12 Dec 1914: British
take over Péronne – Roye
sector to release French
troops for Nivelle's
offensive

Marle

GROUP QU
(XVII)

17 Mar: French
occupy Roye

Roye

La Fère

23 Mar: Germans flood
Oise valley and La Fère

SEVENTH ARMY
(Schubert)

Montdidier

GROUP R
(GD)

18 Mar: French
occupy Noyon; many booby-traps

Noyon

Chauny

5 Apr: Operation Alberich
completed

XXIIII RES

20 Mar: Germans demolish
medieval castle of
Coucy-le-Château

Laon

Coucy-le-
Château

KATHEN
(XXIIII RES)

1 Apr: French reach
Vauxaillon

GROUP
PLÜSCHOW
(XI)

GROUP
EBERHARDT
(X RES)

R. Oise

Vauxaillon

Malmaison

Craonne

0   15 km
0   10 miles

Compiègne

100m
50m
0 m

Compiègne
Forest

R. Aisne

Soissons

The Nivelle Offensive April 1917

The bloody stalemates of Verdun and the Somme had frustrated Allied hopes of a breakthrough in the West in 1916, but the new year found the strategic balance still tilted in the Allied favor. Britain's increased munitions output and mass armies raised through the introduction of conscription, together with the continuing German commitment in Russia (despite political events there early in the year) gave the Allies a superiority of some 3,900,000 troops to 2,500,000. The problem was to find some way of making these numbers tell.

In France, a new star had risen – Robert Nivelle, hero of the recapture of forts Douaumont and Vaux at Verdun (page 108) and enthusiastic proponent of the creeping artillery barrage, had replaced Joffre as commander-in-chief in December 1916. Nivelle believed that a breakthrough was possible in 48 hours by the employment of his Verdun tactics on a larger scale, as long as the most heavily-fortified German positions were avoided. So contagious was his optimism that Lloyd George, the new British prime minister, agreed to the subordination of Haig to Nivelle for the ensuing operations. Strategically, Nivelles's plan offered little that was new (see Strategic View), and any element of surprise was forfeited in part through his own uninhibited remarks. Nonetheless, the main blow was to be delivered by an unprecedented concentration of force –

Micheler's three-army strong Reserve Army Group represented virtually the entire strategic reserve of the French Army.

The offensive
Before the plan could be implemented, however, Ludendorff had launched Operation Alberich, the German withdrawal to the heavily fortified Hindenburg (or Siegfried) Line (page 120). Seemingly unperturbed by this neutralization of his preliminary operation on the Somme, Nivelle ordered the main offensive to proceed as planned. On 9 April, British supporting attacks went ahead at Arras, followed by the Canadian capture of Vimy Ridge (page 124).

The main offensive opened on 16 April between Reims and Soissons, the initial aim being the capture of the heights dominating the Ailette Valley above the plain of Laon, crossed by the Chemin des Dames. After a long preliminary bombardment, 20 French divisions left their trenches at 0630 hrs, led by the elite II Colonial Corps.

Opposing them, the German Seventh Army was expecting the attack, and had been reinforced by the new First Army in anticipation. Despite a high concentration of French air power, German fighters had cleared the skies of French aerial observation. Nivelle's much-vaunted rolling artillery barrage moved too fast

General Nivelle was appointed Joffre's successor in December 1916, largely on the strength of his achievements at Verdun. The disastrous failure of the offensive which bears his name doomed his career and cost France its last chance of an independent, war-winning operation.

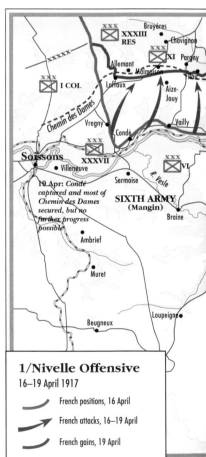

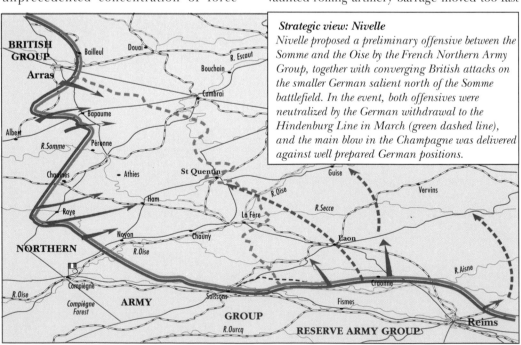

Strategic view: Nivelle
Nivelle proposed a preliminary offensive between the Somme and the Oise by the French Northern Army Group, together with converging British attacks on the smaller German salient north of the Somme battlefield. In the event, both offensives were neutralized by the German withdrawal to the Hindenburg Line in March (green dashed line), and the main blow in the Champagne was delivered against well prepared German positions.

1/Nivelle Offensive
16–19 April 1917

— French positions, 16 April
→ French attacks, 16–19 April
⤻ French gains, 19 April

for the infantry, which was decimated by machine-gun fire. The first French tank attack of the war, sent in during the afternoon of the first day, was doomed by accurate German artillery fire and design weaknesses in the Renault tanks employed; not one of the 128 tanks used reached the German lines. By the third day, the French infantry had fought their way on to the Chemin, but at the cost of sickeningly high casualties: of the expected breakthrough, there was no prospect whatever.

Consequences

The absolute failure of Nivelle's much heralded attack cost over 130,000 casualties in five days for the gain, on the first day, of 600 yds/500 m rather than the expected 6 mls/9.6 km. German losses were far less, though 21,000 of their number were captured. Nivelle cancelled the main effort after the third day, as he had promised the French government, and on the 15th was himself replaced as commander-in-chief by Pétain.

Apart from the loss of life, the mishandling of the last possible hope of a French war-winning offensive proved too much for the long-suffering French Army. Mutinies – described as

One of the many Frenchmen who died on the German wire during the Nivelle offensive. The losses incurred during the offensive would have serious repercussions for the future of the French army. Between 16-25 April, 30,000 were killed, 100,000 were wounded and 4,000 became prisoners of war. Almost 80% of these casualties were suffered in the first day.

"strikes" by the participants – began to spread from 17 April, temporarily paralyzing the French Army on the Western Front and prompting Haig to bring forward his own plans for a British offensive further north. Of the estimated 23,385 mutineers convicted, only 55 were shot – largely through the tact and justice shown by the newly-appointed Pétain, who toured the entire French front personally addressing the dispirited troops and promising an end to costly offensives. He further restored morale by instituting regular and equal tours of duty at the front, leave periods for all units and by improving rest camps behind the line. By mid-June the crisis was past.

"Subjected to four day's combat, hemmed in, deprived of sleep, under constant fire from the German machine gunners and forced to struggle in the rain and mud. They have fought without relief and are now utterly exhausted."

The commander of the Sixth Army's I Corps describing the condition of his men on 20 April

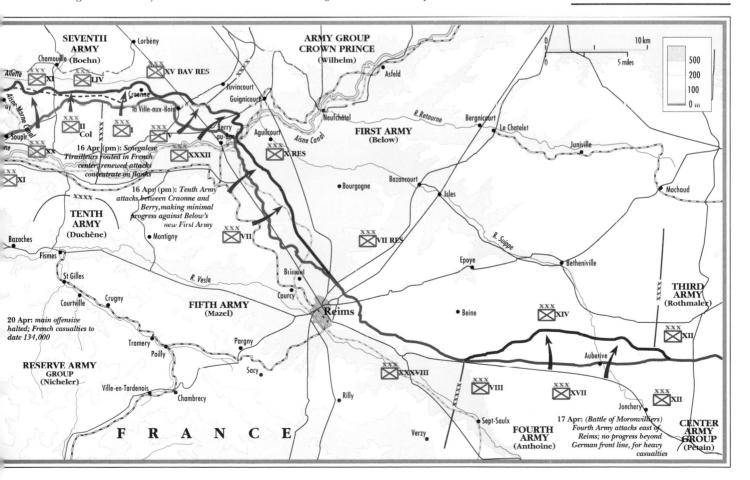

Arras and Vimy Ridge April 1917

Allied plans for 1917 included the resumption of the Somme offensive by the Fourth and Fifth Armies in early February, while Allenby's Third Army was to thrust southeast, blocking a German retreat through the Cojeul and Sensée valleys. The First Army (Horne) was to form a defensive flank by attacking north of the Third, while the French attacked south of the Somme. Three weeks later the French were to launch their assault in the Champagne.

A number of significant changes after the conception of these plans necessitated their modification. Joffre, blamed for French unpreparedness at Verdun, was removed from operational command in December. His replacement, Nivelle, requested that British forces should take over more of the front, freeing French troops for a more ambitious and spectacular offensive. Then, before any Allied offensive could begin, the German withdrawal to the Hindenburg Line (page 120) restricted Allied attacks to the flanks of the abandoned area.

The Arras offensive

The main role in the British attack now fell to Allenby's Third Army. If he were able to break through the German defenses north of the Hindenburg Line, his troops could outflank the new German position. The Germans had anticipated such a move by digging a strong support line from Quéant, near the northern end of the Hindenburg Line, through Drocourt to the north, thereby covering the rear of their old defenses in the Arras area. Allenby's only chance of success, therefore, lay in his ability to break this uncompleted support line, some five miles behind the front defensive system, before German reserves could be brought up.

Since insufficient numbers of tanks were available and a brief bombardment ruled out by the British high command, Allenby was forced to forego the crucial element of surprise. Wire-cutting fire followed by five days' bombardment by 2,879 guns (one to every nine yards of front) was ordered, and the Germans were able to amass considerable reserves of both troops and ammunition in preparation for the assault.

Tactical success, however, was immediate, for a new British gas shell virtually paralyzed the German artillery by killing hundreds of horses, thereby disrupting ammunition supply lines.

The attacking infantry moved forward along

the whole line at 1730hrs, covered by a creeping barrage. In under an hour, the entire German front line was taken. North of the Scarpe the 4th Division seized Fampoux and broke the last German line before the Drocourt–Quéant support line. South of the Scarpe, however, German resistance at Railway Triangle and Telegraph Hill was so powerful that the advance of the 12th and 15th divisions, though not halted, was badly delayed. British cavalry reserves, though moved up, could not be deployed and merely added to the congestion. The opening day had, in both prisoners taken and land occupied, produced better results than in any previous Allied offensive, but a breakthrough had again eluded the British.

Action in the South

On 11 April, part of the Fifth Army (Gough) made a converging attack from the south against the Hindenburg Line to relieve pressure on the Third Army. A pitiful 11 tanks had been gathered, but these, acting as a moving barrage and as wire-cutters, led the 4th Australian Division against German positions at Bullecourt. The Australians penetrated the Hindenburg Line but were immediately counter-attacked from all directions.

The main phase of the offensive came to a close on 14 April, the Allies having missed their strategic objective but captured 13,000 prisoners and some 200 guns, though for great loss in life. The focus of British attention then shifted northward, toward Messines (page 126) and Passchendaele (page 128) in October.

Byng's Canadian Corps advance across "no-man's land", 9 April 1917. In a finely prepared and professionally executed attack the Canadians captured a large part of Vimy Ridge, which had for so long been an impregnable barrier to the Allies.

British troops fix the trench-wall scaling ladders the day before the battle of Arras, 8 April 1917.

"I don't know what the generals wanted to do that attack for, because it was murder. It was often spoken of between us. They had a job to do, of course, but there were too many lives lost."

Rifleman R. Langley,
16th Battalion,
King's Royal Rifle Corps

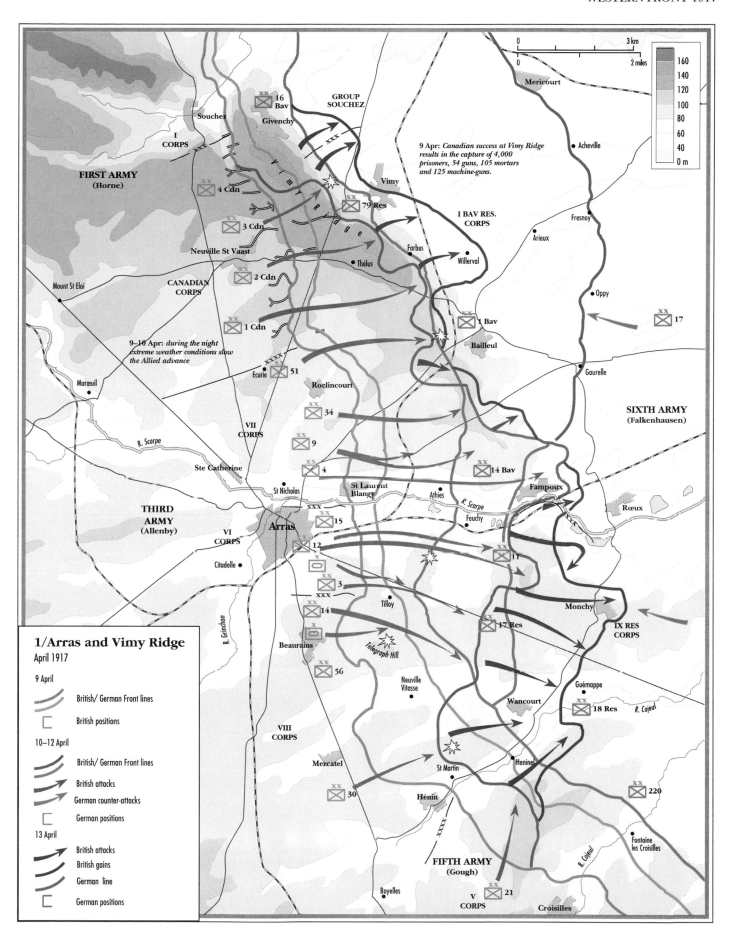

9 Apr: *Canadian success at Vimy Ridge results in the capture of 4,000 prisoners, 54 guns, 105 mortars and 125 machine-guns.*

9–10 Apr: *during the night extreme weather conditions slow the Allied advance*

1/Arras and Vimy Ridge

April 1917

9 April

British/ German Front lines

British positions

10–12 April

British/ German Front lines

British attacks

German counter-attacks

German positions

13 April

British attacks

British gains

German line

German positions

Messines June 1917

Following the disastrous Nivelle offensive (page 122), Pétain, the new French commander-in-chief, resolved to remain on the defensive until American troops and tanks arrived in greater number. Haig, however, now saw the chance to implement his long-cherished plan for an offensive in Flanders. An essential preliminary was an attack on Messines Ridge to straighten the salient just south of Ypres. This attack was entrusted to Plumer's Second Army and scheduled for 7 June.

Preparations

Preparations for an attack on the ridge Messines–Wytschaete (some 5mls/8km long and at most 250ft/76m high) had begun a great deal earlier, for the Germans had held and fortified the ridge since 1914. Such formidable defenses required a new method of attack, and the British had resolved upon the ancient technique of mining. Deep tunnels were dug under the German positions, in some instances to a depth of 90ft/27m and running as far as 60yds/55m behind the first German line. In these tunnels 1 million lb/454,000kg of explosives, were placed destined for simultaneous detonation between hill 60 in the north to St Yves in the south.

The danger to the tunnelers was great. 'Claykickers' sat in the tunnel, leaning against a wooden backrest with their feet at the face and dug out the clay with a spade. Apart from lack of oxygen, there was the ever-present danger of earth collapsing and of German bombardment or break-ins to suspected shafts. Moreover, great care had to be taken to hide removed layers of the terrain, for stacked mounds of clay might be detected by German aircraft, revealing the position of the mines.

By 1917, sophisticated listening instruments, including the geophone, and silent air and water pumps had been introduced, while ammonal had replaced the more volatile gunpowder and guncotton. Plumer's meticulous preparations also involved improvements to roads and railways, frequent patrols to assess the enemy strength, and constant air surveillance. By the day of the assault, only one of the 20 mines had been detected by the Germans.

The assault

For 17 days before the attack, the German positions were subjected to concentrated bombardment. Plumer's plan allocated nine infantry divisions to the assault with three more in reserve. Early on the night of 6–7 June there was a summer storm, with rain, thunder and lightening. When it subsided, the mines were detonated; great billows of scarlet flame erupted along the German front, the ground shook and the noise was so violent that it was heard as far away as southeast England.

The first trench system was immediately attacked, even before all the debris had fallen; then the British and Anzac troops stormed the crest lines. Within two hours some Allied troops had reached their second objective and by 0700hrs Messines itself had fallen. The defenses of Wyschaete were also penetrated and British troops at once began to move down the eastern slopes of the ridge. Guns were quickly brought forward to continue the bombardment. Some 7500 Germans were taken prisoner (the New Zealanders contemptuously cut off their prisoners' trouser buttons and sent them, dazed and compliant, to the rear unescorted) together with 67 artillery pieces, 94 trench mortars and almost 300 machine guns. British losses are estimated at 17,000, German at 25,000.

During the early afternoon Allied tanks and reserve divisions were brought up and by 1510hrs the entire ridge was securely held, all objectives taken.

The Allied troops dug in with such speed that all German counter-attacks the following day were repulsed and some more ground gained. The victory, both rapid and absolute, provided a tonic for the Allied civilian population, now weary and despondent Crown Prince Rupprecht, German commander in Belgium and northeast France was convinced that the Allied success of Messines must be followed-up by further attacks designed on the same principle and was prepared to abandon the low-lying ground to the west of Luys. Plumer envisaged just such a campaign but Haig and Gough overruled him and thereby failed to take the initiative which had been handed to them. Militarily, Messines provided a basic lesson: surprise, and limited, attainable objectives that could he held, should be the tactical aim. It was a lesson largely lost on Haig who, greatly encouraged by this result, was further emboldened in his aggressive planning for new initiatives on the western front.

General Sir Hubert Plumer was the best liked and most trusted army commander in the B.E.F. He made 'Trust, Thoroughness and Training' the keynotes of his generalship and would not commit his troops in any operation that had not been carefully planned and in which the objectives were clearly unobtainable. Both he and his staff regularly visited the trenches making themselves thoroughly aquainted with the men they commanded.

"The waiting infantry felt the shocks and heard the rumble of an earthquake. It seemed as if the Messines Ridge got up and shook itself. All along its flank belched rows of mushroom-shaped masses of debris, flung high into the air."

Capt. W. Grant Grieve
Royal Engineers

British, Australian and Canadian tunnelling companies laid 20 great mines under the German front line defenses, many of them the year before the battle. Only one mine was discovered by the Germans and the remainder were successfully detonated with devastating results. The tunnels ranged from 200 to 2,000 feet in length and the mines were positioned between 50 to 90 feet below the surface. Those Germans who were not immediately killed in the explosions were so bewildered that many were taken prisoner without any show of resistance.

"I suddenly witnessed the most gigantic and at the same time chillingly wonderful firework that ever has been lit in Flanders, a true volcano, as if the whole southeast was spewing fire. A few seconds later we could feel the tremor, like a real earthquake lasting a full minute."

Pastor van Walleghem,
(Parish Priest)

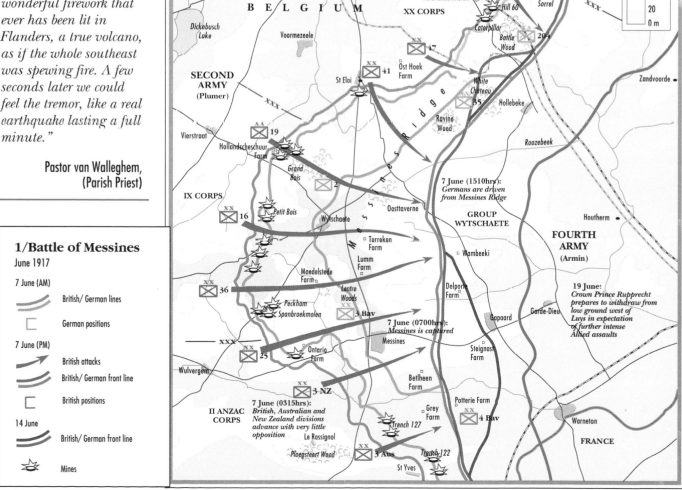

1/Battle of Messines
June 1917

7 June (AM)

⌒ British/ German lines

⌐ German positions

7 June (PM)

➤ British attacks

➤ British/ German front line

⌐ British positions

14 June

➤ British/ German front line

✺ Mines

Map labels:

0 — 2745 metres
0 — 3000 yards

50
40
20
0 m

Zillebeke
Observatory Ridge
XX 23
Verbrandenmolen
Mount Sorrel
XX CORPS
Hill 60
Caterpillar
204
B E L G I U M
Battle Wood
Dickebusch Lake
Voormezeele
XX 47
White Chateau
Zandvoorde
SECOND ARMY (Plumer)
XX 41
Ost Hoek Farm
St Eloi
35
Hollebeke
Ravine Wood
Vierstraat
Roozebeek
XX 19
Hollandscheschuur Farm
Grand Bois
7 June (1510hrs): Germans are driven from Messines Ridge
Houtherm
IX CORPS
XX 2
GROUP WYTSCHAETE
Petit Bois
XX 16
Oosttaverne
Wytschaete
Torrekon Farm
FOURTH ARMY (Armin)
Lumm Farm
Wambeeki
Maedelstede Farm
19 June: Crown Prince Rupprecht prepares to withdraw from low ground west of Luys in expectation of further intense Allied assaults
XX 36
Lentre Woods
Delporte Farm
Peckham
Spanbroekmolen
XX 3 Bav
Gapaard
Garde-Dieu
7 June (0700hrs): Messines is captured
Messines
XXX
XX 25
Ontario Farm
Steignast Farm
Wulvergem
XX 3 NZ
Bethleen Farm
Potterie Farm
7 June (0315hrs): British, Australian and New Zealand divisions advance with very little opposition
Grey Farm
XX 4 Bav
Warneton
II ANZAC CORPS
Le Rossignol
Trench 127
FRANCE
Ploegsteert Wood
XX 3 Aus
Trench 122
St Yves

Passchendaele July–November 1917

The British success at Messines (page 126) had an awesome consequence: Haig came to believe that what had been achieved, swiftly and at relatively little cost, could be repeated, and that a major British breakthrough was possible in Flanders. He now turned his attention to his planned main assault around Ypres.

The Allied military position by mid-1917 was more perilous than it had been since 1914. The German U-boat offensive was at its height, Italy was unable to make progress against Austria, and Russia was evidently on the point of collapse. The United States had entered the war in April, but direct American military contribution was still some way off. Haig made much of the potential of his offensive to close the German U-boat bases at Brugges (within 30mls/48km of the front); more realistically, his initial aim was to dislodge the Germans from their dominating positions on the ridge of high ground between Westroosbeke and Broodseinde before winter.

The operation depended for success on speed, since records from the previous 80 years showed that at best there would probably be only three weeks without rain at that time of year. In the event, the downpour was both early and continuous, rapidly filling the morass of craters created by years of artillery fire.

The main part of the attack was allocated to the Fifth Army (Gough), with one corps of Second Army (Plumer) on its right flank and the French First Army (Anthoine) on its left. Opposed to these was the German Fourth Army (Armin).

The campaign

The offensive was launched on 31 July at 0350hrs, in heavy mist. It quickly became apparent that the attack was not progressing as planned. Three ridges north of Ypres – Bixschoote, St Julien and Pilkem – were taken by the British left flank, but on the right the thrust southeast of Ypres toward the Ypres–Menin road was halted. Ceaseless rain brought further advance to an end, not merely for the infantry, now sinking up to their thighs in mud, but also for the tanks stationed to exploit a breakthrough.

For a further two weeks rain fell without pause, during which time the Germans were able to reorganize and bring up reinforce-ments. The next British attack began on 16 August, when the Fifth Army assaulted the Gheluvelt–Langemarck line. Langemarck was taken but Gough could make little progress, while on the right the advance was again quickly halted. The morale of the British troops began to deteriorate, the staff being damned as much as the mud and the skilful German resistance for their fruitless sacrifice.

Haig now extended the front of the Second Army northward to include the crucial Menin Road area, thereby giving Plumer's Second Army the main target – the Gheluvelt plateau. After careful planning, Plumer launched his attack at 0540hrs on 20 September. Four divisions (two Australian) advanced on a front of less than 3 miles between Klein Zillebeke and Westhoek. The British inched forward against fierce counter-attacks (mustard gas was here used by the Germans for the first time). One division south of the Menin Road almost reached Gheluvelt, while north of the road half of Polygon Wood was taken. Further north, Fifth Army advanced astride the Ypres–Roulers railway almost to Zonnebeke.

The final fierce assault on Passchendaele, Mossel–markt and the ridge beyond was entrusted to the Canadian Corps (Currie). On 6 November at 0600hrs men of the 1st and 2nd divisions, covered by a heavy artillery barrage, made the final drive forward and, for the loss of 2,238 men, took both villages within two hours. Haig was at last content.

Consequences and losses

The campaign had taken pressure off the French, still recovering from the Nivelle offensive, and the British-held Ypres salient had been deepened for some five miles, but these were meager gains.

For both sides the cost was enormous. Some 90,000 British were reported 'missing', more than 40,000 of whom were never found. Most of these had drowned in the mud; even today farmers ploughing the land unearth the bones of these unidentified men. A rough estimate indicates some 300,000 British, more than 8,500 French and 260,000 Germans killed, wounded or unaccounted for.

Tank Corps headquarters had warned that the terrain, broken-up by shelling and rain, was not suitable for a tank assault and the crews soon found themselves unable to keep pace with the advancing infantry.

"The whole earth is ploughed by the exploding shells and the holes are filled with water, and if you do not get killed by the shells you may drown in the craters. Everybody is rushing, running, trying to escape almost certain death."

Musketier Hans Otto Shelter, 231st Reserve Infantry Regiment

A German casualty of the British artillery barrage.

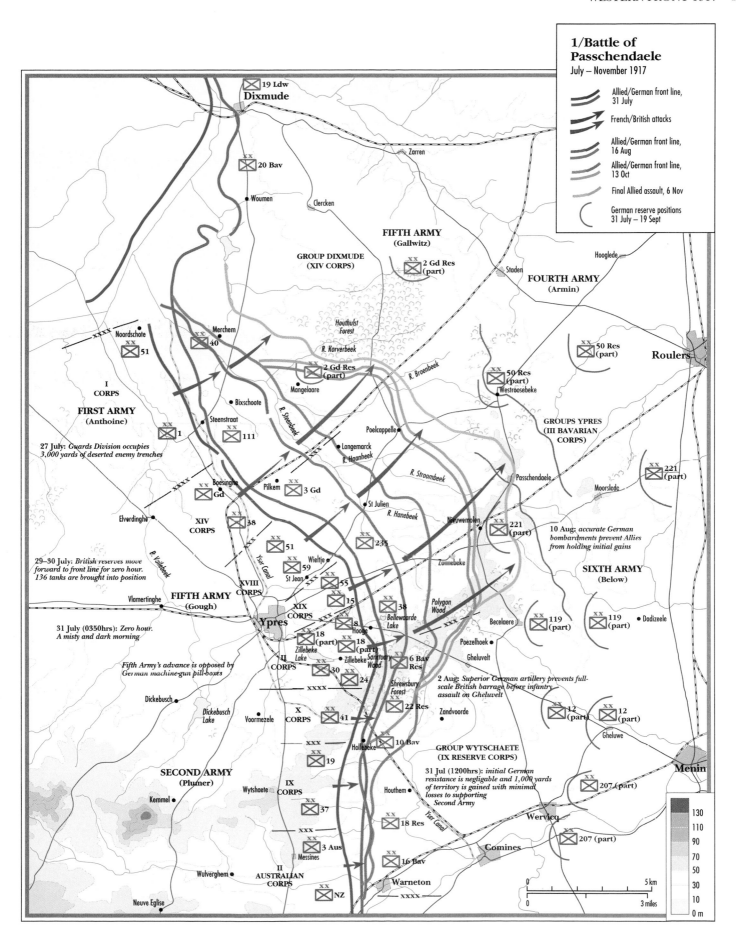

1/Battle of
Passchendaele
July – November 1917

Allied/German front line,
31 July

French/British attacks

Allied/German front line,
16 Aug

Allied/German front line,
13 Oct

Final Allied assault, 6 Nov

German reserve positions
31 July – 19 Sept

19 Ldw
Dixmude

20 Bav

Woumen

Clercken

Zarren

FIFTH ARMY
(Gallwitz)

GROUP DIXMUDE
(XIV CORPS)

2 Gd Res
(part)

Hooglede

Staden

FOURTH ARMY
(Armin)

Houthulst
Forest

R. Korverbeek

Merchem

40

50 Res
(part)

Roulers

Noordschote

51

2 Gd Res
(part)

Mangelaare

R. Broenbeek

50 Res
(part)

Westroosebeke

I
CORPS

Bixschoote

FIRST ARMY
(Anthoine)

Steenstraat

R. Steenbeek

Poelcappelle

R. Stroombeek

Passchendaele

GROUPS YPRES
(III BAVARIAN
CORPS)

221
(part)

Moorsleda

27 July: Guards Division occupies
3,000 yards of deserted enemy trenches

1

111

Langemarck
R. Haanheek

R. Hanebeek

Nieuwemolen

221
(part)

10 Aug: accurate German
bombardments prevent Allies
from holding initial gains

Pilkem

3 Gd

St Julien

Boesinghe
Gd

Elverdinghe

XIV
CORPS

38

R. Vijfdebek

235

Zonnebeke

SIXTH ARMY
(Below)

29–30 July: British reserves move
forward to front line for zero hour.
136 tanks are brought into position

51

Wieltje

59

Yser Canal

St Jean

55

Polygon
Wood

119
(part)

119
(part)

Dadizeele

FIFTH ARMY
(Gough)

Vlamertinghe

XVIII
CORPS

XIX
CORPS

15

Bellewaarde
Lake

38

Becelaere

Ypres

18
(part)

Hooge

8

18
(part)

Poelzelhoek

31 July (0350hrs): Zero hour.
A misty and dark morning

Zillebeke
Lake

Sanctuary
Wood

6 Bav
Res

Ghelavelt

2 Aug: Superior German artillery prevents full-
scale British barrage before infantry
assault on Gheluvelt

II
CORPS

Fifth Army's advance is opposed by
German machine-gun pill-boxes

30

Zillebeke

24

Shrewsbury
Forest

Zandvoorde

12
(part)

12
(part)

Dickebusch

Dickebusch
Lake

Voormezele

X
CORPS

41

22 Res

Gheluwe

10 Bav

GROUP WYTSCHAETE
(IX RESERVE CORPS)

Menin

Hollebeke

207 (part)

SECOND ARMY
(Plumer)

19

31 Jul (1200hrs): initial German
resistance is negligable and 1,000 yards
of territory is gained with minimal
losses to supporting
Second Army

Houthem

Kemmel

Wytschaete

IX
CORPS

37

Yser Canal

Wervicq

18 Res

207 (part)

3 Aus

16 Bav

Comines

Messines

II
AUSTRALIAN
CORPS

Wulverghem

NZ

Warneton

Neuve Eglise

130
110
90
70
50
30
10
0 m

0 ____ 5 km

0 ____ 3 miles

Air War 1 1914–1917

In no area was technological advance so great or so rapid as in the development of aircraft. Derided by most military commanders, aircraft were at first envisaged aids to reconnaissance; their value in this role was proven for many British observers as early as August and September 1914, when the Royal Flying Corps noted German troop movements before the Battle of Mons and then, on 3 September, reported Kluck's change of direction as he wheeled north of Paris. The numbers of aircraft available to the major powers at the outbreak of war reflected their perceived importance: Russia had some 300, Germany about 240, France about 150 and Britain no more than 60.

Aerial photography

Once the Western Front had become static and cavalry patroling impossible, aerial reconnaissance rose in importance. Aircraft were then employed by both sides to photograph enemy trenches, a skill in which the French quickly established a lead.

Mapping improved through the use of overhead photographs, taken by airplanes and dirigibles at a greater height. To cover large areas – the usual requirement – mosaic maps were composed, joined together to form a spread. But only the centers of these photographs were accurate in scale. A refinement for covering large areas was later developed, in which the film was exposed at pre-fixed intervals while the airplane flew at a constant height and speed. The prints were then overlapped to form a uniform, panoramic view of enemy positions.

Airships

Germany's airship 'Zeppelin' fleet had figured strongly in many pre-war predictions, but in fact proved one of the major disappointments of the war. In 1914, Zeppelins dropped bombs on Liége, Antwerp and Warsaw, but proved highly vulnerable to gunfire. Early in 1915, the Germans began making use of the high altitude capability and long endurance of the Zeppelins by sending them against targets in England, where night raids caused some disruption to civil life, but had almost no effect on Britain's war effort. The development of effective warning systems and airplanes capable of climbing to Zeppelin altitudes doomed such raids towards the end of 1916.

Dogfights

Increasing activity in the air inevitably led to combat – the 'dogfights' of the early months of the war, a single airplane against another. Initially airplanes were unarmed, and pilots attempted to shoot each other down with rifles or pistols (some even took with them a brick or heavy stone with the object of dropping it through the flimsy fuselage of an enemy's airplane). Pilots generally avoided dogfights, because airplanes were extremely vulnerable, and parachutes were not issued. Most 'kills' in fact occurred when outmaneuvered pilots hit a high object or caused damage to their airplane by too abrupt a turn.

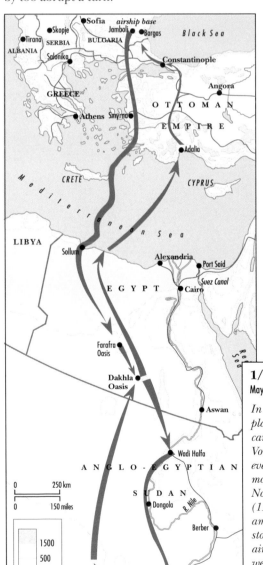

Sub-lieutenant R.A.J Warneford, V.C. who proved the vulnerability of Zeppelins to machine-gun fire by single-handedly destroying an airship as it returned from a raid over southern England on 7 June 1915. Warneford himself was killed 10 days later.

"They hovered over London for a considerable time... They left in no great haste, and the four enemy machines which were ultimately brought down were all hit while they were recrossing the sea."

The Times, 9 July 1917

1/The flight of the L59
May–November 1917

In May 1917, Germany planned to despatch a large airship carrying supplies to Von Lettow-Vorbeck (page 163). The mission was eventually undertaken by a specially modified L59, which departed on 21 November, loaded with 35,000 lb (15,890 Kg) of medicines, ammunition and food. After braving storms and engine problems the airship was recalled by radio message west of Khartoum. The L59 arrived back at Jamboli, Bulgaria on 25 November.

Early airplane armament consisted of machine guns operated by the observer in the front cockpit of a pusher airplane or the rear cockpit of a tractor airplane. In May 1915, however, air warfare was revolutionized by an invention of the Dutch aviation genius Anthony Fokker – the 'interrupter gear' – which allowed a pilot to fire a machine gun sited on the nose of the aircraft and pointing forward without hitting his propeller blades. This led directly to the development of specific 'fighter' airplanes, designed and built solely to destroy other aircraft. Numerous tactical skills evolved, among them the celebrated 'Immelmann turn', invented by the German air ace Max Immelmann and an important factor in the German establishment of temporary air superiority over the Western Front in late 1915. These technical and tactical developments were to change the nature of aerial warfare in the middle years of the war.

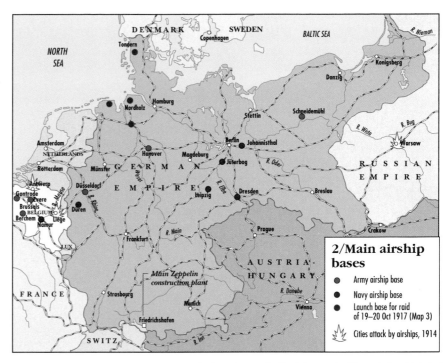

2/Main airship bases

- Army airship base
- Navy airship base
- Launch base for raid of 19–20 Oct 1917 (Map 3)
- Cities attack by airships, 1914

Main Zeppelin construction plant

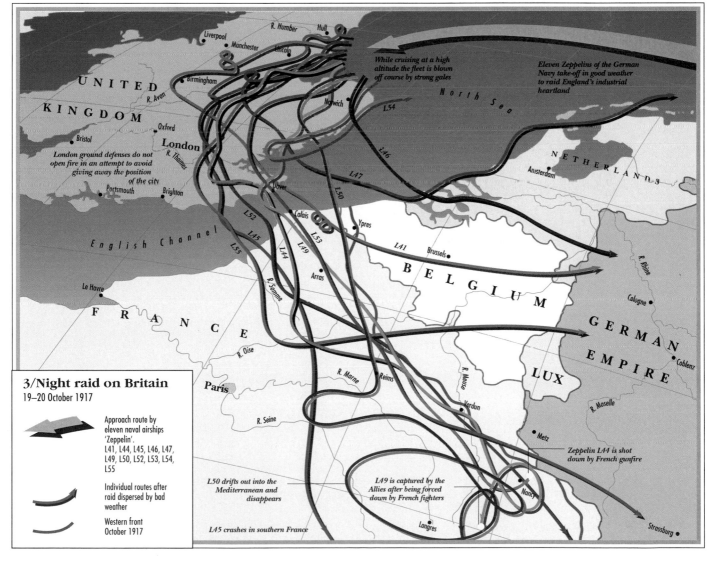

3/Night raid on Britain
19–20 October 1917

Approach route by eleven naval airships 'Zeppelin'. L41, L44, L45, L46, L47, L49, L50, L52, L53, L54, L55

Individual routes after raid dispersed by bad weather

Western front October 1917

While cruising at a high altitude the fleet is blown off course by strong gales

Eleven Zeppelins of the German Navy take-off in good weather to raid England's industrial heartland

London ground defenses do not open fire in an attempt to avoid giving away the position of the city

Zeppelin L44 is shot down by French gunfire

L49 is captured by the Allies after being forced down by French fighters

L50 drifts out into the Mediterranean and disappears

L45 crashes in southern France

Caporetto 24 October–12 November 1917

The Italian-Austrian front ran the entire length of the Alps; for two years both sides had sought, without success, to break through the mountains to the open plains beyond. The Eleventh Battle of the Isonzo ended on 15 September after the Italians had captured the strategically important Bainsizza Plateau but had then outrun their artillery and supplies. The Austrians asked for German help, and Ludendorff seized the opportunity to strike the strategic blow against Italy he intended as the Central Powers' main objective for 1917.

The operation was to be a joint Austro-German offensive by 15 infantry divisions (seven German, eight Austrian) grouped as Fourteenth Army under Otto von Below. Krafft von Dellmensingen, Ludendorff's mountain warfare expert, planned a massive blow between Tolmino and Plezzo, with the intention of breaking through into Friuli and the Venetian plain, trapping the Italian forces in the Carnic Alps. A powerful thrust by Below would quickly seize Cividale and Udine, cutting off the rear of the Italian Second Army and Third Army to its south. Some 1550 guns and more than 400 medium and long-range mortars were brought into position for a planned start date of 20 October.

Cadorna, the Italian commander-in-chief, had allowed a thinly held area to become a virtually unmanned gap between his Second Army and its neighbour, precisely where the Austro-German artillery and infantry were massing. Capello's Second Army comprised 34 divisions to the Central Powers' 35, but many of the Italian units were under strength in both infantry and artillery.

Austro-German tactics (developed by Oskar von Hutier) entailed detachments of infantry, with light artillery and machine guns carried on trucks, thrusting down the roads and valleys to sever Italian communications but leaving strongpoints and defenders on high ground to be picked off later.

Bad weather delayed the offensive 48 hours to the 24th, but at 0200hrs on that day, despite heavy rain, the Central Powers opened a sustained bombardment on a front of some 25mls/40km between Auzza and Monte Rombon. Mainly gas shells were fired because it was generally known that Italian gasmasks were primitive and ineffective.

The campaign

The following day the infantry advanced along the entire front from Monte Rombon to the southern end of the Bainsizza, covered by a thick mist. The Italian wings held, but the center was rapidly overrun and by early afternoon Below's troops were across the river. In freezing conditions on 26 October the Austro-Germans retook the Bainsizza plateau, which earlier the Italians had taken three weeks to capture. Two Italian corps, trapped in the Caporetto area, ceased to exist as fighting units, and Below poured troops through the gap; the Italian front now disintegrated in the entire sector.

The calamity almost overwhelmed Italy. Many troops resisted fiercely, but others gave up without a struggle, and the Second Army was largely reduced to a rabble. Below struck into Friuli on 28 October, and within a further three days had taken 60,000 prisoners and hundreds of guns.

On 25 October the Italian Third Army was obliged to retreat to escape encirclement, and Fourth Army to the north also fell back, fighting stubbornly.

Consequences and losses

The Austro-German advance finally ground to a halt 80mls/130km west of Caporetto on the River Piave, as much because of supply difficulties as stubborn Italian resistance. The Italian Second Army had been virtually wiped out; some estimates put total Italian casualties (including prisoners) as high as 600,000, and only the lack of further Austro-German reserves had prevented the removal of Italy from the war at a stroke.

For the Allies, Caporetto was one of the gravest moments of the war. But on the domestic front there were redeeming factors as Vittorio Orlando replaced the aged Boselli as prime minister. Cadorna's mixed success on the Isonzo front had already raised doubts as to his ability; Italian unpreparedness in the face of the Caporetto Offensive ensured his downfall and the elevation to command of the younger Armando Diaz. The Italian people found a renewed unity of purpose in adversity. A final and all important result of the disaster was the Rapallo Conference in November, which at last set up a Supreme War Council, after three years the first attempt to attain overall Allied unity of command and agreed strategy.

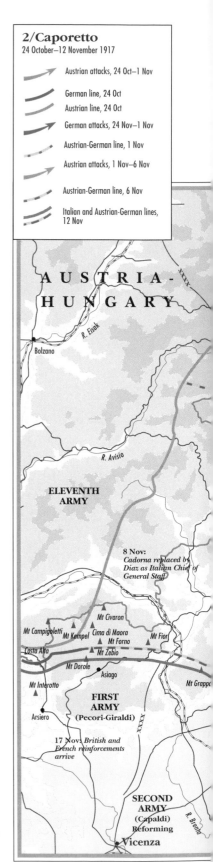

Austrian troops crossing the Isonzo. Under cover of a thick mountain mist the Fourteenth Army broke through the Italian lines almost immediately. Plans for an Italian defensive position on the Tagliamento River were defeated when Below's advance guard established a bridgehead on 2 November. A general retreat to the Piave became unavoidable.

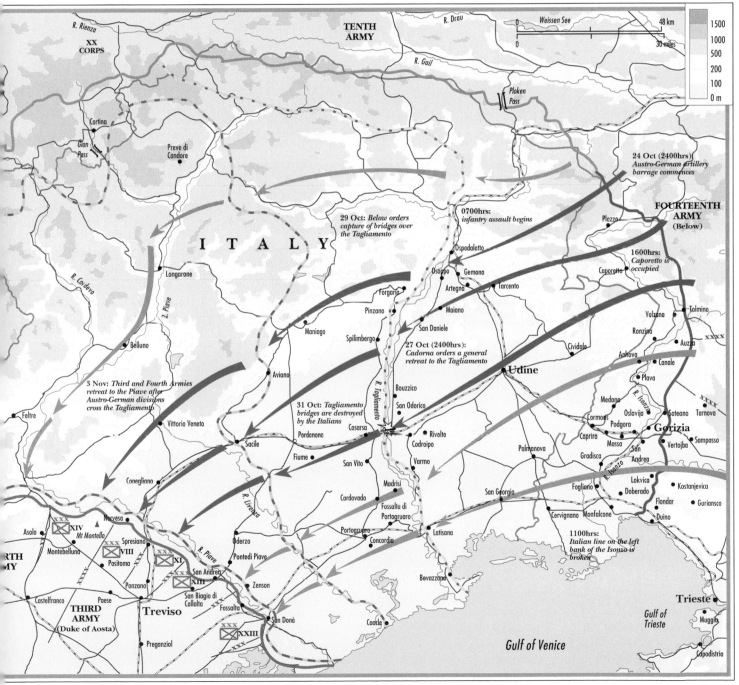

TENTH ARMY

XX CORPS

R. Rienza

R. Drau

R. Gail

Weissen See

0 ___ 48 km
0 ___ 30 miles

1500
1000
500
200
100
0 m

Ploken Pass

Cortina

Gian Pass

Preve di Candore

24 Oct (2400hrs):
Austro-German artillery barrage commences

FOURTEENTH ARMY
(Below)

Plozzo

I T A L Y

29 Oct: *Below orders capture of bridges over the Tagliamento*

0700hrs:
infantry assault begins

Ospedaletto

1600hrs:
Caporetto is occupied

Longarone

R. Cordevo

Osoppo
Gemona

Caporetto

Forgaria

Artegna

Tarcento

Maiano

Volzana

Tolmino

Pinzano

Ronzina

Auzza

San Daniele

xxxx

Maniago

Belluno

Spilimbergo

27 Oct (2400hrs):
Cadorna orders a general retreat to the Tagliamento

Cividale

Anhova

Canale

Aviano

Medana

Plava

3 Nov: *Third and Fourth Armies retreat to the Piave after Austro-German divisions cross the Tagliamento*

Bouzzico

Udine

Cormons

Oslavija

Sateano

Tarnova

xxxx

San Odorico

Podgora

Gorizia

31 Oct: *Tagliamento bridges are destroyed by the Italians*

Vittorio Veneto

Casarsa

Caprira

Mossa

Sampasso

Rivolto

Codroipo

Gradisca

San Andrea

Vertojba

Sacile

Pordenone

Feltre

Fiume

San Vito

Varmo

Palmanova

Fogliano

Lokvica

Kostanjevica

Doberado

Coneglino

Madrisi

Cordovado

Fossalta di Portogruaro

San Giorgio

Cervignano

Monfalcone

Flondar

Gurainsco

XXX
XIV
Mt Montello

Nervesa

Duino

Portogruaro

Concordia

Latisana

Asolo

Spresiano

1100hrs:
Italian line on the left bank of the Isonzo is broken

Montebelluna
RTH
MY

XXX
VIII
Positoma

Ponzano

Oderzo

Pontedi Piave

R. Piave

R. Livenza

Bevazzana

Trieste

XXX
XI

San Andrea

Zenson

Gulf of Trieste

San Biagio di Callalta

Muggia

Castelfranco

Paese

Treviso

Fossalta

Caorle

Capodistria

THIRD ARMY
(Duke of Aosta)

San Donà

XXX
XXIII

Preganziol

Gulf of Venice

The Russian Collapse March–September 1917

In March 1917, following Russia's huge losses during the Brusilov Offensive, civilian and military exhaustion after three years of war, decades of unrest and chronic lack of food, bread riots broke out in Petrograd. The Petrograd garrison, mostly old soldiers, mutinied on 10 March. Cossacks refused to dispel the rioters.

Tsar Nicholas II, visiting the front, tried to return to Petrograd; railwaymen stopped his train. Under pressure from the generals, Nicholas abdicated and a Provisional Government was established under Prince Lvov. The real power in Petrograd, however, soon rested with the Council of Workers' and Soldiers' Deputies (the Soviet). The Provisional Government, established by the Stavka and the Duma and at odds with the Bolshevik-dominated Petrograd Soviet, pledged itself to continue the war. The Soviet, fearful of repressive measures by the officer class, issued on its own authority 'Order Number One', which deprived officers of disciplinary authority. Despite a counter-order from the Provisional Government, Order Number One was broadcast throughout the armed forces and triggered a final breakdown of service discipline. Mutinous soldiers and sailors murdered some officers; others were summarily replaced by soldiers' councils. By the middle of April, an estimated 50 percent of the officer corps had been eliminated by one method or another. Disorder was further stirred up by Bolshevik agitators, notably Lenin, who had returned from Swiss exile in a sealed carriage across Germany and promised redistribution of land in favor of the peasants.

Germany immediately ceased offensive operations in the east through fear of reuniting the Russians in defense of their homeland. Despite this turmoil, the lawyer Alexander Kerensky, appointed war minister on 16 May and leader of the Provisional Government in July, tried to keep faith with Russia's western allies by launching a new offensive in Galicia, again led by Brusilov.

The Kerensky offensive

Also known as the Brusilov offensive, his armies attacked toward Lemberg on 1 July with the limited number of troops still capable of combat duties, the Seventh and Eleventh armies. These thrust into Bothmer's composite Südarmee (four German, three Austrian and one Turkish division) for some 30 miles on a front of 100 miles. Despite considerable success against the Austrian Second and Third Armies, Russian discipline and willingness to fight evaporated as their supply lines broke down and German resistance stiffened.

On 19 July, General Hoffmann, de facto German commander in the east, having quickly secured reinforcements from the west by rail, counter-attacked with an intensive bombardment in the north of the Russian offensive, followed by an assault that rolled up the demoralized Russian armies in rapid succession. The only limit to the German advance was the lack of the logistical means to occupy more territory.

On 1 September activity moved to the north, when the German Eighth Army (von Hutier) attacked the Russian right flank. While a holding force threatened Riga, three divisions crossed the Dvina on pontoon bridges and turned south thereby encircling the fortress. The Russian Twelfth Army streamed eastward in panic and in complete disorder.

The attack was the first employment by Germany of a new method of assault known as 'Hutier tactics' after the commanding general. A short and intensive bombardment was immediately followed by infantry attacks. Gas and smoke shells were extensively used to mask enemy strongpoints while infantry and light guns bypassed them, leaving them to be eliminated later by follow-up units. These tactics were to be employed by the Germans with equal success at Caporetto six weeks later (page 132).

The Battle of Riga effectively ended Russian military activity. Kerensky fled to Moscow and the Bolsheviks began to take over government (the October Revolution). Lenin, Trotsky and other Bolshevik leaders opened peace negotiations with Germany, the preliminaries being concluded at Brest-Litovsk on 15 December, thereby ending hostilities on the Eastern Front. Russia was to degenerate into civil war before the Bolsheviks gained absolute control, but now German attention could be switched entirely to the west before America could intervene.

Russian trenches at the moment of a German gas attack on the eastern front, 1917.

"By playing at war, you are delivering the revolution to the Germans... there is no longer time to exchange diplomatic notes... We have to propose peace to them outright."

Lenin opposing Trotsky's initial intention to continue the war in the east

A soviet official checking documents at the entrance of the Revolutionay Headquarters in Smolny during the October armed uprising. Lenin proclaimed the victory of the socialist revolution on 25 October, 1917.

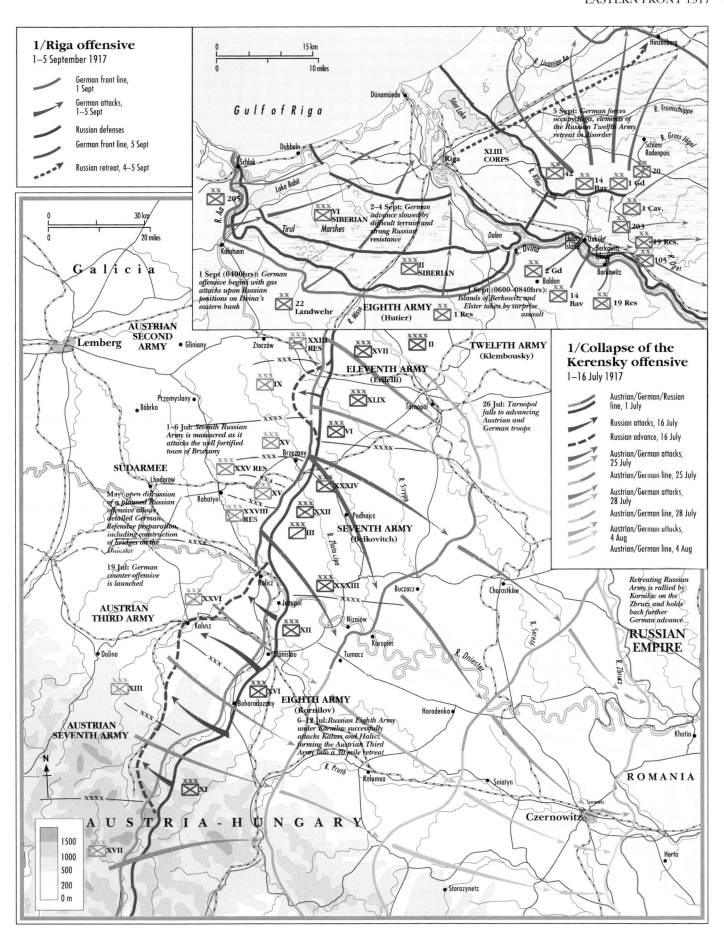

War at Sea The Mediterranean 1914–1918

The naval war in the Mediterranean, an area of more than 100,000 square miles with numerous deep-water harbors, necessarily proved of great complexity. For the Allies a major problem was the difficulty of co-ordinating the operations of three powers – Great Britain, France and Italy – each of which had different aims and preoccupations. Italy sought coastal security, France to retain contact with the North African colonies and Great Britain to guard the route through the Suez Canal to India and the South Pacific.

Goeben and *Breslau*

British Mediterranean power in August 1914 consisted of three battlecruisers, four armored cruisers and support vessels. Their initial task was to protect the movement of French troops from North Africa to southern France from the German battlecruiser *Goeben* and the light cruiser *Breslau*. The two German ships bombarded Algerian ports on 4 August and then used their superior speed to elude pursuit by

2/War in the Adriatic
1914–1918
(Key as main map)

Opposite: A pre-dreadnought shells Turkish defenses during the Allied landings at Suvla Bay, August 1915.

"the Austrian fleet has established a moral ascendency in the Adriatic and has played the part of a weaker force with conspicuous success. Not only has it succeeded in weakening the Italian fleet, but it has immobilised a force very considerably superior to itself."

**British Naval Attaché in Rome
September 1915**

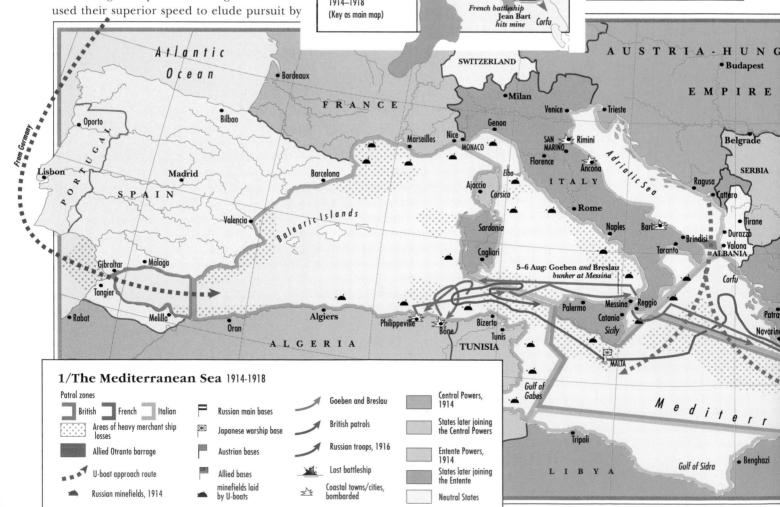

1/The Mediterranean Sea 1914-1918

Patrol zones

British   French   Italian

Areas of heavy merchant ship losses

Allied Otranto barrage

U-boat approach route

Russian minefields, 1914

Russian main bases

Japanese warship base

Austrian bases

Allied bases

minefields laid by U-boats

Goeben and Breslau

British patrols

Russian troops, 1916

Lost battleship

Coastal towns/cities, bombarded

Central Powers, 1914

States later joining the Central Powers

Entente Powers, 1914

States later joining the Entente

Neutral States

two British battlecruisers. The Germans bunkered at Messina, and later at Denusa, before making good their escape to Constantinople, on orders from Berlin. Having foiled British attempts to cut them off, they lay anchored near the entrance to the Golden Horn. On 3 August the British Government had informed Turkey that it was requisitioning two battleships which had been built in Britain for the Turkish Navy and which had been paid for by popular subscription; in response, Turkey agreed to purchase the *Goeben* and *Breslau* from Germany for a mere four million pounds, the German sailors being retained and a German admiral given command of the Turkish navy. These actions collectively tipped the balance in Turkey's decision to enter the war on the side of the Central Powers.

The Adriatic
The main naval activity of 1915 was that of the Gallipoli campaign (page 60) but, with Italy's entry into the war, naval activity also began in the Adriatic. The problem here for the Allies was the existence of a large Austrian fleet with numerous deep-water harbors, repair and docking facilities along the coast of Dalmatia.

As in the North Sea, a direct assault on the enemy fleet was out of the question. The primary Allied task was therefore to prevent Austrian warships from threatening supply routes through the Mediterranean. The Straits of Otranto, no more than 45 miles wide, were closed with a net barrage between Brindisi and Otranto on the Italian peninsula and Serbian-controlled Valona on the Albanian coast. The Austrian surface fleet was thus confined to the Adriatic, though Austrian and German U-boats (the latter transported in sections overland by rail and assembled at Pola) were able to get beneath the nets and sink Allied shipping in the Mediterranean.

The Black Sea
The Russian Black Sea Fleet was superior to that of Turkey, even with the addition of the *Goeben* and *Breslau*. The main force comprised five old battleships, three cruisers, seventeen destroyers and four submarines. On 6 November 1914, Vice-Admiral Eberhardt mined the entrance of the Bosporus and bombarded the Turkish town of Zonguldak, from which coal was shipped (there was no rail link) to Constantinople. Next he bombarded Trebizond, the supply port for Turkish troops in the Caucasus.

Eberhardt continued to attack Zonguldak, but the Germans seized the opportunity to bombard Odessa, where Russian transports were assembling to support the Dardanelles campaign by landing troops on the shores of the Bosporus. This project had to be abandoned when the *Goeben*, earlier damaged, was repaired; the powerful German-Turkish battlecruiser was capable of disrupting any Russian naval activity in the area. In 1916, Russian troops were ferried from Mariampol, safe from enemy attacks, to the recently captured Trebizond, on the north Turkish coast, which was thereafter used as a military port.

No great naval clash occurred in the Black Sea, although submarines claimed victims on both sides and in January 1918 *Goeben* and *Breslau*, in a sortie into the Mediterranean, sank Allied ships in Kusu Bay. *Breslau* hit a mine in the Agean and sank; *Goeben*, though assailed by British bomber and submarine attacks, escaped back into the Black Sea.

Cambrai November – December 1917

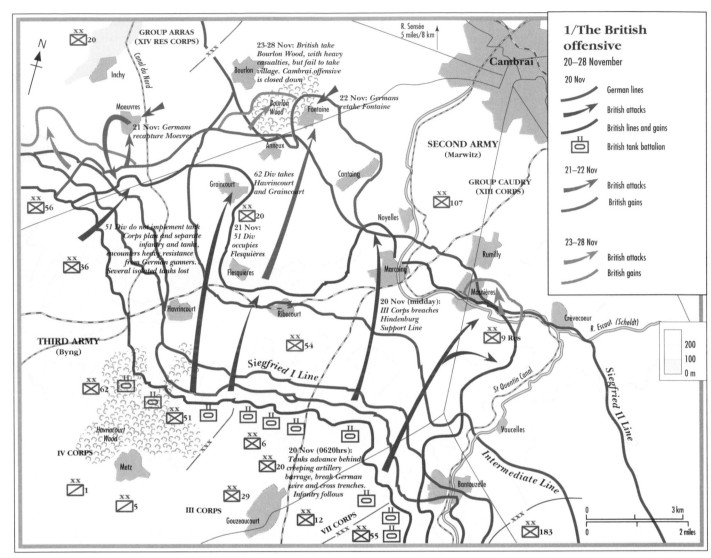

1/The British offensive

20—28 November

20 Nov

German lines

British attacks

British lines and gains

British tank battalion

21—22 Nov

British attacks

British gains

23—28 Nov

British attacks

British gains

200
100
0 m

R. Sensée
5 miles/8 km

GROUP ARRAS
(XIV RES CORPS)

Cambrai

23-28 Nov: British take Bourlon Wood, with heavy casualties, but fail to take village. Cambrai offensive is closed down

Inchy

Bourlon

Bourlon Wood

Fontaine

22 Nov: Germans retake Fontaine

Moeuvres

21 Nov: Germans recapture Moeuvres

Anneux

SECOND ARMY
(Marwitz)

GROUP CAUDRY
(XIII CORPS)

Cantaing

62 Div takes Havrincourt and Graincourt

Graincourt

Noyelles

51 Div do not implement tank Corps plan and separate infantry and tanks, encounters heavy resistance from German gunners. Several isolated tanks lost

21 Nov: 51 Div occupies Flesquières

Rumilly

Flesquières

Marcoing

Mœuvres

Havrincourt

Ribecourt

20 Nov (midday): III Corps breaches Hindenburg Support Line

Mœsnières

THIRD ARMY
(Byng)

Siegfried I Line

9 Res

Crèvecoeur

R. Escaut (Scheldt)

Siegfried II Line

Havrincourt Wood

St Quentin Canal

Vaucelles

IV CORPS

Metz

20 Nov (0620hrs): Tanks advance behind creeping artillery barrage, break German wire and cross trenches. Infantry follows

Intermediate Line

Bantouzelle

III CORPS

Gouzeaucourt

VII CORPS

0   3 km

0   2 miles

November 1917 found the Allies facing a bleak record of failure at Passchendaele, Caporetto and on the Eastern Front. Some success, however local, was needed to preserve morale.

For some time it had seemed to Haig that tanks might be used en masse to good effect in the area around Cambrai. The ground here was firm, the German positions lightly held, and capture of the ridge near Bourlon would provide an uninterrupted view over German rear areas almost as far as Valenciennes. Surprise could be achieved by foregoing the customary preliminary barrage and by camouflaging the tanks themselves; the poor autumn weather might also limit the effect of German spotter aircraft.

Byng, commander of the British Third Army, saw greater opportunities. Once the Hinden-

Left: The British Mark IV tank had a devastating effect on German morale at Cambrai, but the weapon was still in its infancy, and more were lost as a result of mechanical breakdown than enemy fire.

burg Line had been penetrated, his army could pour through the gaps between the Canal du Nord and the St Quentin Canal (Map 1), then seize Cambrai and the Sensée bridges. All German forces south of the Sensée and west of the Canal du Nord could be cut off, and Third Army could thrust toward Valenciennes.

Tank tactics

Tanks worked in threes – an advance guard tank and two infantry tanks, all carrying a bundle of brushwood known as a fascine. The advance guard tank was to smash through the enemy wire and, without crossing the first trench, turn left and sweep it with machine-gun fire.

The two infantry tanks were then to make for the break in the wire. The first was to drop its fascine into the trench, turn left and sweep the trench. The second was to cross the trench on the fascine, make for the support trench, drop its fascine and cross. It too was to turn left and machine-gun the trench. The advance guard tank, yet to cross a trench, was then to cross both trenches on the fascines already laid, drop its own fascine into the third trench, cross and turn left. This was to be repeated along the front.

The battle

The tanks moved off in mist at 0610hrs, supported by a creeping barrage. Surprise was complete; along much of the front, the German defenders panicked and abandoned their trenches (a notable exception was the position around Flesquières, where a single German gun knocked out seven tanks). The front was penetrated in 10 hours to a depth of 5mls/8km. Ahead lay an unfinished German defense line, then open country.

After 10 hours, however, many of the tank crews were exhausted, and no reserves were available. The tanks had in many places outrun their supporting infantry, and German reserves – including Richthofen's "Circus" – were rushed to the front. Further Allied gains were made, but by 27 November two tank brigades had to be withdrawn through fatigue and heavy tank losses (largely through mechanical breakdown). An attempt to exploit the initial breakthrough with cavalry proved disastrous, and the prize of Bourlon continued to evade Third Army. Moreover, Byng's III and IV Corps now found themselves in a dangerous salient.

On 30 November, Marwitz counter-attacked southward from Bourlon and westward from Honnecourt (map 2), employing (for the first time on the Western Front) the infiltration

tactics developed in Russia and employed to devastating effect at Caporetto. German success was almost as dramatic as the initial British assault. The attack from the north was held, but to the south the offensive made strong progress.

Consequences

The British penetrated along a front of 6mls/ l0km and took some 10,000 prisoners and 200 guns on 20 November; 10 days later they lost almost equal casualties and the bulk of the ground they had captured. Both sides lost approximately 45,000 men.

The true debut of the supreme weapon of modern warfare – the tank – had been wasted through lack of reserves and failure to appreciate its true potential. "Fortunately," noted the German High Command, "the enemy was himself taken by surprise at the extent of his success."

General Sir Julian Byng. More optimistic than Haig, he believed that a tank breakthrough at Cambrai would allow his Third Army to advance deep into German-held territory.

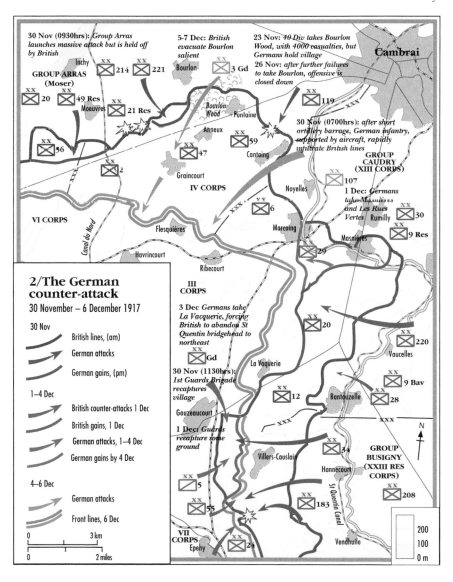

Palestine and Mesopotamia 1917–1918

In spring and summer 1916, British operations under Sir Archibald Murray concentrated on extending the Suez Canal defenses into the Sinai Desert. By the end of the year, the British Egyptian Army had reached El Arish.

The Sinai peninsula was finally cleared of all Turkish forces, Murray was then authorised to launch a limited offensive into Palestine, the main points of entry into which were Gaza and Beersheba. His troops failed in two attempts to take Gaza (26–27 March and 17–19 April).

The British War Office then replaced Murray with Sir Edmund Allenby, from the Western Front, with instructions to take Jerusalem "before Christmas". Allenby insisted on reinforcements; his total force rose to 88,000 men, including the Desert Mounted Corps of horse cavalry and camels.

The campaign

At the Third Battle of Gaza, or Beersheba (Map 2), Allenby left a mere three divisions demonstrating in front of Gaza while moving the bulk of his forces eastward to Beersheba. A spectacular flanking movement by the Desert Mounted Corps took the defenders by surprise, while infantry made frontal attacks on the town. The all-day battle (31 October) ended with an Australian cavalry charge into the town, capturing the water supply intact.

On 2 November Turkish reinforcements mounted a counter-attack, but by 7 November, Allenby's troops had taken Tel esh Sheria, a commanding hill north of Beersheba. He then sent the Desert Mounted Corps across country to the sea. The Turks evacuated Gaza, Eighth Army retreating up the coast, and the Seventh falling back on Jerusalem.

Allenby at first concentrated his pursuit along the coastal sector, driving the Eighth Army back at the Battle of Junction Station, despite shortage of water and severe logistical problems. The Allies broke through Turkish lines before Jerusalem on 8 December and captured it the following day, to tumultuous subsequent celebration in a war-weary Britain.

Mesopotamia

The Allied advance into Palestine had severely weakened the Turkish position in Mesopotamia; a planned offensive had had to be abandoned as troops were transferred to the defense of

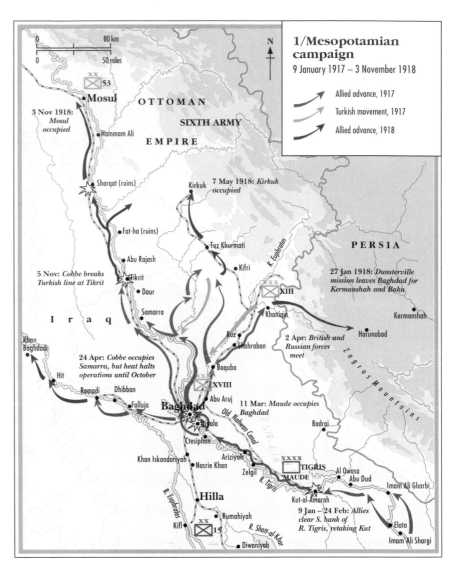

1/Mesopotamian campaign
9 January 1917 – 3 November 1918

→ Allied advance, 1917
→ Turkish movement, 1917
→ Allied advance, 1918

Gaza. Sir Frederick Maude, (British commander since August 1916) had defeated the Turks at the Second Battle of Kut in February, then taken Baghdad after several days of fighting in March.

To consolidate his hold on the city, Maude divided his force into three columns, to advance up the Tigris, Euphrates and Diyala rivers in pursuit of Turkish remnants into central Mesopotamia and in the hope of linking with Russian forces from the Caucasus. He prepared to continue the advance to seize the oil fields of Mosul, but died of cholera in Baghdad on 18 November, leaving it to his successor Sir William Marshall to gain this objective the following year.

Below opposite: A German 10.5cm howitzer, part of a German–Turkish battery near Gaza. Germany supplied a large number of artillery pieces to Turkey, together with a limited number of advisors and senior officers.

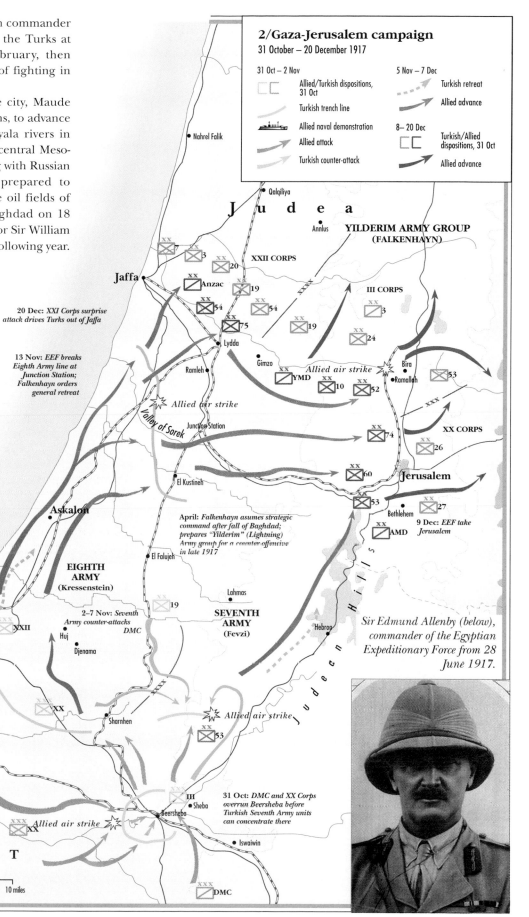

2/Gaza-Jerusalem campaign
31 October – 20 December 1917

31 Oct – 2 Nov
- Allied/Turkish dispositions, 31 Oct
- Turkish trench line
- Allied naval demonstration
- Allied attack
- Turkish counter-attack

5 Nov – 7 Dec
- Turkish retreat
- Allied advance

8– 20 Dec
- Turkish/Allied dispositions, 31 Oct
- Allied advance

20 Dec: XXI Corps surprise attack drives Turks out of Jaffa

13 Nov: EEF breaks Eighth Army line at Junction Station; Falkenhayn orders general retreat

April: Falkenhayn assumes strategic command after fall of Baghdad; prepares "Yilderim" (Lightning) Army group for a counter-offensive in late 1917

5 Nov: Turkish evacuation of Gaza begins (occupied by EEF 7 Nov)

30–31 Oct: bombardment and naval demonstration against Gaza mask EEF concentration against Beersheba; XXI Corps (Bulfin) storms defenses (1–2 Nov)

2–7 Nov: Seventh Army counter-attacks DMC

Sir Edmund Allenby (below), commander of the Egyptian Expeditionary Force from 28 June 1917.

Late Fall: Royal Flying Corps finally wins air superiority in Palestine

31 Oct: DMC and XX Corps overrun Beersheba before Turkish Seventh Army units can concentrate there

British prisoners help identify and collect valuables from the dead.

PART V
1918

Few foresaw in January that the war would end in 1918. The Allies entered the year frustrated, for all their hopes, save in the Near East, had been brought to nought. The German U-boat campaign, though abated through the introduction of the convoy system, still threatened supply routes from America. Time was needed before American forces could arrive on the Western Front to replenish Anglo-French losses. Russia had collapsed. For the moment Great Britain, now again numerically inferior to Germany, had to fall on the defensive. In March 1917 there had been some three Allied troops to every two Germans in the west (178 British, French and Belgian divisions opposed by 129 German divisions), but a year later the trains withdrawing troops from defeated Russia had changed the ratio; now there were four Germans to every three Allies.

Yet it needed a disaster to prod the Allies into the creation of a unified command. That disaster came at Caporetto (page 132). At a conference at Rapallo in November 1917, the formation of a Supreme War Council was agreed upon, to assemble permanently at Versailles. This, however, was little more than a formal committee with no authority on the field. The arrangement would hardly serve, as reports were received in early November of German troops beginning to be withdrawn from the east in evident preparation for a major attack. By the end of March 1918, the Germans mustered 192 divisions in the west; the Allies, partly due to their dispatch of troops to bolster Italy, comprised only 173 divisions – and even that total was achieved by counting the four and a half larger American divisions as two each.

But the establishment of the committee was to have important consequences. The Passchendaele Offensive lost Haig the little confidence that the British Prime Minister, Lloyd George, had ever had in him. Unable to dismiss his senior field commander, Lloyd George sought to curb his powers and freedom of action. To this end he promoted a more vigorous prosecution of the war against Germany's eastern allies, withheld reinforcements bound for Haig's armies and promoted unity of command under a French general. The committee proved impotent in March 1918 when German assaults in the west became imminent. On 26 March Foch was appointed Allied co-ordinator at an emergency meeting of the Supreme War Council; on 3 April, the council went further and appointed him Commander-in-Chief of all Allied forces in France. At last the Allies had achieved unity of command.

Foch's appointment came not a moment too soon, for Ludendorff and selected chiefs of staff of the armies on the Western Front had met at Mons in November to determine German strategy in

After fierce and costly fighting Canadian troops reach the Canal du Nord in the final stages of the war

1918. The Germans lacked the means to mount a general offensive and so conceived a succession of attacks, closely staged and all conducted on a massive scale, that would either break the Allied front or lead to the collapse of their will to resist. In either event, the consequences would be such that no number of American troops arriving on the front could reverse. Faced with the option of seeking victory over either the British or the French, the German High Command opted – probably correctly – for the chance of a British defeat in northern France, where their armies had little space to maneuver and where British and French forces could be separated. This would compromise the French, whereas an attack on the French, where space allowed them to retreat without perilous strategic risk, would not necessarily impair British capacity.

Ludendorff was to launch five great offensives in the west, using, where appropriate, "Hutier" tactics. These tactics, employed to good effect at Riga and overwhelming effect at Caporetto, demanded secrecy prior to attack (in the first offensive, German trains behind the lines continuously shunted to disguise the movement of troops at night), a shock bombardment, followed by a rolling barrage and infantry thrusts at weak defensive points, the stronger being left for later conquest. The trouble with Ludendorff's attacks in the west lay in the fact that they were punching a sack: if the canvas were not penetrated, a vulnerable salient or bulge would result. In all five assaults, Ludendorff undoubtedly achieved tactical victories but no strategic gain. The last of Ludendorff's offensives, in the Champagne–Marne area, beginning on 15 July, designed to pinch out the Reims area, met a similar fate, that of gaining ground but not a breakthrough. Foch, already planning a great counter-attack, was again forewarned of the impending blow by deserters, prisoners and aerial reconnaissance. Ludendorff, though not yet admitting defeat and still hopeful of a further, decisive attack in Flanders, prepared for a general withdrawal from the salient Soissons-Château–Thierry-Reims area to reduce the German front. In some five months he had lost nearly half a million casualties; the Allies had sustained slightly more, but were being replenished at the average rate of 300,000 American troops each month.

The Fourteen Points

Political attempts to end the war were again being made following the issue in an address to Congress on 8 January by President Wilson of his program for peace, the "Fourteen Points". These included open covenants, freedom of the seas in war and peace, removal of trade barriers, armament reductions, adjustment of colonial claims, evacuation of Russian territory and the restoration of Belgium and all occupied French territory, the return of Alsace-Lorraine to France, the drawing of Italian frontiers on lines of nationality, the autonomy of the Austro-Hungarian peoples and the evacuation of Romania, Montenegro and Serbia. Turkish parts of the Ottoman Empire were to be given sovereignty, but other nationalities under Turkish rule to be freed. Poland was to be guaranteed independence and given free access to the sea. All this was to be guaranteed by the League of Nations, an association of states ensuring liberty and territorial integrity for all. These "points", later to be the cause of Allied unease and friction did not meet with universal welcome; while America wished primarily to defeat Germany and then retire into isolation, the Allies and the Central Powers saw a compromise peace and a return to the status quo in different lights. To the Allies it meant a return to the situation in 1914 before the outbreak of war, with Germany punished for her aggression and paying damages; for the Central Powers it meant the situation at the end of 1916, allowing them to keep some of their conquests while being compensated for abandoning the rest. This had been the rock against which all peace feelers had foundered since 1917.

The tide finally turns

Thus, despite Wilson's idealistic proposals, the war continued. With the repulse of Ludendorff's last offensive, Foch gained the initiative and, having gained it, was resolved to give the Germans no respite while his own reserves were assembling. Foch's counter-attack on 18 July eradicated the German Marne salient and, on 20 July, Ludendorff finally abandoned any thought of a renewed attack in Flanders, accepting the need for defensive warfare. Allied attacks continued along the entire front. On 8 August, a carefully concealed British attack on the Somme with 456 tanks broke the German line and

Counting the cost: French troops identify and bury their fallen comrades, July 1918

only came to a halt four days later through lack of reserves and the impediment of the wilderness created by the battles of 1916. The Germans began surrendering after minimal resistance. This day was called by Ludendorff the "Black Day" of the German Army, when its spirit was evidently broken (page 166). Evidence of German decline convinced Foch that the war could be won in 1918. Instead of postponing the attempt until 1919, all Allied armies in the west combined in a simultaneous offensive.

Other fronts

Between 24 October and 4 November, Italian troops, supported by British and French units, defeated the Austrians at the Battle of Vittorio Veneto (page 176) and on 3 November Austria signed an armistice. In the Balkans, Bulgaria signed an armistice on 29 September (page 174) and a month later (30 October) Turkey was obliged to do likewise after Allenby's victories (page 170). In East Africa Germany was finally driven from her colony, despite the brilliant generalship of Lettow-Vorbeck.

Treaty of Brest-Litovsk

The armistice between Germany and Russia had been signed on 3 December, 1917 and a conference was immediately convened at Brest-Litovsk, in eastern Poland, to negotiate an end to Russia's participation in the war. Trotsky, the chief negotiator for the Bolsheviks, attempted to delay the progress of the conference in the hope that civil unrest in Germany might turn into full-scale revolution. Germany's response to such tactics was a continua-

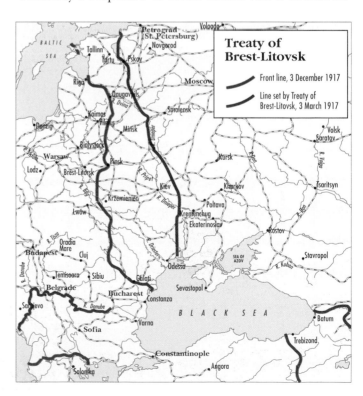

Treaty of
Brest-Litovsk

Front line, 3 December 1917

Line set by Treaty of
Brest-Litovsk, 3 March 1917

tion of its eastern advance. Unable to respond to such a threat, Russia signed the treaty on 3 March 1918. The terms of the document had become increasingly punitive in the face of Russian procrastination and Russia was forced to relinquish the Baltic provinces, the Caucasus, Poland, White Russia, Ukraine and Finland. After the Allied victory in 1918 the borders established at Brest-Litovsk remained predominantly unchanged.

Germany's collapse

Faced with mutiny (page 164), the defeat of her allies, and the exhaustion of her civilian population, Germany had no option but to open peace negotiations. Moreover, both servicemen and civilians became afflicted with the so-called "Spanish influenza" which swept across the globe, becoming the greatest killer of the century so far. Thus to all the demean-ing horrors of the trenches was added fever. It has been estimated that on the Indian sub-continent alone more people died in the pandemic than were killed on all the battlefields of the war combined. To facilitate peace moves, Ludendorff resigned on 27 October. Prince Max of Baden, the newly appointed chancellor, accepted Wilson's terms, a republic was proclaimed and the Kaiser fled to sanctuary in Holland. A German delegation agreed to Allied terms – virtually unconditional surrender – in Foch's railway carriage at Compiègne on 11 November and hostilities ceased at 11:00 on that day. Thus the war, probably the most dreadful and certainly the most costly in life and resources to date, came to an end. The Allies had certainly "won" but whether they had won what they had fought for would be determined by the terms of the peace treaties and the events that sprang therefrom.

British troops storm the ragged remains of the Hindenburg Line.
German attempts to halt the Allied advance and thereby gain more
favorable peace terms were shattered by the force of the Allied assaults

Timeline 1918

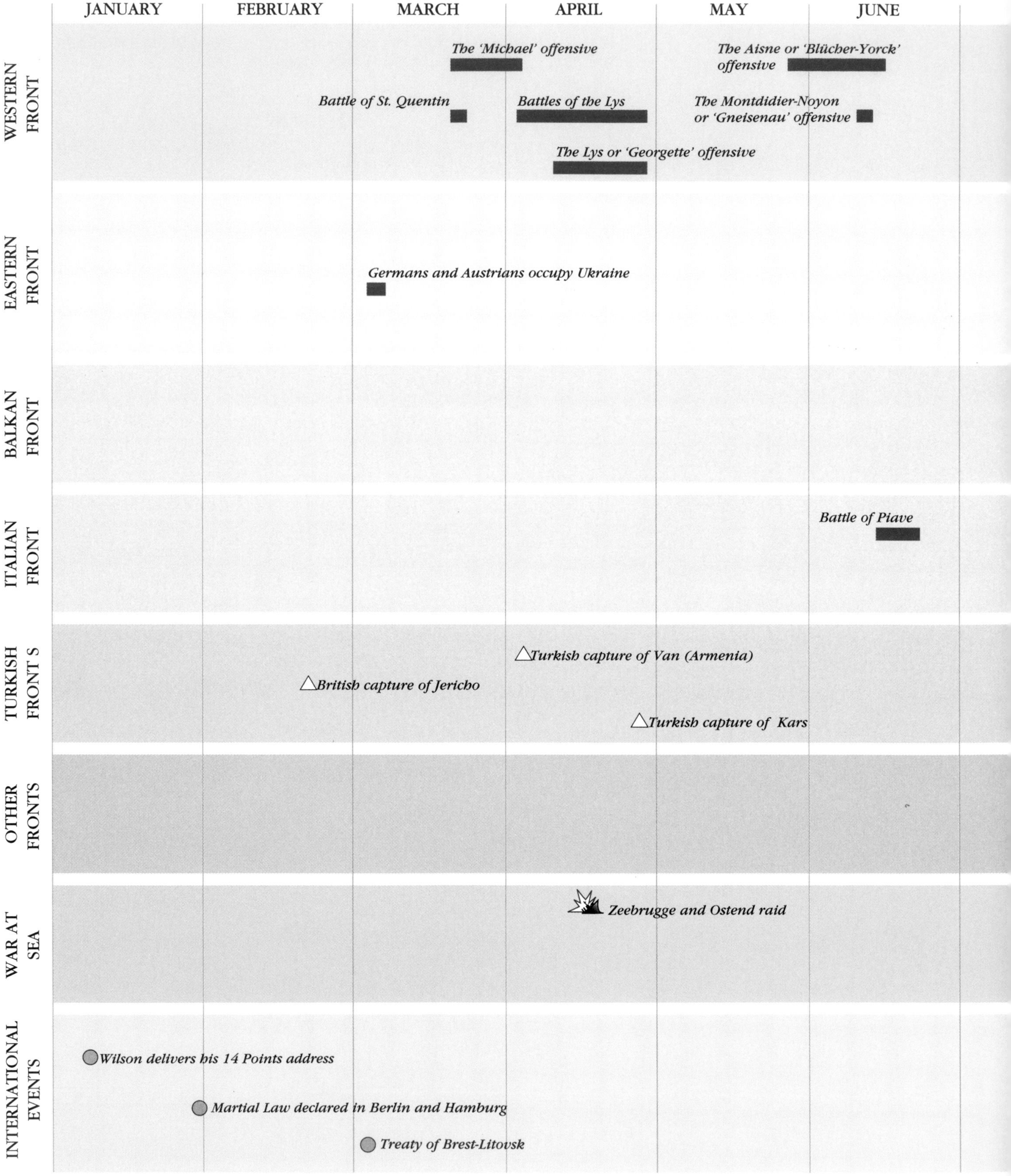

	JANUARY	FEBRUARY	MARCH	APRIL	MAY	JUNE

WESTERN FRONT

The 'Michael' offensive

The Aisne or 'Blücher-Yorck' offensive

Battle of St. Quentin

Battles of the Lys

The Montdidier-Noyon or 'Gneisenau' offensive

The Lys or 'Georgette' offensive

EASTERN FRONT

Germans and Austrians occupy Ukraine

BALKAN FRONT

ITALIAN FRONT

Battle of Piave

TURKISH FRONTS

△Turkish capture of Van (Armenia)

△British capture of Jericho

△Turkish capture of Kars

OTHER FRONTS

WAR AT SEA

Zeebrugge and Ostend raid

INTERNATIONAL EVENTS

◉Wilson delivers his 14 Points address

◉Martial Law declared in Berlin and Hamburg

◉Treaty of Brest-Litovsk

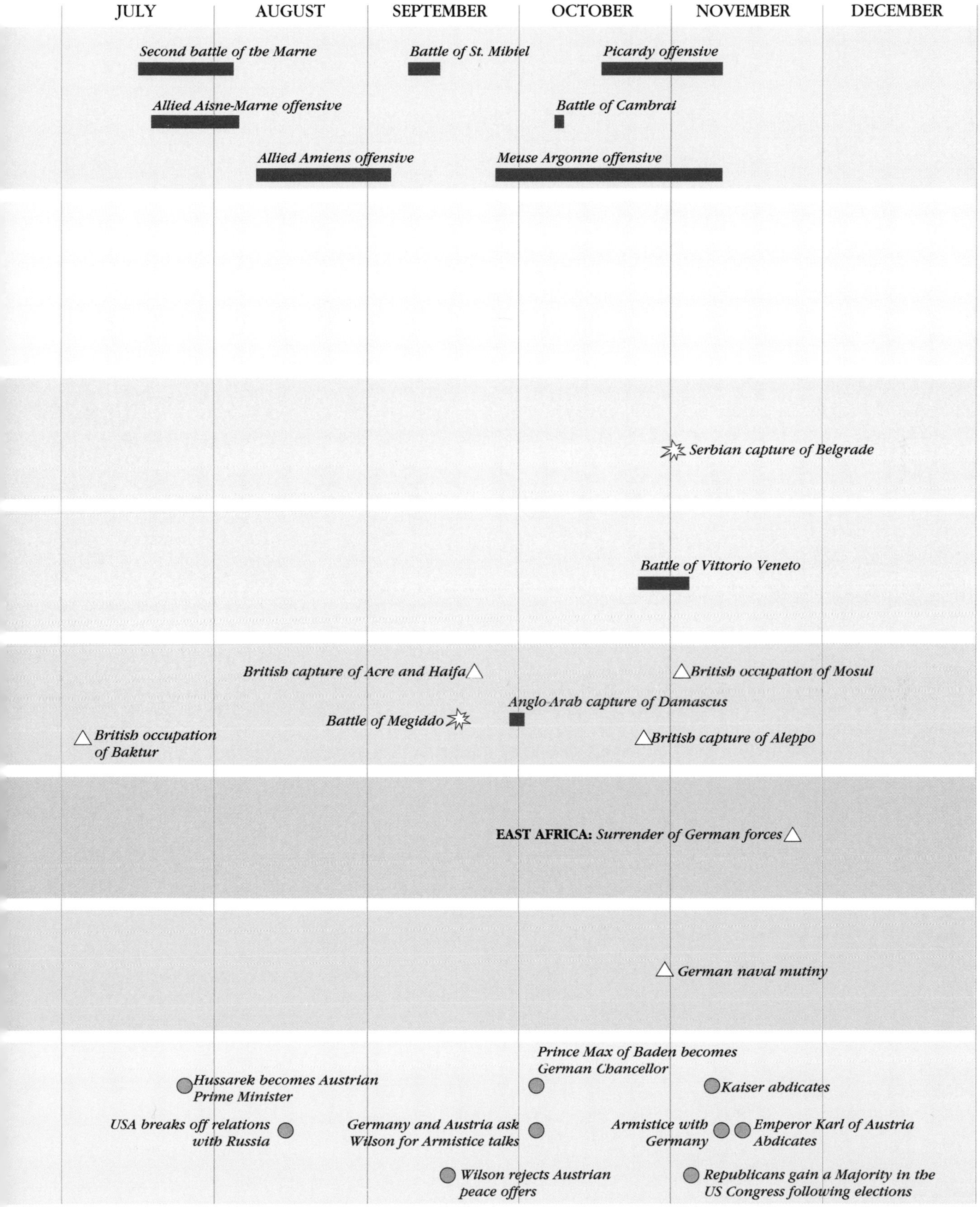

JULY	AUGUST	SEPTEMBER	OCTOBER	NOVEMBER	DECEMBER

Second battle of the Marne

Battle of St. Mihiel

Picardy offensive

Allied Aisne-Marne offensive

Battle of Cambrai

Allied Amiens offensive

Meuse Argonne offensive

✹ *Serbian capture of Belgrade*

Battle of Vittorio Veneto

British capture of Acre and Haifa △

△ *British occupation of Mosul*

Anglo-Arab capture of Damascus

Battle of Megiddo ✹

△ *British occupation of Baktur*

△ *British capture of Aleppo*

EAST AFRICA: *Surrender of German forces* △

△ *German naval mutiny*

Prince Max of Baden becomes German Chancellor

● *Hussarek becomes Austrian Prime Minister*

● *Kaiser abdicates*

USA breaks off relations with Russia ●

Germany and Austria ask Wilson for Armistice talks ●

Armistice with Germany ● ● *Emperor Karl of Austria Abdicates*

● *Wilson rejects Austrian peace offers*

● *Republicans gain a Majority in the US Congress following elections*

Ludendorff's Offensives
Operation 'Michael' March – April 1918

In the middle years of the war, the Central Powers were numerically inferior in the west by nearly two to three; now, after the collapse of Russia and as a result of the flow of troop trains from the Eastern Front to the Western Front, the Germans had amassed a slight and growing advantage in troops. A decisive German attack had to be mounted before American troops could be brought to the front in significant numbers.

Ludendorff's plans

Ludendorff instituted an intensive training program, those units considered the best being developed into 'shock troops' to spearhead his intended offensives. Noting a divergence of British and French interests – the former preoccupied with maintaining their lines with the Channel ports, the latter with protecting Paris – he planned to force a wedge between the two Allied armies, then to destroy the British Army in detail.

For the opening blow, Ludendorff chose the former Somme battlefield between Arras and La Fère; here the Allied armies joined and the ground most favored attack. Meanwhile, in addition to this offensive (codenamed Michael after Germany's patron saint), he continued meticulous preparations for successive operations.

For the Michael offensive, three German armies – Seventeenth (Below), Second (Marwitz) and Eighteenth (Hutier) – were deployed. Against these stood the British Third (Byng) and Fifth (Gough) armies, on the right of the British sector.

Surprise was all-important. Concentrations of men and weapons were carefully concealed, a five-hour bombardment by more than 6,000 guns (planned in minute detail by Colonel Georg Bruchmüller, the war's outstanding artillery expert) was organized for the opening day, and gas and smoke shells were provided in great number. Further aided by mist, some 65 German divisions assaulted a 60-mile British front on 21 March. As at Riga and Caporetto, Hutier tactics were used – troops advancing behind a rolling barrage, bypassing strong-points for mopping-up by following formations.

The campaign

Gough's Fifth Army, thinly spread after taking over part of the French left, collapsed, leaving the Third Army's right flank exposed and forcing it to withdraw. Well organised in depth, Third Army managed to hold the German Seventeenth and Second armies to limited gains, but Hutier's Eighteenth, pressing Gough hard, forced their way across the Somme. All British reserves, and some French units, were dispatched to plug the gap. With Pétain seemingly more interested in protecting Paris than in assisting his allies, Haig appealed for the appointment of a French general with fighting spirit to be given supreme command.

The situation was made even more critical on 23 March when German long-range artillery began bombarding Paris, firing shells at a distance of some 65 miles. The Supreme War Council appointed Foch Allied co-ordinator on 26 March, and he assumed the position of commander-in-chief of Allied forces in France on 3 April.

Meanwhile the German assault was losing some momentum after cutting a deep salient some 40 miles into the Allied line. Only the Eighteenth Army was still making steady gains. Foch's well-placed reserves had halted the thrust at Montdidier, and everywhere the German armies had outrun their supplies, which were brought forward with great difficulty over ground ravaged by three years of almost continuous warfare.

Consequences

Ludendorff then halted Operation Michael. The British had sustained some 163,000 casualties, the French 77,000; German losses were approximately 250,000. Gough was relieved of command and the shattered Fifth Army was then taken over by Rawlinson's Fourth, the remaining troops forming the Reserve Army.

For the German Army, already showing signs of serious decline in fighting capacity, the loss of a high proportion of elite assault troops without the compensation of a strategic victory was disastrous. Moreover, the Allies had at last appointed a single commander-in-chief.

Gen. von Below's Seventeenth Army enjoyed success on the first day of the offensive, only to run into the reserve units of the British Third Army. Nothing his infantry could do in the following days could break the British line on the northern flank.

A group of storm troops attack under cover of a combination of mist and lethal gas. Armed with light machine-guns, trench-mortars and flame-throwers their ultimate goal was to break through to attack enemy artillery positions.

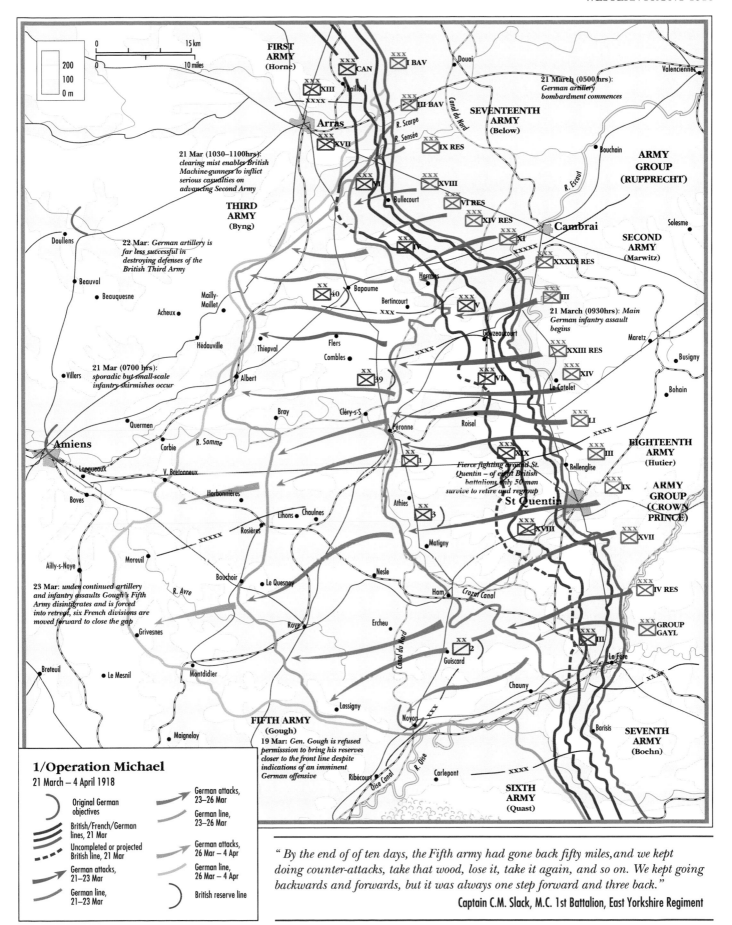

FIRST ARMY (Horne)

XXX CAN

XXX XIII
XXXX

Bailleul

XXX I BAV

Douai

Valenciennes

21 March (0500 hrs): *German artillery bombardment commences*

XXX III BAV

R. Scarpe

Canal du Nord

SEVENTEENTH ARMY (Below)

Arras

R. Sensée

XXX IX RES

Bouchain

R. Escaut

ARMY GROUP (RUPPRECHT)

XXX XVII

21 Mar (1030–1100hrs): *clearing mist enables British Machine-gunners to inflict serious casualties on advancing Second Army*

XXX M

Bullecourt

XXX XVIII

XXX VI RES

Solesme

THIRD ARMY (Byng)

Doullens

XXX XIV RES

Cambrai

SECOND ARMY (Marwitz)

22 Mar: *German artillery is far less successful in destroying defenses of the British Third Army*

Beauval

XXX IV

Hermies

XXX XI
XXXXX

XXX XXXIX RES

Beauquesne

Mailly-Maillet

XX 40

Bapaume

Bertincourt

XXX

XXX V

XXX III

Maretz

21 March (0930hrs): *Main German infantry assault begins*

Acheux

Hédauville

Flers

Gouzeaucourt

XXX XXIII RES

Busigny

21 Mar (0700 hrs): *sporadic but small-scale infantry skirmishes occur*

Thiepval

Combles

XXXX

XXX XIV

Bohain

Villers

Albert

XX 39

XXX VII

Le Catelet

Bray

Cléry-s-S

Roisel

XXX LI
XXXX

Quermen

Péronne

EIGHTEENTH ARMY (Hutier)

Amiens

Corbie

R. Somme

XX 1

XXX XIX

XXX III

Longueaux

V. Bretonneux

Bellenglise

XXX IX

Boves

Athies

XX 3

St Quentin

ARMY GROUP (CROWN PRINCE)

Harbonnières

Fierce fighting around St. Quentin – of eight British battalions only 50 men survive to retire and regroup

Lihons

Chaulnes

XXX XVIII

XXX XVII

Rosières

XXXXX

Matigny

Moreuil

Ailly-s-Noye

Le Quesnoy

Bouchoir

R. Avre

Nesle

XXX IV RES

23 Mar: *under continued artillery and infantry assaults Gough's Fifth Army disintegrates and is forced into retreat, six French divisions are moved forward to close the gap*

Grivesnes

Roye

Ercheu

Ham

Crozat Canal

Canal du Nord

XXX GROUP GAYL

Breteuil

Le Mesnil

Montdidier

Guiscard

XX 2

XXX III

Le Fère

Maignelay

Lassigny

FIFTH ARMY (Gough)

19 Mar: *Gen. Gough is refused permission to bring his reserves closer to the front line despite indications of an imminent German offensive*

Noyon

Chauny

Barisis

SEVENTH ARMY (Boehn)

Ribécourt

Oise Canal

R. Oise

Carlepont

XXXX

SIXTH ARMY (Quast)

1/Operation Michael
21 March – 4 April 1918

) Original German objectives

)))) British/French/German lines, 21 Mar

- - - Uncompleted or projected British line, 21 Mar

→ German attacks, 21–23 Mar

German line, 21–23 Mar

→ German attacks, 23–26 Mar

German line, 23–26 Mar

→ German attacks, 26 Mar – 4 Apr

German line, 26 Mar – 4 Apr

) British reserve line

0   15 km
0   10 miles

200
100
0 m

" *By the end of of ten days, the Fifth army had gone back fifty miles, and we kept doing counter-attacks, take that wood, lose it, take it again, and so on. We kept going backwards and forwards, but it was always one step forward and three back.*"

Captain C.M. Slack, M.C. 1st Battalion, East Yorkshire Regiment

Ludendorff's Offensives

Operation 'Georgette' April 1918

Ludendorff's second thrust, code-named 'Georgette' (see Strategic View), was launched on 9 April on a narrow front against the British line south of Armentières within striking distance of the Channel ports. After an extensive bombardment, the German Sixth Army (Quast) struck the British First (Horne) north of Givenchy on 9 April, concentrating their attack on the sector manned by the remnants of an under-strength Portuguese corps, and immediately gained a dramatic penetration. Only a remarkable stand by vastly-outnumbered units of XI Corps held the line of the rivers Lawe and Lys until reinforcements could be brought up.

The next day, as Horne's position was shored up by units from Second Army under Plumer (recalled from Italy at Horne's request), Rupprecht launched Arnim's Fourth Army both north and south of the Ypres salient. Within three days, Second Army had been forced to give up almost all the gains of the Passchendaele battle (page 128), and German success against IX and XV Corps south of the Douvre had brought them almost within sight of Hazebrouck.

Allied reinforcements

Foch was gathering a reserve force of four infantry and three cavalry divisions from Maistre's Tenth Army behind the British, but, much to Haig's disgust, was unwilling to commit these troops to the line while German forces remained in strength near Paris (page 150). By 21 April, however, a whole army under de Mitry had been assembled, and Plumer was at last able to rest his battered divisions.

A final German attempt to cut off Second Army and the Belgians led to savage fighting around Mt Kemmel from 24 to 29 April, in which German stormtroopers again made significant advances, but de Mitry and Plumer were able to organize counterattacks to stabilize the position. Ludendorff finally discontinued operations at 2200hrs on the 29th.

Consequences

Once again, Ludendorff had failed in his strategic aims, despite having achieved a major tactical success. The British Army had been badly savaged and even the presence of fresh levies from the United Kingdom and reinforcements from other theaters such as Italy, Salonika and Palestine would not enable it to asssume the offensive for many months. But these gains could not offset the failure of the German offensive to break Allied rail communication with the northern front or to cause a repeat of the British collapse of March. Losses were very heavy on all sides (some 76,000 British casualties, 35,000 French, 6,000 Portuguese and 109,000 German), but for the Germans the exhaustion of the offensive capacity of Fourth and Sixth armies without the hoped-for decision was a particularly heavy blow.

Withdrawal of further troops from the East allowed German strength to increase to 208 divisions, of which 80 were now in reserve, but a dozen American divisions had meanwhile arrived in France, and more were assembling or on the way. Ludendorff pressed on rapidly with his plans for attack on the Aisne (page 158), well aware that his elite shock troops had been further depleted and the morale of their survivors shaken.

(page 128), (page 150), (page 158)

> "There is no other course open to us but to fight it out! Every position must be held to the last man: there must be no retirement. With our backs to the wall, and believing in the justice of our cause, each one of us must fight on to the end."
>
> Field Marshal Douglas Haig, Order of the Day, 11 April 1918

Below left: British infantry man a barricade in the streets of Bailleul. The town fell to the Germans on 15 April despite fierce resistance which proved costly to both sides.

Strategic view: Ludendorff
With the failure of operation 'Michael', the most attractive option open to the German High Command was an attack on the British line at Flanders. Possession of the high ground and the proximity of the Channel ports gave the advantage to the Germans and the capture of the strategic railway junction of Hazebrouck would result in the isolation of the British and their possible surrender.

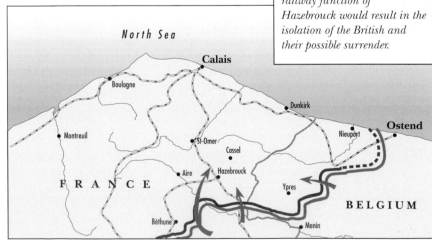

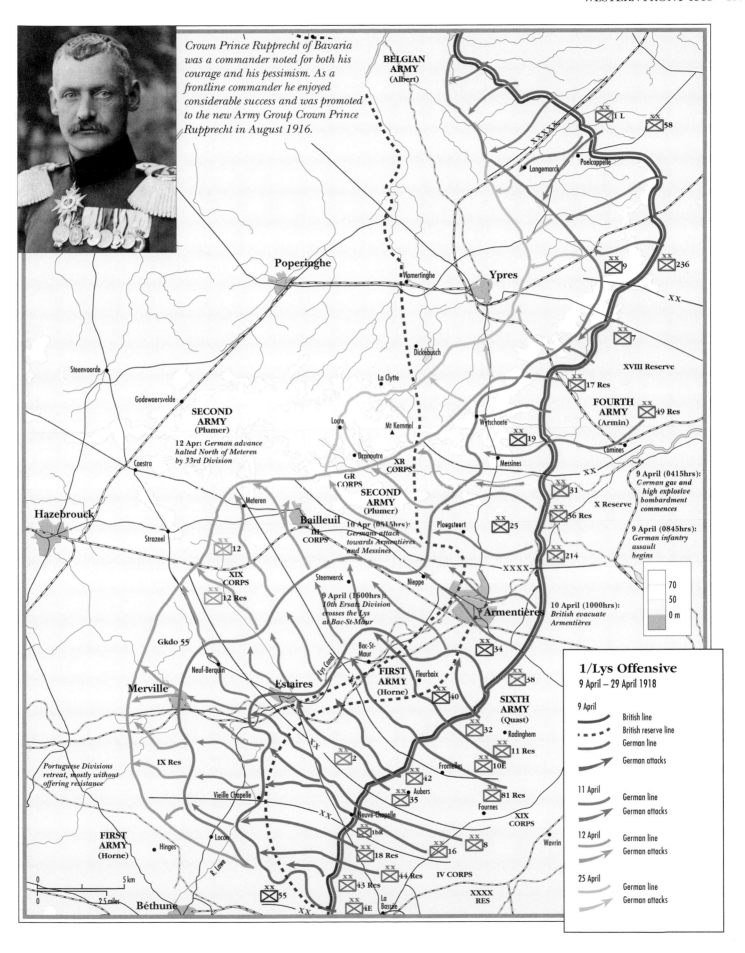

Crown Prince Rupprecht of Bavaria
was a commander noted for both his
courage and his pessimism. As a
frontline commander he enjoyed
considerable success and was promoted
to the new Army Group Crown Prince
Rupprecht in August 1916.

BELGIAN
ARMY
(Albert)

1 L

58

Langemarck

Poelcappelle

Poperinghe

Vlamertinghe

Ypres

9

236

Dickebusch

XX 7

Steenvoorde

XVIII Reserve

La Clytte

17 Res

Godewaersvelde

SECOND
ARMY
(Plumer)

Locre

Mt Kemmel

Wytschaete

FOURTH
ARMY
(Armin)

49 Res

19

12 Apr: German advance
halted North of Meteren
by 33rd Division

Messines

Comines

Caestra

Dranoutre

XR
CORPS

31

X Reserve

9 April (0415hrs):
German gas and
high explosive
bombardment
commences

GR
CORPS

SECOND
ARMY
(Plumer)

56 Res

Meteren

Hazebrouck

Bailleul
III
CORPS

Ploegsteert

25

9 April (0845hrs):
German infantry
assault
begins

Strazeel

10 Apr (0515hrs):
Germans attack
towards Armentières
and Messines

214

12

XXXX

XIX
CORPS

Steenwerck

Nieppe

70

50

12 Res

9 April (1600hrs):
10th Ersatz Division
crosses the Lys
at Bac-St-Maur

Armentières

10 April (1000hrs):
British evacuate
Armentières

0 m

Gkdo 55

Bac-St-
Maur

34

Neuf-Berquin

Estaires

FIRST
ARMY
(Horne)

Fleurbaix

38

1/Lys Offensive
9 April – 29 April 1918

Merville

Lys Canal

40

SIXTH
ARMY
(Quast)

9 April

Portuguese Divisions
retreat, mostly without
offering resistance

32

Radinghem

British line

British reserve line

German line

German attacks

IX Res

XX

2

11 Res

Fromelles

10 E

42

Aubers

35

Fournes

81 Res

11 April

German line

German attacks

Vieille Chapelle

XIX
CORPS

FIRST
ARMY
(Horne)

Hinges

Locon

Neuve-Chapelle

1 bR

16

8

Wavrin

12 April

German line

German attacks

R. Lawe

18 Res

44 Res

IV CORPS

25 April

German line

German attacks

55

43 Res

La
Bassée

XXXX
RES

Béthune

4 E

0   5 km

0   2.5 miles

Zeebrugge and Ostend April-May 1918

The invading Germans created a U-boat base at Bruges in 1914, with docking areas for destroyers and some 30 submarines. Each day two U-boats departed Bruges by the 6ml/9.7km canal to Zeebrugge to search for Allied shipping in the North Sea. Zeebrugge's harbor entrance was protected by a wide mole 1 1/2mls/2.5km long, heavily defended by batteries, naval guns and machine-gun emplacements, with a lighthouse at its northern end.

The plan

By 1918, the German U-boat menace was much reduced by the Allied convoy system but still posed an irritant threat. Rear-Admiral Keyes, commanding Dover Patrol, organised a raid by some 75 vessels to plug the Zeebrugge canal. Eight motorboats and 24 launches led the way on the night of 22–23 April. Their task was to lay a smoke screen over the mole. *Vindictive*, an old cruiser converted to convey the assault force of 733 Royal Marines, was accompanied by two ferries – *Daffodil* and *Iris* – to support her if she were disabled.

The battleship *Warwick*, with smaller ships, acted as escort. Two submarines, their bows packed with explosive, were towed, their task to destroy the bridge connecting the mole to the mainland and thus prevent the Germans bringing up reinforcements. The three "blockships" – *Thetis*, *Intrepid* and *Iphigenia* – were to steam around the mole's open end to the canal mouth, there to be scuttled.

Vindictive and the Marines were scheduled to reach the mole at 2400hrs. An hour earlier, clouds, rain and mist reduced visibility, but 20 minutes before zero hour, the first smoke screens were laid. At 2350hrs, the Germans fired a star shell, *Vindictive* was revealed, caught in a searchlight beam and subjected to gunfire.

As *Vindictive* tried to reach the mole, her starboard anchor jammed. But the commander of *Daffodil* used her bow to push *Vindictive* against the mole, allowing the Marines to land; fierce fighting ensued, the Marines suffering some 75 per cent casualties.

Meanwhile, the towline of one submarine broke, but the other, C3, smashed into the mole bridge. Her crew rowed to safety, after setting the time fuse. Twelve minutes later a great explosion destroyed the bridge, isolating the mole from the mainland.

The three blockships rounded the mole at 0025hrs. The leading vessel, *Thetis*, was raked by fire and shortly ran aground. *Intrepid*, however, got through to the canal and was scuttled, but without closing the canal mouth.

Iphigenia crashed into *Intrepid* while attempting to seal the gap but failed to do so when sunk. Most of the ships crews made good their escape in cutters.

The British flotilla, though badly damaged, limped home to Dover. The raid had limited effect, since U-boats could still get past the sunken ships; a simultaneous raid on Ostend also failed to entomb the U-boats. A further raid on Zeebrugge (9 May) was made by *Vindictive*, the cruiser being scuttled against the lock gates, again without completely closing the entrance.

Consequences

The exploits, though not entirely successful, provided a boost to British morale, at a time when it was sorely needed, went far to reduce German confidence in the impregnability of their harbor defences and greatly demoralised German U-boat crews.

"*Every available space on the mess deck was occupied by casualties. Those who could do so were sitting on the mess stools, awaiting their turn for medical attention. Many were stretched at full length on the deck, the majority being seriously wounded. Some had collapsed and were in a state of coma. I fear many had already passed away. It was a sad spectacle indeed.*"

Captain A.F.B. Carpenter, Commander of H.M.S. Vindictive.

After the raid on Ostend the blockships Brilliant *and* Sirius *lie one mile east of the harbor*

Below right: The commander of the Vindictive, *Captain Carpenter, and other surviving sailors and marines after the raid on Zeebrugge.*

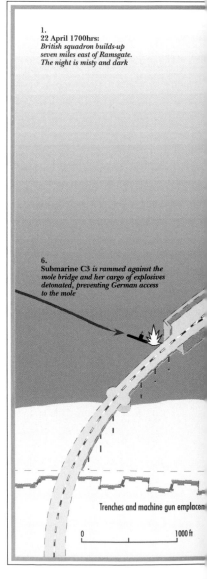

1.
22 April 1700hrs:
British squadron builds-up seven miles east of Ramsgate. The night is misty and dark

6.
Submarine C3 is rammed against the mole bridge and her cargo of explosives detonated, preventing German access to the mole

Trenches and machine gun emplacements

0   1000 ft

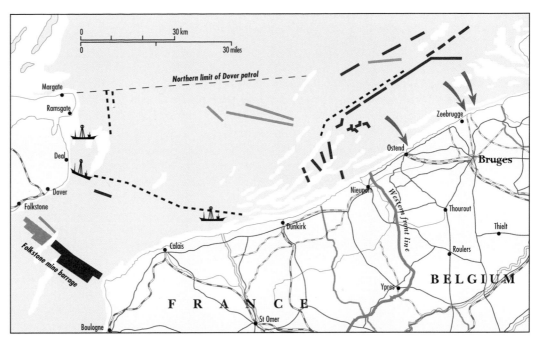

1/Zeebrugge and Ostend
1917–1918

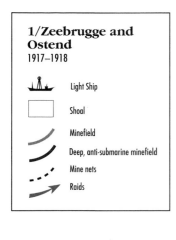

- Light Ship
- Shoal
- Minefield
- Deep, anti-submarine minefield
- Mine nets
- Raids

Northern limit of Dover patrol

Margate

Ramsgate

Deal

Dover

Folkstone

Folkstone mine barrage

Calais

Boulogne

St Omer

Dunkirk

Nieuport

Western front line

Zeebrugge

Ostend

Bruges

Thourout

Thielt

Roulers

Ypres

B E L G I U M

F R A N C E

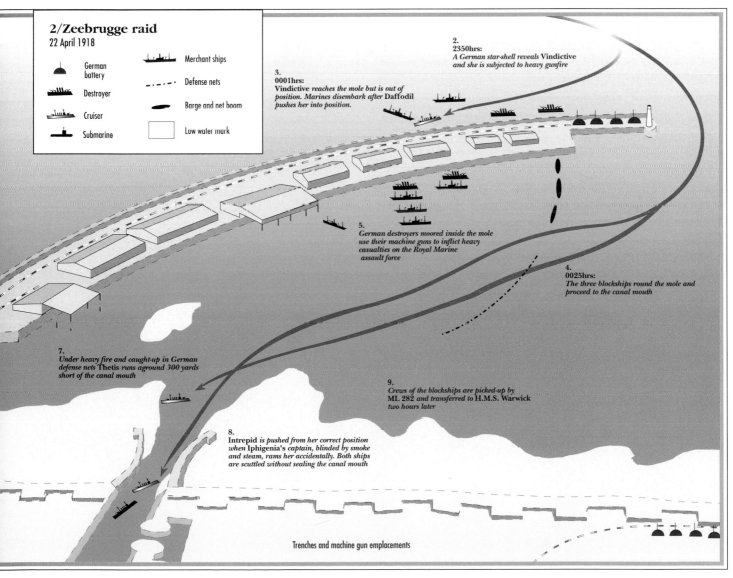

2/Zeebrugge raid
22 April 1918

- German battery
- Destroyer
- Cruiser
- Submarine
- Merchant ships
- Defense nets
- Barge and net boom
- Low water mark

2.
2350hrs:
A German star-shell reveals Vindictive *and she is subjected to heavy gunfire*

3.
0001hrs:
Vindictive *reaches the mole but is out of position. Marines disembark after* Daffodil *pushes her into position.*

5.
German destroyers moored inside the mole use their machine guns to inflict heavy casualties on the Royal Marine assault force

4.
0025hrs:
The three blockships round the mole and proceed to the canal mouth

7.
Under heavy fire and caught-up in German defense nets Thetis *runs aground 300 yards short of the canal mouth*

9.
Crews of the blockships are picked-up by ML 282 *and transferred to H.M.S. Warwick two hours later*

8.
Intrepid *is pushed from her correct position when* Iphigenia's *captain, blinded by smoke and steam, rams her accidentally. Both ships are scuttled without sealing the canal mouth*

Trenches and machine gun emplacements

Air War II 1917-1918

By 1917, with individual duels almost a thing of the past, warfare in the air changed dramatically, aircraft often numbering 50 or more flying in formations at different levels, with the object of clearing the enemy from the skies. Developments proliferated, notably the 'interrupter gear' which, until copied by the Allies, gave Germany air supremacy.

To counter this, the Allies evolved a method of deploying offensive patrols, whereby fighters were assigned to special squadrons to destroy their opponents behind enemy lines, thereby leaving the reconnaissance craft to work unmolested. This briefly restored air initiative to the Allies in 1916 but by 1917 the Germans were not only producing more sophisticated single-seater aircraft but had evolved the 'circus system', which entailed the formation of special squadrons, led by an ace, which could be moved rapidly from one sector of the Western Front to another as occasion demanded. In this way, although outnumbered 3:1 in the air at the time, the Germans were once more ascendant.

Massed formations were used to particularly good effect by the British in Palestine, where they prevented Turkish aircraft even taking off. By this time also aircraft were used to attack infantry and artillery, as well as supply bases and road and rail communication centers to the rear of the line.

Strategic bombing

Strategic bombing became possible with the development of aircraft with greater range and capable of carrying a significant bomb-load. German Gotha G-V heavy, twin-engined bombers, which took over the bombing role of airships when they became vulnerable to improved Allied aircraft, made numerous sorties; on 13 June 1917, for example, in the first daylight raid on London, 14 Gothas killed 162 people and injured 432. Yet, surprisingly, this was attempted in only a haphazard way, for senior military commanders persisted in seeing aircraft as an adjunct to land forces, an ingredient of military activity not a separate arm. Thus a prime Allied target, Germany's industrial heartland, the Ruhr and the Saar, where large quantities of munitions were manufactured, and which were within flying range, was sacrificed for continued fighting over the Western Front at the insistence of Haig

and Foch. The effect of limited strategic bombing, mostly at night, was moral rather than material, despite the increasing number of sorties and bombs dropped.

The first independent air service

On 1 April 1918, in belated recognition of the aircraft's value, the naval and military wings of the British Air Corps (the Royal Naval Air Service and the Royal Flying Corps) were combined to form the Royal Air Force (RAF), the first independent air service. So great had the enlargement of British air power been that while in 1914 the Royal Flying Corps, comprising 165 officers and 1,264 other ranks, took to France a mere 63 aircraft, by the middle of 1918 the RAF consisted of 291,175 officers and other ranks and 22,000 aircraft, making it the greatest air power in the world. The significance of this development lay in the prospect of defeating an enemy by aerial attack, not on the armies in the field but on industrial bases and civilian populations, a form of 'terror' assault that was to be used to awesome effect in subsequent wars.

Baron Manfred von Richtofen was the highest scoring fighter ace of the war with 80 confirmed kills, though many of these were reconnaissance planes. Richtofen met his own death on 21 April, 1918 when he was shot down over Allied lines, probably by a Canadian machine gun battery, though this is still a matter for dispute.

1/The First Gotha Raid on London
13 June 1917

→ Gotha bomber raid, route of main bomber force

Western Front, June 1917

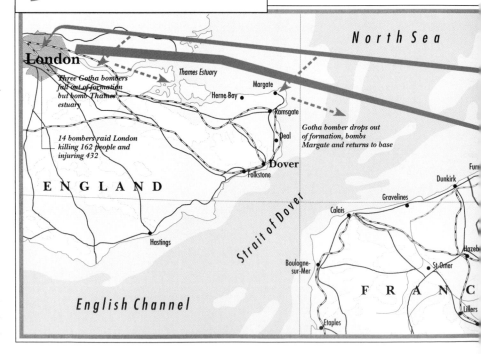

Three Gotha bombers fall out of formation but bomb Thames estuary

14 bombers raid London killing 162 people and injuring 432

Gotha bomber drops out of formation, bombs Margate and returns to base

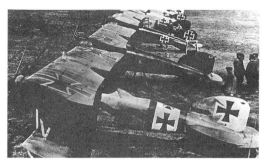

Germany enjoyed considerable success in the air. This was in part due to the development of the 'circus system' for which Richtofen received much of the credit. Richtofen's Albatross D III is second in line.

The most successful combat airplane of the war, the British Sopwith Camel was responsible for the destruction of 1,294 enemy machines. By 1918, 2,500 Camels patrolled the Western Front.

Right: This graphic is based on a German chart showing operational losses over the Western Front. Note the concentration of Allied losses over the front of the Second and Eighteenth Armies on 8–9 August. German aerial victories claimed, contrast strongly with the otherwise 'Black Day' of the German army.

NETHERLANDS

Two Gothas with engine problems abandon raid

Zeebrugge — Terneuzen

Ostend

Bruges — Antwerp

20 Gothas bombers depart from Ghent airfields

Dixmude

All aircraft return to base — Ghent

R. Shelde

Audenarde

Ypres — Menin — Brussels

4 Gothas crash in Belgium

Lille / Roubaix

Carvin

B E L G I U M

WESTERN FRONT AUGUST

Channel Coast — German Armies — Swiss border

Aircraft losses
August 1918
• German   • Allied

Date	4	6	17	2	18	9	7	1	3	5	C	19	A	B
1														
2														
3														
4														
5														
6														
7														
8														
9														
10														
11														
12														
13														
14														
15														
16														
17														
18														
19														
20														
21														
22														
23														
24														
25														
26														
27														
28														
29														
30														
31														

Ludendorff's Offensives

Operation 'Blücher-Yorck', Third Aisne May–June 1918

The third German offensive opened on 27 May when Ludendorff struck along the Chemin des Dames, a diversionary move prior to his overall objective, a decisive blow against the British in Flanders. The German First (von Mudra) and Seventh (Boehn) armies mounted an assault, code-named 'Blücher' against the French Sixth Army (Duchene) on the Aisne. Duchene's out-numbered divisions were surprised in shallow defenses along an inadequately manned line of 25 miles; they collapsed, allowing the Germans to get across the Aisne and reach the Marne on 30 May, making a salient some 20 miles deep and 30 wide. There German impetus faded.

Operation Blücher proved successful, in fact too successful for, designed as a diversion, its initial success had drawn too many reserves to the scene, yet not enough to exploit it. Blocked to their front by the River Marne, the Germans attempted to push west but were held by stubborn Allied resistance, notably by American divisions at Chateau-Thierry.

Ludendorff's next attack, his fourth, was delivered by the Eighteenth Army striking southwesterly and the Seventh Army westerly between the Montdidier and Noyon bulge. But Foch and Pétain had been forewarned by deserters and aerial reconnaisance and defenses had been organised in depth. The German attack opened on 9 June but, although some gains were made, a Franco-American counter-attack (11 June) brought Eighteenth Army's

advance to an end. Seventh Army's attack was likewise halted by 12 June.

Ludendorff then resolved on making one last diversionary attack prior to his intended decisive blow in Flanders. This was designed to pinch out the powerfully defended Reims, Seventh Army (Boehn), advancing up the Marne to meet the First Army (Mudra) and the Third (von Einem) attacking south in the direction of Chalons-sur-Marne. Foch, already planning a counter-offensive and again fore-warned by the usual sources –– deserter prisoners and aerial reconnaisance– pre-empted the attack (15 July) by bombarding German front line positions during the night of 14–15 July.

East of Reims the attack was quickly halted by the French Fourth Army (Gouraud). West of Reims, where defenses were weaker and lacked depth, the German Seventh Army's thrust took it to the Marne, an estimated 14 divisions

A German press photograph shows troops of the German Seventh Army continuing their advance through a ruined village after crossing the Marne.

"This attack has the object of disturbing the present united front of the Entente... thereby creating the possibility of a victorious continuation of the offensive against the British."

German General Order, 1 May

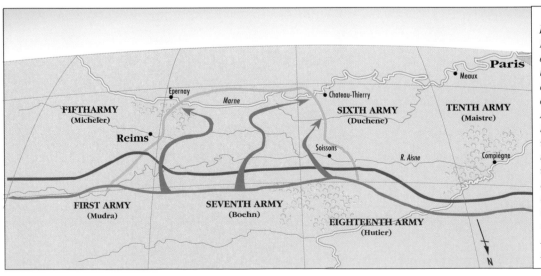

Ludendorff: Strategic view Ludendorff's offensives were designed to win the war before the deployment of the American armies swung the balance entirely in the favor of the Allies. By 30 May the Germans had managed to advance 40 miles in four days and had taken 50,000 prisoners. Paris was under long-range bombardment and French collapse seemed imminent. The German advance was held at Chateau-Thierry by the American 2nd and 3rd Divisions.

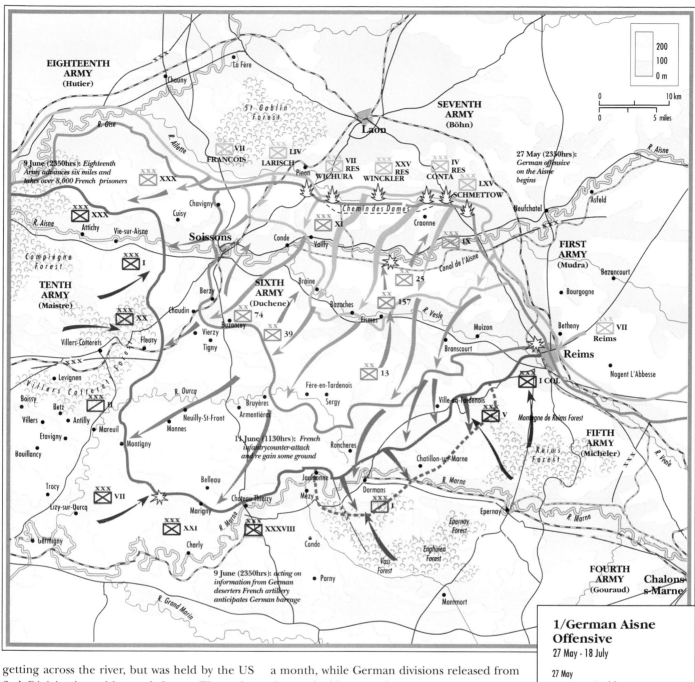

EIGHTEENTH ARMY
(Hutier)

9 June (2350hrs): Eighteenth Army advances six miles and takes over 8,000 French prisoners

SEVENTH ARMY
(Böhn)

27 May (2350hrs): German offensive on the Aisne begins

VII FRANCOIS

LIV LARISCH

Pinon

VII RES WICHURA

XXV RES WINCKLER

IV RES CONTA

LXV SCHMETTOW

Chemin des Dames

XI

IX

FIRST ARMY
(Mudra)

Craonne

Neufchatel

Asfeld

25

157

R. Vesle

TENTH ARMY
(Maistre)

Soissons

SIXTH ARMY
(Duchene)

74

39

13

VII Reims

I COL

Reims

Nogent L'Abbesse

V

Montagne de Reims Forest

FIFTH ARMY
(Micheler)

14 June (1130hrs): French infantry counter-attack and re gain some ground

Belleau

Château Thierry

Marigny

XXI

XXXVIII

I

Dormans

Epernay

FOURTH ARMY
(Gouraud)

Chalons-s-Marne

9 June (2350hrs): acting on information from German deserters French artillery anticipates German barrage

R. Grand Morin

---

getting across the river, but was held by the US 3rd Division's stubborn defense. Then the entire attack was halted when Allied aircraft and artillery destroyed the German bridges, thus disrupting their supply routes.

Consequences and losses

Faced with this situation, Ludendorff, admitting failure, now prepared for a general withdrawal from the Soissons-Château Thierry-Reims salient to shorten the line held by his reduced forces. In five months he had suffered some half a million casualties. Though Allied losses were comparable, they were now being replenished by American troops, some 300,000

a month, while German divisions released from the east had been used up.

Ludendorff had made the mistake of describing his attacks in terms that implied confidence in a decisive victory that would bring peace. Having failed to achieve anything of lasting value, and obliged to retreat, the morale of his troops was badly affected while that of the Allies rose in proportion.

The French counter-attack, taken with the German Marne-Reims attack, is often called the Second Battle of the Marne. From this point, the Allies regained the strategic initiative and held it to the end of the war, the Germans being reduced to hanging on to avert military defeat.

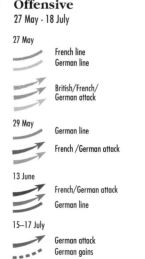

1/German Aisne Offensive
27 May - 18 July

27 May
French line
German line

British/French/
German attack

29 May
German line

French /German attack

13 June
French/German attack

German line

15–17 July
German attack
German gains

The Piave Offensive June – July 1918

In the spring of 1918, Germany transferred troops in Italy to the Western Front in preparation for Ludendorff's great offensives, leaving Austria alone to crush Italy. The arrangement had some strategic sense, since Russia and Romania were now out of the war, but recent events had rendered any big Austrian attack hazardous at best and potentially suicidal.

After four years of war, the morale and fighting spirit of the Austrian Army was much reduced. An infantry division, at the outset numbering more than 11,500 men, now comprised 8,000 at most and usually substantially fewer. But the Austrian Army still mustered some 1,280,000 men, with new conscripts to be trained. Some divisions would of necessity still be tied down in the Ukraine and on the Salonika front, others to maintain order at home, where the civilian population was growing steadily more restive, but some 53 divisions were available for deployment along the Italian Front.

There were other, potent arguments for the Austrians to shun an offensive. All Austrian troops were hungry, many almost starving; there was an acute shortage of horses, a reasonable estimate being that they were one third short of establishment, a deficiency that could not be made good by motorised transport, since adequate fuel and spare parts were lacking. The efficiency of the railway system had rapidly declined during 1918 and by the summer more than a third of locomotives were undergoing repair. Even the quality of personal arms had deteriorated. Not surprisingly, the number of deserters increased every month, many in search of food.

Italian morale, on the other hand, stiffened by patriotic fervor after defeat at Caporetto in 1917 (page 132), was once again high. Moreover, in the spring of 1918 Italy once more had some 59 divisions, including four sent by Great Britain and France. Thus, though an Austrian offensive seemed strategically sound, it would be fraught with danger.

Austrian plans

An Austrian attack might still have succeeded, or may have wrought some havoc, if the Austrian command had reached an agreed strategy and then implemented it; to their cost, they did not. Both Conrad, now commanding on the Trentino Front, and Boroevic, commanding on the Piave, sought command of the main blow. The Archduke Josef resolved matters by a compromise: they were authorized to attack separately. This was the worst of all solutions, since neither commander had sufficient strength to exploit any early success. Moreover, the mountainous terrain and lack of lateral communications prevented mutual support.

The Italian intelligence service was well aware of the impending Austrian blow and countermeasures had been taken. Italian retreat to the Piave in 1917 had given them the lateral lines which the Austrians lacked, enabling rapid movement of troops and supplies from one point to another, often entailing a matter of hours rather than days.

The Austrian offensive

The offensive had been planned to open on 20 May but had to be repeatedly postponed until 15 June, although even then not all was in readiness. High on the list of unresolved problems was Austria's inability to adequately feed front line troops.

Following a diversionary attack on 13 June at Tonale Pass in the west, which was thrown back, the twin Austrian thrusts were launched - Conrad striking in the direction of Verona, Boroevic toward Padua. Diaz, now chief of the Italian General Staff, was well prepared. Conrad's Eleventh Army struck at the Italian Sixth and Fourth armies, behind which Diaz had stationed in reserve the Ninth Army. Limited gains were made but were quickly halted and then thrown back by counter-attacks, Conrad thereafter playing little further part in the campaign.

Boroevic, striking from Conrad's left along the lower Piave, managed to force a wide crossing and advanced some three miles against the Third Army. This success, however, was negated when Italian aircraft bombed the Austrian supply line and the river swelled with unexpectedly heavy rains. Now Italy's lateral lines played their crucial part, for Diaz was able to use them to bring up support from his reserve Ninth Army, which tipped the scales. Unable to get reinforcements from Conrad, and with many of his bridges washed away by the swollen river, Boroevic withdrew his divisions during the night of 22–23 June.

Boroevic, who was promoted to the rank of Field Marshal early in 1918, spent most of the war on the Italian front with the Fifth Army, but he had also served in the Carpathians and at Gorlice-Tarnow, when he relieved the fortress of Przemsyl.

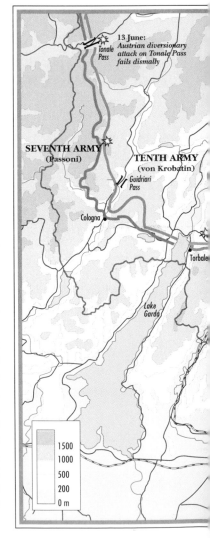

13 June: Austrian diversionary attack on Tonale Pass fails dismally

Tonale Pass

SEVENTH ARMY (Passoni)

TENTH ARMY (von Krobatin)

Guidriari Pass

Cologna

Torbale

Lake Garda

1500
1000
500
200
0 m

Consequences and losses

The Austrians lost some 70,000 men, the Italians approximately 85,000, but the failure of the last Austrian attempt to knock Italy out of the war greatly increased turmoil within the Habsburg empire, which became beyond the Government's power of control.

Diaz, to Foch's disgust, did not immediately move to exploit his success, preferring to mark time until assured of Allied success on other fronts which would make the defeat of the Central Powers inevitable and Italy's task easier.

"Very soon the artillery of the enemy dominated the field to such an extent that one was compelled to ask which of the artillery of the two forces concerned was actually attacking."

Colonel Maximilian Lauer,

An Austrian trench under fire. Hungry deserters from the Austro-Hungarian Army betrayed plans for the offensive and allowed the Italians to plan effective artillery counter strokes. The Italians were rested, well-fed and well-equipped, furthermore they had ample time to strengthen their defenses and co-ordinate their movements.

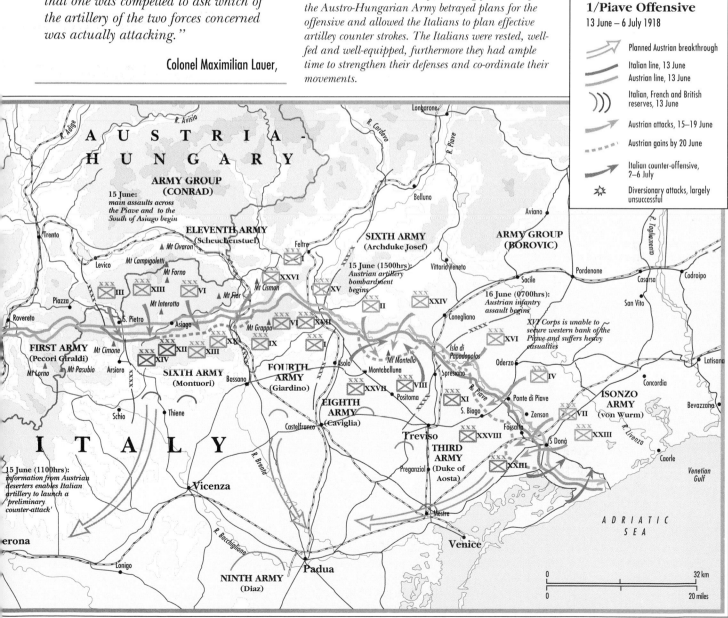

1/Piave Offensive
13 June – 6 July 1918

- Planned Austrian breakthrough
- Italian line, 13 June
- Austrian line, 13 June
- Italian, French and British reserves, 13 June
- Austrian attacks, 15–19 June
- Austrian gains by 20 June
- Italian counter-offensive, 2–6 July
- Diversionary attacks, largely unsuccessful

German East Africa 1914–1918

Three of Germany's four African colonies fell to the Allies early in the war (page 48). German East Africa remained the exception owing to the British inability to spare troops, the bush terrain, and the skill of the German commander, Paul von Lettow-Vorbeck.

German strength was at most 10,000, including German residents and native (Askari) infantry from the outset. The British were heavily outnumbered in 1914, with fewer than 4,000 fighters in Uganda and British East Africa, including settler volunteers, police scouts and 2,300 African troops. Unlike the Germans, they were reluctant at first to arm large numbers of Africans; but by 1918 the King's African Rifles (KAR) had grown from three battalions to 22, in five regiments.

First moves

In October 1914, a British force under Aitken attacked the port of Tanga, from where an advance up the Usambara Railway could be mounted (Map 1). The Germans, alerted to the danger, brought heavy fire to bear on the first Indian units to come ashore; these fled back to the beach. Facing encirclement, the German local commander had virtually abandoned the town, but Lettow-Vorbeck found that the British Empire troops were waiting for daylight before attacking. When they did, they came under fierce fire. Aitken was forced to withdraw in complete chaos. On 25 February 1915, the British announced a naval blockade of the coast. The German garrison was trapped in a state of siege, but the British lacked sufficient troops to exploit the situation.

South Africa intervenes

Early in 1916, South Africa's General Jan Smuts was appointed to the supreme command. He resolved to penetrate German-held territory from the north, while British and Belgian forces attacked from Rhodesia and Belgian Congo (Map 2). Smuts headed around the Pare Mountains to envelop Lettow-Vorbeck's left flank, while the rest of the South African force under Van Deventer kept to his right. On 16 May Lettow-Vorbeck clashed with Van Deventer, but slipped away into the Nguru Mountains. Smuts still hoped to bring Lettow-Vorbeck to a decisive battle, but time and again he evaded the Allied forces after engaging them in costly and

indecisive actions.

Part of the German force surrendered on 28 November 1917, but the remainder, with Lettow-Vorbeck, crossed into Portuguese East Africa (Mozambique). Here Lettow-Vorbeck waged a brilliant guerrilla campaign, inflicting stinging defeats on British Empire and Portuguese forces and retaining the initiative throughout. In September 1918 he reinvaded German East Africa before crossing into Northern Rhodesia, where news of the Armistice reached him on 13 November. Undefeated in the field, Lettow-Vorbeck and his troops marched to the British post at Abercorn to surrender.

Losses

Ninety percent of the original German force died, mostly through disease, or were taken prisoner. The British suffered 60,000 casualties from diseases. Lettow-Vorbeck, with only a few thousand, had tied down 130,000 Allied troops.

Askaris, commanded by German officers, manning a machine gun.

Paul von Lettow-Vorbeck. His skill won the admiration of his opponents; Smuts himself wrote to tell Lettow that he had been awarded the Pour le Mérite.

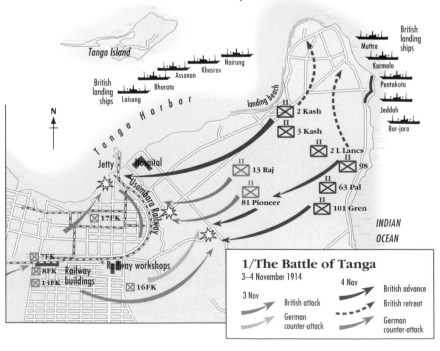

1/The Battle of Tanga
3–4 November 1914

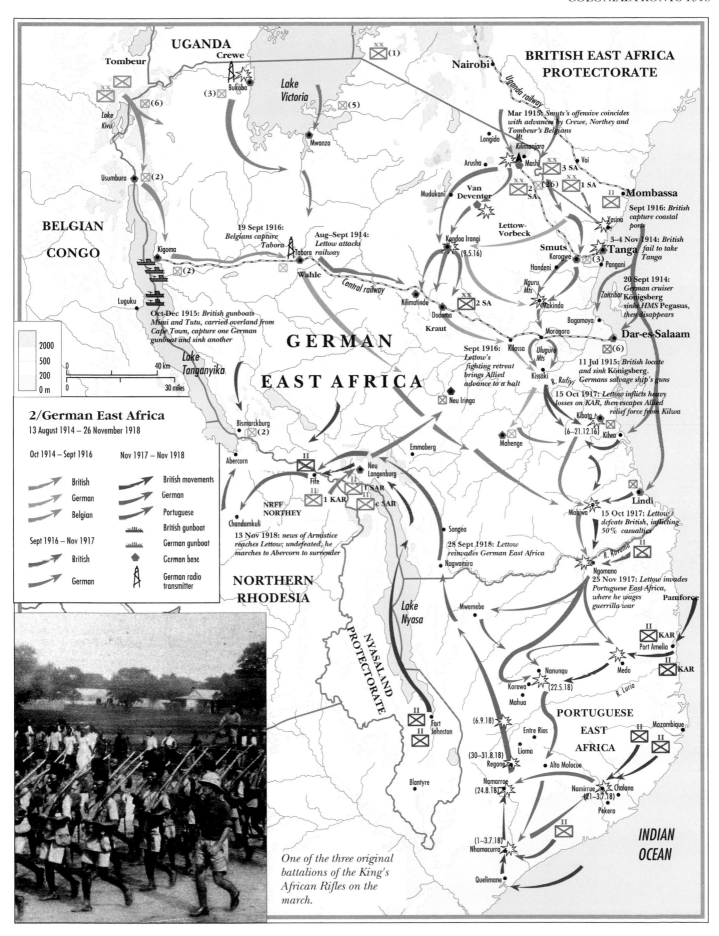

UGANDA

Tombeur

Crewe

⊠ (1)

Nairobi

BRITISH EAST AFRICA PROTECTORATE

Lake Victoria

XX ⊠ (6)

(3) ⊠ Bukoba

Lake Kivu

⊠ (5)

Mwanza

Longido

Mar 1915: Smuts's offensive coincides with advances by Crewe, Northey and Tombeur's Belgians

Mt. Kilimanjaro

Arusha

Mashi

XX 3 SA

Voi

Usumbura ⊠ (2)

BELGIAN CONGO

Mudukani

Van Deventer

XX 2 SA

(26)

XX 1 SA

II ⊠

Mombassa

Sept 1916: British capture coastal ports

19 Sept 1916: Belgians capture Tabora

Aug–Sept 1914: Lettow attacks railway

Kigoma

⊠ (2)

Tabora

Wahle

Kondoa Irangi

(9.5.16)

Lettow-Vorbeck

Yasina

3–4 Nov 1914: British fail to take Tanga

Oct–Dec 1915: British gunboats Mimi and Tutu, carried overland from Cape Town, capture one German gunboat and sink another

Luguku

⊠ (2)

Central railway

Kilimatinde

XX 2 SA

Dodoma

Kraut

Smuts

Korogwe

Handeni

(3)

Tanga

Pangani

20 Sept 1914: German cruiser Königsberg sinks HMS Pegasus, then disappears

Nguru Mts

Makinda

Bagamoya

Morogoro

Dar-es-Salaam

⊠ (6)

Lake Tanganyika

GERMAN EAST AFRICA

Sept 1916: Lettow's fighting retreat brings Allied advance to a halt

Kilossa

Uluguru Mts

Kissaki

R. Rufiyi

11 Jul 1915: British locate and sink Königsberg. Germans salvage ship's guns

2000
500
200
0 m

40 km
30 miles

⊠ Neu Iringa

15 Oct 1917: Lettow inflicts heavy losses on KAR, then escapes Allied relief force from Kilwa

Kibata ⊠

(6–21.12.16)

Kilwa

Bismarckburg ⊠ (2)

Mahenge

2/German East Africa

13 August 1914 – 26 November 1918

Abercorn

Emmaberg

Neu Langenburg

Mahiwa

Lindi

15 Oct 1917: Lettow defeats British, inflicting 50% casualties

Oct 1914 – Sept 1916   Nov 1917 – Nov 1918

British
German
Belgian

British movements
German
Portuguese
British gunboat
German gunboat
German base
German radio transmitter

Fife

II ⊠ 1 KAR

II TSAR

e SAR

NRFF NORTHEY

Chandamkuli

13 Nov 1918: news of Armistice reaches Lettow; undefeated, he marches to Abercorn to surrender

Songea

R. Rovuma

Ngomano

II ⊠

25 Nov 1917: Lettow invades Portuguese East Africa, where he wages guerrilla war

Pamforce

Sept 1916 – Nov 1917

British
German

28 Sept 1918: Lettow reinvades German East Africa

Nagwamira

NORTHERN RHODESIA

Lake Nyasa

NYASALAND PROTECTORATE

Mwemebe

Nanunqu

Korewa

(22.5.18)

Medo

R. Lurio

II ⊠ KAR

Port Amelia

II ⊠ KAR

Mahua

II ⊠ Fort Johnston

II ⊠

(6.9.18)

Entre Rios

Lioma

(30–31.8.18)

Regone

Alto Molocue

Blantyre

Namarroe

(24.8.18)

Namirrue

(21–3.7.18)

Chalana

Pekera

PORTUGUESE EAST AFRICA

Mozambique

II ⊠

II ⊠

II ⊠

(1–3.7.18)

Nhamacurra

INDIAN OCEAN

Quelimane

One of the three original battalions of the King's African Rifles on the march.

Strikes, Mutinies and Revolts 1914–1918

Mutinies and revolts, savagely suppressed by most belligerent nations during the war, were encouraged and sustained by their enemies. Great Britain gave all available help to the Arab uprising against the Turks and Germany smuggled into Russia Lenin and other Bolshevik agitators to undermine the Provisional Government and hasten revolution and Russian collapse (page 134).

Many revolts and mutinies occured too far distant for enemies to support. On 15 February 1915, for example, the 5th Light Infantry, a native regiment of the Singapore garrison, mutinied following disagreements between British and Indian officers which demoralised Indian other ranks and made them prey to sedicious ideas disseminated by Indian nationalists. Here inadequate leadership, not German espionage, was the principal cause of unrest. The mutineers overcame the guard of the prison camp, which held some 300 Germans, mostly pre-war residents of Singapore and the Malay States, who had been interned in 1914, and crews of captured ships. Weapons and ammunition were offered them but fewer than 20 armed themselves. The situation was brought rapidly under control, only 47 British casualties being recorded, including murdered civilians, but the uprising demonstrated that a mutiny by even a small unit could disrupt a distant military outpost.

Greater areas also fell prey to revolt. Tsarist Russia, in particular, had to deal with dangerous disturbances within its borders. One such occurred among the Kazak and Kirghiz tribes in Russian Central Asia in 1916. On 25 June 1916, the Tsar signed a decree for the conscription, for labour or military service, of 250,000 natives of Russian Central Asia, despite a law of 1886 exempting them from military service. At this the inhabitants of Central Asia began organising uprisings. The harvest was abandoned, officials attacked. Confusion ensued over a vast area. Troops, including Cossacks, were rushed in; the uprisings were crushed with the utmost brutality and as many as 100,000 Kazaks may have perished in the grim suppression of 1916. Russian ability to suppress the uprising had been demonstrated, but it was another element in the mosaic that indicated Russia's impending collapse into disorder and revolution.

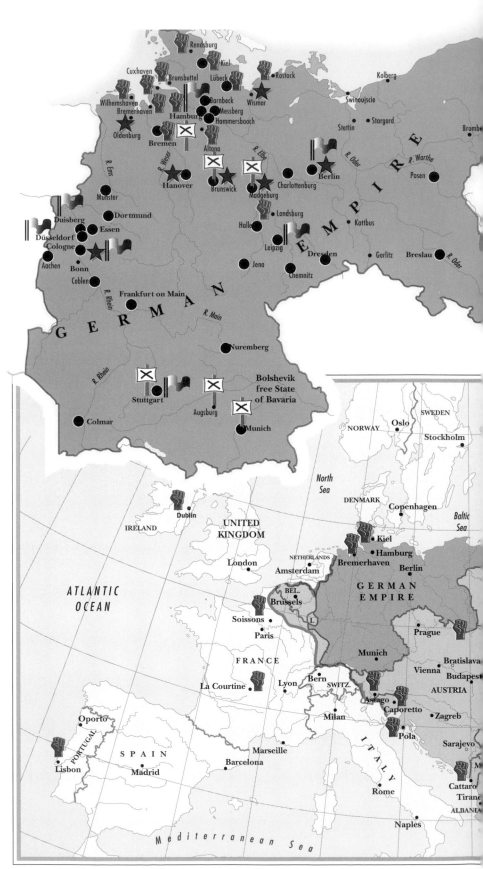

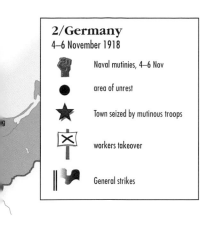

2/Germany
4–6 November 1918

✊ Naval mutinies, 4–6 Nov

⬤ area of unrest

★ Town seized by mutinous troops

⊠ workers takeover

▌▌🏴 General strikes

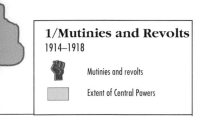

1/Mutinies and Revolts
1914–1918

✊ Mutinies and revolts

▨ Extent of Central Powers

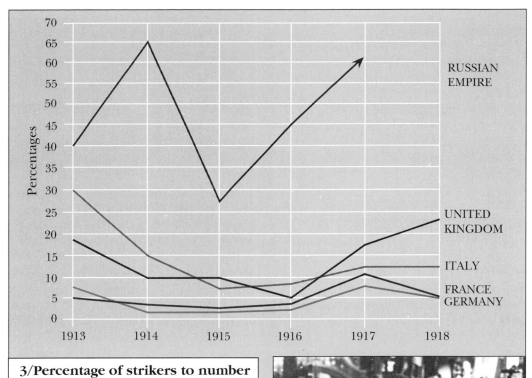

3/Percentage of strikers to number of factory workers 1913–1918

Bolshevik propaganda

Bolshevik propaganda contributed to unrest in Allied areas, among them French and Russian troops in Macedonia and French units on the Western Front in 1917, where the disastrous Nivelle offensive (page 122–123) led 54 French divisions to refuse to go to the front, although all were willing to fight in a defensive capacity - the troops, unlike their commanders, having learned the futility and cost of attack. Early in June, two reliable divisions only stood between the German front line and Paris, some 70 miles to the southwest. Pétain, who replaced Nivelle as commander-in-chief on 15 May, restored order and confidence in the French Army, but for two weeks the front was almost without active French troops.

Nowhere was Bolshevik propaganda more effective than in the German Navy. Mutinies erupted, at Wilhelmshaven on 29 October and then at Kiel, initially in response to a planned but futile challenge to the British Navy in the North Sea to better peace terms. This led to disorders, mutinies and revolts throughout Germany that, within two weeks, turned the country from an autocracy to a republic.

Post-war United Kingdom

Nor was the United Kingdom wholly spared from the insidious danger of revolts, although

A German worker in an ammunition factory in 1918

not until the war's end when demobolization became a disputatious issue. The War Office had produced a seemingly sensible plan whereby the first to be released were to be those most needed in industry. But these were invariably the last to have been conscripted, causing outrage among those who had served longer. Mutinies occurred at the Calais and Folkestone camps; an estimated 3,000 men marched from Victoria Station to occupy the Horse Guards Parade. Canadian troops mutinied at their Rhyl camp when shortage of shipping delayed their return home. The situation, potentially dire, for doubt persisted whether troops could be found who were reliable enough to subdue the mutineers, was solved by Churchill, then Minister of Munitions, who replaced War Office plans with a simple "first in, first out" arrangement, which at once dispelled discontent and was employed to equal satisfaction at the end of the Second World War.

The 'Black Day' of the German Army
August 1918

Ludendorff, following his five attacks in the west (page 158–159), was forced by 20 July to postpone, though not yet abandon, his ultimate aim, a decisive offensive in Flanders. The initiative had finally passed to the Allies; Foch was determined to exploit it without pause, while accumulating his own reserves. The main blow was to be delivered by the British Fourth Army (Rawlinson) and the French First Army (Debeney), which Foch had placed temporarily under British command.

What ensued on 8 August was possibly the most complete surprise attack of the war. Its foundation was the sudden advance of 456 tanks, replacing a forewarning artillery barrage. Secrecy had been strictly maintained, not only against the Germans but from British troops themselves; divisional commanders were told nothing of the intended attack until 31 July, the fighting soldiers' movements were made at night; the times and rates of artillery fire were regulated, so that more guns could be moved into concealed positions without arousing German suspicion. Between 1 and 8 August Rawlinson's Fourth Army was almost doubled in strength, with an additional six infantry divisions, two cavalry divisions, nine tank battalions and a further thousand guns being brought forward. Meanwhile, the bulk of the Canadian Corps, regarded by the Germans as 'storm troops', had been transferred to the Somme.

The campaign
The dispositions of the Fourth Army were designed to allow the main blow to be launched south of the Somme by the Canadian Corps (Currie) on the right and the Australian Corps (Monash) on the left, while III Corps (Butler) moved north of the river to protect the main thrust's flank.

The front of attack was some 14 miles long, opposed by a mere six under-establishment German divisions of Marwitz's second Army. Shrouded by a heavy ground mist, the British tanks moved forward before sunrise on 8 August, with simultaneous artillery barrage and infantry advance, creating the maximum shock of surprise. Canadians and Australians swept over German forward positions. Only to the north of the Somme, where there was a paucity

of tanks, was there any significant check. The day's ultimate objectives, at most eight miles distant, were gained save on the extreme flanks.

Lack of reserves and the fact that the advance rapidly reached the almost impassable edge of the Somme battlefields of 1916 (the whole area comprised a wasteland of derilict trenches and rusty wire entanglements) lost the advance momentum; nor, despite the years of war, had anyone resolved the problem of continuity of advance after a successful thrust. Furthermore, an old problem emerged with every frontal attack: the more it pushed back the enemy, the more it hardened their powers of resistance.

Then, on 21 August, the Third Army, on Fourth Army's left, struck, as on 28 August did the First Army farther north. The Fourth Army, relieved by these distractions, resumed its advance. These thrusts were delivered as part of the new Allied strategy of repeated attacks at related points, each broken off as impetus declined but at once succeeded by another attack nearby.

Consequences and losses
The Fourth Army took 21,000 prisoners between 8 and 12 August, at a loss of 20,000 casualties. This achievement, heralded by surprise, was not in fact the determining factor in marking 8 August, in Ludendorff's words, the 'Black Day' of the German Army. It was not the territory gained nor the casualties sustained that daunted Ludendorff; it was the fact that German units, worn down by attrition, were demoralized and some surrendering with little or at most token resistance. The decline of German fighting power was beyond all doubt and irreversible.

"8 August was the black day of the German Army in the history of this war... Everything I had feared and of which I had so often given warning, had here, in one place, become a reality. Our war machine was no longer efficient."

**Gen. Ludendorff,
'My War Memories'**

"We have passed through many dark days together. Please God these will never return. The enemy has now spent his effort, and I rely confidently upon each one of you to turn to full advantage the opportunity which your skill, courage, and resolution have created."

**Sir Douglas Haig,
Special Order of the Day,
10 September 1918**

German casualties were far heavier than those suffered by the Allies. As was the case throughout the war, the number of killed who received no proper burial was woefully high.

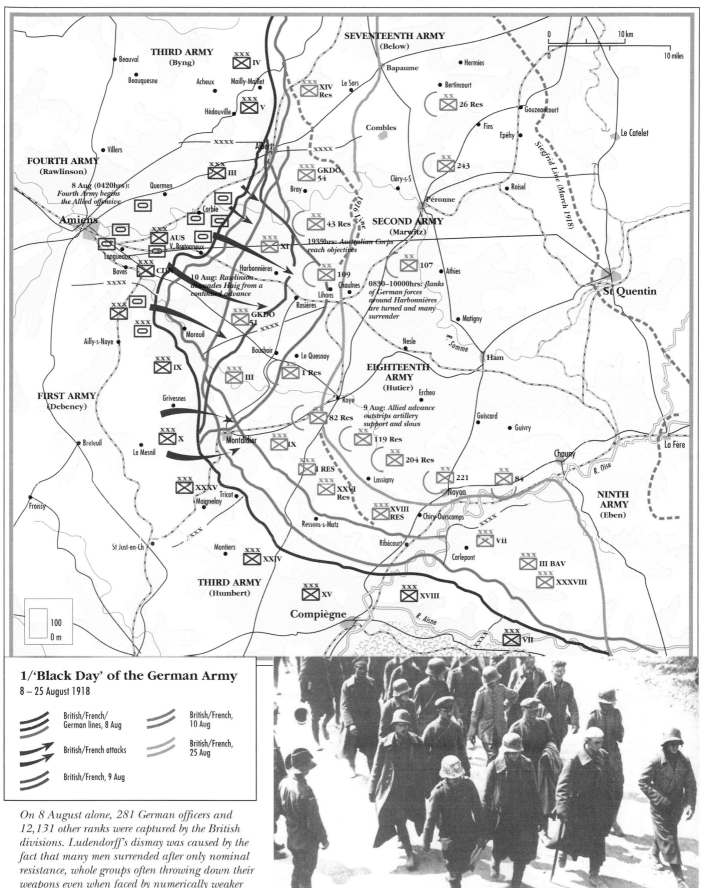

THIRD ARMY
(Byng)

SEVENTEENTH ARMY
(Below)

0   10 km

0   10 miles

Beauval

Beauquesne

Acheux

Mailly-Maillet

Hédauville

Beaufort

Hermies

Bapaume

Bertincourt

26 Res

Gouzeaucourt

Le Sars

XIV
Res

Combles

Clèry-s-S

Fins

Epéhy

Roisel

Le Catelet

FOURTH ARMY
(Rawlinson)

8 Aug (0420hrs):
*Fourth Army begins
the Allied offensive*

Amiens

Villers

Quermen

Corbie

III

GKDO
54

Bray

243

Péronne

Roisel

Siegfrid Line (March 1918)

AUS
V.-Bretonneux

Langueaux

Boves

CDN

XI

43 Res

SECOND ARMY
(Marwitz)

1939hrs: *Australian Corps
reach objectives*

109

107

Athies

St Quentin

Harbonnières

10 Aug: *Rawlinson
dissuades Haig from a
continued advance*

Chaulnes

Lihons

Rosières

0830–10000hrs: *flanks
of German forces
around Harbonnières
are turned and many
surrender*

Matigny

GKDO
51

Moreuil

Ailly-s-Noye

Bouchoir

Le Quesnoy

Nesle

R. Somme

Ham

IX

III

I Res

EIGHTEENTH
ARMY
(Hutier)

Ercheu

Guiscard

Guivry

FIRST ARMY
(Debeney)

Grivesnes

Roye

9 Aug: *Allied advance
outstrips artillery
support and slows*

82 Res

119 Res

204 Res

Chauny

R. Oise

La Fère

Breteuil

X

Le Mesnil

Montdidier

IX

I RES

Lassigny

221

84

Noyon

NINTH
ARMY
(Eben)

Froissy

XXXV

Tricot

Maignelay

XXVI
Res

XVIII
RES

Chiry-Ourscamps

St Just-en-Ch

Montiers

Ressons-s-Matz

Ribécourt

VII

Carlepont

III BAV

XXXVIII

XXIV

THIRD ARMY
(Humbert)

Compiègne

XV

XVIII

R. Aisne

VII

100

0 m

1/'Black Day' of the German Army
8 – 25 August 1918

British/French/
German lines, 8 Aug

British/French,
10 Aug

British/French attacks

British/French,
25 Aug

British/French, 9 Aug

*On 8 August alone, 281 German officers and
12,131 other ranks were captured by the British
divisions. Ludendorff's dismay was caused by the
fact that many men surrendered after only nominal
resistance, whole groups often throwing down their
weapons even when faced by numerically weaker
units of Allied troops.*

The American Offensive September – November 1918

German forces had held the salient around St Mihiel since late 1914; it had formed the basis of their stranglehold on Verdun in 1916, and was now a major obstacle to any Allied offensive into Lorraine. Once the crisis of the German spring offensive had passed, Pershing seized on the elimination of the salient as an opportunity for the AEF to prove its full worth to the Allied cause. The professionalism and courage of his largely inexperienced US First Army in its first independent operation came as a surprise to allies and enemies alike.

The operation
The American staff had planned the elimination of the salient and an immediate advance north-eastward on Metz. Haig argued that a Franco-American push northwards towards Mezières would pose a greater threat to the German armies in northern France, and Foch therefore gave his approval for a limited operation against the salient itself while the larger scheme was prepared.

The First Army, supported by 600 Allied aircraft, attacked on 12 September. The revised plan was simple: American forces would attack both sides of the salient while the French II Colonial Corps applied pressure to its western-most tip. Fuchs, the German commander, had begun to withdraw his troops towards the prepared defences of the Michel Line before the offensive opened, and had to fight a vigorous rearguard action.

The salient was wholly cleared by 16 September. Some 15,000 prisoners and 250 guns were taken at a cost of 7000 killed and wounded in the largest American operation since the Civil War.

Meuse–Argonne
The Meuse–Argonne offensive represented a part of Foch's larger scheme for taking out the

John Pershing, commander of the AEF from 26 May 1917. He allowed US forces to operate under French and British command in spring 1918, but consistently sought an opportunity for decisive, independent US action.

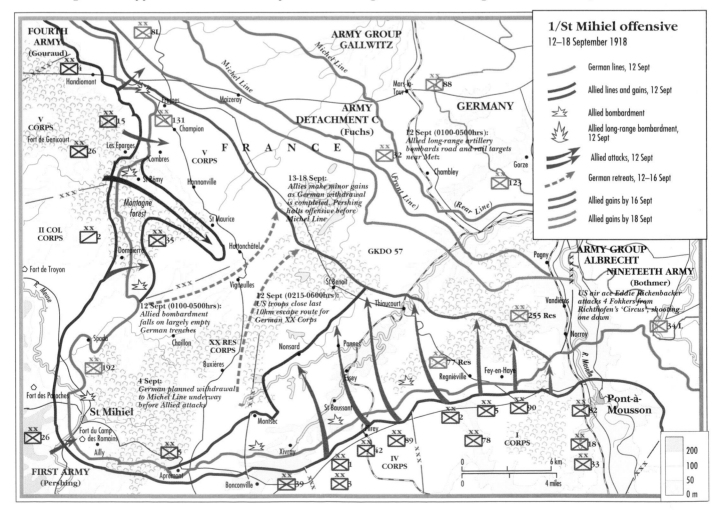

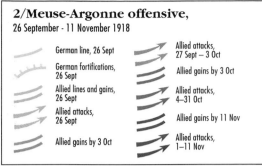

2/Meuse-Argonne offensive,
26 September - 11 November 1918

German line, 26 Sept

German fortifications, 26 Sept

Allied lines and gains, 26 Sept

Allied attacks, 26 Sept

Allied gains by 3 Oct

Allied attacks, 27 Sept – 3 Oct

Allied gains by 3 Oct

Allied attacks, 4–31 Oct

Allied gains by 11 Nov

Allied attacks, 1–11 Nov

huge German salient from Ypres to Verdun. It was directed against a heavily fortified sector of the front on which Ludendorff was unwilling to give ground, in an area where the rugged terrain gave every advantage to the defenders.

The US First Army, three corps abreast, launched its attack at 0525hrs on 26 September; the French Fourth Army, on its left, also attacked. Rapid advance by the Americans was slowed in front of Montfaucon as the Germans quickly brought forward reinforcements Pershing renewed his offensive on 4 October. The First Army, unable to manoeuver, slogged its way slowly forward by costly frontal attacks. The Argonne forest was nevertheless cleared of Germans, allowing the French Fourth Army, on the left, to advance to the River Aisne.

When more American troops from the St Mihiel action were brought up, Pershing regrouped his forces into two armies. The newly-formed second Army (Bullard) prepared to attack northeast between the Meuse and the Moselle, while the First Army (now Liggett) continued slowly northward and finally, at the end of October, broke the German third line.

On 1 November, with rested divisions brought to the front, the First Army smashed through the final German positions northeast and west of Buzancy, allowing the French Fourth Army to get across the Aisne. The Americans, now in the open, raced up the Meuse Valley, reaching Sedan and cut the crucial German supply line between Mézières and Montmédy.

The French, to erase the stain of their 1870 disaster, were, on the highest authority, given the honour of retaking Sedan, despite the ability, after a spectacular drive, of the US 1st Division to take the city. Bullard's Second Army on 10 November launched a drive for Montmédy, but the following day all hostilities in the west were terminated by the Armistice.

An American 14in railroad gun in action in the Argonne in September 1918. US forces adopted the British steel helmet and a mixture of American, British and French equipment.

Megiddo September 1918

Allenby's capture of Jerusalem in December 1917 had provided a much-needed tonic to the Allies, but his scope for further offensives in the new year was severely restricted by the withdrawal of experienced units to France to counter the German spring offensive. It was September 1918 before reinforcements from India and Mesopotamia had brought the Egyptian Expeditionary Force up to strength again.

The EEF's 1918 campaign in Palestine was one of the most boldly planned and decisive in the war. Following Russia's collapse (page 134) Turkey foresaw an imminent German victory overall, and thus sought territorial pickings in the Caucasus rather than reinforcing the strategically more important theater in Palestine. The three Turkish armies in Palestine could muster only 2000 cavalry, 32,000 infantry and about 400 guns in the Fall of 1918, and these forces had to hold an extended line. Against these demoralized formations, Allenby had some 12,000 cavalry, 57,000 infantry and nearly 550 guns. His men, British, Indian, Anzac and Arab, in contrast to the Turks, were experienced, fit and fully supplied.

Objectives

Allenby's basic plan was simple: to strike at the heart of Turkish road and rail communications. Turkish reinforcements and supplies came down the Hejaz Railway, a single line running south from Damascus. The Fourth Army relied directly on this line, while a branch line, turning west at Deraa, supplied the Seventh and Eighth armies. This branch line ran roughly parallel to the Turkish front and, if Allenby could seize key towns along its route, he would cut the line of supply and retreat for both armies.

He planned to delude the Turks into believing an attack would come from the Jordan Valley, while in fact striking on the western coast. Forcing a gap, the bulk of his cavalry would ride north along the coast before swinging in behind the Seventh and Eighth armies. The last great cavalry offensive. Meanwhile, Colonel T. E. Lawrence's Arab irregulars would disrupt the Hejaz Railway itself.

Prior to the planned offensive, three cavalry divisions were secretly moved from the Jordan Valley to the coast. Their redeployment was concealed by movement at night, and numerous other subterfuges were employed to maintain the false impression of an impending attack from the Allied right. Turkish reconnaissance flights were intercepted by the Royal Air Force.

So successful were these ruses that, when the bombardment opened in the west, some 35,000 infantry, 9000 cavalry and almost 400 guns had been secretly positioned along a front of 15mls/24km on the EEF's left wing.

The battle

At 0430hrs on 19 September Allied artillery opened fire on Turkish formations near the coast, followed by an infantry attack. The Turks were overwhelmed. The Desert Mounted Corps pushed through the gap and by 19 September the 5th Cavalry Division had reached Megiddo. On 20 September Allied cavalry swept into Nazareth, just failing to capture Sanders himself.

Remnants of the Eighth Army, spearheaded by the partly-German Asia Corps, attempted to retreat toward the Jordan, but were caught up in the spreading rout of the Seventh Army as Allenby's XX Corps advanced. As they fell back, the Turkish columns were harassed and dispersed by Allied air attacks.

Consequences

On 22 September the Turkish Fourth Army, now dangerously exposed, also began to retreat. Some units escaped northward to surrender near Damascus, while the remainder were cut off and surrendered near Amman. Allenby's forces had advanced more than 300mls/483km, taken 75,000 prisoners, 360 guns and all Turkish transport and equipment, for the loss of 5720 men. Aleppo, Beirut, Damascus and Homs all fell. Turkey sought unilateral peace terms; these were concluded on 30 October 1918.

T E Lawrence ("Lawrence of Arabia"). Raids by Arab irregulars under his leadership tied down large numbers of Turkish troops and played an important part in the Allied success in Palestine in 1917–18.

Strategic View: Allenby
The Egyptian Expeditionary Force commander was a cavalryman by training, and the situation facing him in September 1918 at last seemed to offer the chance of a true cavalry breakthrough. Lawrence's raids on the Hejaz Railway (right) would help to draw Turkish attention inland, while the Desert Mounted Corps was transferred in secrecy to the left flank (dashed arrow). A decisive breakthrough would trap Turkish forces against the Jordan and open the way into Syria (top).

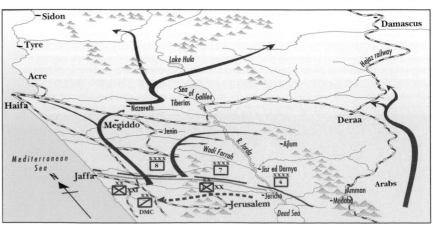

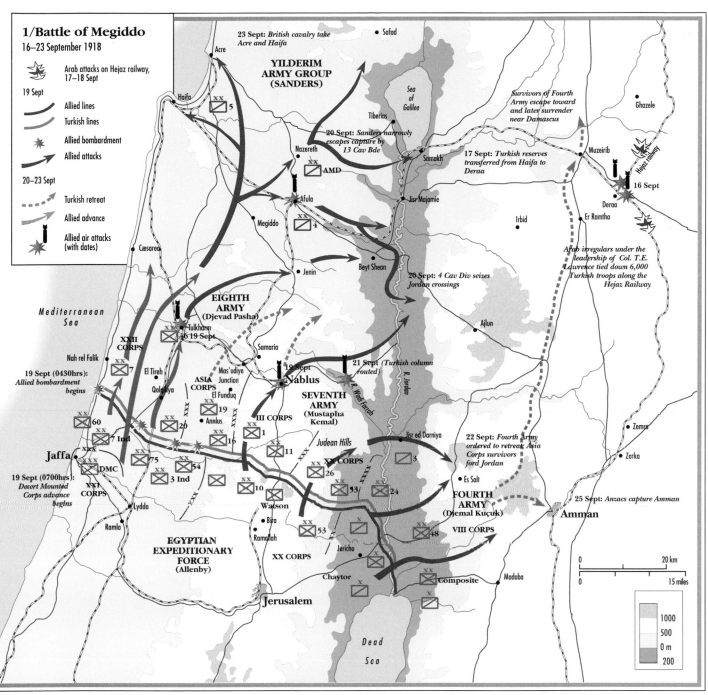

1/Battle of Megiddo
16–23 September 1918

Arab attacks on Hejaz railway, 17–18 Sept

19 Sept

Allied lines

Turkish lines

Allied bombardment

Allied attacks

20–23 Sept

Turkish retreat

Allied advance

Allied air attacks (with dates)

23 Sept: *British cavalry take Acre and Haifa*

YILDERIM ARMY GROUP (SANDERS)

Survivors of Fourth Army escape toward and later surrender near Damascus

20 Sept: *Sanders narrowly escapes capture by 13 Cav Bde*

17 Sept: *Turkish reserves transferred from Haifa to Deraa*

Arab irregulars under the leadership of Col. T.E. Lawrence tied down 6,000 Turkish troops along the Hejaz Railway

20 Sept: *4 Cav Div seizes Jordan crossings*

EIGHTH ARMY (Djevad Pasha)

Mediterranean Sea

19 Sept: *Allied bombardment begins*

19 Sept (0430hrs): *Allied bombardment begins*

XXII CORPS

21 Sept (*Turkish column routed*)

19 Sept

SEVENTH ARMY (Mustapha Kemal)

ASIA CORPS

III CORPS

Judean Hills

22 Sept: *Fourth Army ordered to retreat; Asia Corps survivors ford Jordan*

Jaffa

19 Sept (0700hrs): *Desert Mounted Corps advance begins*

XXI CORPS

25 Sept: *Anzacs capture Amman*

XX CORPS

Amman

EGYPTIAN EXPEDITIONARY FORCE (Allenby)

FOURTH ARMY (Djemal Kuçuk)

VIII CORPS

XX CORPS

Jerusalem

Dead Sea

0   20 km
0   15 miles

1000
500
0 m
200

Arab troops as photographed by T. E. Lawrence. Allenby alloted to the Arabs the task of cutting Turkish lines of communication north and west of Deraa, in the hope of preventing the intervention of Turkish reinforcements from the north. The Arab army was some 8,000 strong and was ordered to attack two days before the main British offensive.

Allied Counter-Offensive September – November 1918

Following German disasters in the west during August, Ludendorff ordered the troops holding the Lys salient and the Amiens area to retire. Then, in September, American forces made their great contribution at St Mihiel and later in the Meuse-Argonne area (page 168). The evidence, daily mounting, of Germany's decline, together with Haig's reiterated conviction that the Hindenburg Line could now be broken, led Foch to seek victory in 1918 by combining all Allied armies in the west in simultaneous offensives.

On 27 September, the day after the opening of the American attacks, Haig's army group thrust against the Hindenburg Line, which was penetrated on 5 October, Boehn's army group managing to withdraw in the face of brave but costly British attacks. British and Belgian forces of King Albert's army group thrust over the Ypres Ridge, but then slowed in the face of supply problems in swampy terrain.

By this time the German high command had lost its nerve. As early as 29 September Ludendorff, studying situation maps at his headquarters at Spa, gave vent to an outburst of passionate recrimination – against his lack of tanks, the defeatist Reichstag, the staff and the restraining humanitarian hand of the Kaiser – until, overcome, he sank to the floor in a fit. That evening he called for an armistice, acknowledging that the Bulgarian collapse (page 174) had unhinged his plans.

In this great German emergency, Prince Max of Baden, a redoubtable negotiator, was appointed chancellor to negotiate peace moves. He asked for time – a few days – before opening negotiations but Hindenburg insisted that peace overtures must be started without delay.

Meanwhile Allied attacks continued without intermission. German hopes of establishing a line west of German territory, to enhance their bargaining powers, were frustrated by a renewed British assault by Rawlinson's Fourth Army, which broke through German defenses on the River Selle (17 October), then Byng's Third Army made a crossing lower down on 20 October. Simultaneously the British and Belgian armies resumed their attacks in Flanders. On 3 October Prince Max sent an appeal for an immediate armistice to President Wilson, based on Wilson's Fourteen Points. An exchange of messages ended on 23 October when Wilson insisted that the Allies would not negotiate with a military dictatorship. On 27 October, Ludendorff resigned to facilitate peace negotiations, Hindenburg retaining his position of overall army commander.

German internal collapse

Meanwhile, from 29 October, a mutiny of the High Seas Fleet, civilian disorders and demonstrations, erupted in metropolitan Germany. At the beginning of November the American First and French Fourth armies broke through the last German positions on the left of their line, while the American Second Army began its assault toward Montmédy.

Prince Max, following Ludendorff's resignation, accepted Wilson's terms, and a republic was proclaimed in Germany; the Kaiser abdicated and fled to sanctuary in Holland. The armistice was concluded on 11 November (page 178) and came into effect at 1100hrs the same day. During the final months of struggle, the Allies lost some 350,000 men, the Germans an even more terrible 500,000.

Above and below left: soldiers of the North Lancashire Regiment advance through scenes of desolation and ruin during the Allied push of September–October 1918

"Today I have been a good deal amongst German prisoners, who are collected in the different cages behind the lines. Souvenirs can be had in the form of money, rings, watches, decorations and so forth... Many of them give quite freely of what they have... certainly they seem to be well contented to be finished with the war and well they might."

Private Adrian Hart, New Zealand Engineers

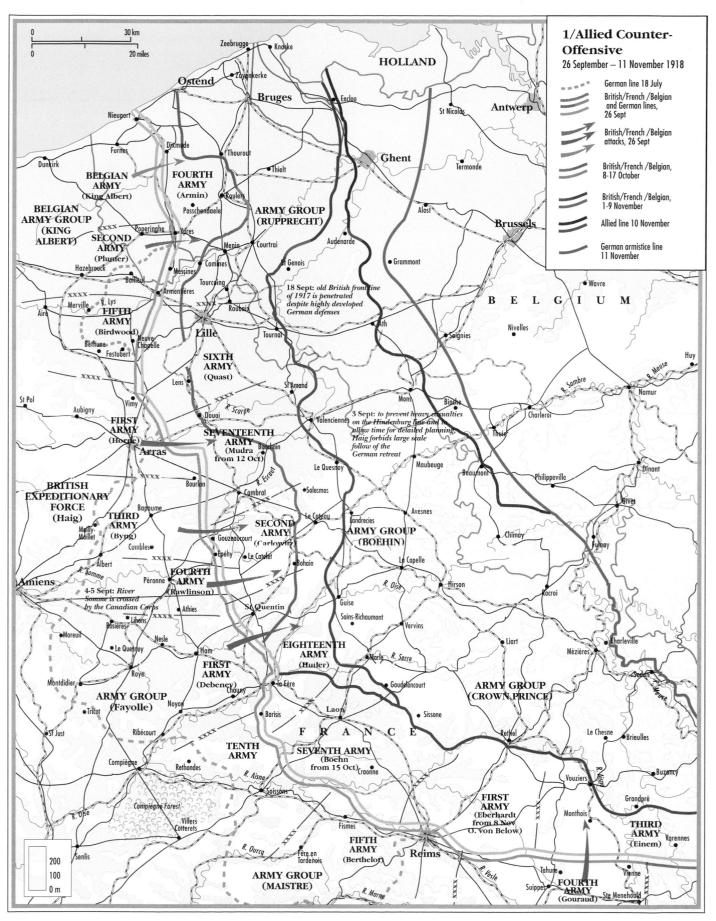

1/Allied Counter-Offensive
26 September – 11 November 1918

German line 18 July
British/French/Belgian and German lines, 26 Sept
British/French/Belgian attacks, 26 Sept
British/French/Belgian, 8-17 October
British/French/Belgian, 1-9 November
Allied line 10 November
German armistice line 11 November

HOLLAND

Zeebrugge
Knocke
Ostend
Zavenkerke
Eecloo
St Nicolas
Antwerp
Bruges
Nieuport
Furnes
Dixmude
Thourout
Thielt
Ghent
Termonde
Dunkirk
BELGIAN ARMY (King Albert)
FOURTH ARMY (Armin)
Roulers
Alost
BELGIAN ARMY GROUP (KING ALBERT)
Passchendaele
ARMY GROUP (RUPPRECHT)
Audenarde
Brussels
Poperinghe
SECOND ARMY (Plumer)
Ypres
Menin
Courtrai
Grammont
Hazebrouck
Messines
Comines
St Genois
Wavre
Bailleul
Tourcoing
Armentières
B E L G I U M
Merville
R. Lys
XXXX
Roubaix
Ath
Nivelles
Aire
FIFTH ARMY (Birdwood)
Lille
Tournai
Soignies
Béthune
Neuve Chapelle
18 Sept: old British front line of 1917 is penetrated despite highly developed German defenses
Huy
Festubert
SIXTH ARMY (Quast)
R. Sambre
St Pol
Lens
St Amand
Mons
Binche
Namur
Aubigny
Vimy
R. Scarpe
Valenciennes
3 Sept: to prevent heavy casualties on the Hindenburg line and to allow time for detailed planning, Haig forbids large scale follow of the German retreat
Charleroi
Thuin
Dinant
FIRST ARMY (Horne)
Douai
SEVENTEENTH ARMY (Mudra from 12 Oct)
Bouchain
Le Quesnoy
Maubeuge
Beaumont
Philippeville
Arras
R. Escaut
Givet
BRITISH EXPEDITIONARY FORCE (Haig)
Bourlon
Cambrai
Solesmes
Avesnes
THIRD ARMY (Byng)
Bapaume
Le Cateau
Landrecies
ARMY GROUP (BOEHIN)
Chimay
Fumay
Mailly-Maillet
Gouzeaucourt
SECOND ARMY (Carlowitz)
La Capelle
Combles
Epéhy
Le Catelet
Bohain
R. Oise
Hirson
Rocroi
Albert
FOURTH ARMY (Rawlinson)
R. Somme
Péronne
St Quentin
Guise
Liart
Charleville
Amiens
4-5 Sept: River Somme is crossed by the Canadian Corps
Athies
Sains-Richaumont
Vervins
Mézières
Moreuil
Rosières
Lihons
Nesle
EIGHTEENTH ARMY (Hutier)
Marle
R. Serre
Sedan
R. Meuse
Le Quesnoy
Ham
FIRST ARMY (Debeney)
Goudelancourt
ARMY GROUP (CROWN PRINCE)
Roye
Montdidier
ARMY GROUP (Fayolle)
Noyon
Chauny
La Fère
Laon
Sissone
Rethel
Le Chesne
Brieulles
St Just
Tricot
Barisis
Buzancy
Ribécourt
TENTH ARMY
SEVENTH ARMY (Boehn from 15 Oct)
Craonne
R. Aisne
Vouziers
Grandpré
Compiègne
Rethondes
R. Aisne
Soissons
FIRST ARMY (Eberhardt from 8 Nov O. von Below)
Monthois
THIRD ARMY (Einem)
Varennes
Compiègne Forest
Villers Cotterets
Fismes
FIFTH ARMY (Berthelot)
Reims
R. Vesle
Tahure
Vienne
R. Ourcq
Fère en Tardenois
Grandpré
Senlis
200
100
0 m
R. Oise
F R A N C E
ARMY GROUP (MAISTRE)
R. Marne
Suippes
FOURTH ARMY (Gouraud)
Ste Menehould

0   30 km
0   20 miles

The Balkans September – November 1918

Before the great Allied attacks in the west developed, a campaign in the Balkans, in Ludendorff's words, "sealed the fate" of the Central Powers. He had still hoped to hold Germany's strong lines in the west, albeit prepared to fall back to other heavily fortified lines, his flanks in Italy and Macedonia being covered, while the German Government negotiated the best possible peace terms.

But on 15 September, the Allies in Salonika mounted a fierce attack on Bulgarian formations, now largely denuded of German troops taken for service in the west. Guillaumat had prepared the plans but during the crisis of June had been recalled to become governor of Paris. He was succeeded by the energetic and capable D'Esperey who, despite the reverses of his army group along the Chemin des Dames in May 1918, remained one of the outstanding French commanders of the war. Having wrung reluctant permission from the Supreme War Council for a major attack, he opened the Battle of the Vardar on 15 September, hitting the Bulgarian line with the First and Second Serbian armies, while employing French and British units on the flanks. His conglomerate force of Serb, Czech, Italian, French and British provided him with some 200,000 men available for duty, against which were ranged approximately twice that number of Bulgarians.

The campaign

Covered by heavy artillery support, the two Serb armies attacked the center of the front, thrusting between units of the French Orient Army. By the night of 17 September the Serbs had penetrated to a depth of 20 miles; the following day, British attacks on the right, while not wholly successful, pinned down Bulgarian reserves.

Meanwhile, west of the Vardar, the entire Bulgarian front had broken under the converging blows of the Serbs and the French, who harried them in pursuit. On 21 September Bulgarian forces of the Vardar also began to retreat. Then British aircraft, bombing the Kosturino Pass, turned the enemy's retreat into disorganised flight.

By 25 September, the Allied assaults had reached the Vardar and the Bulgarian front was split. The British thrust reached Strumitsa during the following day and, on 29 September,

French cavalry took Skoplje. On the same day, with retreating Bulgarians reduced to panic by Allied air attacks, Bulgaria sought, and was granted, a cessation of hostilities.

Consequences

D'Esperey nevertheless kept his Serbian and French troops moving north and was crossing the Danube (10–11 November), determined to march on Budapest and Dresden, when Germany's acceptance of an armistice brought all military activity to an end. D'Esperey's great achievement not only freed the Balkans and opened the way for an advance on Austria's southern borders, but also reinforced Ludendorff of the imperative necessity of securing peace.

Eastern Front

Although hostilities had ended between Germany and Russia, the autonomy of the Balkan states played a crucial role during the conference of Brest-Litovsk, as did that of Poland, Finland and Ukraine. Trotsky, chief Bolshevik negotiator, refused to grant German demands and thereby brought about a recommencement of hostilities on the Eastern Front. Russia, unable to offer resistance, signed a peace treaty on 3 March, the terms of which were even more punative than hitherto. German troops then occupied Ukraine in a last bid to provide grain with which to save the German people from impending starvation in 1918.

Serbian soldiers, supplied with French equipment, under gas attack. The Serbian attack, coming as it did from such seemingly impossible terrain, came as an unpleasant surprise to the Bulgarian defenders.

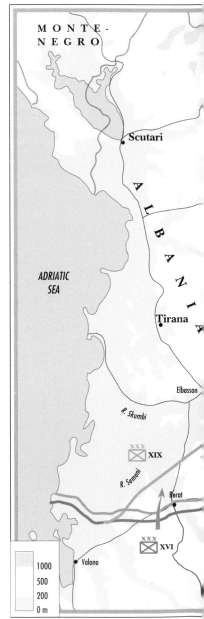

British artillery in the Balkans. During the final campaign the British and Greek Divisions suffered more casualties and enjoyed less success than either the French or the Serbs. Access to the objectives was vulnerable to attack from the heavily defended Bulgarian positions. However, the assaults were successful in that they prevented the reinforcements of the Bulgarian Divisions to the west.

"I expect from you savage vigor."

Gen. Franchet D'Esperey, addressing his officers

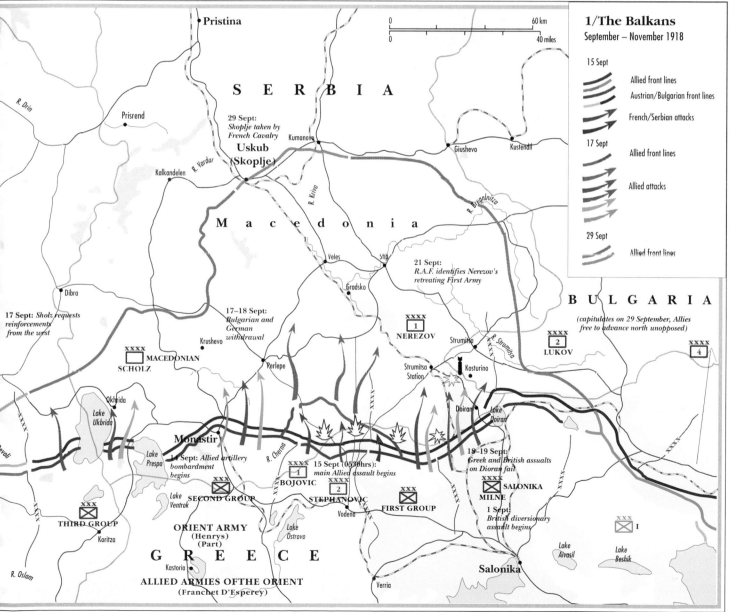

1/The Balkans
September – November 1918

0   60 km
0   40 miles

15 Sept
— Allied front lines
— Austrian/Bulgarian front lines
→ French/Serbian attacks

17 Sept
— Allied front lines
→ Allied attacks

29 Sept
— Allied front lines

S E R B I A

Pristina

R. Drin

Prisrend

29 Sept:
Skoplje taken by French Cavalry
Kumanovo

Uskub
(Skoplje)

Kalkandelen

R. Vardar

Giushevo   Kustendil

R. Kriva

M a c e d o n i a

R. Bregalnitza

Veles

Stip

Dibra

Gradsko

21 Sept:
R.A.F. identifies Nerezov's retreating First Army

B U L G A R I A

17–18 Sept:
Bulgarian and German withdrawal

17 Sept: *Sholz requests reinforcements from the west*

Krushevo

XXXX
1
NEREZOV

(capitulates on 29 September, Allies free to advance north unopposed)

Strumitsa

R. Strumitsa

XXXX
2
LUKOV

XXXX
4

XXXX
MACEDONIAN
SCHOLZ

Perlepe

Strumitsa
Station

Kosturino

Okhrida

Lake
Ukhrida

XXXX

Monastir

R. Cherna

Doiran

Lake
Doiran

XXXX

14 Sept: *Allied artillery bombardment begins*

Lake
Prespa

XXXX
1
BOJOVIC

15 Sept (0530hrs):
main Allied assault begins

XXXX
2
STEPHANOVIC

XXX
FIRST GROUP

18–19 Sept:
Greek and British assaults on Dioran fail

XXX
SALONIKA
MILNE

XXX
SECOND GROUP

Lake
Ventrok

Vodena

1 Sept:
British diversionary assault begins

XXX
THIRD GROUP

Koritza

ORIENT ARMY
(Henrys)
(Part)

Lake
Ostrovo

G R E E C E

XXX
I

Lake
Aivasil

Lake
Beshik

R. Oslam

Kastoria

ALLIED ARMIES OF THE ORIENT
(Franchet D'Esperey)

Verria

Salonika

Vittorio Veneto October 1918

Following Austria's defeat on the Piave in June (page 160), the Italian chief-of-staff, General Diaz, proved extremely reluctant to exploit his success. Uncertain of continued victories and lacking reserves, Diaz had limited himself to minor local operations, ignoring the remonstrations of Foch. Toward the end of October, conditions seemed ripe for a further offensive: Allied maneuvers on the Western Front had made further German intervention in Italy impossible and Austria's internal discord indicated an imminent collapse. Furthermore, in response to his repeated requests for support from his allies, Diaz had been granted reinforcements in the form of French, British, American and Czechoslovakian divisions.

The Italian commander remained reluctant but political events were putting him under increasing pressure to act. On 26 September Bulgaria sued for peace and on 4 October Germany and Austria indicated their acceptance of Wilson's Fourteen Points and asked for an armistice. If peace were to arrive while Italy was militarily inactive, her voice would certainly be weakened during the ensuing negotiations. Political necessity demanded that Diaz take the initiative even though the military statistics proved that victory was still far from assured. The Italians could field 57 divisions and some 7,700 guns while Austria's total force numbered 58 divisions and some 6,000 guns. In the air, the Italians enjoyed numerical superiority with 600 aircraft opposing 564 Austrian.

Preparations

An Italian plan of attack had been devised as early as the end of September by the controller of the operations office, Colonel Cavallero, and this plan had been revised and extended throughout October. A double offensive was proposed. The main assault would be launched on the Piave by the Eighth, Tenth and Twelfth armies, bolstered by experienced British and French divisions. Their objective was to advance as far as Vittorio Veneto, thereby severing all communications between the Austrians in the mountains and those in the Adriatic plain. Meanwhile, the Italian Fourth Army was to penetrate the Austrian front at Monte Grappa to the west, where the army groups of Archduke Josef and Boroevic pivoted.

The exact fighting condition of the forces op-

posing Diaz remained an unknown quantity. Austrian morale was evidently at a low ebb with sedition and desertion rife, but the army's commanders were fully cognizant of the advantages of a continued occupation of Italian territory. If the Austrian army continued to exhibit a willingness and capacity to fight when the armistice was concluded, the terms of the agreement would undoubtedly prove more favorable. It was, therefore, in Austria's best interests to offer strong resistance to an Italian offensive.

The campaign

On 23 October operations began with Fourth Army's secondary thrust in the mountains. Resistance was unexpectedly fierce and the attack was halted with heavy casualties at Monte Grappa. Then, on 24 October, the Italian Eighth Army was likewise halted by the Austrian Sixth Army. However, French troops of the Twelfth Army (Graziani) gained a footing on the left, while British troops of the Tenth Army (Earl of Cavan) gained a sizeable bridgehead on the right, throwing back the Austrian Fifth Army and severing the front on 28 October, reaching Sacile and Vittorio Veneto on 30 October. As Italian reinforcements rushed into the gap, Austrian resistance collapsed.

Belluno was taken on 1 November and the Tagliamento crossed the following day. To the west, British and French troops of the Sixth Army drove to, and took Trento on 3 November. On the same day, an Allied naval expedition captured Trieste, one of Italy's prize objectives, in the Gulf of Venice.

Consequences and losses

Following the breaking of the Austrian front, the retreat degenerated into terrified rout, a defeat that led inexorably to the collapse of the Austro-Hungarian Empire. Austria asked for an armistice on 30 October, which was agreed to and signed on 3 November, hostilities on the Italian front ceasing the following day.

During the campaign, Italy had lost some 40,000 the Austrians 330,000, of whom an estimated 300,000 were prisoners. Total Italian losses throughout the war – 650,000 killed, some 1,000,000 wounded – were less than those sustained by other nations but represent a sacrifice perhaps insufficiently appreciated by the other Allies.

General Amando Diaz, a cautious but competent commander, was promoted to commander-in-chief in November 1917 after the Caporetto disaster.

Austrian machine-gunners inflicted heavy casualties on the advancing Italian Army. Before the battle the Emperor had made a last appeal to his soldiers and his words stirred many to offer unexpectedly stubborn resistance.

"It is my painful duty to inform you that my people have neither the will nor the strength to continue the war... Thus I communicate to you that I have taken the irrevocable decision to ask... for a separate peace and an immediate armistice."

Emperor Karl I, of Austria-Hungary, to Kaiser Wilhelm II, 28 October 1918

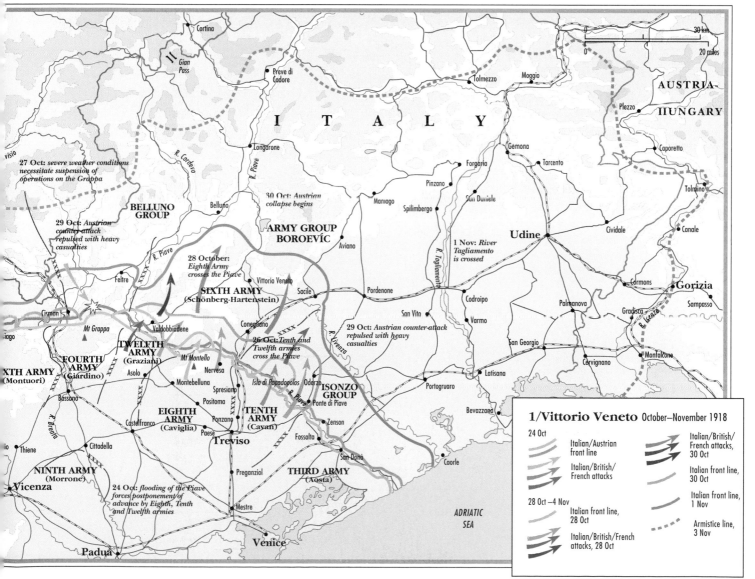

27 Oct: *severe weather conditions necessitate suspension of operations on the Grappa*

29 Oct: *Austrian counter-attack repulsed with heavy casualties*

30 Oct: *Austrian collapse begins*

1 Nov: *River Tagliamento is crossed*

28 October: *Eighth Army crosses the Piave*

29 Oct: *Austrian counter-attack repulsed with heavy casualties*

26 Oct: *Tenth and Twelfth armies cross the Piave*

24 Oct: *flooding of the Piave forces postponement of advance by Eighth, Tenth and Twelfth armies*

AUSTRIA-HUNGARY

ITALY

BELLUNO GROUP

ARMY GROUP BOROEVĬC

SIXTH ARMY (Schönberg-Hartenstein)

TWELFTH ARMY (Graziani)

FOURTH ARMY (Giardino)

XTH ARMY (Montuori)

EIGHTH ARMY (Caviglia)

TENTH ARMY (Cavan)

ISONZO GROUP

NINTH ARMY (Morrone)

THIRD ARMY (Aosta)

1/Vittorio Veneto October–November 1918

24 Oct
Italian/Austrian front line
Italian/British/French attacks

28 Oct –4 Nov
Italian front line, 28 Oct
Italian/British/French attacks, 28 Oct

Italian/British/French attacks, 30 Oct
Italian front line, 30 Oct
Italian front line, 1 Nov
Armistice line, 3 Nov

ADRIATIC SEA

The Armistice November 1918

Ludendorff, by the early fall despairing of victory, still thought that Germany could so exhaust the Allies that favorable peace terms might yet be won. But by September the German rear had begun to collapse. Allenby destroyed the last formidable Turkish army at Megiddo on 19 September (page 170–171); at the same time Allied armies from Salonika at last advanced (page 175). On 29 September, the Bulgarians signed an armistice. The door was thus open for an Allied break into Europe from the east, against which threat Ludendorff had virtually no reserves.

Appeals to President Wilson

On 2 September Ludendorff told the German Government that an immediate armistice was imperative. On 4 October, the German Government duly appealed to President Wilson to open peace negotiations. This appeal was made to Wilson only, not to the Allies in general, in the hope that the idealistic president would agree to easier terms than those likely to be obtained from the war-weary and vengeful Allies. In this they were not mistaken, for Wilson hoped to tie the Germans to his Fourteen Points (which he had enumerated to Congress on 8 January 1918 and which laid down his program for peace) and then, in combination with Germany, to virtually impose the Points on the Allies. Exchanges continued for the best part of three weeks, concluding when Wilson insisted that the Allies and America would not negotiate an armistice with the established military dictatorship.

Ludendorff, to facilitate negotiations, and possibly in part to avoid dismissal, resigned on 27 October. The end was abrupt. The Turkish Government signed an armistice on 30 October and on 3 November the Austrian high command concluded an armistice with Italy.

Unrest in Germany

News in Germany of the negotiations with Wilson brought an almost universal desire to end the war. When Hipper, as commander of the High Seas Fleet, ordered a pre-doomed attack against the British Grand Fleet the crews mutinied. Disorders, revolts and further mutinies, erupted in Germany (p164–165). A Socialist government took power and proclaimed a republic.

Between 7 and 11 November, a German delegation negotiated an armistice with Foch in his railway coach headquarters at Compiègne, agreement being finally reached at 0500hrs on 11 November. The terms provided for the immediate German evacuation of all occupied territory and of Alsace-Lorraine, the surrender of vast quantities of material, including guns and machine-guns, the evacuation of German territory west of the Rhine, the establishment of three Allied bridgeheads over the Rhine, the surrender of all U-boats, the internment of surface warships, the annulment of the Treaty of Brest-Litovsk, and the withdrawal of all German troops in eastern Europe from beyond the German frontier of 1914.

At 1100hrs, the moment when the armistice came into force, German troops were still everywhere on foreign soil (save for a small area of Upper Alsace, conquered by the French in 1914) but, while German land forces remained exhausted but intact, 'home front' collapse left Germany no option but to accept the drastic terms thrust upon her.

Canadian artillery limber cross the Canal du Nord, pursuing the retreating German Army. Well supplied and well fed Allied soldiers such as these backed by the arrival of a huge fresh American Army gave the ordinary German soldier in the field and their commanders a bleak view of any positive outcome of a continued war.

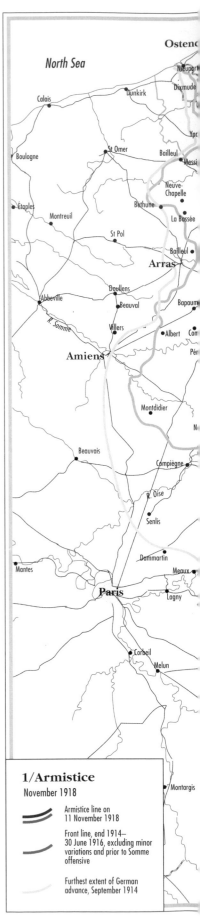

1/Armistice
November 1918

━━━ Armistice line on 11 November 1918

━━━ Front line, end 1914–30 June 1916, excluding minor variations and prior to Somme offensive

─── Furthest extent of German advance, September 1914

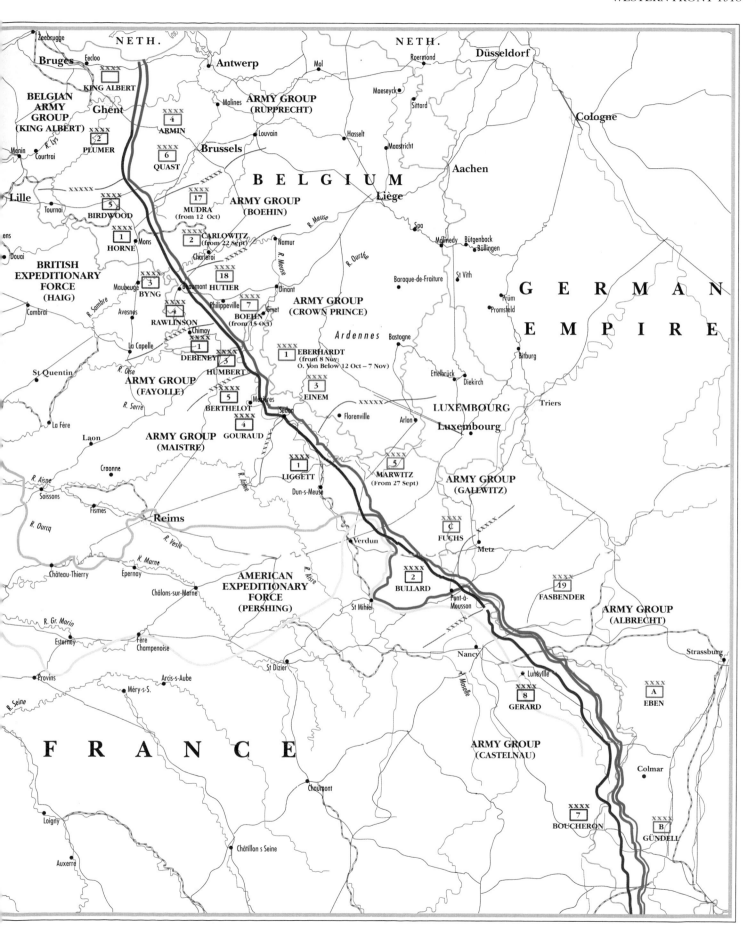

The treaty of Versailles, signed by the Allies and Germany on June 28 1919.

EPILOGUE

Europe had lived through a nightmare of grotesque horror, lifted only with the sudden and almost miraculous German collapse in the autumn of 1918. What caused this abrupt end to four and a quarter years of slaughter? Some historians – notably Sir Basil Liddell Hart – attribute it to an event even before Great Britain was involved: Winston Churchill's mobilization of the Royal Navy on 2 August 1914 to Scapa Flow, which contributed more than any other factor towards ultimate Allied victory by causing the eventual near-starvation of the German people. The harvest of 1917 was particularly poor and, in Germany, the potato ration was reduced to seven pounds a week, the meat ration to 250 grammes. All history shows that it is loss of hope, not loss of lives, that determines the outcome of war. During the terrible Battle of Cannae in August 216 BC, Hannibal's troops killed up to an estimated 70,000 out of 86,000 Roman soldiers, yet Rome survived the last of three crushing defeats in close succession because, despite some faint hearts, the Romans at large thought only of perseverance until victory. The same may be said of the British in 1940. Once hope is gone – as it had in Germany late in 1918 – and the will to resist thereby fatally diminished, the only option is to admit defeat and negotiate for tolerable terms of surrender.

Here Allied propaganda played a great, though not decisive, part. In Great Britain, Lord Northcliffe, a press baron, was summoned to oversee "political warfare". He saturated enemy soldiers with democratic propaganda, emphasizing the relative comforts of internment following surrender. This, though it had greater effect on the demoralized Austrians, was not in itself sufficient to generate German collapse; that could only come about in tandem with grievous military reverses. The sure conclusion is that the immediate cause of German capitulation, for it was no less, was the successes of the Allied armies in 1918. But these did not at once reduce the troops themselves to hopelessness; rather it was the German High Command that, on 8

August, lost its faith in victory. This, as Hart and others have observed, is the deciding factor in warfare: mental impressions of the enemy command and government, not that of their troops, is what tilts the balance between victory and defeat. Napoleon had stipulated that "it is the man, not men, who counts". Seldom has this maxim been better vindicated than in Ludendorff's collapse of confidence in late 1918, as opposed to growing Allied optimism. Ludendorff's conviction of failure turned into hopelessness – the crucial ingredient – by Allied military assaults from Salonika and the collapse of both Bulgaria and Turkey. Ludendorff might yet recover his nerve, victories might be won, but the conviction that defeat was inevitable had taken hold of German service and civilian minds alike. This general impression of hopelessness was paramount in the struggle's conclusion.

Consequences of the war

What did World War One immediately bring about? It is often argued that the nightmare struggle changed European civilization and thus that of the world, beyond recognition. This seems facile, since all the evidence points to its hastening, not causing, the ensuing turbulence. True, three great empires – Russian, Turkish and Austro-Hungarian – collapsed, but these were in any event ripe for disintegration. The Romanov empire, disjointed by the 1905 revolution, could do little more than await another; Austria-Hungary, a conglomerate of disparate races eager for independence, could hardly have survived for much longer, while the Ottoman Empire, long dubbed the "sick man of Europe", was in any event buckling under the weight of corruption, stultifying bureaucracy and internal dissension. It is often said that women in the United Kingdom gained the parliamentary franchise in recognition of their contribution to the war effort; they would shortly have gained it anyway. The male population of Europe had sustained losses on a scale hitherto unknown; the human race reproduced itself and survived in growing – some would argue excessive – numbers. Debts had certainly accrued, most owed by the Allies to America, and destruction had been calamitous, although only in relatively small areas – northeastern France, a corner of Italy and parts of Poland and Serbia. Within a decade, almost all industrialized countries had reached or exceeded their levels of pre-war production.

Many newly proclaimed countries, at first established as democracies, would degenerate into dictatorships, as others did after Europeans withdrew from colonialism in Africa and Asia. That, too, was probably inevitable.

There was one effect of the war, however, that was possibly not inevitable but became ingrained in the human mind up to the present day. Faith in idols was shattered for ever; men no longer worshipped their leaders as heroes. Robert E. Lee was roundly cheered by his defeated troops after the Battle of Gettysburg in 1863; no one cheered Haig. Politicians also became subject to scrutiny and the rapier cruelty of satire.

Losses

Nevertheless, the national losses, both in life, shipping industrial output, were such as to mark a watershed in warfare, for human life and material had been recklessly squandered on an unprecedented scale. Precise figures will never be known, since in many cases statistics were never gathered, and civilian casualties, great though they were, even harder to gauge. Some nations – Russia, Serbia and Bulgaria, for example – suffered more civilian than military loss. Conservative estimates suggest that more than eight million people were killed, with a further 20 million wounded, the wounded usually exceeding the number killed by between two and four to one. These figures take no account of the mental crippling of many thousands, who became incapable of resuming a productive civilian life.

The treaties

Because of its unprecedented cost and waste, the victorious Allies determined to make it the "war to end wars" by treaties imposed on their fallen enemies. Collectively known as the Treaty of Versailles, there were in fact five treaties following the peace.

The Treaty of Versailles, the document signed by the Allies and Germany on 28 June 1919 in the Hall of Mirrors in the Palace of Versailles, took force in the January of the following year. The Germans had earlier accepted Wilson's "Fourteen Points" as the basis for an equitable peace but the Allies now demanded compensation for the damage caused by Germany on land, by sea and in the air. The treaty had been drafted during the Paris Peace Conference early in 1919. This had been dominated by four men – David Lloyd George of Great Britain, Woodrow Wilson of the United States, Georges Clemenceau of France and Vittorio Orlando of Italy, although the last was listened to but largely ignored. None of the defeated nations was permitted any say in shaping the treaty. Thus the Germans were obliged, though with bitter resentment, to stomach the clause attributing "war guilt" to them.

The treaty reduced German territory and population by some 10 percent: Alsace and Lorraine were returned to France, the Saarland was placed under League of Nations supervision until 1935, while small areas in the north were given to Belgium and, after a plebiscite, northern Schleswig was returned to Denmark. Poland, resurrected, was granted much of the formerly German West Prussia and Posen, as well as being given a "corridor" to the Baltic Sea at Danzig, thereby separating East Prussian from metropolitan Germany. Furthermore, all Germany's colonies, in China, Africa and the Pacific, were taken over by either Great Britain, France, Japan or other Allied nations.

This was not the worst of it for Germany, for the clause stipulating her war guilt led to demands for financial compensation for the damage she had caused to Allied territory. An exact sum was impossible to compute, but a commission set it at $33,000,000,000 in 1921. This would inevitably be beyond Germany's means and would dislocate international finances, but the treaty permitted the Allies to take military action if Germany lapsed in her payments.

In addition to all this, to prevent Germany ever again posing a threat to Europe, the treaty, largely at Clemenceau's insistence stipulated that the German Army was to be restricted to 100,000 men, thereby reducing it to the role of a police force. The German general staff was disbanded and the manufacture of armored cars, tanks, submarines, aircraft for service use and poison gas forbidden. All of Germany west of the Rhine and 30 miles east of it was declared a demilitarized zone. For Great Britain, the crowning moment of victory came when the German Fleet was interned at Scapa Flow, although the crews almost at once scuttled their ships.

All of these terms were deeply resented in Germany, where the treaty was seen as a betrayal of their acceptance of the "Fourteen Points" and as being dictated to them. Later the treaty was repeatedly modified, generally in Germany's favor; by 1938 only the territorial articles survived. But the grievance remained. The British and Americans, to their credit, did not seek a peace of revenge that would inevitably in time incite a spirit of revenge in Germany, but France was adamant and would later pay a grievous price.

Treaty of Saint-Germain
Signed near Paris on 10 September 1919 between Austria and the Allied powers, the treaty came into force on 16 July 1920. By its terms, the break-up of the Habsburg Empire was acknowledged and the independence of Czechoslovakia, Hungary, Poland and Yugoslavia recognized. The union of Austria (which had a large minority German population) with Germany was expressly forbidden – another cause of resentment and future disruption. Austria-Hungary's navy was broken up and distributed among the Allies, her army reduced to 30,000 long-service volunteer men. Reparations were demanded but none were actually paid.

Treaty of Neuilly
This was signed on 27 November 1919 and formerly concluded the war between the Allies and Bulgaria, becoming effective on 9 August 1920. By its terms, Bulgaria was forced to cede territory to both Greece and the new Yugoslavia, thus being deprived of access to the Aegean. Bulgaria's army was limited to 20,000 men and reparations demanded, although three-quarters were later remitted.

Treaty of Trianon
The Allies and Hungary signed the Treaty of Trianon on 4 June 1920, by the terms of which Hungary was stripped of some of her territory, which was transferred to Czechoslovakia, Austria,

Yugoslavia, Romania and Italy. In this way, Hungary also lost two-thirds of her population. The Hungarians were not consulted by plebiscite on these arrangements. Hungary's army was restricted to a mere 35,000 men.

Treaty of Sevres
This treaty, signed in 1920 between the Allies and Turkey, stripped the Ottoman Empire of vast areas of land, abolishing the country's sovereignty over Mesopotamia (now Iraq) and Palestine (Israel), which was designated a British mandate. Syria became a French mandate. Turkey also lost territory to Greece and Italy. The Dardanelles became a neutral zone for shipping. These conditions were modified by the Treaty of Lausanne on 24 July 1923 after a prolonged conference. The Lausanne treaty recognized Turkey's boundaries while Turkey made no claim to its former Arab provinces. The Allies, for their part, dropped demands for autonomy for Turkish Kurdistan and cessation of territory to Armenia, abandoned claims to spheres of influence in Turkey and refrained from control over Turkey's armed forces or finances.

Consequences
The Allies, by brushing aside their defeated enemies' dismay at the terms imposed, were in fact losing the peace at the moment they won the war. Great Britain and France had been ruined by the conflict; they no longer held investments in Russia and Turkey, their financial base was disrupted, and income and credit degenerated into debt. Germany, though reduced to capitulation, remained intact and capable of industrial growth. Only America could be considered a complete victor; her territory was both intact and undamaged and she had become the major creditor of all the belligerents.

Other wars
Nor was warfare everywhere at an end, for in eastern Europe new states quickly began organizing their own armies and producing munitions. Armies of intervention were still in Russia, seeking the overthrow of Bolshevism; Russia and Poland would fight each other in 1920, leading to Polish victory (16–25 August) at the Battle of Warsaw, which – temporarily at least – checked Bolshevism's westward

advance. By the Treaty of Riga on 18 March 1921, Russia conceded all of Poland's territorial claims. Between 1920 and 1922 war raged between Greece and Turkey, ending only after huge losses – the Turks somewhat less than 100,000 men, the Greeks in excess of 200,000. The Treaty of Lausanne which superseded that of Sevres, restored to Turkey her Thracian territory to the Maritza River. The Allies evacuated Constantinople and a Turkish republic was established.

These were, in effect, side-shows, for the consequences of the treaties were already becoming dismally apparent. The ruined German economy made it difficult for the Allies to gather the amounts due to them, and in 1923, Germany having perforce fallen into default, Belgian and French troops occupied the Ruhr – a move opposed by the British, fearful that German reparations could only be paid by a surplus of exports, which if achieved would undermine those exports of her own on which she depended.

German finances then degenerated into chaos – by November 1923 there were more than 50 thousand million marks to the pound sterling. By 1931, the economic situation in the western world had collapsed to a point where further German payments were impossible and that clause of the treaty lapsed of necessity.

The rise of Fascism and Communism

Grievances grew throughout much of Europe, fermented by fear, or approval, of Communism and the rise of Fascism. On 28 October 1922, Benito Mussolini's "Black Shirt" movement staged their "March on Rome" and their leader was granted dictatorial powers by the King and Parliament. Germany, meanwhile, had descended into total confusion. The national mood, inflamed by the "iniquities" of the Versailles treaty, domestic deprivation caused by inflation, and fear of Communism proved fertile ground from which Adolf Hitler and his Nazi cronies were to reap a dreadful harvest.

In 1935, Hitler, by then Chancellor, unilaterally annulled the military sections of the Treaty of Versailles. In 1936 he remilitatorized the Rhineland, while at the same time building a new German fleet and conscripting an army far greater than permitted. The Allies lacked the common will to challenge, let alone forbid, these breaches of the treaty.

Thus the Versailles treaties resolved nothing: the very harshness of their terms, and the inability of the Allies to enforce them, leading first to German resentment, then contempt. In November 1918, church bells had rung throughout the victorious countries in Europe, in relief and thanksgiving for the war's end; in truth, they rang only the intermission bell before round two.

Index

Picture page references are shown in *italics*

GENERAL

Bibliography

Aston, George G. *The Biography of the Late Marshal Foch*, Hutchinson, London 1929

Banks, A. *A Military Atlas of the First World War*, Heinemann Educational Books, London 1975

Barker, A.J. *The Neglected War: Mesopotamia, 1914–1918*, Faber, London 1967

Barrie, Alexander *War Underground*, Frederick Muller, London 1962

Bennett Geoffrey *Naval Battles of the First World War*, Batsford, London 1968

Blond, Georges *Verdun*, André Deutsch, London 1965

Bruce, J.M. *The Aeroplanes of the Royal Flying Corps (Military Wing)*, Putman, London 1982

Brusilov, A.A. *A Soldier's Notebook*, Macmillan, London 1930

Burt, R.A. *British Battleships of World War One*, Arms & Armour Press, London 1986

Castle, H.G. *Fire Over England: The German Air Raids of World War I*, Leo Cooper/Secker & Warburg, London 1982

Coombs, Rose E.B. *Before Endeavours Fade: A Guide to the Battlefields of the First World War*, Battle of Britain Prints, London 1976

Cooper, Byran *The Ironclads of Cambrai*, Souvenir Press, London 1967

Costello, John & Hughes, Terry *Jutland 1916*, Weidenfeld & Nicholson, London 1976

Cruttwell, C.R.M.F. *A History of the Great War, 1914–1918*, Clarendon, Oxford 1934

Denton, Kit *Gallipoli: One Long Grave*, Time/Life Books, Sydney 1986

Dupuy, Trevor N. *A Genius for War: The German Army and General Staff 1807–1945*, Macdonald & Jane's, London and Prentice-Hall, NY, 1977

Edmonds, J.E. *A Short History of World War I*, Oxford University Press, London 1951

Ellis, J. *Eye-Deep in Hell: Life in the Trenches, 1914–1918*, Fontana, London 1977

Farrar-Hockley, A. *Death of an Army*, Barker, London 1967; *The Somme*, Batsford, London 1964

Farwell, Byron *The Great War in Africa, 1914–1918*, Viking, London 1987

Ferro, M. *The Great War, 1914–1918*, Routledge, London 1973

Fredette, R.H. *The First Battle of Britain 1917–1918 and the Birth of the Royal Air Force*, Cassel, London 1966

Gardner, Brian *The Big Push*, Cassell, London 1961

Gardner, B. *German East Africa: The Story of the First World War in East Africa*, Cassell, London 1963

Harrington, Charles *Plumer of Messines*, John Murray, London 1935

Horne, Alistair *The Price of Glory*, Macmillan, London 1962

Hough, Richard *The Great War at Sea 1914–1918*, Oxford University Press, Oxford 1983

Howarth, David *The Dreadnoughts*, Time/Life Books, Alexandria, VA 1979

Hoyt, Edwin P. *Guerrilla: Colonel von Lettow-Vorbeck & Germany's East African Empire*, Macmillan, NY; Collier-Macmillan, London, 1981

Ironside, Edmund *Tannenberg: The First Thirty Days in East Prussia*, Blackwood, London 1925

James, Robert Rhodes *Gallipoli*, Batsford, London 1965

Jukes, G. *Carpathian Disaster: Death of an Army*, Ballantine, NY 1971

King, H.F. *Armament of British Aircraft 1909–1939*, Putman, London 1971

Laffin, John *Jackboot: The Story of the German Soldier*, Cassell, London 1965

La Gorce, Paul-Marie de *The French Army*, Weidenfeld & Nicholson, London 1963

Lawrence, T.E. *Revolt in the Desert*, 1927; *Seven Pillars of Wisdom*, 1935; Jonathan Cape, London

Liddell Hart, Basil *A History of the World War*, Faber, London 1934

Livesey, Anthony, *Great Battles of World War I*, Guild Publishing, London 1989

Lucas, James *Fighting Troops of the Austro-Hungarian Army 1868–1914*, Spellmount, Tunbridge Wells, Kent; Hippocrene, NY, 1987

Ludendorff, Paul *My War Memories 1914–1918*, (2 Vols.), Hutchinson, London 1920

Macdonald, L. *They Called It Passchendaele: The Story of the Third Battle of Ypres, and the Men who Fought it*, Michael Joseph, London 1978; *Somme*, Michael Joseph, London 1983

Macksey, K. *The Shadow of Vimy Ridge*, Kimber, London 1965

Macksey, Kenneth & Batchelor, John *A History of the Armoured Fighting Vehicle*, Macdonald, London 1970

Marwick, Arthur *The Deluge: British Society and the First World War*, Bodley Head, London 1965

Middlebrook, Martin *The First Day on the Somme: 1 July 1916*, Allen Lane, London 1971

Miller, Charles *Battle for the Bundu: The First World War in East Africa*, Macdonald & Jane's, London 1974

Norman, Aaron *The Great Air War*, Macmillan, NY; Collier-Macmillan, London, 1968

Palmer, Frederick *Our Greatest Battle: The Neuse–Argonne*, Dodd, Mead, NY 1919

Pitt, Barrie *The Last Act*, Macmillan, London 1962

Reynolds, Quentin *They Fought for the Sky: the Story of the First World War in the Air*, Cassell, London 1958

Seth, Ronald *Caporetto: The Scapegoat Battle*, Macdonald, London 1965

Stallings, Lawrence *The Doughboys: The Story of the AEF 1917–1918*, Harper & Row, NY 1063

Stone, Norman *The Eastern Front 1914–1917*, Hodder & Stoughton, London 1975

Terraine, John *The Road to Passchendaele*, Leo Cooper, London 1977; *White Heat: the New Warfare 1914–1918*, Sidgwick & Jackson, London 1982; *The Great War, 1914–1918: A Pictorial History*, Hutchinson, London 1965

Thayer, John A. *Italy and the Great War*, University of Wisconsin Press, Madison and Milwaukee 1964

Toland, John *No Man's Land: The Story of 1918*, Doubleday, NY; Eyre & Methuen, London, 1980

Warner, Philip *Passchendaele* Sidgwick & Jackson, London 1987

White, C.M. *The Gotha Summer*, Robert Hale, London 1986

Williams, John *Mutiny 1917*, Heinemann, London 1962; *The Home Fronts: Britain, France and Germany, 1914–1918*, Constable, London 1972

Winter, Denis *The First of the Few: Fighter Pilots of the First World War*, Allen Lane, London 1982

Woodward, L. *Great Britain and the War of 1914–1918*, Methuen, London 1967

Woolcombe, Robert *The First Tank Battle: Cambrai 1917*, Arthur Barker, London 1967

Woolf, Leon *In Flanders Fields: The 1917 Campaign*, Longmans Green, London 1959

Wren, J. *The Great Battles of World War I*, Hamlyn, London 1972

Acknowledgements

The publishers would like to thank the following:

Picture Credits

Archiv für Kunst und Geshichte
Bundersarchiv
Codex
Hulton Deutsch Picture Library
Image Select
Imperial War Museum
Popperfoto

Quotations

Lyn MacDonald, *Voices and Images of the Great War*,
Penguin, London 1988
Purnell's *History of the First World War*, BPC Publishing,
London

Text Designed by:
Malcolm Swanston and Isabelle Lewis

Editors:
Stephen Haddelsey, Simon Hall
and Catherine Jones

Maps compiled and produced by:
Peter Gamble
Barry Haslam
Elizabeth Hudson
Isabelle Lewis
David McCutcheon
Kevin Panton
Jeanne Radford
Andrew Stevenson
Malcolm Swanston

Illustration by:
Ralph Orme